PREVENTION'S Stop Dieting and *Lose Weight* Cookbook

PREVENTION'S Stop Dieting and *Lose Weight* Cookbook

Edited by Mary Jo Plutt
and the Food Editors of
PREVENTION Magazine Health Books
Introduction by Mark Bricklin,
PREVENTION Magazine

RODALE PRESS
EMMAUS, PENNSYLVANIA

Copyright © 1994 by Rodale Press, Inc.
Front cover photograph copyright © 1994 by Angelo Caggiano
Interior photographs copyright © 1994 by Angelo Caggiano
Illustration (page 10) copyright © 1994 by Carol Inouye

Front Cover

Recipe: Turkey and Summer Garden Stir-Fry (page 110). *Photographer:* Angelo Caggiano. *Food stylist:* William Smith.

Library of Congress Cataloging-in-Publication Data

Prevention's stop dieting and lose weight cookbook : featuring the 7-step get-slim plan that really works / edited by Mary Jo Plutt and the food editors of Prevention magazine health books; introduction by Mark Bricklin.

      p.   cm.
   Includes index.
   ISBN 0–87596–469–9 paperback
   1. Reducing diets—Recipes. I. Plutt, Mary Jo. II. Prevention (Emmaus, Pa.) III. Title:
   Prevention's stop dieting and lose weight cookbook.
   RM222.2.P718   1994
   641.5'635—dc20   94–8425
                                                              CIP

Distributed in the book trade by St. Martin's Press

2 4 6 8 10 9 7 5 3 1 paperback

Editorial and Design Staff

Editor: Mary Jo Plutt

Senior Editor: Jean Rogers

Contributing Writer: Lisa Delaney

Book Design: Elizabeth Otwell

Cover Design: Kristen Morgan Downey

Interior Layout: Sandy Freeman

Interior Photographer: Angelo Caggiano

Interior Food Stylists: Mariann Sauvion, William Smith

Prop Stylist: Randi Barritt

Recipe Development: Teresa J. Farney, Linda M. Rosensweig,
    Spectrum Communication Services, Inc.

Home Economist, Rodale Food Center: JoAnn Brader

Nutrition Consultants: Sue Roberts, M.S., R.D., L.D.;
    Linda Yoakam, M.S., R.D.

Research Associates: Martha Capwell, Christine Dreisbach

Copy Editor: Jane Sherman

Editor-in-Chief, Rodale Books: Bill Gottlieb

Executive Editor, Prevention Magazine Health Books:
    Debora A. Tkac

Editor, Prevention Magazine: Mark Bricklin

Art Director, Prevention Magazine Health Books:
    Jane Colby Knutila

Research Manager, Prevention Magazine Health Books:
    Ann Gossy Yermish

Contents

Introduction

I have good news: Dieting is dead! The days of "going on a diet" are over. Gone, too, are the feeling of deprivation built into every diet and the slavish devotion to counting calories that was needed to make dieting work. Now we know the true path to permanent weight loss. It's as simple as this: Eat less fat and get more exercise.

The aim of this book is to show you how to do both—through tips from weight-loss experts and a collection of nearly 300 low-fat, high-flavor recipes. And the best part is that eating foods low in fat will do more than just make you look better. It'll make you feel better, too—and give you a fighting chance at a long, healthy life.

The idea that too much fat in the diet is bad for us caught the public attention only in recent times. And for a while, the sole connection was with cholesterol levels. Doctors began to emphasize that fat could drive up serum cholesterol levels more readily even than cholesterol from food.

True. But that was just the beginning. Medical research shows that fat in the high amounts many of us eat is in reality a general biotoxin. In a world that often worries about radioactivity, pesticides and pollution, it's likely that the most powerful long-term poison most of us encounter is on our dinner plate.

As far as your body is concerned, going the low-fat route is something like throwing open the windows in a house that's slowly being filled with carbon monoxide. No, fat won't do you in as fast as CO can, but the danger is still there. You might call high-fat eating a desperate situation played out in slow motion.

There's the chance to do something now. By "throwing open the windows" to low-fat eating, you can stop that slow toxification and even reverse some of the ill effects that may have built up.

Here, in a nutshell, is how changing your way of eating can pay you the biggest dividends you'll ever get.

Low-fat lowers your weight

It sounds hard to believe, but more than one study has shown the same thing: Calories do not make you fat. When large groups of people are studied with an eye toward discovering the habits that make some of them fat, the answer is usually not calories. As men-

tioned, fat consumption and exercise are the key elements.

Here's why: When we eat calories from carbohydrates (as in grains, vegetables and fruit), 23 percent of the little devils get fried to oblivion by the body's metabolic processes before they can be turned into body fat. But with fat, only 3 percent are burned up by the body—the rest are free to attach themselves to your belly or hips.

If you're lucky, none of those calories will actually become permanent fixtures, because your daily activities will consume them as fuel. But, it's a lot harder to be "lucky" when calories come from fat. The ease with which they avoid metabolic burn-up can add 10 to 15 pounds to your body even when your calorie intake isn't really out of bounds.

Can you turn this fact into an action plan?

Researchers at Cornell University in Ithaca, New York, and the University of Götenberg, Sweden, did just that. They took a group of women and put them on a diet. But not the kind of diet you're used to hearing about. The women could eat as much as they wanted to. Calorie counting was out the window. Instead, these women were first given typical American fare to eat, with about 35 to 40 percent of the calories coming from fat. They munched away for 11 weeks.

Then came the big switch. The food they were given to eat had just 20 to 25 percent of calories from fat. Once again, they could eat all they wanted. Eleven weeks later, the women had lost an average of 5.5 pounds. The weight came off because fewer of the calories the women ate were stored as fat.

Being fat is not only a drag on your self-image. Obesity drags down your health, too. Here's how a low-fat lifestyle can help you avoid major assaults on your well-being.

Low-fat can deflate high blood pressure

If you're overweight and your doctor finds your blood pressure to be high, the first thing you'll be told is to lose weight.

You already know the best way to do that.

Low-fat can make you feel younger and stronger. As you get older, you tend to lose a certain amount of muscle. A loss of 10 or more pounds' worth of muscle in a middle-aged person is not unusual. At the same time, many of us—thanks to a high-fat diet—add up to 30 pounds of fat to our frame. Think what that feels like. A new burden to carry around and less muscle to do the job.

Low-fat protects your heart

This is pretty familiar territory, but the main point bears repeating. A high-fat diet is the number one cause of high serum cholesterol, a major risk factor for heart attack. Just how quickly fat does the job was demonstrated in one rather strange experiment.

Researchers took a group of Mexican Indians who usually eat a low-fat, high-fiber diet and presented them with a buffet of rich foods on a daily basis for five weeks. In that relatively short period of time, their LDL cholesterol (the bad kind) shot up by 39 percent. Their triglycerides rose 18 percent, and their weight went up an average of eight pounds.

It was like putting the Cornell experiment into reverse. Give people fatty food to eat and they'll just "naturally" begin to pile on the pounds and lose their protection from heart disease.

Low-fat deflects diabetes

Most people have the idea that a "diabetic diet" consists of little more than avoiding sugar. Today, the American Diabetes Association recommends keeping fat under 30 percent of calories. Why? Because being overweight is a major risk in the development of Type II diabetes, also known as adult-onset diabetes. And eating too much fat just about guarantees you'll get fat. For people who already have diabetes, overweight increases key risks like elevated blood pressure and cholesterol.

One recent study from the University of Colorado Health Sciences Center in Denver actually came up with numbers to quantify the risk of fatty foods. For each additional 40 grams of fat eaten (equal to the fat in one big fast-food burger with large fries), the risk for Type II diabetes may rise threefold.

They also found that reducing carbohydrates in your diet (which used to be considered a good idea) actually increases the chances of impaired glucose tolerance by 56 percent.

In other words, by switching your calories around to get less fat and more carbohydrates (from bread, pasta, vegetables and fruit), you can make a huge difference in how efficiently your body controls its blood sugar.

Low-fat fights off cancer

This discovery is one of the most revolutionary concepts in modern nutrition. Though fairly new, there's already lots of statistical evidence linking lower levels of dietary fat to lower levels of several forms of cancer, including those of the colon, breast, prostate, pancreas, uterus and bladder.

One study even found a strong link between high levels of saturated (mostly animal-source) fats and cancer of the lung in women who don't smoke.

Why higher fat levels promote cancer isn't at all clear, but there is no lack of theories. Possibly, fat works in many ways.

Conversely, the vegetables and fruits that should go a long way toward replacing fat calories in your diet have been identified as having a positive protective effect against several cancers.

Those are the chief benefits of going low-fat. It's likely that new benefits will be discovered in the future. Already, there are studies showing that a low-fat regimen can actually help build muscle. In addition, some animal experiments suggest that a high-fat diet slows down the clearance of harmful hormones produced by stress. And one study indicates that the low-fat approach to health could put more "fight" in your immune system.

Putting it all together, there's no doubt that going low-fat opens lots of windows to better health.

Now that you've thrown the windows open, start cooking!

Mark Bricklin
Prevention Magazine

Extra Health Benefits

Far too often, when it comes to weight loss, we talk about the foods we shouldn't eat. But actually we need to talk about the foods we should eat— foods to ensure superior health. Along with promoting weight loss, the recipes in this book supply one or more of the following health bonuses. These benefits are listed with each recipe.

LOWER CHOLESTEROL   BLOOD BUILDING
BETTER BLOOD PRESSURE   STRONGER BONES
CANCER PROTECTION   STRONGER IMMUNITY

Step Up to a Slimmer You

Are you a prisoner on the diet roller coaster? You're up. You're down. You're up again. And this has been going on for years. You've been on more diets than we've had presidents. But the only thing you've got to show for your efforts is a look of frustration every time you see yourself in the mirror.

So get off that roller coaster. Stop dieting! And lose the weight you want. (Or rather the weight you *don't* want.) Do it without depriving yourself, without saying good-bye to the foods you love and without skipping meals or living on low-cal, no-taste foods you ordinarily couldn't be paid to eat.

The secret to losing weight and keeping it off is to ease into new eating and exercising habits. Get on a program you can live with—now and forever. Is this pie in the sky? No, it's pie in your fridge. (Try the Pineapple Chiffon Pie with Strawberry Sauce on page 312 as a sensationally light dessert.) It's Braised Beef Round (page 137), Bayou Shrimp and Oysters (page 193), Chicken Breasts Marinara over Fettuccine (page 90) and lots more.

Your first step when starting a weight-loss program is to consult your physician and together set achievable goals. Then design a program that will work for you. To help you, we consulted with doctors and weight-loss experts across the country. We asked them for their ideas on an easy, workable, can't-fail program. Here's the step-by-step strategy they recommended.

Step 1: Be Realistic

What is your goal? To look like Cindy Crawford? To fit into your high school prom dress or a string bikini? Maybe it's time for a reality check. Setting your sights too high only sets you up for failure. So give real consideration to how likely it is that you'll be able to reach—and maintain—that "ideal weight" you've been carrying around in your head.

"It's more important to determine if you're at a healthy weight," says George Blackburn, M.D., Ph.D., associate professor of surgery at Harvard Medical School and chief of the Nutrition/Metabolism Laboratory at New England Deaconess Hospital in Boston. A healthy weight is one that can reduce your risk of serious diseases, such as diabetes, heart disease, high blood pressure and osteoarthritis.

To calculate your healthy weight, use the table below. First, find your height. Then find the suggested weight range for your age. Your healthy weight will fall in that range. If you're 5'5" and 36 years old, for instance, you should aim for a weight between 126 and 162 pounds. (Before you get excited about that plump point spread, keep in mind that the higher figures generally apply to men, who have more muscle and bone than women.)

Exactly where you should fall within your healthy weight range

Weighty Matters

Excess pounds affect more than just your silhouette. They can have a direct bearing on your health and may actually lead to the onset of some serious diseases. Use this table to figure out a healthy weight range for your height and age. Lower figures in each range tend to apply to women, and the higher ones are most apt to be appropriate for men.

Height	Weight by Age	
	19 to 34 years	35 years and over
5'0"	97–128	108–138
5'1"	101–132	111–143
5'2"	104–137	115–148
5'3"	107–141	119–152
5'4"	111–146	122–157
5'5"	114–150	126–162
5'6"	118–155	130–167
5'7"	121–160	134–172
5'8"	125–164	138–178
5'9"	129–169	142–183
5'10"	132–174	146–188
5'11"	136–179	151–194
6'0"	140–184	155–199

SOURCE: *Dietary Guidelines for Americans,* U.S. Department of Agriculture/U.S. Department of Health and Human Services.

will be determined by your "happy weight." That's a weight your body will live with (plus or minus five pounds) for two years. It's not one that pleases you—or your ego.

Determining your body's happy weight is a bit tricky at the beginning. The best approach is to follow a sensible weight-loss plan for six to eight weeks, Dr. Blackburn says. At first, you'll lose weight easily. When the pounds seem harder to take off even though you're still following your original plan, your body will probably be approaching its happy weight. After you've reached a weight that you can maintain for three to six months, you've found your happy weight.

If you would like to lose a few more pounds at that point, simply switch from your maintenance program back into your weight-loss mode. But don't get carried away. Be sure to stay within your healthy weight range. If you aim too low, your body will tell you—you'll feel hungry and tired. And you could end up a candidate for a serious rebound effect that would land you back on the diet roller coaster. To avoid that, you'll need to re-think your happy weight.

Step 2: Evaluate Your Current Eating Habits

Do you have eating patterns or habits that keep you from losing weight? Read the statements below and see which ones apply to you. Then take to heart the suggestions our experts offer for healthfully readjusting those habits.

I seldom plan my meals ahead of time.

A healthy weight-loss eating plan doesn't have to be highly structured. But some planning is necessary for managing your fat and calorie intake. To partially structure your eating, pick a few menus that you really like for two meals a day—probably breakfast and lunch. Rotate them for several days each week. "Then you can have some variety at dinner—but it would still be good to have five or six regular menus that you can alternate among," says Thomas Wadden, Ph.D., professor of psychology and director of the Center for Health and Behavior at Syracuse University in New York. "The less you have to think about your menu plans, the better off you'll be."

I tend to eat more than I should at mealtime.

Try portion control. Before sitting down to eat, fill your plate in the kitchen and immediately refrigerate or even freeze the leftovers. That way, you won't be tempted to go back for second and third helpings.

Another approach is to slow down your eating. It could be that you're simply eating too fast and not allowing time for a feeling of fullness to set in. Between bites, put down your fork and fully chew your food. If that approach seems a little boring, add an element of challenge to your meals by using chopsticks. Unless you're adept, you'll really have to take your time.

I can't help snacking between meals.

That's okay—just make those snacks healthy and satisfying. And don't fall into the trap of thinking that snack foods can be only chips, dips, cookies and candy. How about some crusty bread with luscious fruit preserves? Or a microwaved potato topped with salsa and nonfat sour cream? If those things just don't feel like snacks, choose low-fat items like pretzels, rice cakes, fruit and nonfat frozen yogurt. The idea is to pick foods that are low in fat and high in hunger-appeasing complex carbo-hydrates. And recognize that snacks are something you are building into your eating plan so that you can cut back a little at regular meals.

I'd rather snack than eat regular meals.

Go ahead. It's known as grazing, and it's perfectly accept-able—just as long as you choose nutritious foods that are low in fat. And be sure to build variety into your snacks. Throw in fruits, vegetables and plenty of foods rich in complex carbs, such as bread, cereal, rice, pasta, bean dishes and even low-fat pizza. Add some protein items also, such as reduced-fat cheese, hard-cooked eggs (discard the yolks if you're watching your choles-terol intake) and roasted turkey breast or other lean meats.

I usually don't have a lot of time to prepare meals.

No time? No problem. Look for the recipes marked "Quick" in this book. These recipes use no more than ten ingredients. Main dishes take less than 30 minutes to prepare. Appetizers, snacks, side dishes and desserts require less than 15 minutes.

Other ways to keep meal prep to a minimum: At the super-market, pick up precut fresh fruits and vegetables at the salad bar. Look for low-fat frozen dinners and "kits" for preparing fa-jitas or stir-fries. Buy peel-and-eat steamed shrimp or shelled crabmeat. Remember that fish fillets, shellfish, boneless chicken breasts and turkey cutlets cook very quickly.

And keep easy-to-prepare staples, such as low-fat spaghetti sauce, pasta, canned beans, quick-cooking rice and sugar-free dessert mixes, on hand in your pantry. With the timesaving recipes in this book and all the convenience products available, you *can* eat healthy meals without spending a lot of time in the kitchen.

I love to nibble and sample while I cook.

Fine—but take charge of the situation. Before you begin cooking, arm yourself with some slimming snacks that will keep your hands off the food you're preparing. Having a bowl of crunchy air-popped popcorn, crisp raw snow peas or juicy apple wedges to nosh on while you cook will satisfy your habit and keep you from oversampling your entrée.

I never eat breakfast.

You're not doing yourself a big favor. Breakfast is the most important meal of the day, so try to eat something. If you do, chances are you won't snack so much later in the day.

If you're not fond of traditional breakfast fare, then be creative. Try a pita or bagel pizza, some leftover pasta or a small sandwich—eat whatever you like, as long as it's low in fat and calories. And don't feel that you must eat right after getting up. If it takes a little while to get your appetite going, carry something nutritious with you to work and eat it at your desk.

Step 3: Set Up a Fat Budget

If you're a confirmed calorie counter, you might have a little trouble adjusting to this concept. But once you do, you'll find it's a much simpler approach to live with. And doctors say keeping a lid on your fat intake is a real key to successful weight loss.

"Learning to limit your fat intake is the most important step you can take—both for weight loss and for overall health," Dr. Blackburn says. The idea is to cut back on foods high in fat and replace them with low-fat carbohydrate and protein items. And because you'll be dealing with lower numbers, keeping track of the fat grams you eat each day is much easier than counting calories. Here are other reasons for becoming a fat-gram counter.

- One gram of fat contains more than twice as many calories as one gram of carbohydrate or one gram of protein. As a result, when you switch to a low-fat diet, you can usually eat more food than on a fat-heavy diet, for the same calorie cost, and still lose weight.
- Your body is efficient at burning carbohydrate and protein calories. Fat calories, on the other hand (other thigh?), are easily stored by your body—and they're usually stored where you don't want them!
- High-carbohydrate foods are more filling than high-fat foods. So you tend to eat less.
- New low-fat and nonfat versions of your most favorite decadent foods—chocolate brownies, cheeses, salad dressings, sour cream and such—make sticking to a low-fat diet easier than ever before.
- Research shows high-fat diets to be a risk factor for serious diseases such as heart disease, diabetes, osteoarthritis and some cancers.

Use the table on the opposite page to calculate the number of fat grams you're allowed each day: Look up your body's happy weight, then read across to the fat grams column. It's that simple. This figure is based on a diet that gets 25 percent of its total daily calories from fat. That's substantially lower than the 38 to 40 percent most Americans now consume.

The table does not take your activity level into account. So for every 100 calories you burn while working out, you can add three grams of fat to your daily budget. (Use the table on page 13 to help you estimate how many calories you burn when exercising.)

Counting fat grams is similar to counting calories. Simply keep track of the number of grams of fat you eat during the day. And it's actually easier than counting calories because you'll be dealing with lower numbers. You'll easily find the number of fat grams per serving on most food labels and in the nutritional analyses that appear with the recipes in this book. Plus, there is a comprehensive list of common foods at the back of the book so you can check the fat in those items.

Balancing your fat budget is much like balancing your household budget. You know how much you have to "spend," so it's up to you to allocate the funds wisely. Let's say your fat budget is 44 grams per day and you're at a restaurant that just happens to serve the best gourmet ice cream in town. One scoop will set

Setting Up Your Fat Budget

When figuring out any budget, you need to know what your limits are. This table lets you see at a glance how many grams of fat you can eat each day and still keep your weight where you want it. The numbers reflect an eating plan that gets 25 percent of its calories from fat (with no more than one-third of that fat being saturated). Only calories are listed to give you a rough idea of how many you'd be consuming at each weight level, and they are rounded off to the nearest hundred.

You'll notice that men are allowed more fat and calories than women to maintain the same weight. That's not a case of sexist favoritism. It's a reflection of the fact that men have both a higher metabolic rate and more muscle mass than women. The combo merits them more food on the plate. In either case, figures are for sedentary individuals. More exertion will garner you more fat grams and calories.

Your Body's Happy Weight	Fat Grams per Day	Saturated Fat Grams per Day	Calories per Day
Women			
110	36	12	1,300
120	39	13	1,400
130	44	15	1,600
140	47	16	1,700
150	50	17	1,800
160	53	18	1,900
170	56	19	2,000
180	61	20	2,200
Men			
130	50	17	1,800
140	56	19	2,000
150	58	19	2,100
160	61	20	2,200
170	67	22	2,400
180	69	23	2,500
190	75	25	2,700
200	78	26	2,800

you back about 12 fat grams. If you decide to go for it (and it is all right to treat yourself now and then), you'll be left with 32 fat grams for the remainder of the day. That's not a problem if you stick with low-fat fare for the rest of your day's dining.

The beauty of fat budgeting is that you don't have to totally give up your favorite high-fat foods. You can balance them into your budget.

But even though counting fat grams is the latest approach to losing weight, you can't completely disregard calories. Calories tell you the total amount of food energy you're taking in each day. For successful weight loss, you'll need to keep your calorie intake from running wild. But because low-fat foods are generally lower in calories, staying within your calorie budget should come automatically.

Step 4: Build a Healthy Eating Plan

Most of us grew up with the concept of the basic four food groups. We learned in grade school to eat from all four groups every day to have a so-called balanced diet. That concept has been replaced by another one known as the Food Guide Pyramid.

The Pyramid was developed by the U.S. Department of Agriculture to help people visualize how to proportion their food intake. On page 11 is an illustration of the Pyramid. Your goal should be to eat more of the foods at the bottom than at the top. The target foods—grains, pasta, breads, fruits and vegetables—are lower in fat than foods higher up. They also supply important nutrients for overall good health.

You'll note that fats and oils, which appear at the tip of the pyramid, are marked to be used sparingly. Even so, they can fit into a weight-loss plan. Adding a *small amount* of fat to your diet can help satisfy food cravings, preventing overindulgence. Just be sure to choose your fat wisely. Monounsaturated fat is your best choice. Research suggests that it's better for you than other types because it will not increase your risk of heart disease, diabetes or cancer. Monounsaturated fat is mostly found in olive oil, canola oil, macadamia nut oil and avocado oil. Polyunsaturated fat is a second choice, although some doctors have voiced concerns about a possible connection to cancer. Polyunsaturated fat is found in such oils as safflower, sunflower, corn and soybean.

Whether you're losing weight or maintaining an achieved goal, it's important to eat foods from all five of the lower groups of the Pyramid in order to get the vitamins, minerals, protein and fiber you need for a healthful diet. Here are some other tips to follow in your eating plan.

Drink at least eight cups of water a day

It can be plain water or one of the new unsweetened, sodium-free bottled waters. Water is an essential nutrient in any diet. It's especially important in a fiber-rich diet that includes a lot of vegetables and whole grains. Water prevents dehydration, which can lead to kidney damage. It's also important for keeping your digestive system working smoothly.

Best of all, "drinking generous amounts of water is overwhelmingly the number-one way to reduce appetite," Dr. Blackburn says. Sometimes when you think you're hungry, you may just be thirsty. So when hunger pangs strike, first try drinking a glass of water.

Hold back on salt

Excess salt in your diet will cause your body to retain water, which can add to your weight. Salt also is a problem for people with high blood pressure. Most experts recommend limiting your total sodium intake to 2,400 to 3,000 milligrams a day. To cut down on salt when cooking, omit the salt from recipes and use only products described as "salt-free," "low-salt" and "reduced-sodium" on their labels. Compensate for the flavor of salt by using spices, hot peppers, citrus juices and reduced-sodium versions of soy sauce, Worcestershire sauce and other condiments.

Leave the saltshaker off the dinner table. Better yet, fill it with a salt-free seasoning. Or place a small tray of flavored vinegars, herbs and spices on the table for diners to choose from. If your family absolutely insists on having salt on the table, cover half of the holes in the top of the shaker with a piece of tape.

Go light on sweets

Sometimes just a touch of honey, maple syrup, brown sugar or molasses can give life to a recipe. But remember that these sweeteners do have calories. And they can stimulate your appetite, Dr. Blackburn says, so take it easy.

Take a Tour of the Pyramid

This is one case where starting at the bottom has its advantages. The foods lowest on the government's Food Guide Pyramid are your best bets for healthy eating. But even those categories have some options that are smarter choices than others in terms of fat and calories as well as fiber and other vital nutrients. When you get to categories that are higher up on the Pyramid, choosing nutritious foods is more critical.

As to what constitutes a serving, here are some examples. <u>Bread group:</u> 1 slice bread; 1 ounce ready-to-eat cereal; ½ cup cooked cereal, rice or pasta. <u>Vegetable group:</u> 1 cup raw leafy vegetables; ½ cup other vegetables; ¾ cup juice. <u>Fruit group:</u> 1 apple, banana or orange; ½ cup chopped fruit; ¾ cup juice. <u>Milk group:</u> 1 cup milk or yogurt; 1½ ounces natural cheese. <u>Meat group:</u> 2 to 3 ounces cooked lean meat, fish or poultry (note that ½ cup cooked dried beans, 1 egg or 2 tablespoons peanut butter is equivalent to 1 ounce of meat).

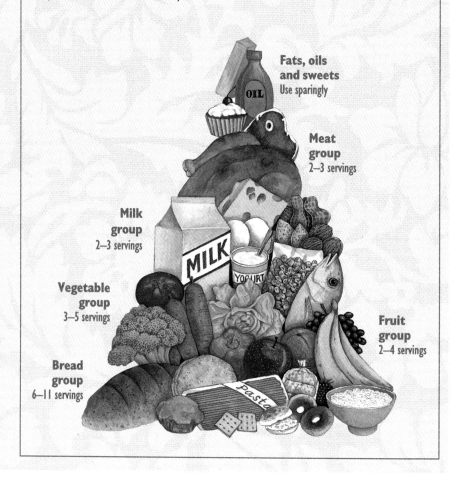

Fats, oils and sweets
Use sparingly

Meat group
2–3 servings

Milk group
2–3 servings

Vegetable group
3–5 servings

Fruit group
2–4 servings

Bread group
6–11 servings

Bread Group

Best Choices

- Whole-grain breads
- Eggless pasta
- No-fat-added hot and ready-to-eat cereals
- English muffins
- Bagels
- Corn tortillas
- Brown rice cooked without added salt
- Oat bran
- Oatmeal
- Couscous
- Nonfat crackers
- Air-popped popcorn
- Pretzels
- Rice cakes

Runners-Up

- Any crackers containing two grams or less of fat per $1/2$ ounce of crackers
- Waffles and pancakes
- Any rice cooked without added salt
- Ready-to-eat cereals containing two grams or less of fat per ounce of cereal
- Egg noodles
- Flour tortillas

Vegetable Group

Best Choice

- Fresh or frozen vegetables served raw, steamed or microwaved and without butter, oil or a sauce

Runners-Up

- Canned vegetables
- Vegetable juices
- Vegetables served with a reduced-fat sauce

Fruit Group

Best Choices

- Fresh fruits
- Frozen fruits without added sugar or syrup

Runners-Up

- Dried fruits
- Fruit juices
- Canned fruits packed in juice or water

Milk Group

Best Choices

- Nonfat dairy products (such as skim milk, sour cream, yogurt, cottage cheese, cream cheese and other cheeses)
- Nonfat dairy desserts (such as pudding and mousse mixes and frozen yogurt)

Runners-Up

- Low-fat dairy products (such as 1% milk, buttermilk, yogurt, cottage cheese and cheeses containing two grams or less of fat per ounce of cheese)
- Low-fat dairy desserts (such as frozen yogurt and other dairy desserts containing two grams or less of fat per four-ounce serving)

Meat Group

Best Choices

- Low-fat fish (such as haddock, flounder, halibut and cod)
- Fish high in omega-3 fatty acids (such as salmon and mackerel)
- Chicken or turkey breast without the skin
- Dried beans, peas or lentils
- Egg whites
- Fat-free egg substitute

Runners-Up

- Shrimp and other shellfish
- Dark-meat poultry without the skin
- Lean meats with all visible fat trimmed (such as pork tenderloin, 95% lean ground beef, beef top round or eye of round, lamb loin, leg of lamb, veal leg and venison)

Fats, Oils and Sweets

Best Choice

- Monounsaturated fats (such as olive, canola, avocado and peanut oils)

Runner-Up

- Polyunsaturated fats (such as corn, safflower, sunflower and soybean oils)

Step 5: Make Exercise Part of Your Lifestyle

The easiest way to lose weight and keep it off is to combine exercise with a low-fat eating plan. The added exercise will help you reach your body's happy weight sooner without having to drastically trim your diet. The reason is that if you try to lose weight by dieting only, you'll lose muscle as well as fat—and less muscle means a slower metabolism.

Another big benefit of exercising is that it'll boost your spirits. By feeling fit and in control, you'll avoid depression that might undermine your resolve, and you'll have a better self-image—making it easier to stick with your weight-loss program.

A good exercise program includes moderate aerobic exercise—like brisk walking, running, bicycling or swimming—at least three days a week. Of course, if you want to lose weight faster, you can exercise more often than that.

As a rule of thumb, for optimum calorie burning and a good cardiovascular workout, your exercise sessions should last a minimum of 30 minutes.

If you choose, add resistance training to your program to help firm up your body and give you a trimmer look. That might involve using weight machines at a fitness center or hand weights at home. Lift weights two or three times a week for 20 minutes in addition to your aerobic exercise session.

Here are some ways to get your workout to work for you.

Don't be overly ambitious when starting out

Like your new eating program, your new exercise program should be something you ease into—especially if you're not exercising now. "If you've never exercised, don't try to take aerobics classes five days a week," says Ronna Kabatznick, Ph.D., psychological consultant to Weight Watchers International. "Instead, start with a 20-minute walk once a day. Then slowly increase the number of days you exercise and the length of your sessions." By easing into your program, you'll prevent stiffness, soreness and even injury if your body isn't conditioned properly.

As a safety precaution, it's a good idea to have a medical checkup before starting any new exercise program. Certain medical problems may suggest a modified program.

Choose an activity you enjoy

The first rule in making exercise part of your lifestyle is to have fun. If you're a nature lover, try hiking, mountain-biking or

Get Moving!

To get the most from your weight-loss program, you'll need to work exercise into your daily routine. It's a sure-fire way to burn extra calories and fat. Just what type of exercise you choose is up to you, of course. You have a lot of options to choose from, including those listed below. The figures given represent how many grams of fat and how many calories you can use up in 30 minutes of the activity.

Activity (30 Minutes)	Fat Grams Burned	Calories Burned	Activity (30 Minutes)	Fat Grams Burned	Calories Burned
Aerobics			Horseback riding		
Low intensity	4	122	Walk	2	75
Medium intensity	6	197	Gallop	8	267
Step aerobics	8	272	Rowing machine		
(7" steps)			Low intensity	4	135
High intensity	9	292	High intensity	9	292
Bicycling			Running		
5½ mph	3	107	5.5 mph	9	292
10 mph	6	185	7.2 mph	9	312
13 mph	9	292	8 mph	11	357
20 mph	12	397	Swimming,	6	187
Cross-country skiing	13	445	moderate pace		
Dancing			Tennis		
Ballroom	4	112	Doubles	4	135
Rock 'n' roll	4	112	Singles	6	190
Square dancing	6	187	Volleyball	5	155
Polka	7	240	Walking		
Gardening	5	172	3 mph	4	135
Golf			4 mph	5	155
Walking (foursome, pulling clubs)	3	112	Yoga	3	102
Walking (twosome, carrying clubs)	5	170			

NOTE: These figures are for a person weighing 127 to 137 pounds. If you weigh less, you'll burn slightly fewer calories and fat grams per half-hour. If you weigh more, you'll burn slightly more calories and grams of fat.

cross-country skiing. If music motivates you, take up ballroom dancing. If you want to meet new people while getting a great workout, join a fitness club. And if you prefer time alone, choose a solo activity such as walking, cycling, in-line skating o swimming. But whatever you do, be sure it's something you enjoy—you'll be more likely to stick with it.

Create variety within your workout

Reduce boredom—and exercise different muscles—by cross-training. In other words, split your workout session into two or three different activities, such as stationary cycling, rowing and stair climbing. Or vary the activities from workout to workout—ride your bike on Mondays, go for a swim on Wednesdays and take an aerobics class on Fridays. By alternating activities, you'll avoid monotony and tone more than one set of muscles.

Exercise with a partner

Having someone to exercise with can be a great motivator on those days when you don't quite feel up to it. Committing to a partner may be the push you need to get you to the gym after a long day at work. Your best choice is someone who also is trying to lose weight. That way you'll both have the same goal in mind.

Incorporate exercise into your daily activities

There are many different ways to increase your physical activity on a daily basis. Instead of taking an elevator, use the stairs; park your car at the far end of a parking lot—or even a few blocks from work; mow your own lawn rather than paying the kid next door.

"Your muscles don't know whether you're digging in the garden or whether you're on the fanciest machine in the gym," says Steven Blair, a doctor of physical education who is director of epidemiology at the Cooper Institute for Aerobics Research in Dallas. Merely moving around more, he says, will help you burn more calories.

Make no excuses—just do it!

Schedule an exercise time during the day and write it on your calendar. Keep your appointment and don't let excuses get in your way.

Step 6: Create Healthy Habits

Bad habits can be hard to break. But the challenge of creating new habits can be exciting. Here are some ways to go about changing your current habits.

Keep tabs on your progress

The first step in adopting healthy new habits is to know exactly where you're coming from and where you're going. By monitoring your progress, you'll be able to recognize weaknesses and alter them in order to create a weight-loss program that works for you. The best device for keeping track of your progress is a diary. Write down such things as the time you ate, what you ate, the portion size and how many fat grams and calories were in the food. Just as important, include any other pertinent information, such as whether you were feeling lonely, whether you were watching television or reading the newspaper while eating, whether you were at a special party or whether you were dining with friends. Also use your diary for recording how many miles you walked, ran or cycled and how often and for how long you exercised.

Write down the information as soon as you finish eating or exercising so you don't forget the particulars. At the end of the day, check whether you stayed within your fat and calorie budgets. Keep the diary for at least four days a week during several random weeks of your weight-loss program. Be sure to include some weekends in your diary.

At the end of each week, review the information you recorded. Look for patterns. If you tended to exceed your fat and calorie budgets on days when you ate out, decide if you need to cut back on dining out—or whether you simply need to select restaurants that have more slimming items on the menu. The diary will help you spot trouble areas so you can make a conscious effort to avoid them or to modify your response to them.

Measure your success

Charting your improvement or photographing your results will give you a little lift every time you check your progress and will encourage you to stay on your program a little bit longer.

To chart your success, use a sheet of graph paper. Draw a straight line along the bottom of the sheet and mark off the line in one-week increments. Then draw a line perpendicular to the horizontal line at the left margin. At the top of the vertical line, write down your starting weight. Mark off the rest of the vertical line in descending, one-pound increments.

At the beginning of each week, record your weight by placing a dot on the chart. (Weigh yourself only once a week and on the same day of each week.) Connect the dots to plot your progress.

You also can use this method for plotting the progress of your exercise program. Instead of marking one-week increments on the horizontal line, mark off daily increments. On the vertical line, mark off the number of miles you walked or jogged or the minutes of your exercise session.

As they say, of course, a picture is worth a thousand words. By taking photographs of yourself before, during and after your weight-loss program you'll be able to see your success. Be sure to share your photographs with friends and family—words of encouragement and recognition are rewarding.

Keep motivation high

The amount of progress you make will vary throughout your program. Slow results, of course, are discouraging and can cause your willpower to waver. But there are ways to avoid falling prey to a case of the blahs. "If you learn to reward yourself by doing something that pleases you, you're going to be more successful," says Kelly Brownell, Ph.D., professor of psychology at Yale University in New Haven, Connecticut. So to keep you on track, try one of the following tactics.

Reward yourself along the way. Imagine that you've already achieved your goal weight. How would you celebrate, other than by eating? Would you treat yourself to a facial or a massage? How about a weekend away at the beach or tickets to a play or concert? Write down your rewards on slips of paper and place them in a jar. Every time you reach a mini-goal, such as losing five pounds or walking a total of 40 miles, pick a slip of paper from the jar. Then pat yourself on the back and treat yourself.

Or bank your results. Set up a weight-loss savings account at home and deposit a quarter or a dollar for each day you stay within your fat or calorie budget. Once you've reached your final goal, go on a spending spree—buy a new, slimming outfit or go on vacation. You've earned it!

Conquer the challenges

As you continue your journey toward your final goal, you'll be met with certain temptations or appetite stimulators. Very often, you'll want to eat whether you're hungry or not. If you know what these challenges are ahead of time, you'll be able to face them head-on with a slimming alternative strategy. Here are some ideas to help.

Emotional eating

- First define the emotion—stress, depression, loneliness, boredom—that triggers overeating. Your food diary can be a helpful tool for doing that.
- Find a listening ear. It may be a friend or a support group of people who also are trying to lose weight. They can listen to your problem and offer you comfort or advice to get you over a hurdle. "It's much more useful to talk about your distress than to eat through it, because eating never solves your problems," says Dr. Wadden.
- Make a list of emotion-busters—things other than food that will make you feel better. Every time you feel stressed or depressed, check your list. Then pamper yourself with a bubble bath or a long walk through the woods as a soothing alternative to eating.
- Indulge wisely. If you simply can't put the brakes on your appetite during emotional times, choose low-fat and low-calorie snacks like flavored popcorn cakes instead of oily potato chips.

Holidays, celebrations and parties

- Slim down your menu. The notion of "eat, drink and be merry" is outdated. You can prepare delicious dishes that are festive yet low in fat and calories. For the holidays, try our recipes beginning on page 336. If you're having an open house, serve some of the snacks and appetizers in this book.
- Plan a celebration around an activity instead of a food. Rather than inviting friends to your home for dinner, have them come over to play a friendly game of volleyball or softball. Or instead of having a dinner party, serve a light snack and then go as a group to the theater or a concert.
- Eat a snack before going to a party. While you're still at home, eat a piece of fruit. That way you have control over what you're eating and you won't be as tempted to fill up on calorie- and fat-laden foods at the party.
- Case the buffet table. Look for those foods that won't push you over your daily fat and calorie budgets.
- Offer to take a dish to the party. Then make it something low in fat, such as a yogurt dip. You'll be assured of having at least one guilt-free food to nosh on during the festivities.

Traveling

• If you're flying to your destination, custom order a meal from the airline. Most airlines offer several menu selections for special dietary needs. When making your reservation, ask about the alternatives available. Often the "diabetic" meal, for instance, is higher in fiber and lower in fat than the regular fare. Low-fat seafood and fruit plate selections also tend to be good weight-watching choices.

• Brown-bag your snacks. Instead of purchasing on-the-run food when traveling by air, car or bus, tote your own nutritious nibbles. You can even pack bagels or individual-serving-size cereals for breakfast in your hotel room.

• Treat yourself at one meal during the day. Stick to basic low-fat breakfast and lunch menus, for instance. For dinner, give yourself some leeway. A regional specialty might hit the spot and keep you from feeling deprived. Just be sure to keep tabs on what you're eating so you can reasonably stay within your fat and calorie budgets.

• Be realistic. Try to stick to your weight-loss plan while traveling, but don't be surprised if you gain a pound or two while away. Just resolve to lose it when you return home.

Dining out

• Choose a restaurant wisely. Stay away from restaurants that are known for serving foods swimming in sauces and buried under butter. If necessary, call the restaurant ahead of time to check if there are any "light" alternatives on the menu.

• Ask questions. Have the waiter or waitress explain in detail how the food is prepared. Don't be afraid to ask if the cream, butter or oil in a dish can be eliminated or reduced. And never hesitate to send your meal back to the kitchen if it was not prepared to your specifications.

• Eat small portions. Order a petite version of an entrée or share your entrée with a companion.

• Order smart when on the run. At fast-food restaurants, opt for baked potatoes without butter (add a bit of ketchup and you won't miss french fries), lettuce salads without extra toppings, grilled chicken or fish sandwiches without the mayonnaise or special sauces and thin-crust pizza with vegetable toppings.

• Stock your office drawers. Keep pretzels, rice cakes, raw veggies and fruit on hand for midmorning or afternoon snacking. You'll find it's much easier on your waistline and pocketbook than eating from a vending machine or snack bar.

**Step 7:
Maintain Your
Healthy Weight**

Congratulations! You've reached your body's happy weight. Now the task is to stay within three to five pounds of that weight. But don't worry—to get this far, you've developed some healthy habits, so it won't be too difficult for you at this stage. Here are some tips for enjoying your new lifestyle while preserving your new, slimmer silhouette.

Continue to keep tabs on what you eat

Maintaining your weight will always require a watchful eye. It's important not to throw out your fat and calorie budgets. Although by now planning your daily menu is probably second nature, it's still essential to stay within your boundaries to avoid overeating. And by occasionally keeping a diary, you'll avoid sudden panic if the scale starts creeping back up again. You'll be able to see where you've been slipping and make changes.

Splurge a little

Don't feel guilty about an occasional piece of cake or pie. By treating yourself on special occasions, you'll find it easier to stick with your new eating habits. "You need a safety valve; otherwise, you might go crazy and overdo it," says Michael Hamilton, M.D., director of the Duke University Diet and Fitness Center in Durham, North Carolina. Just be sure to stay within your daily budgets and to practice portion control.

Stay active

Hopefully, you're enjoying your new physical activities, so keep them up. And remember that the more you exercise, the larger your fat and calorie budgets become.

Be adventuresome with new foods

There's no need to fall into a rut while trying to eat healthier. Experiment with new low-fat recipes, spice blends and exotic fruits and vegetables. You might even want to set aside one night each week for out-of-the-ordinary dining. The recipes in this book can go a long way toward putting low-fat excitement into your meals. And as long as your taste buds are tantalized by the food you're eating, you'll never have to diet again.

Creative Low-Fat Shopping and Cooking

What places do you associate with weight loss? The gym, no doubt, and maybe your workout area at home. Possibly a few other exercise-related spots come to mind. But if you forget to mention the supermarket and your kitchen, you're overlooking two vital sites in the weight-loss war.

Your actions in both locations can make or break your battle of the bulge. Naturally, eating smart is your first line of defense against unwanted pounds. But it's pretty difficult to eat wisely unless you select the healthiest, lowest-fat foods your supermarket has to offer. And then you need to prepare those items in a way that retains their innate goodness. In this chapter, you'll find tips galore for achieving both objectives.

Supermarket Savvy

Your trip to the store begins at home, in more ways than one. Starting that trip on the right foot can go a long way toward making sure you return with foods that will enhance your weight-loss efforts. Here are some suggestions for things to do before you even leave the house.

• Make a shopping list. And promise yourself you'll stick to it. By following your well-planned list, you'll resist temptation.

• Allow plenty of time for shopping. Give yourself time to read labels and find exactly what you need.

• Don't take the kids with you. They're likely to clamor for high-calorie treats.

• Eat something before leaving home, even if it's just an apple or a piece of low-fat cheese. If you shop while you're hungry, you're likely to purchase foods that aren't part of your low-fat plan.

• Take along discount coupons only for foods on your healthy-eating list. Saving a few cents on an item that will undermine your weight-loss strategy is penny-wise and *pounds*-foolish. If you're not sure whether a new product is healthful, take a good look at the label before buying.

When you get to the store, use this mini-guide to the various departments to help you make smart selections.

The produce section

• Select the freshest possible fruits and vegetables. They'll be highest in nutrients. And they'll taste so good you won't want to mask their flavor with fatty sauces or butter.

• Make it a goal to try one new fruit or vegetable each week. The more fresh foods in your standard repertoire, the better.

• If you're pressed for time, take advantage of your grocery's salad bar. You can get precut vegetables, which can form the basis of a healthy stir-fry. Or you can pick up the main ingredients of a salad big enough for your whole family. But avoid high-fat and mega-calorie salad accompaniments such as croutons, bacon bits and regular dressings. (Look for healthier alternatives a few aisles away.) And stay away from mayonnaise-based salads.

The dairy case

• Never buy full-fat dairy products. There are lower-fat versions of almost everything, including butter. And they taste good.

• Beware of nondairy creamers. Many of them are no lower in fat than regular cream or milk. And they often contain saturated vegetable oils, like coconut or palm oil, which can raise your cholesterol levels.

• Many fruit-flavored low-fat yogurts are high in sugar and calories. For a slimmer alternative, buy nonfat plain or vanilla yogurt and stir in fresh fruit.

• Select reduced-calorie margarines or whipped or liquid margarines. If you must have butter, look for reduced-fat brands. Although these products still get 100 percent of their calories from fat, they contain a bit less fat per tablespoon because water has been added to them.

• Don't be fooled by the term "part-skim" on cheese labels. These cheeses may still contain more than two grams of fat per ounce.

• If you use eggs a lot, save fat and cholesterol by purchasing fat-free egg substitute.

The meat counter

• Look for beef cuts labeled loin or round. These are usually leanest. If you have a choice of meat grade, be aware the

"prime" cuts are higher in fat than "choice" cuts. And no matter what grade you buy, trim off all visible fat before cooking the meat.

- Select pork, lamb and veal cuts labeled loin or leg.
- As a basic rule, purchase skinless white-meat poultry. Poultry skin is loaded with fat. And dark meat tends to be higher in fat than the breast meat. That doesn't mean you should never eat chicken or turkey thighs. Just be aware that you'll be getting more fat—and be especially conscientious about trimming off any fat you can see.
- Avoid self-basting poultry. It usually contains added fat.
- Don't assume cold cuts, franks and sausages made with turkey or chicken are slimmer than their beef counterparts. Many still tip the fat scales, so read their labels for fat and calorie information.
- Likewise, be wary of ground turkey and chicken. Skin and dark meat are often included, which drives up the fat content. Instead, ask your butcher to custom-grind skinless white meat.

The fish counter

- Most fresh white-flesh fish are healthy choices.
- All types of fresh shellfish—shrimp, crab, scallops, lobster, oysters, mussels and such—are low in fat. And they'll stay that way if you don't deep-fry them or serve them drenched with butter or smothered by tartar sauce.
- Avoid processed fish sticks and crab cakes. They contain added fat and salt.

The freezer case

- Select frozen entrées or dinners that contain less than ten grams of fat per serving.
- Buy frozen vegetables without sauces or butters and fruits without added sugar or syrups.
- When choosing frozen desserts, pick nonfat versions of yogurt, fruit bars, pops and sorbets. But remember, they're still sugar-sweetened and may be high in calories.
- Beware of tofu-based and other nondairy frozen desserts. These are not always low in fat and calories.

The aisles

- Many low-fat cereals are full of sugar and have very little fiber. Read labels to find those brands that are lowest in sugar

and contain at least two grams of fiber per serving.

• Dried beans, lentils and split peas are probably your best buys in the whole market. They're cheap, loaded with protein, rich in fiber and virtually fat-free. Best of all, they can replace meat in any number of dishes. If you don't have time to cook dried legumes, choose canned versions.

• In the bread section, select whole-grain breads, bagels and English muffins. Stay away from ready-made cornbreads and biscuits—they're usually loaded with fat and sodium. The same can be said for most types of refrigerated bread, biscuit and pizza doughs.

• There's an ever-increasing variety of nonfat or reduced-fat cookies, cakes and other sweets to choose from. But although these are lower in fat, they're still high in sugar and calories. Look at the labels carefully before you buy. Good choices include fig bars, raisin biscuits and graham crackers.

• If you can, choose fat-free crackers. Other good choices include crispbreads, melba toast, matzo crackers, saltines and pretzel crackers. More good snacks are regular pretzels, rice cakes, dried fruit and air-popped popcorn. Do be aware that some of these items are high in sodium, however.

• Ketchup, mustard, Worcestershire sauce, soy sauce, butter-flavored granules and salsas are low in calories and fat but tend to be high in sodium. So look for reduced-sodium versions. Add no-fat flavor to foods by using salt-free seasoning blends, various types of vinegar and hot-pepper sauces.

Deciphering Food Labels

The terms are all so confusing. There's low-calorie, reduced-calorie, light, fat-free and a whole host of others. Food labels can be your best resource in your quest for healthier fare, but you need to know how to read them.

Until recently, nutrition labeling was voluntary, except for fortified foods and foods sporting health claims. Exactly which nutrients were listed and how the information was presented was up to each manufacturer. Under new laws, however, nutrition information is required on virtually all packaged foods, including processed meat and poultry products. Many larger supermarkets may even supply this information for raw fruits and vegetables as well as for fresh meats, poultry and seafood.

When looking at these new labels, you may be overwhelmed by the amount of information. But there's no need to digest all of it before deciding on what to toss into your shopping cart. Instead, check out only the essential elements listed with the chart on page 26.

When you have more time, pay attention to such items as the calcium, vitamin C and iron values. They'll help you make sure you're getting enough of these essential nutrients. You also may be interested in taking a look at the Daily Values. These numbers for total fat, saturated fat, cholesterol, sodium, carbohydrates and fiber let you see how the food you've chosen fits into a healthy diet. Figures are given for both a 2,000-calorie and a 2,500-calorie diet. Since you're probably eating fewer calories, remember that these figures represent upper limits. Your diet should contain less than these amounts.

Glossary of food-label claims

A major aim of the latest label laws has been to standardize the terms used when making health claims. Here's a rundown of some of the most common terms and how manufacturers are allowed to define them according to the Food and Drug Administration guidelines.

Free. One serving contains only trace amounts of or no calories, fat, saturated fat, cholesterol, sodium or sugars. These amounts are so trivial, they barely count in your diet. Something labeled calorie-free, for example, contains fewer than five calories per serving. Fat-free means less than 0.5 gram of fat per serving; sugar-free means less than 0.5 gram of sugar per serving. The words "without," "no" and "zero" also mean the same things.

Good source. One serving contains 10 to 19 percent of the recommended daily intake of fat, carbohydrates, protein, cholesterol, sodium or potassium.

High. One serving contains 20 percent or more of the recommended daily intake of a particular nutrient.

Lean; extra lean. These terms are used to describe the fat content of meats, poultry, seafood and game. An item labeled lean contains less than 10 grams of total fat, less than 4 grams of saturated fat and less than 95 milligrams of cholesterol per serving. Extra lean means less than 5 grams of total fat, less than 2 grams of saturated fat and less than 95 milligrams of cholesterol per serving.

Light; lite. One serving contains one-third fewer calories or half the fat that you'd get in a regular version of the product. And the sodium content of this low-calorie, low-fat food has been reduced by 50 percent. You should be aware that the term *light* can also be used to describe physical properties, such as color and texture—as long as the label explains the usage. Examples include light brown sugar and light olive oil.

Low. Food products carrying this claim are low in one or more specific elements, such as calories or fat, yet they're high enough to figure prominently in your diet. Other terms that mean the same are "little," "few" and "low source of." The specific definitions are:

- Low calorie—contains 40 calories or less per serving
- Low fat—contains three grams or less of total fat per serving
- Low saturated fat—contains one gram or less of saturated fat per serving
- Low cholesterol—contains less than 20 milligrams per serving
- Low sodium—contains less than 140 milligrams per serving
- Very low sodium—contains less than 35 milligrams per serving

More. One serving contains at least 10 percent more of the recommended daily intake of a particular nutrient than its regular counterpart.

Percent fat-free. This claim is a little difficult to explain. The easiest way is to give you an example: If a food contains 5 grams of fat in a 100-gram serving, it can be labeled "95 percent fat-free." The term can be used only on foods that already fall into the category of low fat or fat-free.

Reduced; less. One serving contains 25 percent less of a nutrient than you'd find in a reference food (the regular product or an entirely different product that the food is being compared with).

A food with the "reduced" claim has been nutritionally altered to meet this requirement. This claim may not be made on a product if its reference food already meets the requirement for the "low" claim.

One labeled "less" may or may not have been altered. This second term may also be used when making a comparison claim, as in "Our pretzels have 25 percent less sodium than potato chips."

Nutrition Facts

Serving Size ½ cup (114 g)
Servings per Container 4

Amount per Serving

Calories 120

Calories from Fat 0

	% Daily Value*
Total Fat 0 g	0%
Saturated Fat 0 g	0%
Cholesterol 5 mg	2%
Sodium 170 mg	7%
Total Carbohydrate 17 g	6%
Dietary Fiber 0 g	0%
Sugars 17 g	
Protein 13 g	

Vitamin A 0%	Calcium 40%
Vitamin C 6%	Iron 0%

* Percent Daily Values are based on a 2,000-calorie diet. Your daily values may be higher or lower depending on your calorie needs:

		Calories	2,000	2,500
Total Fat	Less than		66 g	80 g
Sat. Fat	Less than		20 g	25 g
Cholesterol	Less than		300 mg	300 mg
Sodium	Less than		2,400 mg	2,400 mg
Total Carbohydrate			300 mg	375 mg
Dietary Fiber			25 g	30 g

Calories per Gram:
Fat 9 • Carbohydrate 4 • Protein 4

Label Reading Made Easy

Food labels give you just the facts, ma'am. It's up to you to interpret them. Here's a sample label with some suggestions on how to get an accurate "translation."

Serving size. Even though the Food and Drug Administration established serving sizes according to the amounts they say people actually eat, ask yourself if the amount listed seems realistic. All of the nutrition information on the label is based on this serving size—make sure you can stick with this recommended portion so you can accurately calculate the fat and calorie amounts into your daily budgets.

Calories and total fat. Use these numbers when deciding if a food fits into your eating plan. If a snack, for example, contains almost one-third the grams of fat in your daily budget, you'll want to choose a leaner alternative.

Saturated fat and cholesterol. Diets high in saturated fat or cholesterol may be linked to serious diseases, such as heart disease and cancer. So look for low numbers in both areas. No more than 10 percent of your calories should come from saturated fat; use the table on page 7 to calculate how many grams that comes to. As for cholesterol, the American Heart Association recommends a daily intake of no more than 300 milligrams.

Sodium. Try to select foods containing 500 milligrams or less of sodium per serving. High-sodium diets have been linked to high blood pressure.

Dietary fiber. Foods high in fiber are important for keeping your digestive system working smoothly. These foods are especially important in a weight-loss plan because they tend to keep you feeling full longer than foods that are lower in fiber.

The Slim, Trim Kitchen

Take a look around your kitchen. Do you have the tools to make lighter cooking a joy? Here's some equipment that'll ease your task considerably. Since you probably already have some of these items, you won't need to spend a lot of money getting yourself properly outfitted. Just put the remaining things on your wish list and gradually buy them. Before you know it, you'll have a new kitchen to go along with your new outlook on eating.

Blender. This practical appliance is indispensable for making creamy smooth purees, soups and sauces without actually using cream or other high-fat ingredients.

Broiling pan. This pan with a rack is great for broiling or roasting pieces of poultry and meat. Just place the food on the rack and allow the fat to drip into the pan for easy removal.

Egg separator. This little gadget neatly separates the whites from the cholesterol-laden yolks.

Fat skimmer. To remove the fat that rises to the top of homemade stock, soup or stew, use a flat mesh skimmer. Or pour the liquid into a special measuring cup—it's got a spout that reaches to the bottom so you can easily pour off the fat-free portion of the liquid.

Food processor. This handy device can do just about everything a blender can do and more. It cuts, chops, grates and juliennes vegetables within seconds so you have no excuse for stinting on these low-fat foods. If you can afford more than one food processor, get a mini version for small jobs.

Hot-air corn popper. Even the "light" versions of microwave popcorn can have three or four grams of fat per serving. But air poppers allow you to make this crunchy treat without using any oil. To season air-popped corn, squirt it with a shot of no-stick spray, then sprinkle with an herb seasoning or butter-flavored granules.

Kitchen scale. Are you really serving yourself a three-ounce portion of fish? When in doubt, weigh it out. A scale will help you determine proper serving sizes until you can learn to estimate them accurately.

Microwave. This is the ultimate convenience for today's busy health-conscious cook. Foods cook quickly without the need for added fat.

(continued on page 30)

Healthy Swaps

It's amazing how easily you can whittle fat and calories from your diet by making simple substitutions here and there. In most cases, you won't even notice a difference between the standard fatty product and the lighter version. This list of selected items will give you an idea how fast the fat and calorie savings add up.

Instead of:	Use:	Save:
Breads, Cereal and Pasta		
1 blueberry muffin, prepared from a regular mix	1 blueberry muffin, prepared from a light mix	3 grams fat and 39 calories
1 hamburger bun	1 reduced-calorie light hamburger bun	1 gram fat and 39 calories
1 ounce granola	1 ounce low-fat granola	1 gram fat and 30 calories
1 cup cooked egg noodles	1 cup cooked spaghetti	1 gram fat and 16 calories
Dairy		
1 tablespoon butter	1 tablespoon reduced-calorie margarine	4 grams fat and 32 calories
1 ounce cheddar cheese	1 ounce reduced-fat cheddar cheese (4 grams fat per ounce)	5 grams fat and 43 calories
½ cup cottage cheese (4% milk fat)	½ cup nonfat cottage cheese	5 grams fat and 37 calories
1 ounce cream cheese	1 ounce nonfat cream cheese	10 grams fat and 68 calories
1 ounce whole-milk mozzarella cheese	1 ounce reduced-fat mozzarella cheese (3 grams fat per 1 ounce)	3 grams fat and 14 calories
½ cup whole-milk ricotta cheese	½ cup nonfat ricotta cheese	16 grams fat and 136 calories
1 cup whole milk	1 cup skim milk	8 grams fat and 71 calories
1 tablespoon heavy cream	1 tablespoon evaporated skim milk	5 grams fat and 39 calories
½ cup sour cream	½ cup nonfat plain yogurt	23 grams fat and 186 calories

Instead of:	Use:	Save:
Fruits and Vegetables		
I cup canned peach slices (packed in heavy syrup)	I cup canned peach slices (packed in water)	0 grams fat and 132 calories
I cup frozen sweetened strawberries	I cup frozen unsweetened strawberries	0 grams fat and 193 calories
½ cup frozen hash brown potatoes with oil	½ cup frozen hash brown potatoes with no fat	9 grams fat and 91 calories
I cup frozen broccoli spears in butter sauce	I cup frozen broccoli spears, steamed and sprinkled with salt-free seasoning	2 grams fat and 15 calories
Meat, Poultry, Fish and Eggs		
3 ounces ground beef (80% lean)	3 ounces ground turkey breast (no skin added)	17 grams fat and 129 calories
3 ounces boneless beef rib-eye steak	3 ounces boneless beef top round steak	6 grams fat and 38 calories
3 ounces boneless pork loin blade roast	3 ounces pork tenderloin	12 grams fat and 96 calories
3 ounces boneless lamb rib roast	3 ounces lamb arm roast	3 grams fat and 34 calories
3 ounces roasted chicken (dark meat with skin)	3 ounces roasted chicken (breast meat without skin)	10 grams fat and 73 calories
3 ounces canned oil-packed light tuna	3 ounces canned water-packed light tuna	6 grams fat and 70 calories
I egg	2 egg whites	5 grams fat and 42 calories
Miscellaneous		
I tablespoon mayonnaise	I tablespoon nonfat mayonnaise	11 grams fat and 91 calories
I ounce pancake syrup	I ounce reduced-calorie pancake syrup	0 grams fat and 50 calories
I cup prepared canned cream of mushroom soup	I cup prepared 99% fat-free cream of mushroom soup	6 grams fat and 115 calories

No-stick saucepans, skillets and baking pans. These are the most important basics since they'll be the most heavily used items in your new, healthy kitchen. Cookware with a good-quality no-stick coating lets you fry, sauté and bake without adding a lot of fat. To avoid scratching the coating, use only plastic or wooden utensils.

Paper muffin cups. These allow you to make muffins without greasing the pan.

Slow cooker. This is a wonderful appliance for saving time in the kitchen as well as preparing healthy meals. A slow cooker allows lean meats to simmer slowly in their own juices so they become tender like fatty meats. It's also great for preparing long-cooking soups, stews and legumes.

Steamer. Whether you choose a simple stainless-steel basket, an elaborate multi-tiered oriental bamboo variety or a self-contained electric model, a steamer cooks vegetables to crisp-tender perfection. It's also suitable for cooking fish, seafood and boneless chicken breasts or turkey cutlets without added fat.

Stove-top grill. Make low-fat grilling an indoor, year-round event with one of the many stove-top grills available.

Skewers. These are great for grilling or broiling chunks of vegetables, fruits, lean meats and poultry. Just thread the pieces onto the skewers and brush with a juice marinade or some low-fat barbecue sauce during cooking.

Yogurt-cheese maker. This funnel-like gadget lets you make nonfat yogurt cheese, a skinny substitute for cream cheese.

Cook It Lean

Now you're ready for the next step—practicing lighter cooking techniques. The following methods rate top marks for keeping calories and fat to a minimum.

Baking and roasting. These two methods are great for meats, poultry, fish and some vegetables, such as squash and potatoes. Cover the food for part of the cooking time to keep it moist. Use a rack for meats and poultry so that they don't sit in pan drippings and soak them up.

Braising. Also known as stewing, braising refers to cooking food in liquid. It's one of the best methods for tenderizing lean cuts of meat and poultry. An advantage to braising is that the fat seeps into the cooking liquid so you can easily skim it off.

Broiling and grilling. These are excellent alternatives to frying. You cook the food directly under or over a heat source and on a rack to allow the fat to drain away.

Microwaving. Quick and convenient, microwaving is one of the best cooking methods for preserving the nutrients while still keeping the food moist and flavorful. It's ideal for preparing extra-lean foods such as fish fillets and boneless white-meat poultry without a speck of added fat.

Oven-frying. Cooking in this way lets you mimic the texture of fried food without getting the excess fat and calories frying would impart. All you need to do is dip the food, such as skinless chicken breasts or fish fillets, into beaten egg whites and then roll it in fine bread crumbs before baking.

Poaching. Generally used with quick-cooking items like fish or boned poultry, poaching is similar to braising.

Sautéing and stir-frying. These are fine alternatives to cooking in butter or oil. Use a no-stick skillet or wok along with no-stick spray or a small amount of water, defatted broth or citrus juice. If you feel the need for a little oil, pour some into the pan, then wipe it out with a paper towel to leave only a thin coat.

Steaming. By steaming, you can cook vegetables, seafood and some poultry cuts with no added fat.

Starting the Day Right

Orange-Sauced Crêpes
(page 54)

EXTRA HEALTH BENEFITS
Lower Cholesterol
Stronger Immunity

Time: Prep: 15 min.

Makes 8 servings.

Per serving: 166 calories,
1.9 g. fat (10% of calories),
1.4 g. dietary fiber, 3 mg.
cholesterol, 502 mg. sodium.

SLIMMING STRATEGY

You don't always have to
choose the lowest-fat version of a product. The 1%
cottage cheese used here
gives you a creamier
spread than if you used
fat-free cottage cheese—
and fat and calories are
still low.

Curried Cheese Spread

*This mixture keeps for about a week, so you can enjoy it
often. It also makes a good snack spread on whole-grain
crackers.*

 ¾ **cup reduced-fat (1%) cottage cheese**
 2 **tablespoons nonfat mayonnaise**
 1 **tablespoon skim milk**
 ¼ **teaspoon curry powder**
 ⅛ **teaspoon onion powder**
 3 **tablespoons shredded reduced-fat cheddar cheese**
 2 **tablespoons minced fresh parsley**
 8 **English muffins or bagels, split and toasted**

In a blender or small food processor, blend or process the cottage cheese, mayonnaise, milk, curry powder and onion powder
until the cottage cheese is almost smooth.

Transfer the mixture to a container with a tight-fitting cover.
Stir in the cheddar cheese and parsley.

To store: Cover tightly and store in the refrigerator until ready
to serve.

To serve: For each serving, spread 2 tablespoons of the cheese
mixture on each split muffin or bagel.

Chef's Note: If you don't have a blender or small food processor, use a spoon to press the cottage cheese through a fine sieve
or strainer before combining it with the other ingredients.

Breakfast: A Meal Worth Getting Up For

Good morning! It's time to rise and shine with a healthful, hearty breakfast. Breakfast is the most important meal of the day, yet it's the meal most
often missed. However, with the recipes in this chapter, there are no excuses
for skipping this number-one meal.

If your mornings are hectic, try our in-a-hurry breakfasts. Look for the
recipes in this chapter that include storage and serving instructions—these
are delicious foods you can take with you on the way to work or whip up in
minutes before leaving the house. The balance of the recipes are leisurely
breakfast and brunch entrées for when you have more time.

Omelet in an English Muffin

No need to stop at a fast-food restaurant on the way to work. Here's a low-calorie, low-fat version of the popular egg 'n' muffin sandwich. For variety, replace the ham with cooked lean beef, chicken or turkey breast.

½ **cup fat-free egg substitute**
¼ **cup water**
½ **teaspoon dried basil**
⅓ **cup finely chopped fully cooked lean ham**
¼ **cup sliced green onions**
¼ **cup (1 ounce) shredded part-skim mozzarella cheese**
⅓ **cup nonfat ranch-style dressing**
1 **teaspoon prepared mustard**
5 **whole-wheat English muffins, split and toasted**

Spray an unheated large skillet with no-stick spray. Heat the skillet over medium heat.

In a small bowl, beat together the egg substitute, water and basil. Stir in the ham and onions.

Pour the egg mixture into the hot skillet and cook until it begins to set. Using a large spoon, lift and turn the egg mixture so it cooks evenly. Continue cooking until the egg mixture is thoroughly cooked but still glossy and moist on top. Remove the skillet from the heat and stir in the cheese. Set the mixture aside.

In a small bowl, stir together the dressing and mustard. Spread the dressing mixture onto the English muffin halves.

Spoon the egg mixture onto half of the English muffin halves. Top with the remaining English muffin halves.

To store: Individually wrap each sandwich in freezer wrap and freeze until ready to serve.

To serve: Thaw overnight in the refrigerator.

Remove the freezer wrap and wrap each sandwich in foil. Bake at 350° about 25 minutes or until heated through.

Or vent the freezer wrap and heat each sandwich in a microwave oven on medium power (50%) for 1 minute. Rotate the sandwich a half-turn; heat on medium about ½ to 1 minute more.

Quick

EXTRA HEALTH BENEFITS
Lower Cholesterol
Stronger Immunity

Times: Prep: 23 min.
Cooking: 2 min.
Microwaving: 1½ min. (opt.)
Reheating: 25 min. (opt.)

Makes 5 servings.

Per serving: 190 calories, 2.5 g. fat (12% of calories), 1.4 g. dietary fiber, 7.7 mg. cholesterol, 632 mg. sodium.

SLIMMING STRATEGY

A study at Kent State University in Ohio found that breakfasts eaten at home average 28 percent of calories from fat. Those eaten out average 35 percent. At-home breakfasts also tend to have more vitamins and minerals.

Good Morning Muffins

Reminiscent of carrot cake, these low-calorie muffins can double as either an on-the-go breakfast or a sugar-free dessert.

Times: Prep: 20 min.
Baking: 20 min.
Microwaving: 15 sec. (opt.)

Makes 10 muffins.

Per muffin: 119 calories, 3.2 g. fat (23% of calories), 2.1 g. dietary fiber, 0 mg. cholesterol, 58 mg. sodium.

¾ **cup unbleached flour**
¾ **cup whole-wheat flour**
¼ **cup oat bran**
1½ **teaspoons baking powder**
½ **teaspoon ground cinnamon**
⅛ **teaspoon ground allspice**
¼ **teaspoon grated orange peel**
¾ **cup orange juice**
1 **lightly beaten egg white**
2 **tablespoons canola oil**
2 **tablespoons honey**
1 **medium carrot, shredded**

Spray 10 muffin cups with no-stick spray (or line the cups with paper baking cups); set aside.

In a medium bowl, stir together the unbleached flour, whole-wheat flour, oat bran, baking powder, cinnamon and allspice.

In a small bowl, combine the orange peel, orange juice, egg white, oil and honey. Add to the flour mixture and stir just until combined. Stir in the carrots.

Spoon the batter into the muffin cups, filling each about three-quarters full. Bake at 400° about 20 minutes or until a toothpick inserted near the centers comes out clean. Remove the muffins from the muffin cups. Cool completely on a wire rack.

To store: Individually wrap each muffin in freezer wrap and freeze until ready to serve.

To serve: Thaw overnight at room temperature. Or thaw and reheat each muffin in a microwave oven on high power (100%) for 15 to 20 seconds.

Chef's Note: When you have extra zucchini from the garden, shred it and use in place of the carrots.

SLIMMING STRATEGY

Here are some easy ways to cut fat from your own muffin recipes. Use 2 egg whites or ¼ cup fat-free egg substitute in place of each whole egg. Replace whole milk with skim milk. Reduce the oil to 1 tablespoon per cup of flour.

Peach-Bran Muffins

EXTRA HEALTH BENEFITS
Lower Cholesterol
Stronger Immunity

Times: Prep: 15 min.
Baking: 20 min.
Microwaving: 15 sec. (opt.)

Makes 10 muffins.

Per muffin: 125 calories,
3.1 g. fat (21% of calories),
2.8 g. dietary fiber, 0 mg.
cholesterol, 93 mg. sodium.

One or two of these fruity muffins and a glass of low-fat milk make an ideal hurry-up breakfast.

     1 **cup skim milk**
    ⅓ **cup chopped dried peaches**
     1 **cup whole-wheat flour**
    ½ **cup unbleached flour**
    ¼ **cup bran cereal**
     2 **tablespoons packed brown sugar or ¼ cup honey**
  1½ **teaspoons baking powder**
     1 **lightly beaten egg white**
     2 **tablespoons canola oil**

Spray 10 muffin cups with no-stick spray (or line the cups with paper baking cups); set aside.

In a small bowl, combine the milk and peaches. Let stand for 5 minutes.

Meanwhile, in a medium bowl, stir together the whole-wheat flour, unbleached flour, cereal, brown sugar or honey and baking powder.

Stir the egg white and oil into the milk and peaches. Add to the flour mixture and stir just until combined.

Spoon the batter into the muffin cups, filling each cup about half full. Bake at 400° about 20 minutes or until a toothpick inserted near the centers comes out clean. Remove the muffins from the muffin cups. Cool completely on a wire rack.

To store: Individually wrap each muffin in freezer wrap and freeze until ready to serve.

To serve: Thaw overnight at room temperature. Or thaw and reheat each muffin in a microwave oven on high power (100%) for 15 to 20 seconds.

Chef's Note: For variety, replace the peaches with other types of dried fruit, such as raisins, blueberries, cranberries, cherries, currants or a mixed-fruit combo.

SLIMMING STRATEGY
You can lighten muffin and quick-bread recipes by substituting applesauce or pureed prunes for half of the fat. Use ½ cup applesauce or ¼ cup prune puree for each ½ cup of fat you're replacing.

Three-Grain Granola

Despite its "healthy" reputation, granola—especially the commercial variety—is often alarmingly high in fat and calories. This homemade version is considerably better for you.

> 2 **cups puffed rice**
> 1⅓ **cups bran flakes**
> ½ **cup old-fashioned rolled oats**
> ¼ **cup raisins**
> 2 **tablespoons toasted wheat germ**
> ½ **cup unsweetened apple juice**
> 2 **tablespoons honey**

In a medium bowl, combine the puffed rice, bran flakes, oats, raisins and wheat germ.

In a small bowl, stir together the apple juice and honey. Pour over the puffed rice mixture and toss until moistened.

Spray a 15" × 10" baking pan with no-stick spray. Spread the puffed rice mixture in the pan. Bake at 300° about 30 minutes or until golden brown, stirring twice during baking.

Transfer the granola to a large piece of foil. Let the mixture cool, then break it into pieces.

To store: Transfer the granola to a container. Cover loosely and store at room temperature until ready to serve. (Do not cover tightly because the cereal will not stay crisp.)

To serve: For each serving, place ¾ cup granola in a cereal bowl and add ½ cup skim milk.

Chef's Note: If you want to splurge a little, stir ¼ cup flaked coconut into the cereal mixture before baking. You'll get an extra 35 calories and 2.4 grams of fat in each serving.

EXTRA HEALTH BENEFITS
Lower Cholesterol
Cancer Protection
Blood Building
Stronger Immunity

Times: Prep: 10 min.
Baking: 30 min.

Makes 4 servings.

Per serving (with milk): 250 calories, 1.5 g. fat (5% of calories), 3.5 g. dietary fiber, 2 mg. cholesterol, 218 mg. sodium.

Apple-Apricot Turnovers

Times: Prep: 50 min.
Rising: 1 hr. 35 min.
Baking: 15 min.
Microwaving: 2 min. (opt.)

Makes 6 turnovers.

Per turnover: 228 calories, 2 g. fat (7% of calories), 5.1 g. dietary fiber, 0 mg. cholesterol, 49 mg. sodium.

SLIMMING STRATEGY

If you like to drink coffee with your turnover, be sure not to fatten it up with a high-cal whitener like heavy cream or half-and-half. Also be aware that commercial nondairy creamers often contain a lot of saturated fat. An excellent alternative is nonfat dry milk powder. You can even keep a small container of it in your desk for coffee at the office.

Don't compromise your healthy eating habits with high-calorie, fat-laden Danish pastries. When you have a yen for fruit-filled pastry, try these satisfying turnovers. Although they take a little while to make, they're not complicated. And you can keep the extras in the freezer for those mornings when you need to brown-bag your breakfast.

> 2 **cups whole-wheat flour**
> 1 **package active dry yeast**
> ½ **cup unsweetened apple juice**
> 1 **tablespoon honey**
> 1 **tablespoon reduced-calorie margarine**
> 2 **lightly beaten egg whites**
> 1 **can (20 ounces) pie-sliced apples, drained**
> ½ **cup apricot all-fruit spread**
> ¼ **teaspoon ground cinnamon**
> ¼ **teaspoon ground nutmeg**
> ¼ **teaspoon vanilla**

In a large bowl, stir together 1 cup of the flour and the yeast. Set the mixture aside.

In a small saucepan, combine the apple juice, honey and margarine. Heat just until warm (120° to 130°). Stir to completely melt the margarine.

Stir the juice mixture and egg whites into the flour mixture. Using an electric mixer, beat on low speed just until combined. Then beat on medium speed for 3 minutes. Using a spoon, stir in enough of the remaining flour to make a soft dough. Transfer to a floured surface. Knead in enough of the remaining flour to make a smooth, moderately stiff dough.

Spray a medium bowl with no-stick spray. Place the dough in the bowl and turn it over to coat all sides with the spray. Cover the bowl with a clean towel and let the dough rise in a warm place about 1 hour or until doubled in size.

Punch down the dough and cover it with the towel. Let rest for 10 minutes. On a floured surface, roll the dough to an 18" × 12" rectangle. Cut into 6 squares, 6" each.

Spray a cookie sheet with no-stick spray; set aside.

In a small bowl, combine the apples, fruit spread, cinnamon, nutmeg and vanilla. Spoon a rounded ⅓ cup of the apple mixture onto 1 side of each square of dough. Moisten the edges of the dough with water, then fold the other side of the dough over the apple mixture. Using the tines of a fork, seal the edges of the dough. Place the pastries on the cookie sheet. If desired, cut a small slit in each pastry.

Cover the pastries with the towel and let rise about 35 minutes or until they are almost doubled in size. Bake at 375° for 15 to 20 minutes or until golden brown. Transfer to a wire rack and cool completely.

To store: Individually wrap each pastry in freezer wrap and freeze until ready to serve.

To serve: Thaw overnight at room temperature. Or microwave each pastry on medium power (50%) about 2 minutes.

Chef's Note: To speed up preparation time, use quick-rising yeast. The dough will rise in about a third less time.

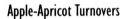

Apple-Apricot Turnovers

EXTRA HEALTH BENEFITS
Lower Cholesterol
Stronger Immunity

Time: Prep: 8 min.

Makes 4 servings.

Per serving: 222 calories, 3.3 g. fat (13% of calories), 1.1 g. dietary fiber, 13 mg. cholesterol, 906 mg. sodium.

SLIMMING STRATEGY

Reduced-fat cheeses aren't always lower in cholesterol. So if you're watching your cholesterol intake, check the label.

Savory Cheese Pockets

Here's a savory vegetable breakfast sandwich that can also double as a slimming brown-bag lunch entrée. Pack the sandwich while it's still frozen so that it'll still be cold at lunchtime.

> 1 **cup reduced-fat (1%) cottage cheese**
> 1 **tablespoon skim milk**
> ½ **cup shredded zucchini**
> ¼ **cup (1 ounce) shredded reduced-fat cheddar cheese**
> ½ **teaspoon dillweed**
> ¼ **teaspoon onion powder**
> 2 **6" whole-wheat pita breads**

In a blender or small food processor, blend or process the cottage cheese and milk until smooth.

Transfer the cottage cheese mixture to a small bowl. Stir in the zucchini, cheddar cheese, dillweed and onion powder.

Cut each pita crosswise in half to form 2 pockets. Fill each pocket with the cheese mixture.

To store: Individually wrap each sandwich in freezer wrap and freeze until ready to serve.

To serve: Thaw overnight in the refrigerator.

EXTRA HEALTH BENEFITS
Lower Cholesterol
Cancer Protection
Stronger Immunity

Times: Prep: 5 min.
Chilling: overnight
Cooking: 2 min.
Microwaving: 2 min. (opt.)

Fruited Bulgur

Bulgur wins high marks for its impressive fiber content. Adding dried fruit and a little skim milk to the bulgur turns this side-dish grain into a delicious hot cereal.

> 1 **cup bulgur**
> 1 **cup water**
> 1 **cup apricot nectar**
> ⅓ **cup mixed dried fruit bits**
> 1 **tablespoon oat bran**
> 1 **tablespoon honey**

Place the bulgur in a colander and rinse under cold running water. Drain the bulgur and transfer it to a container with a tight-fitting cover. Add the water, apricot nectar, fruit bits, oat bran and honey; stir until well combined. Cover and refrigerate overnight.

For each serving, place ¾ cup of the mixture in a small saucepan. Bring to a boil, stirring once or twice. Then transfer the mixture to a cereal bowl and add ¼ cup milk.

Or, to heat in a microwave oven, place ¾ cup of the mixture in a microwave-proof cereal bowl. Cook on high (100% power) for 1½ to 2 minutes or until the cereal is heated through, stirring occasionally. Add ¼ cup skim milk.

Chef's Note: Store this cereal in your refrigerator for only 2 to 3 days. For longer storage, freeze individual servings in self-closing freezer bags.

Nutty Pineapple Cream Cheese on Raisin Bread

Peanut butter is notoriously high in fat. But you can still enjoy it if you eat it in moderation. These breakfast sandwiches extend it—while retaining its nutty taste—by combining the spread with nonfat cream cheese.

　1　**container (8 ounces) nonfat cream cheese**
　2　**tablespoons peanut butter**
　1　**can (8 ounces) crushed pineapple (packed in juice), drained**
　10　**slices raisin bread**

In a small bowl, stir together the cream cheese and peanut butter. Then stir in the pineapple.

Spread the mixture on half of the bread slices. Then top each with a remaining bread slice.

To store: Individually wrap each sandwich in freezer wrap and freeze until ready to serve.

To serve: Thaw overnight in the refrigerator. Or microwave each sandwich on high power (100%) for 25 to 30 seconds.

Chef's Note: This mixture is also delicious on bagels or toasted English muffins.

Makes 4 servings.

Per serving (with milk): 245 calories, 1.7 g. fat (6% of calories), 7 g. dietary fiber, 1 mg. cholesterol, 99 mg. sodium.

Quick

EXTRA HEALTH BENEFIT
Stronger Immunity

Times: Prep: 12 min. Microwaving: 25 sec. (opt.)

Makes 5 servings.

Per serving: 240 calories, 5.2 g. fat (19% of calories), 2.1 g. dietary fiber, 8 mg. cholesterol, 507 mg. sodium.

Breakfast Pizzas

If you're the type of person who likes pizza for breakfast, we have a treat for you! This beef and vegetable "pie" is low in fat and calories.

EXTRA HEALTH BENEFITS
Blood Building
Stronger Bones
Stronger Immunity

Times: Prep: 38 min.
Baking: 15 min.
Reheating: 20 min. (opt.)
Microwaving: 3 min. (opt.)

Makes 4 servings.

Per serving: 296 calories, 7.8 g. fat (24% of calories), 2.8 g. dietary fiber, 30 mg. cholesterol, 331 mg. sodium

1	package active dry yeast
½	cup warm water (105° to 115°)
2	teaspoons canola oil
¾	cup unbleached flour
½	cup rye flour
4	ounces (85% lean) ground beef
1	cup sliced fresh mushrooms
1	cup chopped onions
¾	cup chopped sweet red peppers
½	cup nonfat plain yogurt
¼	cup nonfat mayonnaise
¼	teaspoon curry powder
¾	cup (3 ounces) shredded part-skim mozzarella cheese

In a small bowl, stir together the yeast, water and oil. Let stand for 10 minutes.

Using a spoon, stir in the unbleached flour and enough of the rye flour to make a smooth, moderately stiff dough. (If the dough becomes too difficult to stir with the spoon, use your hands to knead in enough of the remaining rye flour to make the dough smooth and moderately stiff.) Divide the dough into quarters and shape into smooth balls. Cover the balls with a clean towel and let rest for 10 minutes.

Meanwhile, spray an unheated large skillet with no-stick spray. Heat the skillet over medium heat. Add the ground beef, mushrooms, onions and peppers and cook about 8 minutes or until the meat is browned and the vegetables are tender, stirring occasionally to break up the meat.

Drain the beef mixture in a strainer or colander, then transfer it to a large plate lined with 3 layers of paper towels. Blot the top of the mixture with additional paper towels. Set the mixture aside.

Spray 2 cookie sheets with no-stick spray. On the cookie sheets, pat each ball of dough into a 6" circle, building up the edges. Bake at 425° for 5 minutes.

Meanwhile, in a small bowl, stir together the yogurt, mayonnaise and curry powder. Spread on the hot crusts and sprinkle with the meat mixture and cheese. Bake for 10 to 12 minutes more or until the cheese is melted and the pizzas are heated through. Serve hot or transfer the pizzas to wire racks and cool completely.

To store: Individually wrap each pizza in freezer wrap and freeze until ready to serve.

To serve: Thaw overnight in the refrigerator.

Remove the freezer wrap and wrap each pizza in foil. Bake at 350° about 20 minutes or until heated through.

Or unwrap each thawed pizza and place on a microwave-proof plate. Cover loosely with plastic wrap. Reheat in a microwave oven on medium power (50%) for 1½ minutes. Rotate the plate a half-turn and heat on medium about 1½ minutes more.

Chef's Note: If you forget to thaw the pizzas ahead of time, give them an extra 10 minutes or so in the oven. Or increase the microwave time of each pizza to 5 minutes; rotate the pizza a half-turn after 2 minutes.

SLIMMING STRATEGY

There are solid reasons to eat a good breakfast, including that this morning meal helps rev up your metabolism. People who don't eat breakfast have metabolic rates 4 to 5 percent below normal, according to studies done at George Washington University in Washington, D.C. As a result of this metabolic slump, a breakfast skipper could expect to gain 1 pound in 7 weeks—even without increasing calorie intake.

Bagels to Go

In the morning before you head off for work, grab one of these low-fat sandwiches from the freezer. By the time you get to the office, the sandwich will be thawed and you'll be able to enjoy a nutritious breakfast.

- ½ **cup nonfat cream cheese**
- ¼ **cup chopped dates**
- ½ **teaspoon grated orange peel**
- 1 **tablespoon orange juice**
- ⅛ **teaspoon ground allspice**
- 4 **white or whole-wheat bagels, split and toasted**

In a small bowl, stir together the cream cheese, dates, orange peel, orange juice and allspice.

Spread 1 side of each bagel with the cheese mixture. Top with the remaining bagel half.

To store: Individually wrap each sandwich in freezer wrap and freeze until ready to serve.

To serve: Thaw overnight in the refrigerator. Or microwave each sandwich on high power (100%) for 20 to 30 seconds.

Fast-Track Breakfast

Fruit-flavored yogurt gives this shake its thick and creamy texture without contributing unwanted fat. This recipe makes several servings, so you can freeze any leftovers for other mornings. Just pack in single-serving containers to freeze, then allow it to thaw overnight in the refrigerator. Stir well before drinking.

- 2 **containers (8 ounces each) low-fat blueberry or straw-berry yogurt**
- 1¼ **cups skim milk**
- ¾ **cup fresh or frozen blueberries or strawberries**
- 3 **tablespoons nonfat dry milk powder**
- 2 **teaspoons honey**

In a blender, blend the yogurt, milk, berries, milk powder and honey until smooth.

Casserole of Eggs and Asparagus

EXTRA HEALTH BENEFIT
Stronger Immunity

Times: Prep: 23 min.
Baking: 15 min.

Makes 4 servings.

Per serving: 118 calories,
3.4 g. fat (26% of calories),
0.9 g. dietary fiber, 72 mg.
cholesterol, 129 mg. sodium.

Here's a cheesy egg casserole that will fit into most weight-loss plans. It's low in calories, fat and cholesterol. Serve it with fresh fruit and Good Morning Muffins (page 36).

4 **egg whites**
1 **egg or ¼ cup fat-free egg substitute**
2 **tablespoons water**
2 **tablespoons + ½ cup skim milk**
1 **tablespoon unbleached flour**
1 **teaspoon reduced-sodium chicken bouillon powder**
¾ **teaspoon dried sage**
½ **teaspoon onion powder**
Pinch of ground black pepper
¼ **cup (1 ounce) shredded part-skim mozzarella cheese**
1 **package (10 ounces) frozen cut asparagus, thawed and well drained**
3 **ounces chopped cooked turkey breast**

Spray an unheated large skillet with no-stick spray. Heat the skillet over medium heat.

In a small bowl, beat together the egg whites, egg or egg substitute and water. Pour into the skillet. Cook until it begins to set. Using a large spoon, lift and turn the egg mixture so it cooks evenly. Continue cooking until the egg mixture is thoroughly cooked but still glossy and moist. Remove the skillet from the heat and set aside.

In a small saucepan, use a wire whisk to stir together the 2 tablespoons milk and flour. Stir in the remaining ½ cup milk, bouillon powder, sage, onion powder and pepper. Cook and stir over medium heat until the mixture thickens and begins to gently boil. Stir in the cheese. Remove from the heat.

Spray an 8" round baking dish with no-stick spray; set aside. In a medium bowl, combine the asparagus and turkey. Stir in the cheese sauce, then gently fold in the cooked egg mixture. Transfer to the baking dish. Bake at 350° for 15 to 20 minutes or until heated through.

Chef's Note: When fresh asparagus is at its peak, use 1 pound of fresh spears. Trim the woody bottoms from the spears, then cut the stalks into 1" pieces. Steam the asparagus just until tender before adding it to the casserole.

SLIMMING STRATEGY

A piece of seasonal fruit offers just the right amount of sweetness to round out a quick, low-fat brunch. For something fast and warm, halve and section a grapefruit. Drizzle with a little maple syrup and broil until warm. Or take advantage of fresh summer berries and top them with low-fat vanilla yogurt.

Potato Frittata Italiano

Begin your day right with this hearty low-calorie egg dish. If Italian seasoning doesn't suit your fancy, flavor this dish with half a teaspoon of your favorite herb and omit the garlic.

 2 cups refrigerated or thawed frozen hash brown potatoes with no fat
¼ cup sliced green onions
 2 medium tomatoes, seeded and chopped
 4 egg whites
 2 eggs or ½ cup fat-free egg substitute
¼ cup grated Parmesan cheese
 3 tablespoons water
½ teaspoon dried Italian seasoning
¼ teaspoon garlic powder
⅛ teaspoon ground black pepper

Spray the bottom and sides of an unheated 10" skillet with no-stick spray. Heat the skillet over medium-low heat. Add the potatoes and onions. Cook for 4 to 5 minutes or until the potatoes are just tender, stirring frequently. Stir in the tomatoes. Then cook for 2 minutes more or until heated through, stirring occasionally.

Meanwhile, in a medium bowl, beat together the egg whites, eggs or egg substitute, cheese, water, Italian seasoning, garlic powder and pepper. Carefully pour over the vegetables. Cook over low heat until it begins to set. Using a spatula, lift the edges to allow the uncooked egg mixture to flow underneath. Continue cooking until the egg mixture is nearly set but still moist on top.

Cover and let stand for 3 to 4 minutes or until the surface is set. To serve, cut into wedges.

EXTRA HEALTH BENEFIT
Stronger Immunity

Times: Prep: 9 min.
Cooking: 10 min.
Standing: 3 min.

Makes 4 servings.

Per serving: 184 calories, 4.6 g. fat (22% of calories), 2.6 g. dietary fiber, 111 mg. cholesterol, 228 mg. sodium.

SLIMMING STRATEGY

Not all hash brown potatoes are created equal! Some are loaded with fat. So be sure to take a look at the nutrition information on the label before tossing those taters into your shopping cart.

Eggs and Beef on an English Muffin

EXTRA HEALTH BENEFIT
Stronger Immunity

Times: Prep: 22 min.
Baking: 15 min.

Makes 4 servings.

Per serving: 166 calories,
4.2 g. fat (23% of calories),
0.7 g. dietary fiber, 119 mg.
cholesterol, 373 mg. sodium.

If this reminds you a little of eggs Benedict, it's not surprising. The big difference, of course, is that this version is a lot lower in fat. You can credit the egg substitute, lean beef and a light mustard sauce that replace the traditional poached eggs, ham and hollandaise sauce.

EGGS AND BEEF
  2 **English muffins, split and toasted**
  3 **ounces beef round steak**
  4 **egg whites**
  2 **eggs or ½ cup fat-free egg substitute**
  2 **tablespoons skim milk**
     Pinch of ground black pepper

SAUCE
  ⅓ **cup skim milk**
  1 **teaspoon cornstarch**
  1 **teaspoon Dijon mustard**
  ½ **teaspoon reduced-sodium chicken bouillon powder**
  ¼ **teaspoon lemon juice**
  1 **tablespoon minced fresh parsley**

For the eggs and beef: Spray an 8" × 8" baking dish with no-stick spray. Arrange the muffin halves, cut sides up, in the baking dish; set aside.

Spray an unheated small skillet with no-stick spray. Heat the skillet over medium-high heat. Add the beef and cook for 2 minutes. Turn the beef over and cook about 3 minutes more for medium doneness. Transfer the beef to a cutting board, then bias-slice it across the grain into thin strips. Arrange the strips on the muffin halves.

Spray an unheated large skillet with no-stick spray. Heat the skillet over medium heat.

In a small bowl, beat together the egg whites, eggs or egg substitute, milk and pepper. Pour into the skillet. Cook until it begins to set. Using a large spoon, lift and turn the egg mixture so it cooks evenly. Continue cooking until the egg mixture is thoroughly cooked but still glossy and moist on top. Remove the skillet from the heat.

Spoon the egg mixture on top of the steak strips. Cover with foil and bake at 350° about 15 minutes or until heated through.

For the sauce: Meanwhile, in a small saucepan, use a wire whisk to stir together the milk, cornstarch, mustard, bouillon powder and lemon juice. Cook and stir until the mixture thickens and begins to gently boil. Cook and stir for 2 minutes more.

To serve, spoon the sauce over the English muffin stacks. Sprinkle with the parsley.

Chef's Note: You can easily double this recipe. Assemble the English muffin stacks in a 13" × 9" baking dish.

Be Smart about Eggs

Is there room for eggs in a healthy diet? You bet your frittata there is! Even the American Heart Association says that three or four eggs a week are permissible.

The main objection most people have to whole eggs is the cholesterol content (about 213 milligrams in a large egg). A secondary concern is the fat content, but that's not as bad as you might think: five grams in a yolk and none in the white. Still, if eggs are a regular item on your breakfast table, you'd be wise to find ways to keep cholesterol and fat under control. Here are a few suggestions.

• You'll notice that many recipes in this book call for egg substitute. This readily available product comes in both refrigerated and frozen forms. It's made mostly of egg whites, contains no cholesterol and has fewer calories than whole eggs. Egg substitute is ideal for omelets, frittatas, scrambled eggs, pancakes, muffins, casseroles, quiches, sauces and other dishes that call for whole eggs. Use $\frac{1}{4}$ cup egg substitute in place of each egg.

• If you shy away from egg substitute, buy whole eggs and use just the whites. For cooking and baking purposes, two whites are equivalent to one whole egg.

• A compromise alternative is to stretch one yolk by adding several extra whites. This works well for omelets, frittatas, scrambled eggs and other dishes where the yellow color is important.

• Some brands of whole eggs are reputed to have less cholesterol than usual. Look for them near the regular eggs in your market's refrigerated case. In a similar vein, there's at least one brand of reduced-cholesterol blended eggs. It comes in a carton like egg substitute and is used the same way. In both of these cases, the fat content is no lower than usual.

• Bear in mind that what often accompanies eggs—butter, bacon, cheese and cream—is far worse than the eggs themselves. So ship off the offenders and shape up your breakfasts.

Mushroom-Carrot Omelet

Times: Prep: 9 min.
Cooking: 8 min.

Makes 2 servings.

Per serving: 66 calories,
0.4 g. fat (5% of calories),
0.8 g. dietary fiber, 1 mg.
cholesterol, 229 mg. sodium.

This version of a French omelet tastes just like the classic but with less fat, fewer calories and almost no cholesterol. Serve it with Peach-Bran Muffins (page 38) for an easy brunch.

½ **cup sliced fresh mushrooms**
⅓ **cup coarsely shredded carrots**
3 **tablespoons water**
¼ **cup reduced-fat (1%) cottage cheese**
⅔ **cup fat-free egg substitute**
¼ **teaspoon dried marjoram**
   Pinch of cracked black pepper

In a small saucepan, combine the mushrooms, carrots and 2 tablespoons of the water. Bring to a boil, then reduce the heat. Cover and simmer about 3 minutes or until the carrots are just tender; drain. Stir in the cottage cheese. Set aside.

Spray an unheated 10" skillet with slanted sides with no-stick spray. Heat the skillet over medium heat.

In a small bowl, beat together the egg substitute, the remaining tablespoon of water, marjoram and pepper. Pour into the skillet. Using a spatula, lift the edges to allow the uncooked egg mixture to flow underneath. Continue cooking until the egg mixture is set but still glossy and moist on top.

Spoon the vegetable-cheese mixture across the center of the omelet. Fold the sides of the omelet over the mixture. Transfer the omelet to a serving plate.

Chef's Note: There's a trick to successfully transferring an omelet to a serving plate without breaking it. Slide the omelet to the edge of the skillet, then slowly tilt the skillet and push the omelet onto the plate.

Mushroom-Carrot Omelet

Oven-Crisped French Toast with Apricot Sauce

You might think French toast is off-limits on a sensible eating plan, but this dish has the potential to be quite low in fat. Egg whites and skim milk slim it down considerably. And baking the bread slices rather than frying them in butter keeps the fat low. An added advantage to the baking method is that you won't run out of space on the griddle—all the slices fit on a single cookie sheet.

FRENCH TOAST
- 4 egg whites
- ½ cup skim milk
- ½ teaspoon ground cinnamon
- ½ teaspoon vanilla
- 8 slices whole-wheat or white bread

SAUCE
- 2 tablespoons water
- 1½ teaspoons cornstarch
- 1 can (6 ounces) apricot nectar
- 1 tablespoon honey

For the French toast: Spray a cookie sheet with no-stick spray; set aside. In a shallow bowl, beat together the egg whites, milk, cinnamon and vanilla.

Dip the bread slices, 1 at a time, into the egg mixture, coating both sides. Place them on the cookie sheet.

Bake at 450° for 6 minutes. Turn the bread slices over and bake about 5 minutes more or until golden brown.

For the sauce: Meanwhile, in a small saucepan, use a wire whisk to stir together the water and cornstarch. Stir in the apricot nectar and honey. Cook and stir over medium heat until the mixture thickens and begins to gently boil. Cook and stir for 2 minutes more.

To serve, arrange 2 slices of the French toast on each plate. Serve with the warm sauce.

Chef's Note: Next time you make this French toast, try slices of seven-grain, cracked wheat or raisin bread.

EXTRA HEALTH BENEFITS
Lower Cholesterol
Stronger Immunity

Times: Prep: 12 min.
Baking: 11 min.

Makes 4 servings.

Per serving: 205 calories, 1.8 g. fat (8% of calories), 2.9 g. dietary fiber, 1 mg. cholesterol, 289 mg. sodium.

Orange-Sauced Crêpes

EXTRA HEALTH BENEFIT
Stronger Immunity

Times: Prep: 28 min.
Baking: 15 min.

Makes 4 servings.

Per serving: 249 calories,
4.2 g. fat (15% of calories),
2.9 g. dietary fiber, 15 mg.
cholesterol, 116 mg. sodium.

Any morning that starts with these crêpes is bound to be good!

CRÊPES
  2 **lightly beaten egg whites**
  ¾ **cup skim milk**
  ½ **cup whole-wheat flour**

FILLING
  ¾ **cup part-skim ricotta cheese**
  ¼ **cup raisins**
  1 **tablespoon honey**

SAUCE
  2 **tablespoons water**
  2 **teaspoons cornstarch**
  1 **teaspoon grated orange peel**
  1 **cup orange juice**
  1 **teaspoon honey**
  1 **can (10½ ounces) mandarin orange sections (packed in water), drained**

For the crêpes: In a small bowl, use a wire whisk to stir together the egg whites, milk and flour just until combined.

Spray an unheated, 6" no-stick skillet with no-stick spray. Heat the skillet over medium heat, then remove the skillet from the heat.

Ladle about 2 tablespoons of the batter into the skillet. Immediately rotate the skillet so the batter forms a circle in the bottom. Return the skillet to the heat. Cook about 1 minute or until the crêpe is brown on 1 side. Using a rubber spatula, loosen the edges. Turn the skillet upside down and remove the crêpe. Repeat with the remaining batter to make 8 crêpes, occasionally letting the skillet cool slightly and spraying it with no-stick spray.

For the filling: In a small bowl, combine the ricotta cheese, raisins and honey.

To assemble: Spray an 8" × 8" baking dish with no-stick spray; set aside. Spoon a rounded tablespoon of the ricotta mixture on the center of the uncooked side of each crêpe. Form each into a packet by folding 2 opposite sides to the center, overlapping the edges slightly. Then fold in the remaining 2 sides.

Place the packets in the baking dish, overlapping slightly. Cover with foil and bake at 350° for 15 to 20 minutes or until heated through.

For the sauce: Meanwhile, in a small saucepan, stir together the water and cornstarch. Then stir in the orange peel, orange juice and honey. Cook and stir until the mixture thickens and begins to gently boil. Cook and stir for 2 minutes more. Gently stir in the oranges.

To serve, arrange 2 crêpes on each plate. Serve with the warm sauce.

Chef's Note: Save time by making the crêpes ahead. Let them cool, then stack the bunch and cover with plastic wrap. Refrigerate for up to 4 days. For longer storage, freeze the crêpes. They'll be easier to separate later if you place 2 pieces of wax paper between each pair. Wrap airtight. When ready to use, thaw the crêpes in the refrigerator overnight or at room temperature until pliable.

Orange-Sauced Crêpes

Whole-Wheat Pancakes with Pear Sauce

EXTRA HEALTH BENEFITS
Lower Cholesterol
Stronger Immunity

Times: Prep: 25 min.
Cooking: 10 min.

Makes 4 servings.

Per serving: 291 calories,
5.6 g. fat (17% of calories),
5.5 g. dietary fiber, 1 mg.
cholesterol, 187 mg. sodium.

You can make a really nice, simple sauce for all sorts of pancakes and waffles by cooking pears with pear nectar. For variety, try apples with apple juice or cider or combine peaches with peach nectar.

SAUCE

> 1 cup cored and chopped pears
> 1 can (6 ounces) pear nectar
> 1 teaspoon packed brown sugar
> ⅛ teaspoon ground nutmeg
> 1 tablespoon water
> 1½ teaspoons cornstarch

PANCAKES

> 1 cup whole-wheat flour
> ½ cup unbleached flour
> 2 teaspoons packed brown sugar
> 1½ teaspoons baking powder
> ⅛ teaspoon ground nutmeg
> 1 cup skim milk
> 4 teaspoons canola oil
> 2 egg whites

For the sauce: In a small saucepan, combine the pears, pear nectar, brown sugar and nutmeg. Bring to a boil, then reduce the heat. Cover and simmer about 3 minutes or just until the pears are tender.

In a cup, combine the water and cornstarch, then stir into the pear mixture. Cook and stir until the mixture thickens and begins to gently boil. Cook and stir for 2 minutes more. Remove the saucepan from the heat and cover to keep the sauce warm.

For the pancakes: In a medium bowl, stir together the whole-wheat flour, unbleached flour, brown sugar, baking powder and nutmeg.

In a small bowl, stir together the milk and oil. Add to the flour mixture. Stir just until combined.

In a clean small bowl, beat the egg whites until stiff peaks form. Gently fold into the batter.

Spray an unheated griddle or large skillet with no-stick spray. Heat the griddle or skillet over medium heat. For each pancake, pour about ¼ cup of the batter onto the griddle or skillet,

SLIMMING STRATEGY

A spritz of no-stick spray adds only 2 calories and just a trace of fat to your recipe. Compare that with the tablespoon of butter you would use to grease the griddle. Butter contains 102 calories and 11.5 grams of fat.

spreading the batter to about a 4" circle. Cook until the pancakes are bubbly and dry around the edges. Then turn over and cook until golden brown.

To serve, arrange 2 pancakes on each plate. Serve with the warm sauce.

Whole-Wheat Pancakes with Pear Sauce

Skewered Sesame Chicken (page 78), Sun-Dried Tomato Crostini with Goat Cheese (page 67), Chick-Pea Crunchies (page 64) and Dilled Shrimp (page 84)

Herbed Yogurt Cheese

EXTRA HEALTH BENEFIT
Lower Cholesterol

Times: Prep: 3 min.
Chilling: 9 hr.

**Makes ½ cup or
2 servings.**

Per ¼ cup: 44 calories,
0.3 g. fat (6% of calories),
0.4 g. dietary fiber, 1 mg.
cholesterol, 100 mg. sodium.

*This is an extremely easy recipe. The only thing that takes
time is draining the yogurt until it's as thick as cream
cheese.*

> 1   **cup nonfat plain yogurt (made without gelatin)**
> ¼ **cup finely chopped tomatoes**
> 2   **tablespoons minced fresh basil**
> 1   **tablespoon minced fresh dill**
> 1   **tablespoon minced fresh chives**
> ¼ **teaspoon freshly ground black pepper**

Line a fine-mesh sieve with a double thickness of cheesecloth
or a coffee filter. Place the sieve over a bowl. Spoon the yogurt
into the sieve. Refrigerate about 8 hours or overnight, until all
the extra whey has drained from the yogurt.

Discard the liquid in the bowl. Transfer the yogurt to a small
bowl. Stir in the tomatoes, basil, dill, chives and pepper. Cover
and refrigerate for at least 1 hour for the flavors to blend.

Chef's Note: For a beautiful presentation, place the spread in
a pastry bag fitted with a medium to large star tip. Pipe the
spread onto crackers, small pieces of toast (cut into fancy shapes
with small cookie cutters) or vegetable slices, such as cucumber,
radish, zucchini or carrot rounds.

Piquant Yogurt Cheese

EXTRA HEALTH BENEFITS
Lower Cholesterol
Better Blood Pressure

Times: Prep: 3 min.
Chilling: 8 hr.

*This peppy spread uses yogurt cheese (well-drained yogurt)
as a healthy alternative to full-fat cream cheese. The mixture
is especially good on whole-grain crispbreads or toasted pita
wedges.*

> 1   **cup nonfat plain yogurt (made without gelatin)**
> ½ **cup chopped tomatoes**
> ¼ **cup finely chopped green onions**
> 1   **tablespoon minced fresh cilantro**
> 2   **teaspoons lime juice**
> ¼ **teaspoon ground cumin**
> ⅛ **teaspoon ground red pepper**

Line a fine-mesh sieve with a double thickness of cheesecloth or a coffee filter. Place the sieve over a bowl. Spoon the yogurt into the sieve. Refrigerate about 8 hours or overnight, until all the extra whey has drained from the yogurt.

Discard the liquid in the bowl. Transfer the yogurt to a small bowl. Add the tomatoes, onions, cilantro, lime juice, cumin and pepper. Stir just until combined. If desired, cover and chill in the refrigerator until ready to serve.

Chef's Note: You can easily turn this spread into a dip for crisp raw vegetables. Just stir in enough milk to get the desired consistency.

Makes 1 cup or 4 servings.

Per ¼ cup: 16 calories, 0.1 g. fat (7% of calories), 3.2 g. dietary fiber, 0 mg. cholesterol, 17 mg. sodium.

Say (Yogurt) Cheese!

Nonfat yogurt cheese is an excellent substitute for both regular cream cheese and sour cream. It's especially good in dips and as a spread for toast, bagels, muffins and fruit breads. And it's very simple to prepare.

Line a fine-mesh sieve with a double thickness of cheesecloth or a coffee filter. Place the sieve over a bowl. Spoon the nonfat yogurt into the sieve. Refrigerate about eight hours or overnight, until all the extra whey has drained from the yogurt. Discard the whey and transfer the yogurt cheese to a bowl.

Be sure to use a brand of yogurt that contains no gelatin or other thickeners that would prevent the whey from draining out. You can tell if the yogurt is a good candidate for draining by scooping out a large spoonful and seeing if the depression left behind starts to fill with liquid within a half-hour.

Here's how yogurt cheese compares with cream cheese and sour cream.

Food (1 ounce)	Calories	Fat Grams	% Calories from Fat
Nonfat yogurt cheese	17	trace	5
Cream cheese	98	10	90
Nonfat cream cheese	30	0	0
Sour cream	61	6	86
Nonfat sour cream	28	0	0

Dutch Garden Dip

The pretty colors might remind you of tulip season.

- ⅓ cup nonfat plain yogurt
- 1 tablespoon nonfat mayonnaise
- 1 tablespoon finely chopped sweet red peppers
- 1 tablespoon finely chopped yellow peppers
- 1 tablespoon finely chopped celery
- 2 teaspoons finely chopped shallots
- 2 teaspoons minced fresh tarragon or ½ teaspoon dried tarragon

In a small bowl, stir together the yogurt, mayonnaise, red and yellow peppers, celery, shallots and tarragon. Transfer the dip to a serving bowl. If desired, cover and chill in the refrigerator until serving time.

Madras Curry Dip

Curry powder is a blend of many spices, and it can vary considerably from manufacturer to manufacturer. If you like yours hot, choose one labeled Madras curry powder.

- ¾ cup nonfat plain yogurt
- ¼ cup nonfat mayonnaise
- 1 teaspoon Madras or other curry powder
- 1 clove garlic, minced
- Assorted fresh vegetables, cut up

In a small bowl, stir together the yogurt, mayonnaise, curry powder and garlic. Transfer the dip to a serving bowl. Serve with the vegetables for dipping.

Chef's Note: Although you may serve this dip with practically any assortment of vegetables, curry seems to complement cauliflower, carrots, artichokes and asparagus especially well.

Crispy Wonton Chips

Quick

EXTRA HEALTH BENEFITS
Lower Cholesterol
Better Blood Pressure

Times: Prep: 5 min.
Baking: 5 min.

**Makes 60 chips or
10 servings.**

Per 6 Chips: 42 calories,
0.5 g. fat (11% of calories),
0 g. dietary fiber, 0 mg. cholesterol, 0 mg. sodium.

These chips are so low in fat and calories that you can munch on them without feeling guilty. The wonton wrappers used to make the chips store well in the refrigerator or freezer, so you can always have some on hand to satisfy your chip cravings.

30 wonton wrappers (3" square)

Spray 2 large cookie sheets with no-stick spray. Arrange the wonton wrappers in a single layer on the cookie sheets.

Spray the wonton wrappers with no-stick spray. Using a pizza cutter or sharp knife, cut each diagonally in half.

Bake at 350° about 5 minutes or until the wonton wrappers are lightly brown and crisp.

Chef's Note: You can vary the taste of the chips by using different flavors of no-stick spray, such as regular, olive oil and butter. You can also add some zest to the chips by lightly sprinkling the wonton wrappers with ground red pepper or chili powder before baking them.

Chick-Pea Crunchies

EXTRA HEALTH BENEFIT
Lower Cholesterol

Times: Prep: 5 min.
Baking: 30 min.

**Makes 1 cup or
4 servings.**

Per ¼ cup: 55 calories,
1.3 g. fat (21% of calories),
2.3 g. dietary fiber, 1 mg.
cholesterol, 232 mg. sodium.

These savory little nibbles are high in fiber, so they'll boost your intake at the same time that they satisfy your between-meal munchies.

**1 cup canned chick-peas (garbanzo beans), rinsed and
    drained**
1 tablespoon grated Parmesan cheese
1 teaspoon sour-cream-flavored granules
½ teaspoon curry powder
    Pinch of ground red pepper

Pat the chick-peas dry with paper towels; set aside. In a medium bowl, stir together the cheese, sour cream granules, curry powder and pepper. Add the chick-peas and toss until well coated.

Spray an 8" round baking pan with no-stick spray. Transfer the chick-peas to the pan. Bake at 350° about 30 minutes or until dry and golden, stirring every 5 minutes. Cool completely and store in an airtight container.

Fresh Tomato Salsa

Serve this spicy salsa with low-fat chips, such as the Crispy Wonton Chips on page 62. It's also good as a topping for baked potatoes or poached chicken or fish.

3   **medium tomatoes, finely chopped**
1   **small onion, finely chopped**
2   **fresh green chili peppers, seeded and finely chopped (wear disposable gloves when handling)**
2   **teaspoons cider vinegar**
1   **teaspoon minced fresh cilantro (optional)**

In a small bowl, stir together the tomatoes, onions, peppers and vinegar. If desired, stir in the cilantro. Cover tightly and chill in the refrigerator for at least 1 hour to blend the flavors.

Chef's Note: When handling fresh chili peppers, you'll want to protect your hands with disposable gloves or plastic bags. That's because the peppers contain volatile oils that can result in irritating or painful burns to your skin. Be especially careful not to touch your eyes before thoroughly washing your hands.

EXTRA HEALTH BENEFITS
Lower Cholesterol
Better Blood Pressure

Times: Prep: 10 min.
Chilling: at least 1 hr.

Makes 2½ cups or 10 servings.

Per ¼ cup: 13 calories, 0.1 g. fat (9% of calories), 0.7 g. dietary fiber, 0 mg. cholesterol, 4 mg. sodium.

SLIMMING STRATEGY

Be realistic about calories. Even foods that are very low in calories—and fat—can have an unfavorable impact on your weight-loss plan if you eat them by the bagful. Before you indulge, multiply the number of calories in a serving by the number of servings you're <u>really</u> likely to eat. The total may shock you into being more prudent.

Coffee-Break Cheese Spread

Quick

EXTRA HEALTH BENEFITS
Lower Cholesterol
Cancer Protection
Better Blood Pressure
Blood Building

Time: Prep: 5 min.

Makes 1 cup or 4 servings.

Per ¼ cup: 96 calories, 2.1 g. fat (18% of calories), 1.2 g. dietary fiber, 1 mg. cholesterol, 73 mg. sodium.

Need a midmorning snack? Tease your appetite with this spread served on miniature rice cakes or toasted mini bagels.

½ cup nonfat cottage cheese
1 tablespoon skim milk
1 tablespoon smooth peanut butter
1 teaspoon honey
¼ teaspoon ground cinnamon
½ cup raisins

In a blender or small food processor, blend or process the cottage cheese, milk, peanut butter, honey and cinnamon until well combined.

Transfer the mixture to a container. Stir in the raisins. Cover and store in the refrigerator until ready to serve.

Halt!

When snacking becomes uncontrollable, it's time to H-A-L-T. Ask yourself why you're overeating. Is it because you're Hungry, Angry, Lonely or Tired? If so, here are a few specific ways to prevent those feelings from turning into frantic eating.

Hunger. Obviously, your body will crave food when you're hungry. So one of the most effective ways to prevent bingeing is to keep yourself from getting ravenous. If well-balanced, normally spaced meals aren't enough to keep your hand out of the cookie jar, make sure you have a supply of healthful foods such as fresh fruits and vegetables to munch throughout the day.

Anger. When you're angry, negative energy courses through your body in need of a channel. Addressing the source is the ideal response, but it's less threatening to many people to use some of that energy in other ways, such as eating. As a result, the anger dissipates, but the source of irritation remains. Either resolve to handle these situations as they arise or learn to blow off steam in other ways, such as by exercising.

Loneliness. Food can seem like terrific company when you're feeling abandoned or unwanted. But you know it's a fickle friend. A smarter solution is to figure out what kind of contact you need when you're lonely, then go after it. Initiate that contact!

Tiredness. It's all too easy to use food as a pick-me-up when you're fatigued. Make sure you get a full night's sleep whenever possible. And turn to exercise instead of food to rouse your mind and body when you become overtired.

Sun-Dried Tomato Crostini with Goat Cheese

A baguette is the classic long, narrow loaf of French bread. Most types of French bread contain little or no fat, which is why they go stale easily. You can use leftover bread to make simple crackerlike snacks.

    8 ounces baguette bread, cut into 16 slices
    2 teaspoons olive oil
    1 clove garlic, halved
   10 sun-dried tomatoes
    2 ounces goat cheese, crumbled
    1 flat anchovy fillet, finely chopped
    1 tablespoon minced fresh parsley
    1 teaspoon balsamic vinegar
   ¼ teaspoon freshly ground black pepper

Place the bread slices on a large cookie sheet. Lightly brush the tops with the oil and rub with the garlic. Bake at 350° for 8 to 10 minutes or until golden. Transfer the slices to a wire rack and cool.

Meanwhile, in a small bowl, cover the tomatoes with boiling water and soak for 4 minutes. Drain the tomatoes and finely chop them.

In a medium bowl, stir together the tomatoes, cheese, anchovies, parsley, vinegar and pepper. Spoon on top of the bread slices and serve.

Chef's Note: You can easily prepare the components of these canapés ahead of time and assemble the snacks just before serving. Store the tomato mixture in the refrigerator. Place the completely cooled bread slices in a self-closing plastic bag. Both will keep for several days.

Quick

Times: Prep: 15 min.
Baking: 8 min.

Makes 8 servings.

Per serving: 116 calories, 2.8 g. fat (22% of calories), 0.9 g. dietary fiber, 4 mg. cholesterol, 196 mg. sodium.

Sun-Dried Tomato Crostini
with Goat Cheese

EXTRA HEALTH BENEFITS
Lower Cholesterol
Better Blood Pressure

Times: Prep: 5 min.
Cooking: 4 min.

Makes 4 servings.

Per serving: 43 calories,
1.2 g. fat (21% of calories),
0.5 g. dietary fiber, 0 mg.
cholesterol, 22 mg. sodium.

Golden Spiced Bananas

*Craving something sweet? Try these honey-glazed bananas.
It's just like eating candy, but healthier!*

> 1 medium ripe banana
> Juice of 1 lemon
> 2 teaspoons reduced-calorie margarine
> 1 teaspoon ground cinnamon
> ½ teaspoon honey
> ¼ teaspoon ground nutmeg

Cut the banana into ¼"-thick slices. Sprinkle both sides of the slices with the lemon juice.

Melt the margarine in a large no-stick skillet. Stir in the cinnamon, honey and nutmeg. Add the banana slices. Cook for 2 to 3 minutes or until golden. Using a spatula sprayed with no-stick spray, gently turn the slices over. Cook for 2 to 3 minutes more or until golden. Serve warm.

EXTRA HEALTH BENEFIT
Lower Cholesterol

Times: Prep: 5 min.
Chilling: at least 1 hr.

**Makes 2 cups or
16 servings.**

Per 2 tablespoons:
28 calories, 0.4 g. fat (15%
of calories), 0 g. dietary
fiber, 7 mg. cholesterol,
107 mg. sodium.

Tuna Salad Spread

This spread is wonderful served on party bread slices, toasted miniature bagel halves or Melba toast rounds or as a filling for celery. For an easy garnish, top each with a small celery leaf or sprig of cilantro or parsley.

> 1¾ cups cooked and flaked tuna
> 3 tablespoons nonfat mayonnaise
> 1 stalk celery, finely chopped
> 2 shallots, finely chopped
> 2 tablespoons minced fresh cilantro or parsley

In a medium bowl, stir together the tuna and mayonnaise until well combined and smooth. Stir in the celery, shallots and cilantro or parsley. Cover and chill in the refrigerator for at least 1 hour to blend the flavors.

Chef's Note: Fresh tuna steaks are readily available. They're easy to grill or sauté, and you can use the leftovers in a spread such as this. The steaks look like pieces of beef tenderloin, and they even have a meaty texture. They range in color from light to dark red, depending on the species. No matter which type you prefer, make sure the pieces look a little shiny; the longer fish stands, the more it loses its glistening, healthy look. If you don't have fresh tuna, substitute a 12½-ounce can of water-packed tuna; drain it well before using.

Chinese Eggplant Salad on Cucumber Rounds

Eggplant makes a wonderful base for a robust, low-calorie vegetable dip. And because it's roasted rather than fried, it stays quite low in fat.

> 1   **eggplant (10 to 12 ounces)**
> ¼   **cup loosely packed fresh cilantro leaves**
> 1   **tablespoon grated ginger root**
> 1   **tablespoon reduced-sodium soy sauce**
> 2   **cloves garlic**
> 2   **teaspoons Oriental sesame oil**
> 1   **teaspoon rice vinegar**
> 1   **large cucumber**
> ¼   **cup chopped roasted sweet red peppers**

Place the eggplant on a piece of foil and prick it with a fork in several places. Bake at 350° for 20 to 25 minutes or until the skin is charred and the eggplant is tender when pierced with a fork. Remove from the oven and cool slightly.

When the eggplant is cool enough to handle, use a sharp knife to peel off the skin. Discard the skin. Transfer the eggplant to a food processor. Add the cilantro, ginger, soy sauce, garlic, oil and vinegar. Process until coarsely chopped.

To serve, slice the cucumber into ¼"-thick rounds. Spoon the eggplant mixture on top of the rounds. Garnish each with the roasted peppers.

Chef's Note: Don't overblend the eggplant mixture. It will look better if it's still a little chunky.

EXTRA HEALTH BENEFITS
Lower Cholesterol
Cancer Protection

Times: Prep: 5 min.
Baking: 20 min.

Makes 4 servings.

Per serving: 54 calories, 2.5 g. fat (24% of calories), 1.6 g. dietary fiber, 0 mg. cholesterol, 156 mg. sodium.

Blazing Trail Mix

Here's a great portable snack for whenever you need a low-calorie energy boost.

EXTRA HEALTH BENEFITS
Lower Cholesterol
Stronger Immunity

Times: Prep: 10 min.
Baking: 15 min.

**Makes 8 cups or
16 servings.**

Per ½ cup: 97 calories,
0.6 g. fat (5% of calories),
1.5 g. dietary fiber, 0 mg.
cholesterol, 128 mg. sodium.

    2 cups shredded miniature wheat or bran squares
    1 cup unsalted thin pretzel sticks, broken into pieces
    ½ cup cooked lentils
    ½ cup quick-cooking rolled oats
    ½ cup raisins
    ½ cup chopped dried apples
    ¼ cup honey
    2 teaspoons curry powder
    ½ teaspoon ground coriander
    ¼ teaspoon ground cumin
    ¼ teaspoon paprika
    ⅛ teaspoon ground red pepper

In a 13" × 9" baking pan, combine the wheat or bran squares, pretzels, lentils, oats, raisins and apples.

In a small bowl, stir together the honey, curry powder, coriander, cumin, paprika and pepper. Drizzle the honey mixture over the cereal mixture. Toss until evenly coated.

Bake at 350° for 15 to 20 minutes or until crisp, stirring occasionally. Store in an airtight container or self-closing plastic bags.

Peach Pops

There is nothing more convenient than having a healthy snack waiting for you in the freezer.

EXTRA HEALTH BENEFITS
Lower Cholesterol
Better Blood Pressure

Times: Prep: 10 min.
Freezing: 9 hr.
Standing: 5 min.

Makes 4 servings.

Per serving: 63 calories,
0.2 g. fat (3% of calories),
1 g. dietary fiber, 1 mg.
cholesterol, 32 mg. sodium.

    3 medium ripe peaches, peeled, pitted and sliced (about
       1½ cups)
    1 cup skim milk
    ¼ cup pineapple juice
    2 teaspoons grated lemon peel
    1 teaspoon lemon juice
    1 teaspoon vanilla

In blender or food processor, blend or process the peaches, milk, pineapple juice, lemon peel, lemon juice and vanilla until smooth.

Pour the mixture into 4 (6- to 8-ounce) paper cups. Cover with foil and freeze until partially frozen. Insert a wooden ice-pop stick in the center of each and freeze at least 8 hours or until completely frozen.

To serve, let the pops stand at room temperature for 5 minutes. Then gently peel the paper cup from the frozen pop.

Chef's Note: You can easily prepare these pops with other fruits, such as apricots, strawberries or bananas.

Artichoke Quiche Squares

By eliminating the crust from this quiche, a lot of fat and calories are cut.

- ½ **cup fat-free egg substitute**
- 3 **tablespoons dry seasoned bread crumbs**
- 1 **tablespoon reduced-calorie mayonnaise**
- ½ **teaspoon dried thyme**
- ¼ **teaspoon garlic powder**
- ¼ **teaspoon hot-pepper sauce**
- 1 **package (10 ounces) frozen artichoke hearts, thawed and chopped**
- ¾ **cup (3 ounces) shredded reduced-fat Swiss cheese**
- ½ **cup chopped green onions**

In a large bowl, stir together the egg substitute, bread crumbs, mayonnaise, thyme, garlic powder and pepper sauce. Add the artichokes, cheese and onions. Mix until well combined.

Spray an 8" × 8" baking pan with no-stick spray. Spoon the artichoke mixture into the pan.

Bake at 350° for 25 to 30 minutes or until bubbly and golden. Cool for 5 minutes, then cut into 16 squares.

EXTRA HEALTH BENEFITS
Lower Cholesterol
Cancer Protection

Times: Prep: 5 min.
Broiling: 4 min.

Makes 16 pizza circles or 4 servings.

Per 4 pizza circles: 39 calories, 1.1 g. fat (20% of calories), 1.3 g. dietary fiber, 10 mg. cholesterol, 187 mg. sodium.

SLIMMING STRATEGY

Be wary when a package of mozzarella cheese boasts that it contains "no cholesterol." That doesn't necessarily mean it's also low in fat. One ounce of imitation mozzarella has 90 calories and 7 grams of fat. But typical brands of the real thing clock in at 80 calories and 6 grams for part-skim cheese, 60 calories and 3 grams for reduced-fat cheese and 40 calories and no fat for nonfat cheese.

Zucchini Pizzarettes

Satisfy your craving for pizza with these zucchini tidbits. They have all the flavor of pizza, but they're low in calories and fat.

- **1 medium zucchini**
- **⅓ cup canned low-sodium tomato sauce**
- **2 ounces cooked and crumbled turkey sausage**
- **¼ cup (1 ounce) shredded part-skim mozzarella cheese**
- **1 tablespoon grated Parmesan cheese**
- **¼ teaspoon dried basil**
- **¼ teaspoon crushed red pepper**

Spray a large cookie sheet with no-stick spray. Cut the zucchini crosswise into 16 slices, each ½" thick. Place the slices on the cookie sheets.

Spread each slice with 1 teaspoon of the sauce. Top with the turkey sausage. Then sprinkle each with equal amounts of mozzarella and Parmesan cheeses, basil and pepper.

Broil 3" to 4" from the heat for 4 to 5 minutes or until the cheese melts.

Zucchini Pizzarettes

Hot Crab Cakes with Yogurt Tartar Sauce

Crab cakes can be fairly high in fat, especially when they're deep-fried. But these mini patties are prepared with low-fat ingredients and just lightly sautéed in a touch of oil.

SAUCE
- ½ cup nonfat plain yogurt
- 1 tablespoon reduced-calorie mayonnaise
- 1 tablespoon minced fresh dill
- 2 cloves garlic, minced
- 1 teaspoon fresh lime juice

CRAB CAKES
- ¼ cup fat-free egg substitute
- 1 tablespoon Dijon mustard
- 1 tablespoon nonfat plain yogurt
- 2 teaspoons reduced-sodium soy sauce
- ¼ teaspoon hot-pepper sauce
- 8 ounces cooked crabmeat, cartilage removed
- ⅓ cup finely chopped celery
- ¼ cup finely chopped green onions
- 1 teaspoon canola oil

For the sauce: In a small bowl, stir together the yogurt, mayonnaise, dill, garlic and lime juice. Set the sauce aside.

For the crab cakes: In a medium bowl, stir together the egg substitute, mustard, yogurt, soy sauce and pepper sauce. Add the crab, celery and onions. Mix until combined.

Form the crab mixture into 16 patties. Add ½ teaspoon of the oil to a large no-stick skillet and heat over medium heat. Add half the crab patties. Cook for 4 minutes. Turn the patties over and cook about 4 minutes more or until golden. Cook the remaining patties using the remaining ½ teaspoon of oil.

Serve the crab cakes with the sauce.

Chef's Note: Always pick over crabmeat to remove any little bits of shell and pieces of cartilage that might be in with the meat. Then flake the meat with your fingers to break up large pieces. For purposes of this recipe, you don't need to buy the most expensive crab. The meat labeled claw meat, special or backfin is cheaper than jumbo lump backfin. If your budget is tight, opt for artificial crab, also known as surimi.

EXTRA HEALTH BENEFIT
Stronger Immunity

Times: Prep: 15 min.
Cooking: 16 min.

Makes 16 crab cakes or 4 servings.

Per 4 crab cakes:
118 calories, 3.5 g. fat (27% of calories), 0.4 g. dietary fiber, 51 mg. cholesterol, 468 mg. sodium.

Italian Nachos

Here's the best of two cultures!

3 6" whole-wheat pita breads
1 cup (4 ounces) shredded nonfat or reduced-fat mozzarella cheese
1 tablespoon grated Parmesan cheese
1 teaspoon dried basil
1 teaspoon dried oregano
½ teaspoon dried thyme
¼ teaspoon paprika
¼ teaspoon freshly ground black pepper

Line 2 large cookie sheets with foil, then spray with no-stick spray. Cut each pita bread into 1½" triangles. Then split each triangle to form 2 single-layer triangles. Place the pita pieces on the cookie sheets in a single layer; set aside.

In a small bowl, combine the mozzarella and Parmesan cheeses, basil, oregano, thyme, paprika and pepper. Sprinkle over the pita pieces.

Bake at 350° for 10 to 15 minutes or until the pitas are golden and the cheese is melted. Cool slightly before serving.

Chef's Note: Lining the cookie sheets with foil makes cleanup fast and easy.

Sidebar

EXTRA HEALTH BENEFIT
Lower Cholesterol

Times: Prep: 10 min.
Baking: 10 min.

Makes 4 servings.

Per serving: 89 calories, 1 g. fat (<1% of calories), 0.5 g. dietary fiber, 6 mg. cholesterol, 430 mg. sodium.

Hot Spinach Puffs

These easy spinach balls are served with spicy mustard as a dipping sauce.

1 package (10 ounces) frozen chopped spinach, thawed and squeezed to remove excess moisture
1 cup dry seasoned bread crumbs
¼ cup grated onions
¼ cup fat-free egg substitute
¼ cup grated Parmesan cheese
1 tablespoon reduced-calorie margarine, melted
⅛ teaspoon ground nutmeg
    Hot Chinese, spicy Dijon or honey mustard

In a medium bowl, combine the spinach, bread crumbs, onions, egg substitute, cheese, margarine and nutmeg.

Sidebar

EXTRA HEALTH BENEFITS
Lower Cholesterol
Cancer Protection

Times: Prep: 10 min.
Baking: 10 min.

Makes 20 balls or 10 servings.

Per 2 balls: 65 calories, 1.9 g. fat (25% of calories), 1.2 g. dietary fiber, 2 mg. cholesterol, 158 mg. sodium.

Mix until well combined. Form into 20 balls.

Spray a cookie sheet with no-stick spray. Place the balls on the cookie sheet and bake at 350° for 10 to 15 minutes or until lightly brown. Serve with the mustard.

Chef's Note: If you're making these for a party or other busy occasion, you can do most of the work ahead. Form the spinach mixture into balls and refrigerate them. Pop them into the oven just before serving.

Fruit Kabobs in Honey Mustard

If you've never experienced the blend of honey, mustard and fruit, you're in for a treat! The sweet-spicy marinade gives fruit an extra, unexpected dimension.

- ¼ **cup rice vinegar**
- 1 **tablespoon honey**
- 1 **teaspoon poppy seeds**
- 1 **teaspoon Dijon mustard**
- 1 **large plum, pitted and sliced**
- 1 **large nectarine, pitted and sliced**
- 1½ **cups whole strawberries**
- ½ **cup green grapes**

In a medium bowl, stir together the vinegar, honey, poppy seeds and mustard. Cut any large slices of the plums or nectarines crosswise in half. Add the plums, nectarines, strawberries and grapes to the vinegar mixture. Toss until coated. Cover and marinate in the refrigerator for 1 hour, stirring occasionally.

Drain the fruit, reserving the marinade. Thread the fruit onto 6" bamboo skewers. Brush with the marinade before serving.

Chef's Note: You can easily substitute other fruit, according to what's in season. Melon balls, pineapple chunks, banana slices, orange sections, fresh fig halves, apple chunks and mango pieces are among the alternatives.

EXTRA HEALTH BENEFITS
Lower Cholesterol
Cancer Protection
Better Blood Pressure
Stronger Immunity

Times: Prep: 4 min.
Marinating: 1 hr.

Makes 4 kabobs or 4 servings.

Per kabob: 82 calories, 0.9 g. fat (9% of calories), 2.8 g. dietary fiber, 0 mg. cholesterol, 34 mg. sodium.

Mushrooms à l'Italienne

EXTRA HEALTH BENEFITS
Lower Cholesterol
Better Blood Pressure
Stronger Immunity

Times: Prep: 5 min.
Cooking: 5 min.
Marinating: at least 1 hr.

Makes 1½ cups or 6 servings.

Per ¼ cup: 23 calories, 0.3 g. fat (10% of calories), 1 g. dietary fiber, 0 mg. cholesterol, 6 mg. sodium.

For variety, you could replace the mushrooms with sliced zucchini, yellow squash, baby carrots or cherry tomatoes.

- ⅓ cup water
- 3 tablespoons lemon juice
- 2 tablespoons white wine vinegar
- ½ teaspoon dried marjoram
- ¼ teaspoon dried oregano
- ¼ teaspoon dried thyme
- 1 clove garlic, halved
- 1 bay leaf
- 1 pound small fresh mushrooms
- 1 tablespoon nonfat Italian salad dressing

Mushrooms à l'Italienne

SLIMMING STRATEGY

When you need a quick marinade for fresh vegetables or pasta, use commercial nonfat salad dressing. Choose Italian dressing when you want a zesty marinade, and pick a garlic-and-herb blend when something more delicate is needed.

In a medium saucepan, combine the water, lemon juice, vinegar, marjoram, oregano, thyme, garlic and bay leaf. Bring to a boil. Add the mushrooms and return to a boil, then reduce the heat. Cover and simmer about 5 minutes or until the mushrooms are tender.

Remove the saucepan from the heat. Remove and discard the garlic and bay leaf. Stir in the salad dressing. Transfer the mushrooms and liquid to a glass container. Cool slightly, then cover and marinate in the refrigerator for at least 1 hour before serving.

Chili-Spiced Scallops

Use peanut oil to stir-fry these sweet-and-spicy scallops. It's high in heart-healthy monounsaturated fat and adds a nutty flavor. But remember . . . use just a little oil; you don't need extra calories or fat.

EXTRA HEALTH BENEFIT
Stronger Immunity

Times: Prep: 8 min.
Cooking: 10 min.

Makes 8 servings.

Per serving: 95 calories,
1.7 g. fat (16% of calories),
0.1 g. dietary fiber, 23 mg.
cholesterol, 362 mg. sodium.

⅓ **cup chili sauce**
1½ **tablespoons reduced-sodium soy sauce**
1 **tablespoon defatted low-sodium chicken broth**
2 **teaspoons honey**
½ **teaspoon ground ginger**
¼ **teaspoon crushed red pepper**
2 **teaspoons peanut oil**
1 **bunch green onions, cut into 2" pieces**
4 **cloves garlic**
1¼ **pounds bay scallops**

In a small bowl, stir together the chili sauce, soy sauce, broth, honey, ginger and pepper; set aside.

Spray an unheated, large no-stick skillet with no-stick spray. Add the oil and heat over medium heat. Then add the onions and garlic. Cook and stir for 5 minutes or until the onions are tender but not brown. Using a slotted spoon, remove the onions and garlic. Discard the garlic and set the onions aside.

Add the scallops to the skillet. Cook and stir for 2 minutes. Stir in the sauce mixture and cook for 3 to 4 minutes more or until the scallops turn opaque, stirring frequently. Using the slotted spoon, remove the scallops and toss them with the onions.

Chef's Note: Serve the scallops either warm and tossed with angel hair pasta or chilled on lettuce-lined plates.

SLIMMING STRATEGY

It's the oldest trick in the book—and it works. Before you go to a party, eat something filling but low in fat at home. (Fruit is good; so is a big bowl of unsalted air-popped popcorn.) You won't be so apt to dig into the goodies on the buffet table.

Skewered Sesame Chicken

Serve these Oriental skewers as a hearty snack or on a bed of shredded lettuce or Chinese cabbage for a light meal.

EXTRA HEALTH BENEFITS
Stronger Immunity

Times: Prep: 8 min.
Marinating: at least 15 min.
Broiling: 6 min.

Makes 12 skewers or 4 servings.

Per 3 skewers:
123 calories, 3.4 g. fat (26% of calories), 0.5 g. dietary fiber, 49 mg. cholesterol, 212 mg. sodium.

¼ cup defatted low-sodium chicken broth
2 tablespoons minced fresh parsley
2 tablespoons finely chopped green onions
1 tablespoon reduced-sodium soy sauce
2 teaspoons Oriental sesame oil
1 teaspoon grated ginger root
¼ teaspoon ground coriander
12 ounces skinless, boneless chicken breasts, cut into ½"-wide strips
1 tablespoon sesame seeds

If using bamboo skewers, place them in a shallow dish or pan and cover with water. Set aside to soak.

In a medium bowl, stir together the broth, parsley, onions, soy sauce, oil, ginger and coriander. Add the chicken and toss until well coated. Cover and marinate in the refrigerator for at least 15 minutes.

Drain the chicken and discard the marinade. Thread the chicken strips onto 6" metal or the soaked bamboo skewers in a loose accordion fashion. Sprinkle with the sesame seeds.

Place the skewers on the rack in a broiling pan. Broil 4" from the heat for 3 minutes. Turn the skewers over and broil for 3 to 5 minutes more or until the chicken is no longer pink.

Chef's Note: The longer the chicken marinates, the more flavorful it will be.

Skewered Sesame Chicken

SLIMMING STRATEGY

Don't go it alone. Involve your family with your weight-loss plans. Let your children look through some low-fat cookbooks for pictures of foods they think they would like. To the extent that it's practical, let them help in the preparation of those dishes.

50 Fast Snacks

The way to outsmart those munchies and stay slim is by stocking up on snacks that you can nibble on whenever the urge strikes. The following treats are low in fat and calories (generally less than 100 calories and 2 grams of fat per item).

1. 1 cup nonfat, sugar-free, flavored yogurt
2. 1 cup dry unsweetened cereal
3. ½ cup unsweetened applesauce
4. 5 cauliflower florets with 1 tablespoon creamy nonfat salad dressing for dipping
5. ½ large square plain Ry-Krisp cracker
6. 1 slice reduced-calorie whole-wheat bread with 2 teaspoons all-fruit spread
7. ¼ cup nonfat ricotta cheese topped with 1 tablespoon toasted wheat germ
8. 4 ounces fruit sorbet
9. 10 jelly beans
10. 1 banana
11. 1 prepared envelope of instant oatmeal
12. 2 nonfat Fig Newtons
13. 1 square graham cracker
14. 3 ounces frozen nonfat yogurt
15. 1 prepared envelope of sugar-free instant cocoa mix
16. 1 hard pretzel
17. 10 dried apricot halves
18. 1 apple
19. 4 ounces nonfat cottage cheese
20. ½ cup sugar-free flavored gelatin
21. ½ ounce reduced-fat Swiss cheese
22. 2 nacho-flavored rice cakes
23. 1 frozen fruit-juice bar
24. 3 ounces surimi with cocktail sauce
25. ½ cup canned fruit (packed in juice)
26. ½ cup sugar-free pudding prepared with skim milk
27. 3 cups air-popped corn
28. 7 animal crackers
29. 1 shredded-wheat biscuit drizzled with 1 tablespoon honey
30. 1 orange
31. 6 ounces grapefruit juice
32. 5 whole-grain melba rounds
33. 2 gingersnaps
34. 2 ounces thinly sliced turkey breast wrapped around 4 melon balls
35. 5 fat-free saltines
36. 1 fortune cookie
37. 2 ounces water-packed tuna
38. 5 mini rice cakes
39. 1 cooked low-fat frank, cut into chunks and served with honey-mustard sauce for dipping
40. 1 medium kiwifruit
41. 1 cup strawberries
42. 2 pieces hard candy
43. 1 carrot with 2 tablespoons nonfat creamy salad dressing for dipping
44. ½ cup zucchini slices topped with 2 tablespoons salsa
45. 1 tomato
46. 1 celery stalk stuffed with 1 tablespoon nonfat cream cheese
47. 1 cup vegetable-juice cocktail mixed with a dash of Worcestershire sauce and lemon juice, served with ½ celery stalk
48. 6 ounces no-salt bouillon
49. 1 kosher dill-pickle spear
50. 1 cup herbal tea

Chilled Provençal Asparagus

*Here's an easy appetizer that can double as a first course or
as a hearty snack.*

16 asparagus spears
 2 cups seeded and chopped tomatoes
 ½ cup chopped red onions
 ¼ cup minced and loosely packed fresh basil
 2 tablespoons minced fresh parsley
 1 clove garlic, minced
 1 tablespoon capers, rinsed and drained
 1 tablespoon red wine vinegar
 1 teaspoon olive oil
 ¼ teaspoon freshly ground black pepper
    Juice of 1 lemon

In a large saucepan with a tight-fitting lid, bring about 1" of
water to a boil. Place the asparagus in a steamer basket and set
the basket in the saucepan, making sure the basket sits above
the water. Cover the saucepan; steam for 5 minutes or until the
asparagus is crisp-tender.

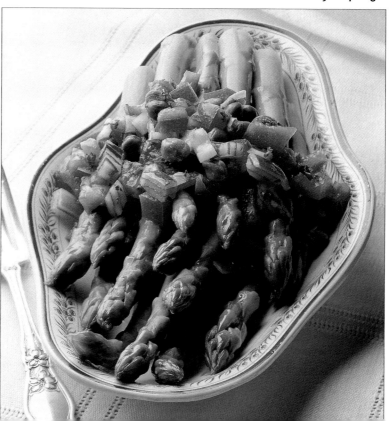

Chilled Provençal Asparagus

Transfer the asparagus from the basket to a large plate or shallow container. Chill in the refrigerator for at least 1 hour.

Meanwhile, in a medium bowl, combine the tomatoes, onions, basil, parsley, garlic, capers, vinegar, oil and pepper. Set aside at room temperature for at least 15 minutes to blend the flavors.

For each serving, place 4 spears on a salad plate. Sprinkle with the lemon juice, then top each serving with the tomato mixture.

Snow Peas Bursting with Goodness

Nonfat ricotta cheese makes an ideal low-fat filling for raw or lightly blanched vegetables. Here it's jazzed up with tangy sun-dried tomatoes and garlic.

10 sun-dried tomatoes
¾ cup nonfat ricotta cheese
 1 tablespoon grated Parmesan cheese
 1 tablespoon minced fresh chives
 2 cloves garlic, crushed
    Pinch of ground white pepper
32 snow peas, ends and strings removed

In a small bowl, cover the tomatoes with boiling water and soak for 4 minutes. Drain the tomatoes and finely chop them.

In a medium bowl, stir the tomatoes, ricotta and Parmesan cheeses, chives, garlic and pepper until well combined; set aside.

In a medium saucepan, bring a small amount of water to a boil. Add the snow peas and cook for 2 minutes. Immediately drain and rinse with very cold water. Using the tip of a sharp knife, cut open 1 long side of each snow pea.

Spoon the cheese mixture into a pastry bag fitted with a small star tip. Pipe into each snow pea to fill. Or use a small spoon to fill each snow pea.

Chef's Note: If snow peas are unavailable, use mushroom caps, hollowed-out cherry tomatoes or small potatoes (steam them until tender, then scoop out the centers).

EXTRA HEALTH BENEFITS
Lower Cholesterol
Cancer Protection
Stronger Immunity

Time: Prep: 15 min.

Makes 4 servings.

Per serving: 97 calories, 0.7 g. fat (6% of calories), 2.3 g. dietary fiber, 1 mg. cholesterol, 93 mg. sodium.

Cherrystone Clams in Red Pepper Mayonnaise

Times: Prep: 18 min. Cooking: 5 min.

Makes 32 appetizers or 8 servings.

Per 4 appetizers: 38 calories, 0.4 g. fat (10% of calories), 0.2 g. dietary fiber, 12 mg. cholesterol, 92 mg. sodium.

For a stunning presentation, serve these clams on the half shell on a bed of rock salt or on a platter lined with leaves of ornamental kale.

  1 **sweet red pepper**
 ½ **cup water**
  2 **tablespoons lemon juice**
  1 **tablespoon minced fresh tarragon or 1 teaspoon dried tarragon**
  2 **shallots, halved**
  2 **cloves garlic, minced**
  1 **bay leaf**
32 **cherrystone clams, scrubbed**
  3 **tablespoons nonfat mayonnaise**
  2 **tablespoons minced fresh parsley (optional)**

To roast the pepper, cut it lengthwise in half and remove the stem, seeds and inner membranes. Place the pepper halves, cut sides down, on a cookie sheet. Broil 5" from the heat about 10 minutes or until the skin begins to blister. Then place the pepper halves in a clean paper bag, close it and let stand for 30 minutes.

Meanwhile, in a large heavy saucepan, combine the water, lemon juice, tarragon, shallots, garlic and bay leaf. Bring to a boil, then add the clams. Reduce the heat, cover and simmer about 5 minutes or until the clams open. Drain; discard the liquid and any clams that did not open. Cool until easy to handle.

Remove the clams from their shells, transfer to a bowl and cover to keep warm. Reserve 32 of the shell halves.

Using a knife, pull the skin from the red pepper. Discard the skin. In a food processor or blender, puree the pepper.

In a medium bowl, stir together the pureed pepper and the mayonnaise. Add the clams, then toss until coated.

To serve, place 1 clam in each of the reserved shell halves. If desired, garnish the tops with the parsley.

Chef's Note: Always choose clams that have tightly closed shells, which indicates they're alive. If the shells are slightly agape, tap them lightly with your finger. If they don't close, don't buy them. Keep the clams refrigerated until you need them, and plan to use them within a day of purchase.

SLIMMING STRATEGY

You may be surprised to learn that reduced-fat products are not always as low in calories as you might assume. Be sure to read the nutritional information on the back of the package and not just the bold claims on the front.

Times: Prep: 6 min.
Cooking: 2 min.
Marinating: 8 hrs.

Makes 6 servings.

Per serving: 58 calories,
0.9 g. fat (14% of calories),
0.4 g. dietary fiber, 72 mg.
cholesterol, 79 mg. sodium.

Dilled Shrimp

Here's an easy no-oil marinade that's appropriate for all types of seafood. For best results, allow the shrimp to marinate for at least 8 hours to absorb the flavors of the marinade (but try not to let it stand for more than 12 hours or the shrimp will become chewy).

> 12 **ounces medium shrimp, peeled and deveined**
> 2 **lemon slices**
> 1 **bay leaf**
> ¾ **cup water**
> ¼ **cup tarragon vinegar**
> ¼ **cup minced fresh dill or 2 tablespoons dillweed**
> 1 **small stalk celery, chopped**
> 2 **green onions, chopped**
> 1 **head Boston or bibb lettuce**

Place the shrimp, lemon slices and bay leaf in a medium saucepan and add just enough water to cover the shrimp. Bring to a boil, then reduce the heat. Simmer, uncovered, about 2 minutes or until the shrimp turn pink.

Drain the shrimp and discard the liquid, lemon slices and bay leaf. Transfer the shrimp to a medium glass bowl. Add the ¾ cup water, the vinegar, dill, celery and onions. Stir until mixed. Cover and marinate in the refrigerator for 8 to 12 hours, stirring occasionally.

Drain the marinated shrimp and discard the marinade. To serve, arrange the shrimp on a serving plate or platter lined with the lettuce.

Chef's Note: Fresh shellfish should always look and smell good. Avoid any that have a sulfur or ammonia odor.

Dilled Shrimp

Mussels with Caper Vinaigrette

Capers are the pickled buds of a shrub that's native to the Mediterranean. They add just the right degree of piquancy to this seafood appetizer. Be sure to rinse them before using to remove excess sodium.

½ cup water
¼ cup clam juice
1 tablespoon black peppercorns
16 large mussels, scrubbed
½ cup chopped roasted sweet red peppers
2 tablespoons capers, rinsed, drained and chopped
1 tablespoon white wine vinegar
2 teaspoons thyme
1 teaspoon lemon juice
1 teaspoon grated lemon peel
¼ teaspoon freshly ground black pepper

In a large Dutch oven, bring the water, clam juice and peppercorns to a boil. If necessary, remove the beards from the mussels.

Add the mussels to the boiling liquid. Return just to a boil, then reduce the heat. Cover and simmer about 5 minutes or until the shells open. Drain and discard the liquid and any mussels that did not open. Cool until easy to handle.

Remove the mussels from their shells and transfer to a medium bowl. Reserve 16 of the shell halves.

Add the roasted peppers, capers, vinegar, thyme, lemon juice, lemon peel and black pepper to the bowl. Toss until well mixed. If desired, cover and chill in the refrigerator for up to 6 hours.

To serve, spoon the mussel mixture into the reserved shell halves.

Chef's Note: Using roasted red peppers from a jar will save you time when making this recipe. But if you prefer to roast your own, here's how: Cut fresh sweet red peppers lengthwise in half and remove the stems, seeds and inner membranes. Place the pepper halves, cut sides down, on a cookie sheet. Broil 5" from the heat about 10 minutes or until the skin chars and blisters. Then place the peppers in a clean paper bag, close it and let stand for 30 minutes to let the skins steam loose. Use a knife to pull off the skins; discard the skins and chop the peppers.

Quick

EXTRA HEALTH BENEFITS
Cancer Protection
Blood Building

Times: Prep: 10 min.
Cooking: 5 min.

Makes 16 appetizers or 4 servings.

Per 4 appetizers:
92 calories, 2 g. fat (11% of calories), 0.4 g. dietary fiber, 45 mg. cholesterol, 324 mg. sodium.

SLIMMING STRATEGY

Take it easy on yourself! Losing weight takes skill and is a long-term process. Don't berate yourself for lapses. Just put them behind you and try to do better in the future.

Chicken and Three-Pepper Fajitas (page 92)

Spicy Barbecued Chicken Breasts

Chili sauce is superlow in fat and calories and makes a wonderfully spicy base for homemade barbecue sauce.

¼ **cup chili sauce**
2 **tablespoons reduced-calorie and -sodium ketchup**
1 **tablespoon honey**
1 **tablespoon red wine vinegar**
1 **teaspoon ground ginger**
1 **teaspoon Dijon mustard**
¾ **teaspoon ground black pepper**
¼ **teaspoon garlic powder**
¼ **teaspoon ground red pepper**
1 **pound skinless, boneless chicken breast halves**

To prepare the grill for cooking, spray the unheated grill rack with no-stick spray. Then light the grill according to the manufacturer's directions. Place the rack on the grill.

Meanwhile, for the sauce, in a small saucepan, stir together the chili sauce, ketchup, honey, vinegar, ginger, mustard, black pep-

Spicy Barbecued
Chicken Breasts

per, garlic powder and red pepper. Bring to a boil, then remove from the heat; set aside.

Rinse the chicken and pat dry with paper towels. Place the chicken on the rack over the coals. Grill, uncovered, for 5 minutes. Turn the chicken over and brush with the sauce. Grill for 5 to 10 minutes more or until the chicken is no longer pink. Brush with the remaining sauce before serving.

Apricot-Glazed Chicken Breasts

Preserves contain no fat and make an excellent sauce for poultry. Here, apricot preserves are mixed with orange juice and spices to fashion a quick topping for chicken breasts. Serve this glazed chicken with couscous and steamed beans for a complete dinner.

   1 **pound skinless, boneless chicken breast halves**
   ¼ **teaspoon paprika**
   1 **teaspoon canola oil**
   2 **cloves garlic, minced**
   ⅓ **cup reduced-calorie apricot preserves**
   ¼ **cup orange juice**
   1 **tablespoon minced fresh cilantro**
   ¼ **teaspoon ground nutmeg**
   ¼ **teaspoon ground allspice**

Rinse the chicken and pat dry with paper towels. Sprinkle the chicken with the paprika.

Spray an unheated, large no-stick skillet with no-stick spray. Heat the skillet over medium-high heat. Add the chicken and cook for 4 minutes. Turn the chicken over and cook for 4 to 6 minutes more or until the chicken is no longer pink. Transfer to a serving platter and cover to keep warm.

Add the oil to the skillet. Add the garlic. Cook and stir for 30 seconds. Stir in the preserves, orange juice, cilantro, nutmeg and allspice. Bring to a gentle boil. Remove from the heat and pour over the chicken.

Chef's Note: Cilantro is a green herb that also goes by the names Chinese parsley and fresh coriander. Although it resembles flat-leaf parsley, it's got a distinctive flavor that can't be duplicated with any other ingredient.

Quick

EXTRA HEALTH BENEFITS
Better Blood Pressure
Stronger Immunity

Times: Prep: 5 min.
Cooking: 9 min.

Makes 4 servings.

Per serving: 177 calories, 2.7 g. fat (14% of calories), 0.4 g. dietary fiber, 66 mg. cholesterol, 97 mg. sodium.

Chicken Breasts Marinara over Fettuccine

EXTRA HEALTH BENEFITS
Better Blood Pressure
Cancer Protection
Stronger Immunity

Times: Prep: 14 min.
Cooking: 35 min.

Makes 4 servings.

Per serving: 227 calories,
2.8 g. fat (11% of calories),
2.6 g. dietary fiber, 52 mg.
cholesterol, 133 mg. sodium.

Gone are the days when a made-from-scratch Italian sauce required several hours of simmering. This marinara sauce is just as tasty as a traditional one but takes only 30 minutes.

- ¼ **cup finely chopped onions**
- 1 **tablespoon water**
- 3 **cups coarsely chopped plum tomatoes (with juices) or 1 can (28 ounces) low-sodium tomatoes (with juices), cut up**
- 1½ **cups water**
- ¼ **cup finely chopped celery**
- 1 **tablespoon minced fresh parsley**
- 1 **tablespoon red wine vinegar**
- 1 **teaspoon dried oregano**
- 1 **teaspoon dried thyme**
- 1 **clove garlic, minced**
- 1 **bay leaf**
- 4 **skinless, boneless chicken breast halves (about 12 ounces total)**
- 2 **cups hot cooked fettuccine**
- 2 **tablespoons finely shredded fresh Parmesan cheese**

For the sauce, in a medium saucepan, combine the onions and the 1 tablespoon water. Cover and cook over medium-low heat for 5 minutes, stirring occasionally. (If necessary, add more water during cooking to prevent the onions from browning.)

Stir in the tomatoes (with juices), the 1½ cups water, celery, parsley, vinegar, oregano, thyme, garlic and bay leaf. Bring to a boil, then reduce the heat to medium-low. Gently simmer, uncovered, about 30 minutes or until the sauce is the desired consistency. Remove and discard the bay leaf.

Meanwhile, spray an unheated large skillet with no-stick spray. Heat the skillet over medium heat. Rinse the chicken and pat dry with paper towels. Add to the skillet and cook for 4 minutes. Turn the chicken over and cook for 4 to 6 minutes more or until the chicken is no longer pink.

To serve, slice each chicken breast half at an angle into

SLIMMING STRATEGY

Are you eating too much at mealtime? Try this trick: Put a large sauce-pan of water on the stove when you sit down to eat. When the water boils, in about 10 to 15 minutes, get up and make a pot of herb tea. By the time you go back to the table, you probably won't feel like eating much more.

¼"-thick slices. Then arrange the slices, fanning them, on top of the fettuccine. Spoon some sauce over each serving and sprinkle with the cheese. Serve with the remaining sauce.

Chef's Note: If there is any leftover sauce, freeze it to serve over pasta as a side dish for another meal.

Chicken Breasts Marinara over Fettuccine

Chicken and Three-Pepper Fajitas

EXTRA HEALTH BENEFITS
Lower Cholesterol
Blood Building
Stronger Immunity

Times: Prep: 15 min.
Chilling: 1 hr.
Cooking: 10 min.

Makes 4 servings.

Per serving: 318 calories,
5 g. fat (14% of calories),
3.1 g. dietary fiber, 49 mg.
cholesterol, 75 mg. sodium.

Fajitas are typically made by marinating poultry or meat in a mixture of oil and lime juice. This healthier version eliminates the oil. Then lime juice is drizzled over the chicken just before serving in order to retain the delightful tart flavor.

- 1 **clove garlic, minced**
- ½ **teaspoon ground cumin**
- ½ **teaspoon chili powder**
- ¼ **teaspoon reduced-sodium soy sauce**
- 12 **ounces skinless, boneless chicken breasts, cut into ½"-wide strips**
- ½ **cup chopped and loosely packed fresh cilantro**
- 1 **medium yellow pepper, cut into 2" × ⅛" strips**
- 1 **medium sweet red pepper, cut into 2" × ⅛" strips**
- 1 **medium green pepper, cut into 2" × ⅛" strips**
- 1 **medium onion, thinly sliced and separated into rings**
- 3 **tablespoons lime juice**
- 8 **small whole-wheat tortillas**

In a medium bowl, stir together the garlic, cumin, chili powder and soy sauce. Stir in the chicken until coated. Then stir in the cilantro. Cover and refrigerate for 1 hour.

Spray an unheated, large no-stick skillet with no-stick spray. Heat the skillet over medium-high heat. Add the chicken and cook and stir for 3 to 4 minutes or until the chicken is no longer pink. Transfer the chicken to a large bowl. Cover to keep warm.

Add the yellow, red and green peppers to the skillet. Cook and stir for 4 to 6 minutes or until the peppers are crisp-tender. Transfer the peppers to the bowl with the chicken.

Add the onions to the skillet and cook and stir about 3 minutes or until the onions are crisp-tender.

Return the chicken and peppers to the skillet. Drizzle the lime juice over the mixture and stir until combined. Remove the skillet from the heat.

To serve, place the mixture on the tortillas and roll up. Serve immediately.

SLIMMING STRATEGY

Did you know that ½ cup of uncooked red, green, yellow or purple sweet peppers has more than a day's supply of vitamin C? And the red peppers contain more than 25 percent of the recommended daily allowance of vitamin A. All of this is important because it's essential to get enough nutrients when you're watching your weight.

Chicken Curry in a Hurry

Here's a quick dish inspired by the flavorful curries of India. This one pairs tender strips of chicken with a low-fat yogurt sauce and brown rice. All you need to add to make a complete meal is a vegetable, such as steamed zucchini or roasted sweet peppers, and some piquant commercial chutney.

½ cup nonfat plain yogurt
½ cup nonfat mayonnaise
3 tablespoons finely chopped onions
1 teaspoon ground ginger
1 teaspoon curry powder
1 pound skinless, boneless chicken breasts, cut into ½"-wide strips
1 teaspoon paprika
½ teaspoon ground black pepper
2 cups hot cooked brown rice

In a small bowl, stir together the yogurt, mayonnaise, onions, ginger and curry powder; set aside.

Place the chicken in a medium bowl. Combine the paprika and pepper. Sprinkle over the chicken and toss until coated.

Spray an unheated, large no-stick skillet with no-stick spray. Heat the skillet over medium-high heat. Add the chicken. Cook and stir for 3 to 4 minutes or until the chicken is no longer pink.

Stir in the yogurt mixture. Cook and stir for 2 minutes. Serve over the rice.

Quick

EXTRA HEALTH BENEFIT
Stronger Immunity

Times: Prep: 7 min.
Cooking: 5 min.

Makes 4 servings.

Per serving: 281 calories, 2.5 g. fat (8% of calories), 2 g. dietary fiber, 66 mg. cholesterol, 481 mg. sodium.

SLIMMING STRATEGY

Do it for yourself! A very common reason for wanting to lose weight is to look good for someone else. But that's a sure prescription for failure. If you're dieting for any reason that is not internally motivated, you're unlikely to succeed.

Waldorf Chicken Salad

EXTRA HEALTH BENEFIT
Stronger Immunity

Time: Prep: 13 min.

Makes 4 servings.

Per serving: 213 calories, 5.6 g. fat (24% of calories), 2.3 g. dietary fiber, 59 mg. cholesterol, 142 mg. sodium.

This recipe has an advantage over traditional Waldorf salad. It adds lean protein for a main-dish salad.

> 2 cups cooked and cubed chicken breast
> 2 cups cored and chopped Granny Smith apples
> 1 cup chopped celery
> 1/4 cup raisins
> 2 tablespoons reduced-calorie mayonnaise
> 2 tablespoons low-fat plain yogurt
> 1/4 teaspoon ground nutmeg
> 1/4 teaspoon ground cinnamon
> Ground black pepper (to taste)
> Lettuce leaves

In a large bowl, combine the chicken, apples, celery and raisins.

In a cup, stir together the mayonnaise, yogurt, nutmeg and cinnamon. Add to the chicken mixture and toss until coated. Season to taste with the pepper. Serve on lettuce-lined salad plates.

Pronto Poultry

In a hurry and need a super fast entrée? Then quickly poach or microwave boneless, skinless chicken breasts or turkey tenderloins and top them with a purchased low-fat sauce (such as salsa, spaghetti, sweet-and-sour or barbecue). Or sprinkle them with a salt-free seasoning (such as lemon-pepper, herb or dried Italian).

To poach the poultry: Bring about an inch of water to a boil in a large skillet. Carefully add the poultry and simmer, covered, for 15 to 20 minutes or until the pieces are no longer pink.

To microwave the poultry: Start with 1 pound of chicken breast halves or whole turkey tenderloins. If using turkey, cut each piece crosswise in half. Arrange the pieces in a microwave-proof dish with the thicker parts facing the rim. Cover with plastic wrap. Vent the wrap by pulling back a small corner. Cook on high power (100%) for 3 minutes. Rotate the dish a half-turn, then cook on high about 3 minutes more or until the juices run clear when the thickest part of the poultry is pierced with a fork.

Chicken and Spuds Salad

Frozen hash brown potatoes can be a real time-saver. Here we use them to make a quick potato salad that we enhance with cooked chicken breast. Be aware, however, that some brands of hash browns are high in fat. Read the labels and choose one that is fat-free.

   4 **cups frozen hash brown potatoes with no fat**
   2 **cups cooked and cubed chicken breast**
 ½ **cup chopped celery**
 ½ **cup sliced green onions**
 ¼ **cup chopped green peppers**
 ⅓ **cup nonfat mayonnaise**
 ⅓ **cup nonfat plain yogurt**
 1½ **tablespoons prepared mustard**
 ¼ **teaspoon celery seeds**
     Ground black pepper (to taste)
 ⅛ **teaspoon paprika**

Place the potatoes in a small saucepan and add enough water to cover. Bring to a boil, then reduce the heat. Cover and simmer about 10 minutes or until the potatoes are nearly tender. Drain well. Transfer to a medium bowl and cool to room temperature, about 20 minutes.

Add the chicken, celery, onions and green peppers to the potatoes. In a small bowl, stir together the mayonnaise, yogurt, mustard and celery seeds. Add to the potato mixture and toss until well coated. Season to taste with the pepper. Sprinkle with the paprika.

Cover and chill in the refrigerator for at least 4 hours to blend the flavors.

EXTRA HEALTH BENEFIT
Stronger Immunity

Time: Prep: 15 min.

Makes 4 servings.

Per serving: 306 calories, 6.6 g. fat (20% of calories), 1 g. dietary fiber, 63 mg. cholesterol, 360 mg. sodium.

Chicken and Grape Salad in Pitas

Chicken salad can be quite low in fat if you dress it properly. In this case, we combine low-fat yogurt and nonfat mayonnaise for a creamy but light dressing. You can serve the chicken salad in pita bread, as suggested here, or you can turn it into an interesting luncheon dish by mounding it in a cantaloupe half.

½ **cup low-fat lemon yogurt**
1 **tablespoon nonfat mayonnaise**
1 **teaspoon minced fresh rosemary**
2 **cups cooked and cubed chicken breast**
½ **cup halved green grapes**
4 **6" whole-wheat pita breads**
4 **lettuce leaves**

In a medium bowl, stir together the yogurt, mayonnaise and rosemary. Fold in the chicken and grapes.

To serve, cut the top from each pita. Line each pita with a lettuce leaf and spoon in about ¾ cup of the chicken mixture.

Chicken and Grape
Salad in Pitas

The Fairest Fowl

Pitas Stuffed with Chicken-Apple Salad

The combination of chicken and fruit is particularly appealing. Serve these sandwiches for a light lunch in the middle of summer.

- 2 cups cooked and cubed chicken breast
- 2 medium red apples, cored and chopped
- 1 can (8 ounces) crushed pineapple (packed in juice), well drained
- ½ cup chopped celery
- ⅓ cup low-fat lemon yogurt
- ¼ cup nonfat mayonnaise
- ¼ teaspoon celery seeds
- 4 6" whole-wheat pita breads
- 4 lettuce leaves

In a medium bowl, combine the chicken, apples, pineapple and celery.

In a small bowl, stir together the yogurt, mayonnaise and celery seeds. Add to the chicken mixture and toss until well coated.

To serve, cut the top from each pita. Line each pita with a lettuce leaf and spoon in about 1 cup of the chicken mixture.

Chef's Note: This sandwich filling is best served within 2 hours. If it stands longer, the acid in the pineapple will tend to soften the chicken.

Quick

EXTRA HEALTH BENEFIT
Stronger Immunity

Time: Prep: 15 min.

Makes 4 servings.

Per serving: 346 calories, 6.4 g. fat (17% of calories), 2.9 g. dietary fiber, 63 mg. cholesterol, 493 mg. sodium.

SLIMMING STRATEGY

If you just can't eat sandwiches without mayonnaise, use the nonfat or low-fat variety. If you insist upon real mayonnaise, spread a little around the edges only. You'll use less than usual, and your tongue will be fooled into thinking there's mayo throughout the sandwich.

Tuscan Chicken Legs with Spinach Fettuccine

Just keep a few staple ingredients on hand and you'll be able to enjoy this easy dish anytime. Round out the meal with a package of frozen Italian mixed vegetables.

- 1 **pound skinless chicken legs**
- 1 **teaspoon garlic powder**
- ½ **teaspoon ground black pepper**
- 2 **teaspoons olive oil**
- 1 **can (14½ ounces) salt-free tomatoes (with juices), cut up**
- ¼ **teaspoon dried oregano**
- ¼ **teaspoon dried basil**
- 4 **cups hot cooked spinach fettuccine**

Rinse the chicken legs and pat dry with paper towels. Lightly sprinkle with the garlic powder and pepper. Add the oil to a large no-stick skillet and heat over medium-high heat. Add the chicken and cook for 2 to 3 minutes or until lightly brown on all sides.

Stir in the tomatoes (with juices), oregano and basil. Bring to a boil, then reduce the heat. Cover and simmer about 20 minutes or until the chicken is no longer pink. Serve with the fettucine.

Lemon-Garlic Roasted Cornish Hens

EXTRA HEALTH BENEFITS
Better Blood Pressure
Stronger Immunity

Times: Prep: 5 min.
Roasting: 45 min.
Standing: 10 min.

Makes 8 servings.

Per serving: 163 calories,
4.4 g. fat (25% of calories),
0.1 g. dietary fiber, 0 mg.
cholesterol, 77 mg. sodium.

Lemon and garlic tucked underneath the skin add no-fat flavor to these Cornish hens. Serve the birds with a wild-rice pilaf and steamed asparagus for a company-special meal.

4 Cornish game hens (1–1½ pounds each)
2 tablespoons minced garlic
1 lemon, thinly sliced and seeded

Rinse the game hens and pat dry with paper towels. Starting at the neck opening of each hen, use your fingers to gently loosen the skin from the meat to create a pocket on each side of the breast. Leave the skin attached to the breast bones.

Rub the garlic onto the meat underneath the skin. Then place the lemon slices underneath the skin. Place the hens, breast side up, on a rack in a large shallow roasting pan. Skewer the neck skin to the back of the hens and tie the legs to the tails. Insert a meat thermometer in the thickest part of a thigh.

Roast, uncovered, at 350° for 45 to 60 minutes or until the thermometer registers 180° to 185° and the hens are no longer pink.

Loosely cover with foil and let stand for 10 minutes before carving. Remove and discard the skin and the lemon slices before serving.

Lemon-Garlic Roasted
Cornish Hens

Orange-Glazed Chicken Thighs

Start with reduced-calorie orange marmalade, add a few spices, and you have an easy low-calorie glaze for chicken.

    1   pound skinless chicken thighs
    ¼   teaspoon ground cinnamon
    ¼   teaspoon ground black pepper
    1   teaspoon canola oil
    ⅓   cup reduced-calorie orange marmalade
    ⅓   cup defatted low-sodium chicken broth
    ⅓   cup orange juice
    ⅛   teaspoon ground nutmeg
    ⅛   teaspoon ground ginger
        Orange slices (optional)

Rinse the chicken and pat dry with paper towels. Lightly sprinkle with the cinnamon and pepper; set aside.

Add the oil to a large no-stick skillet and heat over medium-high heat. Add the chicken and cook for 3 to 4 minutes or until lightly brown on all sides.

Push the chicken to the side of the skillet. Stir in the marmalade, broth, orange juice, nutmeg and ginger. Stir until well combined. Then push the chicken back to the center of the skillet. Cover and cook over medium heat about 15 minutes or until the chicken is no longer pink, stirring occasionally.

To serve, transfer to a shallow serving dish. If desired, garnish with the orange slices.

Quick

EXTRA HEALTH BENEFITS
Better Blood Pressure
Stronger Immunity

Times: Prep: 3 min.
Cooking: 18 min.

Makes 4 servings.

Per serving: 137 calories, 4 g. fat (27% of calories), 0.5 g. dietary fiber, 57 mg. cholesterol, 89 mg. sodium.

SLIMMING STRATEGY

Most of the fat in chicken and turkey is located in the skin, and removing the skin will get rid of it. But the thighs also have fat deposits running through the meat. Pare off what you can see from the outside. And when you're using boneless thighs, trim as much as you can from the interior.

Chicken Roasted with Winter Vegetables

Times: Prep: 15 min.
Roasting: 1 hr.
Standing: 10 min.

Makes 6 servings.

Per serving: 188 calories,
3.7 g. fat (18% of calories),
2 g. dietary fiber, 79 mg.
cholesterol, 129 mg. sodium.

This chicken is stuffed with vegetables instead of a high-calorie bread dressing.

1 broiler-fryer chicken (about 3 pounds)
1 clove garlic, minced
4 sprigs fresh rosemary
4 small potatoes, quartered
3 medium carrots, halved and quartered
1 small onion, quartered
1 small fennel bulb, chopped
½ cup water

Rinse the chicken and pat dry with paper towels. Remove any excess fat from inside the chicken. Starting at the neck opening, use your fingers to gently loosen the skin from the meat to create a pocket on each side of the breast. Leave the skin attached to the breast bones.

Rub the garlic onto the meat underneath the skin. Then place the rosemary underneath the skin. Place the chicken, breast side up, on a rack in a shallow roasting pan. Loosely stuff with some of the potatoes, carrots, onions and fennel. Place the remaining vegetables in the pan around the chicken. Skewer the neck skin to the back of the chicken and tie the legs to the tail. Insert a meat thermometer in the thickest part of a thigh. Pour the water in the bottom of the pan.

Roast, uncovered, at 400° for 30 minutes. Turn the vegetables over and roast, uncovered, about 30 minutes more or until the thermometer registers 180° to 185° and the chicken is no longer pink.

Transfer the vegetables from the pan to a serving dish and keep warm. Loosely cover the chicken with foil and let stand for 10 minutes before carving. Serve the chicken with the vegetables. Remove and discard the skin before eating.

SLIMMING STRATEGY

Here's a surefire way to water down your appetite: Drink 2 cups of water before each meal. That will suppress your appetite—and guarantee exercise (to and from the restroom).

Chef's Note: This chicken would go especially well with a rice or barley pilaf. To make either, cook some diced onions and garlic in a little defatted low-sodium broth until soft. Then add 1 cup of quick-cooking rice or barley, additional defatted broth (check the package for the amount) and a few pinches of your favorite dried herb. Cover and cook according to the package directions. For added zest, stir in some grated orange peel.

Chicken Roasted with Winter Vegetables

Grilled Cornish Hens Teriyaki

EXTRA HEALTH BENEFIT
Stronger Immunity

Times: Prep: 10 min.
Grilling: 35 min.

Makes 4 servings.

Per serving: 190 calories, 5.3 g. fat (26% of calories), 0.1 g. dietary fiber, 0 mg. cholesterol, 377 mg. sodium.

Cornish hens are miniature chickens that weigh no more than 2½ pounds. They're handy to use when you're in the mood for a grilled or roasted whole chicken but don't want leftovers. Here we marinate a pair of hens in an Oriental sauce mixture, then cook them on the grill.

- 2 tablespoons reduced-sodium soy sauce
- 1 tablespoon honey
- 1 teaspoon sesame seeds, toasted
- ½ teaspoon Oriental sesame oil
- 1 clove garlic, minced
- 2 Cornish game hens (1–1½ pounds each), halved and skin removed

In a large shallow dish, combine the soy sauce, honey, sesame seeds, oil and garlic. Rinse the game hens and pat dry with paper towels. Place in the soy sauce mixture and turn to coat evenly. Cover with plastic wrap and marinate in the refrigerator for 10 minutes.

To prepare the grill for cooking, spray the unheated grill rack with no-stick spray. Then light the grill according to the manufacturer's directions. Place the rack on the grill.

Remove the hens from the marinade and discard the marinade. Place the hens, bone side up, on the rack over the coals. Insert a meat thermometer in the thickest part of a thigh. Grill, uncovered, for 15 minutes. Turn the hens over and grill, uncovered, for 20 to 30 minutes more or until the thermometer registers 180° to 185° and the hens are no longer pink.

Chef's Note: If you prefer to broil the Cornish game hens, coat the rack of a broiling pan with no-stick spray and place the hens on the rack. Broil 5" from the heat for 15 minutes. Turn the hens over and broil about 15 minutes more or until the juices run clear when the thickest part of a thigh is pierced with a sharp knife or fork.

SLIMMING STRATEGY

Go nuts! When the craving for nuts hits, grab some chestnuts. They pack fewer calories and less fat than any other type of nut. To roast them, cut an ✕ in the flat side of each shell. Place on a cookie sheet and bake at 400° for 20 minutes, or until cooked through (test one). Peel while they're still warm.

Lemon-Sesame Turkey Cutlets

A sprinkling of sesame seeds enlivens this Japanese-style turkey dish. Toasting the seeds first brings out their nutty flavor so you can get away with using a small amount. That's important because sesame seeds are relatively high in fat.

- 4 teaspoons lemon juice
- 2 teaspoons honey
- 2 teaspoons reduced-sodium soy sauce
- 1 pound turkey breast cutlets
- ⅛ teaspoon ground black pepper
- 4 teaspoons sesame seeds, toasted

In a small bowl, stir together the lemon juice, honey and soy sauce; set aside.

Rinse the turkey and pat dry with paper towels. Sprinkle each cutlet with the pepper. Spray an unheated, large no-stick skillet with no-stick spray. Heat the skillet over medium-high heat. Add the turkey and cook for 1 minute. Turn the cutlets over and cook for 2 to 3 minutes more or until the turkey is no longer pink.

Pour the lemon juice mixture over the turkey and cook until the mixture comes to a boil.

To serve, transfer the turkey and juice mixture to a serving dish. Sprinkle with the sesame seeds.

Chef's Note: To toast the sesame seeds, place them in a small no-stick skillet. Cook and stir over medium heat for 2 to 3 minutes or until lightly brown.

Quick

EXTRA HEALTH BENEFIT
Stronger Immunity

Times: Prep: 4 min.
Cooking: 3 min.

Makes 4 servings.

Per serving: 163 calories, 3.4 g. fat (19% of calories), 0.5 g. dietary fiber, 66 mg. cholesterol, 169 mg. sodium.

Lemon-Sesame Turkey Cutlets

The Fairest Fowl

Times: Prep: 4 min.
Cooking: 3 min.

Makes 4 servings.

Per serving: 143 calories, 2.9 g. fat (19% of calories), 0 g. dietary fiber, 68 mg. cholesterol, 132 mg. sodium.

SLIMMING STRATEGY

When cooking healthy, it's best to use no added fat. But if you do need to add a bit for sautéing, pour a little into your pan and spread it around with a paper towel to leave just a thin coat. And choose vegetable oils high in monounsaturates and polyunsaturates because they won't increase your risk of heart disease. Olive, canola, safflower and sunflower oils are smart selections.

Turkey Piccata

Piccata is a classic Italian dish that is typically served with a sauce made from pan drippings and lemon juice. This lightened version eliminates the drippings and drizzles the lemon juice over the cooked turkey for the same tangy taste without the fat.

- 1 **pound turkey breast tenderloins, cut crosswise into ¾"-thick strips**
  Ground black pepper
- 1 **teaspoon olive oil**
- 1 **large clove garlic, minced**
- 1 **tablespoon lemon juice**
- 4 **teaspoons capers, rinsed and drained**

Lightly sprinkle the turkey with the pepper. Add the oil to a large no-stick skillet and heat over medium heat. Add the turkey and garlic and cook for 2 minutes. Turn the strips over and cook for 1 to 2 minutes more or until the turkey is no longer pink.

Remove the skillet from the heat and drizzle the lemon juice over the turkey. Sprinkle with the capers. Serve immediately.

Turkey Tenderloins
in Golden Apple Sauce

The microwave does more than save you time—it can lend a helping hand when you're trying to cook healthier. Cooking these turkey tenderloins in the microwave rather than sautéing them in butter cuts a hefty amount of fat from the recipe. Serve the turkey with a mixture of white and wild rice for a low-fat accompaniment.

TURKEY

- ½ **cup chopped celery with leaves**
- ¼ **cup water**
- ¼ **cup sliced green onions**
- 1 **tablespoon minced fresh parsley**
- 2 **turkey breast tenderloins (about 1 pound total), halved crosswise**

SAUCE

- ½ **cup peeled and chopped tart apple**
- ¼ **cup orange juice**
- 2 **teaspoons reduced-calorie orange marmalade**

For the turkey: In a 2- to 2½-quart round, microwave-proof casserole, combine the celery, water, onions and parsley. Rinse the turkey and pat dry with paper towels. Place on top of the vegetables in a spoke pattern, overlapping the pointed ends of the tenderloins in the center if necessary.

Cover and cook in a microwave oven on high power (100%) for 3½ minutes. Turn the turkey over and cook, covered, on high for 3 to 4 minutes more or until the turkey is no longer pink.

For the sauce: In a small saucepan, cook the apples, orange juice and marmalade over medium heat about 4 minutes or until the apples are tender but still hold their shape.

Pour the sauce over the turkey and serve.

Chef's Note: Turkey tenderloins are oblong in shape and can easily become overcooked at the tapered ends when microwaved. To avoid this, cut the tenderloins crosswise in half. Then arrange the pieces in a round dish, with the thicker ends facing the rim.

Turkey Divan with Peaches

Here's a divine dish! And it's all the more so because it's minus the heavy cream sauce and egg yolks that characterize classic turkey divan.

- 2 turkey breast tenderloins (about 1 pound total)
- 1 package (16 ounces) frozen cut broccoli
- ½ cup nonfat sour cream
- 2 tablespoons nonfat mayonnaise
- ½ teaspoon onion powder
- ¼ teaspoon garlic powder
- 1 can (16 ounces) peach halves (packed in juice), drained
- 2 tablespoons grated Parmesan cheese

Poach the turkey according to the directions on page 94. Cook the broccoli according to the package directions, but without adding the salt.

Meanwhile, in a small bowl, stir together the sour cream, mayonnaise, onion powder and garlic powder.

Spray a shallow baking pan with no-stick spray. Add the turkey, then arrange the broccoli and peach halves around the tenderloins. Spoon the sour cream mixture on top and sprinkle with the cheese.

Broil 6" to 7" from the heat for 5 to 6 minutes or until the sour cream mixture is puffy and lightly brown.

Turkey and Summer Garden Stir-Fry

Turkey and Summer Garden Stir-Fry

Turkey breast meat is just about the leanest meat there is. When it's sliced into thin cutlets, it cooks in minutes. That makes it perfect for both watching your waistline and getting dinner on the table pronto.

   1 teaspoon ground black pepper
   1 teaspoon paprika
   1 teaspoon garlic powder
   1 pound turkey breast cutlets, cut into ½"-wide strips
   2 teaspoons olive oil
1½ cups sliced yellow summer squash
   1 cup cubed green or sweet red peppers
   4 ounces snow peas, ends and strings removed
   ½ teaspoon dried Italian seasoning

Combine the black pepper, paprika and garlic powder in a pie plate. Roll the turkey strips in the mixture until coated.

In a wok or large skillet, heat 1 teaspoon of the oil over medium-high heat. Add the turkey and stir-fry for 3 to 4 minutes or until the turkey is no longer pink. Transfer the turkey to a plate and cover to keep warm.

Heat the remaining 1 teaspoon of oil in the wok or skillet. Add the squash, green or red peppers and snow peas. Stir-fry for 3 to 4 minutes or until the vegetables are crisp-tender. Sprinkle with the Italian seasoning. Reduce the heat to medium. Stir in the turkey and cook for 1 to 2 minutes or until heated through.

Quick

EXTRA HEALTH BENEFITS
Better Blood Pressure
Blood Building
Stronger Immunity

Times: Prep: 10 min.
Cooking: 7 min.

Makes 4 servings.

Per serving: 181 calories, 4.5 g. fat (22% of calories), 1.6 g. dietary fiber, 66 mg. cholesterol, 72 mg. sodium.

Times: Prep: 10 min.
Chilling: at least 2 hr.
Grilling: 1¼ hr.
Standing: 10 min.

Makes 8 servings.

Per serving: 141 calories,
2.1 g. fat (14% of calories),
0 g. dietary fiber, 68 mg.
cholesterol, 113 mg. sodium.

SLIMMING STRATEGY

In the summer, take
advantage of nature's
fruitful bounty for low-
calorie desserts. Eat the
fruit raw or do something
special like grilling it. You
could, for instance, thread
thick peach slices on
skewers, brush them with
orange juice and grill
about 4 minutes per side.
Serve with a sprinkle of
toasted coconut.

Grilled Lemon-Lime Turkey

You'd never guess the secret ingredient in this dish: lemon-lime soda. It's used as a marinade and adds a pleasant hint of tartness and sweetness to grilled turkey breast.

> 1 bone-in turkey breast half (2–3 pounds)
> 1½ cups or 1 can (12 ounces) sugar-free lemon-lime soda
> 2 tablespoons canola oil
> ¼ cup reduced-sodium soy sauce
> 1 tablespoon prepared horseradish
> 1 teaspoon garlic powder
> 4 cups hot cooked rice

Rinse the turkey and pat dry with paper towels. Place in a large self-closing plastic bag. In a small bowl, stir together the soda, oil, soy sauce, horseradish and garlic powder. Pour the soda mixture over the turkey in the bag. Seal the bag and marinate the turkey in the refrigerator for at least 2 hours, turning the bag occasionally.

To prepare the grill for cooking, spray the unheated grill rack with no-stick spray. Then light it according to the manufacturer's directions. Place the rack on the grill. (If using a charcoal grill, place a foil pan in the center of the fire box to catch the drippings. Arrange the hot coals around the pan.)

Remove the turkey from the bag and discard the marinade. Place the turkey, skin side up, on the rack. (If using a charcoal grill, make sure the turkey is over the drip pan, not over the coals.) Insert a meat thermometer in the thickest part of the breast. Cover and grill for 1¼ to 1½ hours or until the thermometer registers 170° to 175° and the turkey is no longer pink in the center. Loosely cover with foil and let stand for 10 minutes before slicing. Remove and discard the skin before serving. Serve with the rice.

Chef's Note: Marinade that's been in contact with any raw ingredient such as poultry, meat, fish or seafood may be contaminated with undesirable organisms. Your best bet is to discard it. However, if you have enough left over to use as a sauce, transfer it to a clean saucepan and bring it to a full boil. Let it cook for a few minutes before using.

Add Flavor with Marinades

One of poultry's selling points is its mild flavor, which marries well with all sorts of other ingredients. A second plus is its low fat content. The only time those attributes can become a drawback is when you broil or grill skinless pieces. Without added fat, the meat can become tough and dried out. Without a sauce, accompanying vegetables or other flavor enhancers, the poultry can be quite bland.

Marinades can remedy both situations. These flavorful liquids, which don't need a speck of fat to be delicious, infuse poultry with big flavor and help it stay moist during cooking. White meat does best with light-tasting mixtures; dark meat can take something a bit stronger.

Mix the marinade in a glass or other nonreactive dish, add the poultry pieces and turn them to coat them all over. Refrigerate for at least an hour; flip the pieces occasionally. To cook, remove the pieces from the dish and grill or broil as usual. Baste often with the leftover liquid, then discard whatever remains. (If there's enough marinade left and you want to turn it into sauce, boil it for a few minutes to kill any bacteria that might be present from the raw meat.)

Below are a few sample combinations that may inspire you to create blends of your own.

• Orange juice, tomato puree, honey, grated orange peel, minced garlic, chopped thyme and ground black pepper
• Lemon juice, minced garlic, chopped oregano and snipped chives
• Yogurt, chopped mint, minced garlic and hot-pepper sauce
• White wine vinegar, chopped basil, minced shallots and ground black pepper
• Lime juice, yogurt, curry powder and minced garlic
• Buttermilk, ground cumin, ground ginger, turmeric, chopped coriander and minced garlic
• Chicken stock, orange juice, soy sauce, grated ginger and five-spice powder

Apricot-Rosemary Turkey Breast

EXTRA HEALTH BENEFITS
Better Blood Pressure
Blood Building
Stronger Immunity

Times: Prep: 2 min.
Cooking: 10 min.
Roasting: 1¾ hr.
Standing: 10 min.

Makes 10 to 12 servings.

Per serving: 246 calories, 1.1 g. fat (4% of calories), 0.3 g. dietary fiber, 120 mg. cholesterol, 78 mg. sodium.

This entrée is ultra-easy to prepare. The turkey roasts with barely any attention needed, and the glaze is a snap to prepare using apricot nectar, honey and rosemary.

1½ **cups apricot nectar**
¼ **cup honey**
1 **tablespoon minced fresh rosemary**
1 **bone-in turkey breast (4–6 pounds)**
1 **cup water**
1 **tablespoon cornstarch**

For the glaze, in a medium saucepan, stir together the apricot nectar, honey and rosemary. Bring to a boil, then reduce the heat to medium. Simmer, uncovered, for 10 to 15 minutes or until the glaze reduces to about 1 cup.

Rinse the turkey and pat dry with paper towels. Spray the rack in a roasting pan with no-stick spray. Place the turkey breast, skin side up, on the rack. Insert a meat thermometer in the thickest part of the breast. Roast, uncovered, at 325° for 1¾ to 2 hours or until the thermometer registers 170° to 175° and the turkey is no longer pink in the center. During the last 15 minutes of roasting, brush ¼ cup of the glaze over the turkey breast.

Remove the turkey from the oven and loosely cover it with foil. Let stand for 10 minutes before slicing. Remove and discard the skin before serving.

Meanwhile, for the sauce, in a small bowl, stir together the water and cornstarch. Stir into the remaining ¾ cup of glaze in the saucepan. Cook and stir over medium heat until the mixture thickens and begins to boil. Cook and stir for 2 minutes more. Serve the sauce with the turkey.

Chef's Note: If you don't have fresh rosemary, use dried. Buy the leaves whole and crush them just before using to bring out their flavor. The usual rule of thumb is to use ⅓ as much dried as fresh. So in this recipe, that would come to 1 teaspoon dried rosemary.

Mustard-Roasted Turkey Breast

When roasting poultry, it's best to leave the skin on so the meat doesn't dry out as it cooks. Contrary to popular opinion, none of the fat from the skin seeps into the flesh. Just remember to discard the skin before eating because it does contain a lot of fat. This recipe is ideal for the holidays, parties or a buffet table. And leftovers—should there be any—make great sandwiches.

1 **bone-in turkey breast (3½–4 pounds)**
1 **tablespoon Dijon mustard**
½ **cup defatted low-sodium chicken broth**
   Italian parsley sprigs (optional)

Rinse the turkey and pat dry with paper towels. Use your fingers to gently loosen the skin from the meat to create a pocket on each side of the breast. Leave the skin attached to the breast bones. Rub the mustard onto the meat underneath the skin.

Spray the rack in a roasting pan with no-stick spray. Place the turkey breast, skin side up, on the rack. Insert a meat thermometer in the thickest part of the breast. Roast, uncovered, at 325° for 15 minutes.

Baste the turkey with the broth and continue roasting for 1¼ to 1¾ hours more or until the thermometer registers 170° to 175° and the turkey is no longer pink in the center. Remove the turkey from the oven and loosely cover with foil. Let stand for 10 minutes before slicing.

To serve, remove and discard the skin. Slice the turkey and arrange it on a platter. If desired, garnish with the parsley.

EXTRA HEALTH BENEFITS
Better Blood Pressure
Stronger Immunity

Times: Prep: 5 min.
Roasting: 1½ hr.
Standing: 10 min.

Makes 10 servings.

Per serving: 141 calories, 2.1 g. fat (14% of calories), 0 g. dietary fiber, 68 mg. cholesterol, 113 mg. sodium.

Pitas with Turkey-in-the-Slaw

EXTRA HEALTH BENEFIT
Stronger Immunity

Time: Prep: 15 min.

Makes 6 servings.

Per serving: 178 calories, 3.8 g. fat (20% of calories), 1.7 g. dietary fiber, 29 mg. cholesterol, 220 mg. sodium.

Here's a great make-ahead sandwich filling—the cabbage stays crunchy hours after the filling has been made.

> 6 ounces cooked turkey breast, cubed
> 1½ cups shredded cabbage
> 2 medium carrots, coarsely shredded
> ¾ cup (3 ounces) shredded part-skim mozzarella cheese
> 6 ounces low-fat or nonfat peach yogurt
> ½ teaspoon ground black pepper
> 3 6" pita breads, cut in half

In a medium bowl, combine the turkey, cabbage, carrots and cheese. Stir together the yogurt and pepper, then add to the turkey mixture. Stir until combined.

To serve, spoon about ½ cup of the turkey mixture into each pita pocket.

Chef's Note: If you're taking this sandwich to work with you, pack the filling separately from the bread and assemble the sandwich just before eating. That way the bread won't get soggy.

Turkey, Macaroni and Fruit Salad

EXTRA HEALTH BENEFITS
Better Blood Pressure
Cancer Protection
Blood Building
Stronger Immunity

Times: Prep: 15 min.
Cooking: 10 min.

Makes 4 servings.

Per serving: 396 calories, 2.6 g. fat (6% of calories), 2.9 g. dietary fiber, 31 mg. cholesterol, 66 mg. sodium.

Savor the tanginess from the yogurt and the sweetness from the fruit in this salad. If you feel daring, mix and match your own favorite combinations of yogurt and fruit.

> 2 cups elbow macaroni
> 2 large navel oranges
> 2 tablespoons orange juice (if necessary)
> 2 kiwifruits, peeled and sliced
> 6 ounces cooked turkey breast, cut into ½" cubes
> 1 medium red apple, cored and chopped
> 1 container (8 ounces) low-fat or nonfat strawberry yogurt
> ¼ teaspoon ground ginger

Cook the macaroni according to the package directions, but without adding the salt. Drain, then rinse with cold water and drain again. Transfer to a large bowl.

Meanwhile, peel the oranges. Section them over a small bowl to catch the juices. If necessary, add enough of the additional orange juice to make a total of 2 tablespoons. Cut the kiwi slices in half.

Add the oranges, orange juice, kiwi, turkey and apples to the macaroni. In a small bowl, stir together the yogurt and ginger. Add to the macaroni mixture and gently toss until coated.

Potatoes Stuffed with Turkey Ham

This entrée is cooked in the microwave, so you can whip it up in no time flat. For variety, use smoked turkey breast.

- **2 large baking potatoes**
- **½ cup nonfat plain yogurt**
- **1 cup chopped cooked turkey ham**
- **½ cup finely chopped onions**
- **½ cup finely chopped green peppers**
- **¼ teaspoon ground black pepper**

Wash and scrub the potatoes, then pat dry. Use a fork to prick the potatoes. Place on a microwave-proof plate and cover with plastic wrap. Vent the wrap by pulling back a small corner. Cook in a microwave oven on high power (100%) for 5 minutes. Rotate the plate a half-turn, then cook on high for 5 to 7 minutes more or until the potatoes are tender. Let stand, covered, for 5 minutes.

Cut each potato lengthwise in half. Scoop out the pulp, leaving ¼"-thick shells. Set the shells aside. In a medium bowl, mash the potato pulp with a potato masher. Stir in the yogurt until well combined. Then stir in the turkey ham, onions, green peppers and black pepper.

Pile the mixture into each potato shell. Transfer the shells to the plate and cover with plastic wrap. Vent the wrap. Cook on high for 3 to 4 minutes or until heated through.

Chef's Note: If you can spare the time and prefer your potatoes cooked in a conventional oven, bake them at 400° for 40 to 60 minutes or until tender.

Quick

EXTRA HEALTH BENEFITS
Lower Cholesterol
Cancer Protection
Stronger Immunity

Times: Prep: 10 min.
Microwaving: 13 min.

Makes 4 servings.

Per serving: 118 calories, 1.7 g. fat (12% of calories), 1.9 g. dietary fiber, 16 mg. cholesterol, 311 mg. sodium.

Times: Prep: 15 min.
Cooking: 10 min.

Makes 4 servings.

Per serving: 183 calories,
4.2 g. fat (21% of calories),
0.8 g. dietary fiber, 23 mg.
cholesterol, 364 mg. sodium.

Orzo and Smoked Turkey Salad

*Orzo is a tiny rice-shaped pasta with all of the nutrient bene-
fits of other pastas: It's low in fat and sodium, has no cholesterol and is high in B vitamins. If orzo is unavailable, use
macaroni in this slimming pasta salad.*

> 1 **cup orzo**
> 6 **ounces smoked turkey breast, cut into ¼" cubes**
> ½ **cup thinly sliced green onions**
> ¼ **cup finely shredded red cabbage**
> ¼ **cup chopped and loosely packed fresh cilantro**
> 3 **tablespoons lemon juice**
> 2 **tablespoons nonfat mayonnaise**
> 2 **teaspoons olive oil**

Cook the orzo according to the package directions, but without adding the salt. Drain, then rinse with cold water and drain
again.

In a large bowl, combine the orzo, turkey, onions, cabbage
and cilantro.

In a small bowl, stir together the lemon juice, mayonnaise and
oil. Add to the orzo mixture and toss until well coated.

Orzo and Smoked Turkey Salad

Black Bean Chili with Turkey

This spicy Southwest-style chili uses ground turkey instead of beef. Serve it topped with nonfat plain yogurt and chopped green onions.

- 1 **pound ground turkey**
- 1 **cup coarsely chopped onions**
- 1 **sweet red pepper, coarsely chopped**
- 2 **jalapeño chili peppers, seeded and finely chopped (wear disposable gloves when handling)**
- 2 **cloves garlic, minced**
- 1 **can (28 ounces) salt-free tomatoes (with juices), coarsely chopped**
- 1 **can (16 ounces) black beans, rinsed and drained**
- 1 **tablespoon chili powder**
- 2 **teaspoons ground cumin**
- 1 **teaspoon ground coriander**
- ½ **teaspoon dried oregano**
- ½ **teaspoon dried marjoram**
- ¼ **teaspoon crushed red pepper**
- ¼ **teaspoon ground cinnamon**
- ½ **cup coarsely chopped and loosely packed fresh cilantro**

In a large saucepan, cook the turkey, onions, sweet peppers, jalapeño peppers and garlic over medium heat 8 minutes or until the turkey is no longer pink and the vegetables are tender.

Stir in the tomatoes (with juices), beans, chili powder, cumin, coriander, oregano, marjoram, crushed pepper and cinnamon. Bring to a gentle boil, then reduce the heat. Cover and simmer for 5 minutes. Then stir in the cilantro and serve.

Chef's Note: Like regular chili, this version freezes well, so you can pack up leftovers for a future meal. Or do something a little different: Use the chili as burrito filling. Just roll some up in flour tortillas and serve with salsa, nonfat sour cream and additional fresh cilantro.

EXTRA HEALTH BENEFITS
Better Blood Pressure
Blood Building
Stronger Immunity

Times: Prep: 18 min.
Cooking: 13 min.

Makes 4 main-dish servings.

Per serving: 312 calories, 3.6 g. fat (10% of calories), 6.5 g. dietary fiber, 66 mg. cholesterol, 120 mg. sodium.

Turkish Eggplant with Turkey

Bulgur, a form of dried cracked wheat, is a nutritious staple in the Middle East. You'd be wise to incorporate it into your family's diet because it's high in dietary fiber. In this dish, bulgur's nutty flavor blends with dill and yogurt to produce an exotic delicacy.

EXTRA HEALTH BENEFITS
Better Blood Pressure
Cancer Protection
Stronger Immunity

Times: Prep: 7 min.
Cooking: 8 min.
Baking: 25 min.

Makes 6 servings.

Per serving: 255 calories, 2.2 g. fat (7% of calories), 6.4 g. dietary fiber, 45 mg. cholesterol, 112 mg. sodium.

 1 **cup bulgur**
 1 **cup boiling water**
 1 **large eggplant**
 1 **pound ground turkey**
 1 **cup chopped onions**
 1 **cup coarsely chopped fresh mushrooms**
 ½ **cup chopped sweet red peppers**
 2 **cloves garlic, minced**
 1 **tablespoon minced fresh dill**
 ½ **teaspoon ground black pepper**
 2 **cups nonfat plain yogurt**

Place the bulgur in a colander and rinse under cold running water. Drain and transfer it to a medium bowl. Pour the boiling water over the bulgur, then let stand at room temperature while preparing the filling.

For the filling, cut the eggplant lengthwise in half. Remove the pulp from both halves, leaving ½"-thick shells. Coarsely chop the pulp.

In a large no-stick skillet, cook the eggplant pulp, turkey, onions, mushrooms, red peppers and garlic over medium heat about 8 minutes or until the turkey is no longer pink and the vegetables are tender. Stir in the bulgur, dill and black pepper.

Spray a 13" × 9" baking dish with no-stick spray. Place the eggplant shells in the dish and spoon the turkey mixture into them. (Some of the filling will fall over the sides of the shells.) Cover the dish with foil and bake at 350° for 25 to 30 minutes or until the bulgur is tender and the filling is heated through. Serve with the yogurt.

Chef's Note: When buying eggplant, look for heavy, shiny ones that have almost-black skins and bright green stem caps. The skin should feel firm when you press it with your thumb. Store in the refrigerator in a covered container or wrapped in plastic to minimize moisture loss, and use as soon as possible.

Turkey Hash in a Flash

Here's a low-fat variation on old-fashioned corned beef hash.

- 8 ounces ground turkey
- 1 cup chopped onions
- 2 cups frozen hash brown potatoes with no fat, thawed
- ¼ cup grated Parmesan cheese
- 1 teaspoon onion powder
- 1 teaspoon garlic powder
- ½ teaspoon ground sage
- ½ teaspoon ground thyme
- ½ teaspoon ground black pepper

In a medium no-stick skillet, cook the turkey and onions over medium heat about 5 minutes or until the turkey is no longer pink and the onions are tender, stirring occasionally.

Add the potatoes. Cook and stir for 2 to 3 minutes or until the potatoes are tender. Stir in the cheese, onion powder, garlic powder, sage, thyme and pepper.

Chef's Note: If you can't find fat-free frozen hash browns at your supermarket, replace them with 2 cups of peeled and diced fresh potatoes.

Quick

EXTRA HEALTH BENEFIT
Stronger Immunity

Times: Prep: 6 min.
Cooking: 7 min.

Makes 4 servings.

Per serving: 174 calories, 3 g. fat (16% of calories), 2.2 g. dietary fiber, 38 mg. cholesterol, 157 mg. sodium.

How Lean Is That Ground Turkey?

Ground turkey can be a low-fat alternative to hamburger, but you have to be careful when you buy it to make sure you really are getting a lean product.

Your best choice is ground breast meat, which gets about 5 percent of its calories from fat. If dark meat is mixed in, the fat content will rise. And it will go even higher if skin has been incorporated into the mixture.

As always, read the label carefully to determine what's in the package. If there is no label, quiz the butcher. Or take matters into your own hands—buy a turkey breast and grind it yourself. Use a food grinder with a coarse blade. Or cut the meat into one-inch chunks and chop it in your food processor, but try not to puree it. However you grind the meat, be sure to first remove and discard the skin and any visible fat. Package the meat in small portions and freeze it until you're ready to use it.

Turkey Tetrazzini

EXTRA HEALTH BENEFITS
Blood Building
Stronger Immunity

Times: Prep: 10 min.
Cooking: 17 min.
Baking: 10 min.

Makes 4 servings.

Per serving: 339 calories,
6.4 g. fat (17% of calories),
1.3 g. dietary fiber, 72 mg.
cholesterol, 228 mg. sodium.

Traditional tetrazzini recipes feature a rich Parmesan and cream sauce. Here we've cut the fat by using skim milk and a modest amount of Parmesan. We've also simplified the procedure by using ground turkey instead of precooked meat.

> 4 ounces spaghetti
> 1 pound ground turkey
> 1 cup chopped fresh mushrooms
> 1¼ cups skim milk
> 2 tablespoons cornstarch
> 1 teaspoon garlic powder
> 1 teaspoon ground black pepper
> ½ cup chopped sweet red peppers
> ¼ cup grated Parmesan cheese
> 2 tablespoons sliced almonds

Cook the spaghetti according to the package directions, but without adding the salt. Drain well.

In a large no-stick skillet, cook the turkey and mushrooms over medium heat about 5 minutes or until the turkey is no longer pink and the mushrooms are tender, stirring occasionally.

In a small bowl, stir together the milk, cornstarch, garlic powder and black pepper. Stir into the turkey mixture. Cook and stir until the mixture slightly thickens and begins to gently boil. Cook and stir for 2 minutes more. Remove the skillet from the heat. Stir in the spaghetti and red peppers.

Spray a 9" × 9" baking dish with no-stick spray. Transfer the spaghetti mixture to the dish. Sprinkle the cheese and almonds on top. Bake at 350° about 10 minutes or until the mixture bubbles and the top is lightly brown.

Chef's Note: This makes a nice buffet dish. To double the recipe, increase the ingredients accordingly and use a 12" × 7½" baking dish.

Red Peppers Stuffed with Turkey

Stuffed peppers are a family favorite. This recipe uses ground turkey and rice to make a low-fat filling for them. Some varieties of green bell peppers turn bright red when fully ripe and make an especially nice presentation. Besides giving the peppers a more mellow flavor, the ripening process greatly increases their vitamin A content.

  8 **ounces ground turkey**
  4 **sweet red peppers**
½ **cup cooked rice**
½ **cup finely chopped onions**
½ **cup finely chopped carrots**
¼ **cup finely chopped celery**
1½ **teaspoons dried oregano**
  1 **teaspoon dried thyme**
  1 **teaspoon minced fresh parsley**

In a medium no-stick skillet, cook the turkey over medium heat about 5 minutes or until it is no longer pink, stirring occasionally. Drain the turkey in a strainer or colander, then transfer it to a large plate lined with 3 layers of paper towels. Blot the top with additional paper towels; set aside.

Slice off the stem ends of the peppers and remove the seeds and inner membranes.

In a medium bowl, stir together the turkey, rice, onions, carrots, celery, oregano, thyme and parsley. Spoon into the pepper shells.

Place the peppers in an 8" × 8" baking dish and add just enough water to cover the bottom of the baking dish. Cover with foil and bake at 350° for 40 minutes. Remove the foil and bake about 15 minutes more or until the tops are lightly brown. Serve immediately.

Extra Health Benefits
Cancer Protection
Stronger Immunity

Times: Prep: 7 min.
Cooking: 5 min.
Baking: 55 min.

Makes 4 servings.

Per serving: 137 calories, 1.4 g. fat (9% of calories), 2.6 g. dietary fiber, 34 mg. cholesterol, 59 mg. sodium.

Roulade of Turkey and Spinach

EXTRA HEALTH BENEFIT
Stronger Immunity

Times: Prep: 15 min.
Baking: 55 min.
Standing: 5 min.

Makes 8 servings.

Per serving: 131 calories, 2 g. fat (14% of calories), 1 g. dietary fiber, 35 mg. cholesterol, 202 mg. sodium.

This is meat loaf with a twist. It's turkey formed into a jelly roll with a spinach-cheese filling, making it special enough for entertaining.

MEAT ROLL

- ⅔ **cup fine dry plain bread crumbs**
- ⅓ **cup finely chopped onions**
- ¼ **cup fat-free egg substitute or 2 lightly beaten egg whites**
- ¼ **cup low-sodium tomato paste**
- ½ **teaspoon dried thyme**
- ¼ **teaspoon ground coriander**
- ¼ **teaspoon ground black pepper**
- 1 **pound ground turkey**

FILLING

- ½ **cup reduced-fat cottage cheese**
- 2 **tablespoons fat-free egg substitute or 1 lightly beaten egg white**
- 1 **tablespoon grated Romano cheese**
- 1 **tablespoon grated Parmesan cheese**
- 2 **tablespoons minced fresh parsley**
- 1 **cup chopped spinach**
   Bottled low-sodium spaghetti sauce, heated (optional)

For the meat roll: In a large bowl, stir together the bread crumbs, onions, ¼ cup egg substitute or 2 egg whites, tomato paste, thyme, coriander and pepper. Add the turkey and combine until well mixed; set aside.

For the filling: In a medium bowl, stir together the cottage cheese, 2 tablespoons egg substitute or 1 egg white, Romano and Parmesan cheeses and parsley. Add the spinach and combine until well mixed.

To assemble: On a piece of foil about 15" long, form the turkey mixture into a 10" × 8" rectangle. Spread the spinach mixture on top, keeping the spinach mixture within ½" of the edges. Beginning from a short side, gently lift the foil to roll up the turkey and spinach, jelly-roll style, into a tight roll.

Press the ends of the roll to seal. Carefully transfer the meat roll, seam side down, to a rack in a 13" × 9" baking pan. Cover with foil. Bake at 350° for 20 minutes, then remove the foil. Continue baking for 30 to 35 minutes more or until the turkey is no longer pink. Let stand for 5 minutes before slicing. If desired, serve with the heated spaghetti sauce.

Chef's Note: If you have any leftover turkey roll, freeze individual slices for later. Thaw the slices in the refrigerator and serve them cold or reheat them briefly in the microwave.

Turkey Sloppy Joes

Reduced-sodium tomato products help keep the sodium level to a minimum in this dish. Even if you're not on a salt-restricted diet, it's best to keep an eye on your sodium intake. Otherwise, your body will tend to retain water, which will show up as unwanted pounds on the scale.

  1 **pound ground turkey**
  1 **small onion, thinly sliced and separated into rings**
  ½ **cup chopped green peppers**
  ½ **cup reduced-calorie and -sodium ketchup**
  ¼ **cup salt-free tomato sauce**
1½ **teaspoons chili powder**
  ½ **teaspoon garlic powder**
  ¼ **teaspoon celery seeds**
  4 **whole-wheat hamburger buns, split and toasted**

In a large no-stick skillet, cook the turkey, onions and peppers over medium heat about 5 minutes or until the turkey is no longer pink and the vegetables are tender.

Stir in the ketchup, tomato sauce, chili powder, garlic powder and celery seeds. Bring to a boil, then reduce the heat to low. Cover and simmer for 15 minutes.

To serve, spoon about ½ cup of the mixture on the bottom half of each bun, then replace the tops.

Chef's Note: If you have any leftover meat mixture, cover and refrigerate it for up to 2 days. Before serving, bring the mixture to a boil.

Quick

EXTRA HEALTH BENEFITS
Blood Building
Stronger Immunity

Times: Prep: 5 min.
Cooking: 20 min.

Makes 4 servings.

Per serving: 286 calories, 4.3 g. fat (14% of calories), 2.9 g. dietary fiber, 66 mg. cholesterol, 555 mg. sodium.

EXTRA HEALTH BENEFITS
Blood Building
Stronger Immunity

Times: Prep: 10 min.
Cooking: 10 min.

Makes 4 servings.

Per serving: 254 calories,
4.1 g. fat (15% of calories),
2.7 g. dietary fiber, 66 mg.
cholesterol, 385 mg. sodium.

Mushroom-Turkey Burgers

Bite into a big, juicy burger—but make it a low-fat turkey burger rather than a fatty hamburger.

- **1 pound ground turkey**
- **2 cloves garlic, minced**
- **1 teaspoon paprika**
- **1 teaspoon ground black pepper**
- **2 teaspoons reduced-calorie margarine**
- **2½ cups sliced fresh mushrooms**
- **2 tablespoons nonfat mayonnaise**
- **4 whole-wheat hamburger buns, split and toasted**
- **4 lettuce leaves**

In a medium bowl, combine the turkey, garlic, paprika and pepper until well combined. Shape into 4 patties, each ¾" thick.

Spray an unheated, large no-stick skillet with no-stick spray. Heat the skillet over medium heat. Add the patties to the skillet and cook for 3 minutes. Turn the patties over and cook for 3 to 5 minutes more or until the patties are no longer pink. Transfer to a plate and cover to keep warm.

Add the margarine to the skillet and heat until melted. Then add the mushrooms; cook and stir over medium-high heat about 4 minutes or until the mushrooms are tender.

To serve, spread the mayonnaise on the buns. Place some lettuce and a turkey patty on the bottom half of each bun, then spoon on the mushrooms and replace the tops.

Salad of Duck Breast with Raspberry Dressing

Flavored vinegar is a wonderful way to season foods without adding fat and calories. In this salad, a splash of raspberry vinegar adds a sweet-sour note to the mayonnaise dressing. If you don't have raspberry vinegar, you can use ½ teaspoon of raspberry jelly mixed with 1 tablespoon of rice vinegar or red wine vinegar.

12 ounces cooked duck breast meat, skin removed
 1 can (8 ounces) whole water chestnuts, drained and quartered
 ¾ cup chopped watercress
 ¼ cup nonfat mayonnaise
 1 tablespoon raspberry vinegar
 1 head red leaf lettuce
 1 tablespoon chopped fresh parsley (optional)
 4 slices French bread

Cut the duck breast meat into 2" × ½" pieces. In a large bowl, gently combine the duck, water chestnuts and watercress.

In a small bowl, stir together the mayonnaise and vinegar. Pour over the duck mixture and gently toss until coated. Cover and chill in the refrigerator for at least 1 hour to blend the flavors.

To serve, line salad plates with the lettuce and gently mound some of the duck mixture in the middle of each. If desired, sprinkle with the parsley to garnish. Serve with the bread.

Chef's Note: If you don't have any cooked duck on hand, you can use cooked chicken or turkey breast instead.

EXTRA HEALTH BENEFITS
Blood Building
Stronger Immunity

Times: Prep: 9 min.
Chilling: at least 1 hr.

Makes 4 servings.

Per serving: 256 calories, 6.5 g. fat (23% of calories), 1.3 g. dietary fiber, 65 mg. cholesterol, 455 mg. sodium.

Bombay Grilled Duck

Duck breast is a nice change of pace from chicken and turkey. Here it gets Far East flavor from soy sauce, ginger and sesame oil.

EXTRA HEALTH BENEFITS
Blood Building
Stronger Immunity

Times: Prep: 10 min.
Marinating: 24 hr.
Grilling: 7 min.

Makes 4 servings.

Per serving: 309 calories, 8.2 g. fat (25% of calories), 1 g. dietary fiber, 87 mg. cholesterol, 238 mg. sodium.

1 tablespoon finely chopped ginger root
1 tablespoon reduced-sodium soy sauce
3 cloves garlic, minced
1 teaspoon Oriental sesame oil
½ teaspoon ground cinnamon
1 pound skinless, boneless duck breasts, fat removed
1 tablespoon chopped mango chutney
2 cups hot cooked rice

In a large self-closing plastic bag, combine the ginger, soy sauce, garlic, oil and cinnamon. Rinse the duck and pat dry with paper towels. Add to the bag. Seal the bag and marinate in the refrigerator for 24 hours, turning the bag occasionally.

To prepare the grill for cooking, spray the unheated grill rack with no-stick spray. Then light the grill according to the manufacturer's directions. Place the rack on the grill.

Remove the duck from the bag and discard the marinade. Place the duck on the rack over the coals. Cover and grill for 4 minutes. Turn the duck over and spoon the chutney over each breast. Cover and grill for 3 to 4 minutes more or until the juices run clear when the duck is pierced. Serve with the rice.

SLIMMING STRATEGY

You might think duck is off-limits in a prudent diet. But domestic duckling is an acceptable alternative to chicken and turkey. Through genetics and breeding, ducks are now meatier, tastier and leaner than they were in the past. But as with chicken and turkey, it's important to remove the fatty skin before eating.

Getting to the Meat of the Matter

Mustard-Yogurt Lamb
Kabobs on a Bed of
Couscous (page 153)

Gingered Beef Satays over Brown Rice

EXTRA HEALTH BENEFIT
Stronger Immunity

Times: Prep: 9 min.
Marinating: 2 hr.
Broiling: 9 min.

Makes 4 servings.

Per serving: 247 calories,
4.7 g. fat (18% of calories),
2.3 g. dietary fiber, 48 mg. cholesterol, 151 mg. sodium.

The spicy ginger-soy marinade used here gives bold flavor to lean round steak and helps tenderize it.

- 2 tablespoons water
- 2 tablespoons lemon juice
- 2 teaspoons reduced-sodium soy sauce
- 2 teaspoons grated ginger root or ½ teaspoon ground ginger
- 1 teaspoon caraway seeds
- ½ teaspoon ground coriander
- ½ teaspoon ground turmeric
- ½ teaspoon ground red pepper
- 1 clove garlic, minced
- 12 ounces boneless beef round steak, trimmed of all visible fat and cut into 1" cubes
- 1 medium onion, finely chopped
- 2 cups hot cooked brown rice

In a medium bowl, combine the water, lemon juice, soy sauce, ginger, caraway seeds, coriander, turmeric, pepper and garlic. Add the beef and onions, then stir until well combined. Cover and marinate in the refrigerator for 2 hours, stirring occasionally.

Drain the beef, reserving the marinade. Thread the beef onto small metal skewers or bamboo skewers that have been soaked in cold water for 20 minutes. Place the kabobs on the rack in a broiling pan. Broil 4" from the heat, turning the kabobs frequently, for 9 to 12 minutes or until cooked to desired doneness.

Meanwhile, in a small saucepan, bring the reserved marinade to a boil. Brush over the kabobs. Serve the kabobs on top of the rice.

Chef's Note: For a hearty appetizer, serve these kabobs on a lettuce-lined platter and use the cooked marinade as a dipping sauce.

Gingered Beef Satays over Brown Rice

Tournedos of Beef Athené

Tournedos are beef steaks cut from the lean tenderloin. Here we pair them with a chunky tomato-basil sauce that's a healthy alternative to the classic fatty mushroom sauce usually served with them.

- **1 cup coarsely chopped tomatoes**
- **¼ cup finely chopped red onions**
- **1 tablespoon minced fresh basil or 1 teaspoon dried basil**
- **1 teaspoon minced fresh thyme or ½ teaspoon dried thyme**
- **4 beef tenderloin steaks (about 3 ounces each), cut ¾" to 1" thick and trimmed of all visible fat**
- **¼ cup defatted low-sodium beef broth**
  Basil leaves (optional)
- **3 cups hot cooked couscous**

In a medium bowl, stir together the tomatoes, onions, basil and thyme; set aside.

Spray an unheated large skillet with no-stick spray. Heat the skillet over medium-high heat. Add the steaks and brown on both sides. Then pour in the broth and cook, uncovered, for 5 minutes. Turn the steaks over and cook about 5 minutes more or until cooked to desired doneness; drain the steaks.

To serve, arrange the steaks on a serving platter. Spoon the tomato mixture over the steaks. If desired, garnish the platter with the basil leaves. Serve with the couscous.

Quick

EXTRA HEALTH BENEFITS
Blood Building
Stronger Immunity

Times: Prep: 4 min.
Cooking: 10 min.

Makes 4 servings.

Per serving: 350 calories, 9.1 g. fat (24% of calories), 6.9 g. dietary fiber, 71 mg. cholesterol, 160 mg. sodium.

SLIMMING STRATEGY

Shake the salt habit by relying more on herbs to perk up the flavor of meat. Herbs that especially complement beef include basil, bay leaf, chili powder, cumin, garlic, ginger, marjoram, oregano, parsley, rosemary, sage, savory, tarragon and thyme.

Tournedos of Beef Athené

Rib Steaks with Papaya Salsa

Times: Prep: 15 min.
Broiling: 14 min.

Makes 4 servings.

Per serving: 358 calories,
11.2 g. fat (28% of calories),
3.1 g. dietary fiber, 68 mg.
cholesterol, 177 mg. sodium.

*The papaya-and-tomato salsa used here makes a refreshing
low-fat topping for pork, poultry and fish as well as beef.*

- 1 small papaya, peeled, seeded and coarsely chopped
- ½ cup chopped green onions
- ½ cup chopped green peppers
- ½ cup chopped tomatoes
- ½ cup chopped and loosely packed fresh basil
- 2 tablespoons balsamic vinegar
- ¼ teaspoon chili powder
- 3 drops hot-pepper sauce
- ¼ cup vegetable juice cocktail
- 2 tablespoons lime juice
- 2 tablespoons minced fresh parsley
- 2 garlic cloves, minced
- 4 beef rib-eye steaks (about 4 ounces each), cut about ¾" thick and trimmed of all visible fat
- 2 cups hot cooked brown rice

For the salsa, in a small bowl, stir together the papaya, onions, green peppers, tomatoes, basil, vinegar, chili powder and pepper sauce; set aside.

Spray the rack of a broiling pan with no-stick spray. In another small bowl, stir together the vegetable juice, lime juice, parsley and garlic. Brush both sides of the steaks with the juice mixture, then place the steaks on the rack.

Broil 3" from the heat for 7 minutes. Turn the steaks over and broil for 7 to 8 minutes more for medium doneness or until cooked to desired doneness.

To serve, spoon some of the salsa on top of each steak. Serve with the rice.

SLIMMING STRATEGY

Beware of "all or nothing" thinking. Some people assume that if they aren't doing everything in their weight-loss plan with total perfection, they might as well give up. But keep in mind that nobody's perfect. Even if you blow your diet one-fifth of the time, you're still 80 percent on target. And that's not bad.

Getting to the Meat of the Matter

Warm Salad of Steak Strips and Spinach

EXTRA HEALTH BENEFITS
Blood Building
Stronger Immunity

Times: Prep: 15 min.
Broiling: 12 min.

Makes 4 servings.

Per serving: 145 calories,
3.9 g. fat (23% of calories),
1.7 g. dietary fiber, 48 mg.
cholesterol, 376 mg. sodium.

A tangy ginger dressing adds delightful flavor to this warm main-dish salad without contributing any fat.

> 1 **beef top round steak (12 ounces), cut ¾" thick and trimmed of all visible fat**
> 2 **cups spinach cut in ½"-wide shreds**
> 1½ **cups bite-size broccoli florets**
> ¼ **cup rice vinegar**
> 2 **tablespoons defatted low-sodium beef broth or water**
> 2 **tablespoons reduced-sodium soy sauce**
> 1 **teaspoon honey**
> ½ **teaspoon grated ginger root**
> 1 **clove garlic, minced**

Place the steak on the rack in a broiling pan. Broil 3" from the heat for 6 minutes. Turn the steak over and broil for 6 to 8 minutes more or until cooked to desired doneness; cool. Slice across the grain on the diagonal into ⅛"-thick strips. Then cut each strip lengthwise in half and transfer the strips to a large bowl; set aside.

Place the spinach in a colander and set aside. Fill a large saucepan with water and bring to a boil. Add the broccoli and blanch for 30 seconds. Immediately pour the hot water and broccoli over the spinach in the colander. (The hot water will blanch, but not cook, the spinach.) Drain the spinach and broccoli well and add them to the steak.

In a small bowl, stir together the vinegar, broth or water, soy sauce, honey, ginger and garlic. Pour over the steak and vegetables. Toss until coated. Arrange on a platter and serve.

Warm Salad of Steak Strips and Spinach

Braised Beef Round

Long, slow braising keeps beef moist and makes it tender.
You could also use a boneless round rump roast for this dish.

1 tablespoon minced fresh parsley
½ teaspoon dried oregano
1 small clove garlic, minced
¼ teaspoon dried basil
  Pinch of ground thyme
1 beef bottom round roast (2 pounds), trimmed of all
  visible fat
½ cup finely chopped onions
¼ cup finely chopped carrots
¼ cup finely chopped celery
1 cup defatted low-sodium beef broth
½ cup coarsely chopped tomatoes
1 bay leaf
  Ground black pepper (to taste)
2 pounds hot cooked new potatoes

In a small bowl, stir together the parsley, oregano, garlic, basil and thyme; set aside. Using the tip of a small, sharp knife, make ½"-deep incisions about 2" apart in the beef. Fill each incision with some of the parsley mixture.

Place the beef on the rack in a broiling pan. Broil 4" from the heat about 4 minutes on each side or until the surface is browned. Drain the beef, then pat dry with paper towels.

Meanwhile, in a large skillet, combine the onions, carrots, celery and 1 tablespoon of the broth. Cover and cook over medium-low heat about 5 minutes or until the vegetables are tender, stirring occasionally. Transfer the vegetables to a 4-quart Dutch oven. Then place the beef on top of the vegetables.

In a small saucepan, combine the remaining broth, the tomatoes and bay leaf. Bring to a boil, then reduce the heat. Simmer, uncovered, for 5 minutes. Pour over the beef. Cover tightly. Bake at 325° about 2 hours or until the beef is tender.

To serve, remove and discard the bay leaf. Skim and discard the fat from the top of the vegetable mixture. Thinly slice the beef. Season to taste with the pepper. Transfer the beef to a platter with the potatoes and spoon the vegetable mixture over the beef.

EXTRA HEALTH BENEFITS
Better Blood Pressure
Blood Building
Stronger Immunity

Times: Prep: 20 min.
Baking: 2 hr.

Makes 8 servings.

Per serving: 330 calories, 9 g. fat (25% of calories), 2.7 g. dietary fiber, 109 mg. cholesterol, 74 mg. sodium.

SLIMMING STRATEGY

A fat-free way to brown beef before braising or stewing is to broil it. Simply place the meat on the rack in a broiling pan. Place 4" from the heat and cook for about 4 minutes per side, until the surface is browned. Pat dry with paper towels to remove any fat from the surface.

London Broil with Roasted Green and Yellow Squash

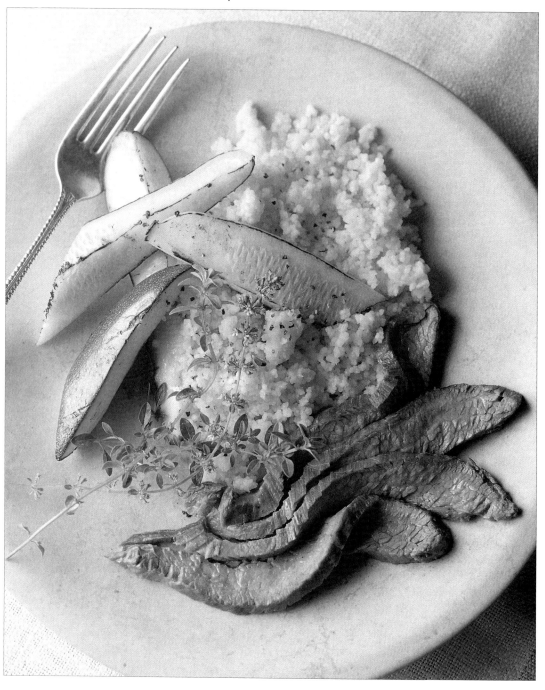

Getting to the Meat of the Matter

London Broil with Roasted Green and Yellow Squash

Flank steak, typically used to make London broil, is a little higher in fat than other lean cuts of beef. To keep the overall fat content of the meal down, this recipe calls for low-fat squash and couscous to accompany the steak.

　1　**beef flank steak (1 pound), trimmed of all visible fat**
　¾　**cup red wine vinegar**
　2　**tablespoons reduced-sodium soy sauce**
　1　**tablespoon honey**
　1　**teaspoon grated ginger root**
　1　**clove garlic, minced**
　1　**bay leaf**
　1　**pound small zucchini**
　4　**small yellow summer squash**
2½　**cups hot cooked couscous**

Use a meat fork to pierce both sides of the steak. Place the steak in a 13" × 9" baking dish. In a small bowl, stir together the vinegar, soy sauce, honey, ginger, garlic and bay leaf. Pour over the steak. Cover and marinate in the refrigerator for at least 6 hours, turning the steak once or twice.

Drain the steak, reserving the marinade. In a small saucepan, bring the reserved marinade to a boil. Meanwhile, cut the zucchini and yellow squash lengthwise in halves or quarters.

Place the vegetables on the rack in a broiling pan, leaving room for the steak. Broil the vegetables 6" from the heat for 10 minutes, turning them and rearranging them as needed to cook evenly.

Place the steak on the rack with the vegetables and broil for 6 minutes. Turn the steak over and broil about 8 minutes more or until the vegetables are tender and the steak is cooked to desired doneness. (The vegetables will take about 20 minutes total and the steak about 14 minutes total.)

To serve, thinly slice the steak across the grain on the diagonal. Arrange the slices on a large serving platter with the vegetables. Serve with the couscous.

EXTRA HEALTH BENEFITS
Blood Building
Stronger Immunity

Times: Prep: 3 min.
Marinating: at least 6 hr.
Broiling: 24 min.

Makes 4 servings.

Per serving: 414 calories, 11 g. fat (24% of calories), 8.7 g. dietary fiber, 57 mg. cholesterol, 386 mg. sodium.

Old-Fashioned Pot Roast

EXTRA HEALTH BENEFITS
Better Blood Pressure
Blood Building
Stronger Immunity

Times: Prep: 20 min.
Cooking: 2¾ hr.

Makes 4 servings.

Per serving: 374 calories,
9.3 g. fat (22% of calories),
6.6 g. dietary fiber, 109 mg.
cholesterol, 139 mg. sodium.

Of course you can still have pot roast! Simply switch to a lean cut of beef like top or bottom round. And use cooking techniques that don't add extra fat, such as browning the meat under the broiler and boiling down the pan juices to thicken them.

  1 **beef top or bottom round roast (1 pound), trimmed of all visible fat**
  ¾ **cup water**
  1 **can (14½ ounces) tomatoes (with juices), finely chopped**
  ¼ **teaspoon dried thyme**
  4 **black peppercorns**
  1 **small bay leaf**
  1 **pound baby carrots**
12 **ounces new potatoes, halved or quartered**
  2 **stalks celery, cut into 1" pieces**
  ½ **medium onion, sliced**
  1 **tablespoon minced fresh parsley**

Place the beef on the rack in a broiling pan. Broil 4" from the heat about 4 minutes on each side or until the surface is browned. Drain the beef, then pat with paper towels.

Spray a large deep skillet with no-stick spray. Place the beef, water, tomatoes (with juices), thyme, peppercorns and bay leaf in the skillet. Bring to a boil, then reduce the heat. Cover and simmer for 2 hours. Add the carrots, potatoes, celery and onions. Cover and simmer over low heat for 45 to 60 minutes more or until the beef and vegetables are tender, adding more water if necessary when the cooking liquid evaporates.

To serve, transfer the beef and vegetables to a serving platter. Cover with foil to keep warm. Skim the fat from the cooking juices. Stir in the parsley. Bring the juices to a boil. Boil, uncovered, about 2 minutes or until slightly thickened. Remove and discard the bay leaf. Drizzle the juices over the beef and serve.

Chef's Note: Roasts usually are not sold in 1-pound pieces, so ask the butcher to cut off the amount you need for this recipe and freeze the remaining piece to use at another time.

Veggie-Beef Burgers

Chock-full of vegetables and topped with a no-fat horseradish sauce, these burgers are a tasty and healthy change from ordinary patties.

EXTRA HEALTH BENEFITS
Cancer Protection
Stronger Immunity

Times: Prep: 11 min.
Cooking: 4 min.
Broiling: 8 min.

Makes 4 servings.

Per serving: 156 calories, 4.6 g. fat (27% of calories), 1 g. dietary fiber, 52 mg. cholesterol, 142 mg. sodium.

SAUCE

- ½ **cup nonfat plain yogurt**
- 1 **tablespoon minced fresh dill**
- 2 **teaspoons prepared horseradish**
- 1 **teaspoon sweet pickle relish**

BURGERS

- 2 **tablespoons defatted low-sodium chicken broth**
- ½ **cup grated onions**
- ½ **cup shredded zucchini**
- ½ **cup shredded carrots**
- 12 **ounces ground sirloin beef**
- 2 **teaspoons steak sauce**

Ground Rules

Ground meat is a godsend for preparing fast meals because it cooks so quickly. You can't always be sure, however, how much fat it contains. Many markets do label their beef, and in that case, choose ground beef that is at least 90 percent fat free. When it comes to pork and lamb, you probably won't have a choice. In those cases—or when you end up with fattier beef—here are some easy ways to reduce the meat's fat content.

• When browning the meat or cooking burgers, never add oil to the skillet. Instead, use a no-stick skillet sprayed with no-stick spray.

• You can also brown meatballs or burgers in the oven or under the broiler. To blot up any rendered fat after cooking, transfer the cooked meat to a large plate lined with paper towels and pat off the excess.

• After browning crumbled ground meat, drain the meat in a colander. Then transfer it to a large plate lined with three layers of paper towels. Blot the top of the meat with additional paper towels. If the meat still looks shiny, transfer it to clean paper towels. Note that you can use this technique even when the meat is browned with onions, garlic or other vegetables.

• To reduce the fat content of cooked crumbled meat even more, return the meat to the colander and pour hot (not boiling) water over it. Let the meat drain for 5 minutes before continuing with your recipe. You'll lose a little flavor, but if you're using the meat in spaghetti sauce, a casserole or any other dish that has lots of other ingredients, it won't make a big difference.

For the sauce: In a small bowl, stir together the yogurt, dill, horseradish and relish; set aside.

For the burgers: In a small no-stick skillet, bring the broth to a boil. Reduce the heat to medium and add the onions, zucchini and carrots. Cook and stir for 4 to 5 minutes or until the vegetables are tender and the liquid has evaporated.

Transfer the vegetable mixture to a medium bowl. Add the beef and steak sauce. Mix until well combined. Shape into 4 patties, each ¾" thick.

Spray the rack of a broiling pan with no-stick spray. Place the burgers on the rack. Broil 3" from the heat for 5 minutes. Turn the burgers over and broil about 3 minutes more for medium-rare doneness or until cooked to desired doneness.

To serve, top each burger with the sauce.

Chef's Note: Serve these burgers with noodles or baked potatoes. Or make them into sandwiches by placing the patties in reduced-calorie buns. Add chopped tomatoes and cucumbers, if desired, then top with the horseradish sauce.

Veggie-Beef Burgers

Times: Prep: 10 min.
Cooking: 9 min.

Makes 4 servings.

Per serving: 303 calories, 8.7 g. fat (24% of calories), 4.6 g. dietary fiber, 52 mg. cholesterol, 395 mg. sodium.

SLIMMING STRATEGY

For an easy, low-fat Mexican topping, stir a small amount of chili powder or cumin, or chopped cucumbers, green onions or your favorite fresh vegetable, into nonfat sour cream or plain yogurt. Or top your entrée with salsa; 2 tablespoons of a low-fat brand contains only about 8 calories and no fat.

Loose Beef Fajitas

For fast fajitas, this version uses ground sirloin instead of the usual beef flank strips. Sirloin has only 33 percent of calories from fat, whereas flank steak has 44 percent.

- 12 ounces ground sirloin beef
- 1 cup chopped onions
- ½ cup chopped green peppers
- ½ cup chopped sweet red peppers
- 2 cloves garlic, minced
- 2 teaspoons chili powder
- ½ teaspoon ground cumin
- 1 cup chunky salsa
- ½ cup chopped tomatoes
- 8 warm corn or flour tortillas

In a large no-stick skillet, cook the beef, onions, green and red peppers and garlic over medium heat about 5 minutes or until the beef is browned and the vegetables are tender, stirring frequently.

Stir in the chili powder and cumin and cook for 1 minute. Add the salsa and tomatoes. Bring to a gentle boil, then reduce the heat. Simmer, uncovered, for 4 to 5 minutes or until the liquid reduces slightly, stirring occasionally.

To serve, spoon some of the beef mixture just below the center on each of the tortillas. Fold the bottom edge of each tortilla over the filling, then fold in the sides and roll up to enclose the filling.

Pork Medallions in Spiced Tomato Sauce over Noodles

The tenderloin is the leanest cut of pork. Here it's simmered with a full-flavored sauce and served over noodles to make an entire dinner for less than 350 calories.

- 1 pork tenderloin (12 ounces), cut into ¼"–½"-thick slices
- ½ teaspoon dried oregano
- ¼ teaspoon ground black pepper
- 1 teaspoon olive oil
- ½ cup chopped red onions
- 1 teaspoon ground cinnamon
- ¼ teaspoon ground nutmeg
- 2 cups seeded and chopped tomatoes
- ¼ cup defatted low-sodium chicken broth
- 1 tablespoon grated lemon peel
- 2 cloves garlic, minced
- 4 cups hot cooked wide noodles
- 2 tablespoons chopped fresh Italian parsley

Sprinkle both sides of the pork slices with the oregano and pepper. Add the oil to a large no-stick skillet and heat over medium heat. Then add the pork to the skillet and cook for 2 minutes. Turn the slices over and cook for 2 to 4 minutes more or until the pork is no longer pink. Transfer to a plate and cover to keep warm.

Add the onions, cinnamon and nutmeg to the skillet. Cook and stir for 2 minutes. Then add the tomatoes, broth, lemon peel and garlic. Cook and stir for 4 to 5 minutes or until the liquid has evaporated.

To serve, place the noodles on a large platter. Sprinkle with the parsley and arrange the pork on top. Then spoon the tomato mixture on top of the pork.

EXTRA HEALTH BENEFITS
Better Blood Pressure
Blood Building
Stronger Immunity

Times: Prep: 10 min.
Cooking: 10 min.

Makes 4 servings.

Per serving: 332 calories, 4.6 g. fat (13% of calories), 3.5 g. dietary fiber, 55 mg. cholesterol, 55 mg. sodium.

SLIMMING STRATEGY

Pork tenderloin gets only 26 percent of its calories from fat, so it is almost as lean as chicken breast without skin (19 percent). Center loin, pork leg and lean ham also are good pork choices.

Times: Prep: 5 min.
Cooking: 6 min.

Makes 4 servings.

Per serving: 296 calories,
6 g. fat (18% of calories),
1.8 g. dietary fiber, 62 mg.
cholesterol, 72 mg. sodium.

Cranberry-Glazed Pork Chops

*For some reason, fruit always complements the flavor of
pork. This dish features dried cranberries, which are a
refreshing change from the apples, pineapple or raisins that
often accompany pork chops.*

4 **pork loin chops (about 4 ounces each), cut about
¹/₂" thick and trimmed of all visible fat**
¹/₄ **teaspoon ground black pepper**
2 **teaspoons cornstarch**
³/₄ **cup apple-cranberry juice**
¹/₂ **cup dried cranberries**
1 **tablespoon minced fresh tarragon**
1 **tablespoon minced fresh parsley**
1 **teaspoon honey**
2 **cups hot cooked brown rice**

Sprinkle both sides of the chops with the pepper; set aside.

Spray an unheated, large no-stick skillet with no-stick spray.
Heat the skillet over medium heat. Add the chops and cook for
3 minutes. Turn the chops over and cook for 2 to 3 minutes
more or until no longer pink. Transfer to a plate and set aside.

In a small bowl, stir the cornstarch into the apple-cranberry
juice until dissolved. Then add the juice mixture to the skillet,
stirring and scraping to loosen any brown bits from the bottom.
Stir in the cranberries, tarragon, parsley and honey. Cook and
stir until slightly thickened.

Add the chops to the skillet. Spoon the sauce over the chops;
cook for 1 to 2 minutes more or until heated through. Serve with
the rice.

Sweet-and-Sour Pork Stir-Fry

Extra Health Benefit
Stronger Immunity

Times: Prep: 19 min.
Marinating: 4 hr.
Cooking: 6 min.

Makes 4 servings.

Per serving: 364 calories,
7.4 g. fat (18% of calories),
3.2 g. dietary fiber, 47 mg.
cholesterol, 343 mg. sodium.

This dish uses a no-fat method for stir-frying. The meat and vegetables cook in a few tablespoons of marinade rather than oil. If you use this technique with other stir-fry recipes, use water or broth for the cooking liquid.

½	**cup pineapple juice**
3	**tablespoons cider vinegar**
2	**tablespoons finely chopped onions**
2	**tablespoons reduced-sodium soy sauce**
1	**teaspoon grated ginger root**
1	**clove garlic, minced**
12	**ounces boneless pork loin chops, trimmed of all visible fat**
1	**ripe pineapple**
1	**teaspoon cornstarch**
1	**green pepper, cut into thin strips**
1	**sweet red pepper, cut into thin strips**
2	**cups hot cooked rice**

In a medium bowl, stir together the pineapple juice, vinegar, onions, soy sauce, ginger and garlic.

Thinly slice the pork against the grain into bite-size pieces. Stir into the juice mixture. Cover and marinate in the refrigerator for 4 to 6 hours.

Meanwhile, cut the pineapple lengthwise in half, leaving the crown intact. Use a sharp knife to loosen the flesh from the peel of one pineapple half. (Wrap the remaining pineapple half with plastic wrap and refrigerate it for another use.) Then use a spoon to scoop out the flesh. Cut the flesh into ½" bite-size pieces. Set the pineapple pieces and shell aside.

Drain the pork, reserving ½ cup of the marinade. Discard the remaining marinade.

Spray an unheated wok or large skillet with no-stick spray. Heat the wok or skillet over medium-high heat. Add 3 table-spoons of the reserved marinade. Add the pork and cook and stir about 2 minutes or until the pork is no longer pink. Using a slotted spoon, transfer the pork to a plate. Stir together the remaining reserved marinade and the cornstarch. Then stir into the juices in the wok or skillet. Cook and stir just until thickened. Immediately add the green and red peppers. Cook and stir about 2 minutes more or until the peppers are crisp-tender.

Then stir in the pineapple and pork. Heat through.

To serve, spoon the pork mixture into the pineapple shell. Serve immediately with the rice.

Chef's Note: To achieve paper-thin slices when cutting pork, partially freeze it first. Twenty minutes should do it.

Ham and Oriental Vegetable Stir-Fry

The beauty of a stir-fry is that it usually contains lots of vegetables, and this recipe is no exception. You might be surprised to see ham in a weight-loss book, but it's fairly lean as long as excess fat is trimmed away. (Ham is high in sodium, however, so take that into consideration if you're watching your intake.)

  2 **tablespoons cornstarch**
⅓ **cup water**
  1 **tablespoon reduced-sodium soy sauce**
  1 **teaspoon hoisin sauce**
  2 **cloves garlic, minced**
½ **teaspoon ground ginger**
¼ **teaspoon crushed red pepper**
  1 **tablespoon Oriental sesame oil**
  1 **cup sliced carrots**
  1 **cup green pepper strips**
  1 **cup coarsely chopped green onions**
  2 **cups shredded Chinese cabbage**
10 **ounces low-sodium fully cooked, lean ham, cubed**
  3 **cups hot cooked cellophane or lo mein noodles**

In a small bowl, stir the cornstarch into the water. Then stir in the soy sauce, hoisin sauce, garlic, ginger and red pepper.

Add the oil to a wok or large skillet and heat over medium-high heat. Add the carrots, green pepper strips and onions. Stir-fry for 3 minutes. Then add the cabbage, ham and cornstarch mixture. Stir-fry for 4 to 5 minutes or until the vegetables are crisp-tender and the liquid slightly thickens. Serve over the noodles.

Chef's Note: The beauty of this recipe is that it's a great way to use up whatever vegetables you might have lying around. Pea pods, cauliflower, broccoli, asparagus, mushrooms and summer squash work as well as the vegetables specified.

EXTRA HEALTH BENEFIT
Stronger Immunity

Times: Prep: 20 min. Cooking: 7 min.

Makes 4 servings.

Per serving: 326 calories, 6.2 g. fat (17% of calories), 1.1 g. dietary fiber, 37 mg. cholesterol, 763 mg. sodium.

SLIMMING STRATEGY

Maybe it's not nice to fool Mother Nature, but it's okay to fool yourself. Thinly slicing meat across the grain and cutting vegetables on the bias make small portions look like a lot because the food takes up more room on your plate. You'll think you've eaten more than you really have.

Lamb Chops in Parchment

Lamb Chops in Parchment

Here's a wonderfully easy dish that'll dazzle your guests. The sophisticated flavors and artful presentation will impress all. Serve the chops with steamed baby carrots and a salad of romaine lettuce tossed with oil-free vinaigrette.

4 **lamb loin chops (about 4 ounces each), cut ¾" thick and trimmed of all visible fat**
½ **cup nonalcoholic red wine**
2 **tablespoons finely chopped green onions**
2 **tablespoons minced fresh parsley**
2 **cloves garlic, minced**
10 **ounces red potatoes, sliced ½" thick**
8 **ounces mushrooms, thinly sliced**
2 **tablespoons minced fresh dill**

Place the chops in a large self-closing plastic bag. In a small bowl, stir together the wine, onions, parsley and garlic. Pour over the chops. Seal the bag and marinate in the refrigerator for 30 minutes, turning the bag occasionally.

Cut parchment paper into 4 squares, 12" each. Fold each square in half, then trim into large hearts. Open the paper hearts.

Remove the chops from the bag, reserving the marinade. Place a chop on half of each paper heart. Top with the potatoes, mushrooms and dill. Then sprinkle 1½ teaspoons of the marinade on top of each vegetable mound.

For each packet, fold the paper over the chop and vegetables and align the edges. Make a small fold at the top edge, crease and repeat to make a double seal. Work your way around the edge, making a double seal. When you reach the pointed end, twist the parchment to hold the folds in place. Make sure the edges are tightly sealed.

Place the packets on a large cookie sheet. Bake at 350° about 20 minutes or until the paper is browned and puffed. Carefully cut a large X in the top of each packet and fold back the points. Check to see if the lamb has cooked to medium-rare doneness and the vegetables are tender. If not, close the packets and bake about 5 minutes more.

To serve, transfer the packets to dinner plates.

Chef's Note: If parchment paper is unavailable, you can use foil. Because the foil doesn't make as nice a presentation, transfer the chops and vegetables to dinner plates before serving.

EXTRA HEALTH BENEFITS
Better Blood Pressure
Blood Building
Stronger Immunity

Times: Prep: 35 min.
Marinating: 30 min.
Baking: 20 min.

Makes 4 servings.

Per serving: 138 calories, 3.3 g. fat (20% of calories), 1.2 g. dietary fiber, 33 mg. cholesterol, 44 mg. sodium.

SLIMMING STRATEGY

Here's how to kill two birds with one stone. Instead of having dessert, sit down after dinner and plan your meals for the following day. You'll be feeling full, so you won't be tempted to go overboard in your planning. And your mind will be occupied, so you won't have time to notice that you're skipping dessert.

Dolmades

Times: Prep: 10 min.
Cooking: 20 min.

Makes 4 servings.

Per serving: 298 calories,
8.2 g. fat (25% of calories),
1.9 g. dietary fiber, 35 mg.
cholesterol, 230 mg. sodium.

*Dolmades (pronounced dohl-MAH-theez) are stuffed grape
leaves, vegetables or fruit. Here we use grape leaves and fill
them with a savory lamb-and-rice mixture. We've cut fat
from this traditional Greek dish by using lean beef and just
enough lamb to give the little packets their customary flavor.*

24 **bottled grape leaves, rinsed and dried**
 1 **cup coarsely chopped uncooked long-grain rice**
 2 **ounces ground beef (80% lean)**
 2 **ounces ground lamb**
 2 **ounces feta cheese, crumbled**
 2 **tablespoons minced fresh mint**
 2 **teaspoons grated lemon peel**
 ¼ **teaspoon garlic powder**
 2 **cups low-sodium tomato juice**
 ¼ **teaspoon hot-pepper sauce**

Place the grape leaves, with the vein sides up, on a work surface. Using a knife or kitchen scissors, remove the stems from
the leaves. Discard the stems and set the leaves aside.

In a medium bowl, combine the rice, beef, lamb, cheese, mint,
lemon peel and garlic powder until well mixed.

Place 2 teaspoons of the mixture on each leaf, about 1" from
the stem end. Fold the stem end of the leaf over the filling. Then
fold in the sides and roll
up to enclose the filling.

Place the bundles, seam
side down, in a large skillet. Pour in the tomato
juice and add the pepper
sauce. Bring to a boil, then
reduce the heat. Partially

Dolmades

simmer for 20 to 30 minutes or until the filling is cooked through. Using a slotted spoon, transfer the bundles to a serving platter. Serve warm or chilled.

Chef's Note: Coarsely chopping the rice helps it to cook more quickly. Use a blender or food processor and pulse it just until the rice grains are no longer whole. Look for grape leaves in the specialty section of your supermarket. If you have difficulty locating them, try a gourmet shop or Greek market. Before using the leaves, be sure to rinse them well to remove excess sodium.

Mustard-Yogurt Lamb Kabobs on a Bed of Couscous

You don't need a standard oil-and-vinegar marinade to get great taste out of lamb kabobs. Yogurt works just as well and gives the meat a delicious tangy flavor.

   1 **cup nonfat plain yogurt**
   3 **tablespoons honey-flavored Dijon mustard**
   ½ **teaspoon ground cumin**
   ½ **teaspoon ground coriander**
   ¼ **teaspoon paprika**
  12 **ounces boneless lean lamb, trimmed of all visible fat and cut into 1" cubes**
   1 **medium green pepper, cut into 1" pieces**
   1 **medium yellow summer squash, cut into 1" pieces**
   4 **cups hot cooked couscous**

In a medium bowl, stir together the yogurt, mustard, cumin, coriander and paprika. Add the lamb, peppers and squash. Toss until well coated. Cover and marinate in the refrigerator for 30 minutes, stirring once.

Spray the rack of a broiling pan with no-stick spray; set aside. Thread equal amounts of the lamb, peppers and squash onto 4 metal skewers. Place the kabobs on the rack. Brush any of the remaining marinade over the kabobs. Broil 4" from the heat for 7 to 9 minutes for medium doneness, turning the kabobs frequently. Serve on a bed of couscous.

EXTRA HEALTH BENEFIT
Stronger Immunity

Times: Prep: 15 min.
Marinating: 30 min.
Cooking: 7 min.

Makes 4 servings.

Per serving: 379 calories, 6.4 g. fat (15% of calories), 9.5 g. dietary fiber, 61 mg. cholesterol, 402 mg. sodium.

Extra Health Benefits
Better Blood Pressure
Stronger Immunity

Times: Prep: 4 min.
Cooking: 5 min.
Broiling: 9 min.

Makes 4 servings.

Per serving: 366 calories,
8.8 g. fat (22% of calories),
7.4 g. dietary fiber, 80 mg.
cholesterol, 78 mg. sodium.

Noisettes of Lamb

When you're in a hurry, here's a slimming entrée that's not only quick but also elegant.

  2 **tablespoons defatted low-sodium beef broth or water**
  2 **teaspoons ground coriander**
  1 **teaspoon crushed black peppercorns**
  1 **clove garlic, minced**
  4 **lamb loin chops (about 4 ounces each), cut about 1"
      thick and trimmed of all visible fat**
  1 **cup couscous**
  ½ **cup seeded and chopped tomatoes
      Cilantro or parsley sprigs (optional)**

In a small bowl, stir together the broth or water, coriander, peppercorns and garlic. Rub over the surface of the lamb chops.

Place the chops on the rack in a broiling pan. Broil 4" from the heat for 5 minutes. Turn the chops over and continue broiling about 4 minutes more or until cooked to desired doneness.

Meanwhile, cook the couscous according to the package directions. After removing it from the heat, stir in the tomatoes.

To serve, spoon the couscous mixture onto a serving platter. Arrange the chops on top. If desired, garnish with the cilantro or parsley sprigs.

Chef's Note: *Noisette* is the French word for hazelnut, but it also refers to tender, round slices of meat taken from the rib or loin of lamb, beef or veal.

Venison Schnitzel

Venison is a good choice for those watching their weight—it's so low in fat and calories that it even outshines skinless chicken breast.

1½ **cups fine dry plain bread crumbs**
1 **tablespoon grated Parmesan cheese**
½ **teaspoon dried basil**
½ **teaspoon garlic powder**
4 **boneless venison steaks (about 4 ounces each), trimmed of all visible fat**
1 **teaspoon garlic-and-herb salt-free seasoning**
¼ **teaspoon ground black pepper**
2 **large egg whites**
2 **teaspoons olive oil**

In a small bowl, stir together the bread crumbs, cheese, basil and garlic powder until the mixture forms fine crumbs. Transfer the crumbs to a large piece of wax paper; set aside.

Using a meat mallet, pound each steak to ¼" thickness. Rub the surface of the steaks with the herb seasoning and pepper.

In a shallow bowl, lightly beat the egg whites with a fork. Dip the steaks in the egg whites. Then roll each steak in the crumb mixture, evenly coating both sides.

Add the oil to a large no-stick skillet and heat over medium heat. Add the steaks and cook for 3 minutes. Turn the steaks over and cook for 3 to 5 minutes more or until cooked to desired doneness for the venison.

Chef's Note: If venison is unavailable, use 4 pork loin butterfly chops, 4 ounces each.

Quick

EXTRA HEALTH BENEFIT
Stronger Immunity

Times: Prep: 8 min.
Cooking: 6 min.

Makes 4 servings.

Per serving: 320 calories, 7.4 g. fat (21% of calories), 1.4 g. dietary fiber, 97 mg. cholesterol, 391 mg. sodium.

Broiled Rabbit with Chili-Fennel Sauce

EXTRA HEALTH BENEFITS
Better Blood Pressure
Stronger Immunity

Times: Prep: 3 min.
Cooking: 12 min.
Broiling: 15 min.

Makes 4 servings.

Per serving: 288 calories, 8.4 g. fat (26% of calories), 2 g. dietary fiber, 48 mg. cholesterol, 89 mg. sodium.

People always say that rabbit tastes like chicken. Well, it's got something else in common with chicken—it's low in fat and calories. Here it gets a flavor boost from mixed spices and chili peppers.

RABBIT
- 1 tablespoon ground cinnamon
- 1 teaspoon ground coriander
- ½ teaspoon ground cumin
- ⅛ teaspoon ground white pepper
- 1 rabbit (about 2 pounds), cut into 8 pieces

SAUCE
- ½ cup chopped onions
- 2 cloves garlic, minced
- 1¼ cups defatted low-sodium chicken broth
- ½ cup chopped fennel
- 1 tablespoon canned diced green chili peppers
- 1 tablespoon minced fresh cilantro
- 2 teaspoons fresh lime juice
- 1 teaspoon honey
- 2 cups hot cooked brown rice

For the rabbit: In a small bowl, stir together the cinnamon, coriander, cumin and white pepper. Rub over the surface of the rabbit pieces.

Spray the rack of a broiling pan with no-stick spray. Place the rabbit on the rack. Broil 4" from the heat for 8 minutes. Turn the pieces over and broil for 7 to 12 minutes more or until tender and the juices run clear when the meat is pierced with a fork.

For the sauce: Meanwhile, in a medium saucepan, cook and stir the onions and garlic in 2 tablespoons of the broth for 2 minutes. Then add the remaining broth, the fennel and chili peppers. Bring to a boil, then reduce the heat. Simmer, uncovered, about 10 minutes or until the fennel is tender.

Transfer the mixture to a blender or food processor. Blend or process until smooth. Transfer to a serving bowl and stir in the cilantro, lime juice and honey. Spoon the sauce over the rabbit and serve with the rice.

Chef's Note: You can easily make the sauce ahead. Store it, covered, in the refrigerator and reheat just before serving.

Habañero

Thai

Jalapeño

Hungarian cherry

Bell

Spice It Up!

Have you ever tried to eat a huge plate of spicy Mexican, Thai, Szechuan or Indian fare? It's nearly impossible. Those foods seem to quiet the appetite better than blander dishes. One possible reason is that the flavor is so intense—thanks mostly to hot peppers—that you don't need as much. Besides, it's hard to pig out on fiery foods. Your taste buds just won't let you.

Spicy foods also speed up the metabolism. The faster your metabolism, the more heat your body produces—and the more fat you're likely to burn. So stock up on chili peppers and use them often.

If you're confused about which peppers are which and how hot they are, here's a general rule: The smaller and redder peppers, like cayenne and tabasco, are hotter; the larger and greener peppers, like poblano and Anaheim, are milder. The accompanying photo shows the relative warmth of several commonly available peppers.

One piece of advice: When working with fresh chili peppers (or even dried ones), wear disposable gloves or cover your hands with plastic bags. Hot peppers contain volatile oils that can result in irritating or painful burns to your skin. Be careful not to touch your face, especially your eyes, until you've removed the gloves or washed your hands well to get rid of the offending oil. Be sure also to wash your cutting board in warm soapy water to remove traces of the oil.

Sensational Fish and Seafood

Catfish Creole

Extra Health Benefits
Better Blood Pressure
Blood Building
Stronger Immunity

Times: Prep: 5 min.
Cooking: 20 min.

Makes 4 servings.

Per serving: 301 calories,
3.9 g. fat (12% of calories), 0.5
g. dietary fiber, 49 mg. cholesterol, 80 mg. sodium.

Here's an authentic-tasting Louisiana dish that's lower in calories and fat than standard versions. Best of all, it takes only minutes to make. Serve it with crusty bread for an honest-to-goodness Creole meal.

12 ounces skinless fresh or frozen catfish fillets
($\frac{1}{2}$"–1" thick)
2 cups water
1 cup long-grain rice
1 can (16 ounces) low-sodium stewed tomatoes (with juices)
2 teaspoons dried minced onions
1 teaspoon reduced-sodium chicken bouillon powder
$\frac{1}{2}$ teaspoon dried oregano
$\frac{1}{4}$ teaspoon garlic powder
$\frac{1}{8}$ teaspoon hot-pepper sauce

If using frozen fish, let it stand at room temperature for 10 to 20 minutes or until partially thawed.

Meanwhile, in a small saucepan, bring the water to a boil. Stir in the rice. Return to a boil, then reduce the heat. Cover and simmer for 20 minutes or until the rice is tender and the water is absorbed.

Using a very sharp knife, cut the catfish into $\frac{3}{4}$" pieces; set aside. In a medium saucepan, combine the tomatoes (with juices), onions, bouillon powder, oregano, garlic powder and

Catfish Creole

hot-pepper sauce. Bring to a boil, then stir in the catfish. Cover and cook over medium heat for 5 to 8 minutes or until the fish flakes easily when tested with a fork and is opaque all the way through. Serve the fish mixture over the rice.

Chef's Note: If you can't find low-sodium stewed tomatoes, substitute low-sodium canned tomatoes and chop them before using.

Swordfish Steamed with Mushrooms

Adding just a touch of balsamic vinegar to this dish gives it a refreshingly piquant flavor without contributing any extra calories. If you don't have balsamic vinegar, use cider vinegar or rice vinegar.

  2 **cups thinly sliced fresh mushrooms**
  1 **large onion, thinly sliced**
  3 **tablespoons defatted low-sodium chicken broth**
  ½ **teaspoon lemon-pepper seasoning**
  4 **swordfish steaks (4 ounces each), cut 1" thick**
  1 **tablespoon balsamic vinegar**

Spray an unheated, large no-stick skillet with no-stick spray. Heat the skillet over medium heat. Add the mushrooms, onions and 1 tablespoon of the broth to the skillet. Cook and stir about 5 minutes or until the vegetables are just tender. Stir in the remaining 2 tablespoons of broth and the seasoning.

Place the swordfish in a single layer on top of the vegetables. Cover and cook over medium heat for 8 to 10 minutes or until the fish flakes easily when tested with a fork and is opaque all the way through.

Transfer the swordfish to a warm serving platter. Then stir the vinegar into the vegetables in the skillet. Spoon the vegetable mixture over the swordfish.

Chef's Note: Balsamic vinegar has a dark color and a pungent, sweet flavor that comes from an elaborate aging process. Although it used to be quite expensive and hard to find, balsamic vinegar is now available in most large supermarkets—and at a price you can afford.

Quick

EXTRA HEALTH BENEFITS
Better Blood Pressure
Stronger Immunity

Times: Prep: 13 min.
Cooking: 13 min.

Makes 4 servings.

Per serving: 150 calories, 4.3 g. fat (26% of calories), 1.1 g. dietary fiber, 39 mg. cholesterol, 96 mg. sodium.

SLIMMING STRATEGY

To convert die-hard meat eaters into fish lovers, serve them firm fish like swordfish, monkfish, shark and fresh tuna. These types have a more meaty taste and texture than orange roughy, flounder, cod, catfish and other mild, delicate fish.

EXTRA HEALTH BENEFITS
Lower Cholesterol
Cancer Protection
Stronger Immunity

Times: Prep: 15 min.
Cooking: 6 min.

Makes 4 servings.

Per serving: 199 calories,
2.2 g. fat (10% of calories),
1.8 g. dietary fiber, 27 mg.
cholesterol, 372 mg. sodium.

SLIMMING STRATEGY

Soften margarine at room
temperature before using
it, especially as a spread
on bread or muffins.
Chances are you'll use less
because it'll be easy to
apply a very thin layer. If
you forget to soften your
margarine, place it in the
microwave for a few sec-
onds—but be careful not
to melt it.

Halibut Aloha

*In just minutes you can have a low-calorie Oriental meal on
the table. To keep calories down, make sure to use fruit
packed in juice instead of heavy syrup.*

> 12 **ounces skinless fresh or frozen halibut steaks or fillets
>   (½"–1" thick)**
> 2 **stalks celery, thinly sliced**
> 1 **carrot, thinly sliced**
> ⅔ **cup orange juice**
> ¼ **teaspoon ground ginger**
> 1 **can (11 ounces) pineapple and mandarin orange
>   sections or 1 can (15¼ ounces) pineapple tidbits
>   (packed in juice)**
> 1 **tablespoon cornstarch**
> 2 **tablespoons reduced-sodium soy sauce**
> 1 **tablespoon vinegar**
> 1 **tablespoon honey**

If using frozen fish, let it stand at room temperature for 10 to
20 minutes or until partially thawed. Using a very sharp knife,
cut the halibut into 1" pieces; set aside.

In a medium saucepan, combine the celery, carrots, orange
juice and ginger. Bring to a boil, then stir in the halibut. Cover
and cook over medium heat for 4 to 6 minutes or until the fish
flakes easily when tested with a fork and is opaque all the way
through. Using a slotted spoon, carefully transfer the halibut to a
plate and set aside.

Meanwhile, in a strainer over a small bowl, drain the pineapple and mandarin orange sections or the pineapple tidbits.

In another small bowl, stir together 2 tablespoons of the fruit
juice and the cornstarch. Then stir in the soy sauce, vinegar and
honey. Stir into the vegetable mixture in the saucepan. Cook
and stir until the mixture thickens and begins to gently boil.
Cook and stir for 2 minutes more.

Add the halibut and the fruit. Cover and cook about 1 minute
or until heated through.

Chef's Note: Rice is the perfect accompaniment for this
Chinese dish. But for variety, you might consider cellophane
noodles or lo mein noodles.

Haddock in Creamy Orange-Basil Sauce

You'll be fooled! The sauce is rich and creamy, yet it's low in calories and fat. Serve this grand dish with a wild-and-white-rice pilaf.

  2 **ounces light cream cheese**
  ⅓ **cup defatted low-sodium chicken broth**
  ⅓ **cup orange juice**
  1 **small carrot, coarsely shredded**
  1 **teaspoon dried basil**
  12 **ounces skinless haddock fillets (¼"–½" thick)**
  ¼ **cup reduced-fat cottage cheese**
  2 **teaspoons unbleached flour**
      Orange twists (optional)
      Fresh basil or parsley sprigs (optional)

Place the cream cheese in a small bowl; set aside to soften. Meanwhile, in a large skillet, stir together the broth, orange juice, carrots and dried basil. Cover and bring to a boil, then carefully add the haddock. Reduce the heat, cover and gently simmer for 3 to 6 minutes or until the fish flakes easily when tested with a fork and is opaque all the way through. Using a slotted spatula or spoon, carefully transfer to a serving platter. Reserve the cooking liquid. Cover the haddock with foil to keep warm.

Stir the cottage cheese and flour into the cream cheese. Stir about ⅓ cup of the hot cooking liquid into the cream cheese mixture. Then stir the cream cheese mixture into the remaining cooking liquid. Cook and stir over medium heat about 2 minutes or until heated through. Spoon the sauce over the haddock. If desired, garnish the platter with orange twists and fresh basil or parsley.

Chef's Note: You can substitute most any other herb for the basil. Marjoram, thyme, oregano and dill are all good choices.

Quick

EXTRA HEALTH BENEFIT
Stronger Immunity

Times: Prep: 17 min.
Cooking: 5 min.

Makes 4 servings.

Per serving: 142 calories, 3.6 g. fat (22% of calories), 0.8 g. dietary fiber, 55 mg. cholesterol, 209 mg. sodium.

SLIMMING STRATEGY

You can enjoy creamy cheese sauces without taking in a lot of fat. Simple adjustments to most recipes can lighten them up considerably. Always stop to consider whether reduced-fat cheeses, skim milk and nonfat sour cream or yogurt can be substituted for fattier ingredients.

Sole Poached with Italian Vegetables

EXTRA HEALTH BENEFITS
Cancer Protection
Stronger Immunity

Times: Prep: 15 min.
Cooking: 3 min.

Makes 4 servings.

Per serving: 156 calories,
2.9 g. fat (17% of calories),
1.4 g. dietary fiber, 57 mg.
cholesterol, 175 mg. sodium.

Colorful and lightly seasoned, these vegetables also go well with other mild fish such as flounder, orange roughy, cod, haddock and halibut.

- 1 **cup defatted low-sodium chicken broth**
- 1 **medium tomato, peeled and chopped**
- 1 **small green pepper, cut into thin bite-size strips**
- 1 **small onion, thinly sliced**
- 1 **cup thinly sliced fresh mushrooms**
- 1 **clove garlic, minced**
- ⅛ **teaspoon ground black pepper**
- 4 **skinless sole fillets (about 4 ounces each and ¼"–½" thick)**
- 2 **tablespoons grated Parmesan cheese**

In a large skillet, combine the broth, tomatoes, green peppers, onions, mushrooms, garlic and black pepper. Cover and bring to

Sole Poached with Italian Vegetables

a boil, then carefully add the sole. Reduce the heat, cover and gently simmer for 3 to 6 minutes or until the fish flakes easily when tested with a fork and is opaque all the way through.

Using a slotted spatula or spoon, carefully transfer the sole to a serving platter. Then spoon the vegetable mixture over the sole. Sprinkle with the cheese.

Poached Halibut with Tomato Yogurt

Poaching is an ultrasimple way to prepare fish, especially nice firm steaks that won't fall apart as they cook. The tangy cucumber sauce that we're using with this halibut also goes with cod, salmon and orange roughy.

    1 cup water
    2 bay leaves
  ½ teaspoon onion powder
  ¼ teaspoon ground black pepper
    4 halibut steaks (1 pound total), cut 1" thick
  ¾ cup nonfat plain yogurt
  ½ of a small cucumber, seeded and shredded
    1 small tomato, seeded and chopped
    2 green onions, thinly sliced
    1 tablespoon chopped parsley

In a large skillet, combine the water, bay leaves, onion powder and pepper. Cover and bring to a boil, then carefully add the halibut. Reduce the heat, cover and gently simmer for 8 to 12 minutes or until the fish flakes easily when tested with a fork and is opaque all the way through.

Meanwhile, for the sauce, in a small bowl, stir together the yogurt, cucumbers, tomatoes, onions and parsley.

To serve, use a slotted spatula to carefully transfer the halibut to a serving platter. Serve with the sauce.

Chef's Note: You could turn this fish into a Greek gyro sandwich. Flake the fish and stuff it into a pita bread. Add some shredded lettuce and top the whole thing off with the tomato-yogurt sauce.

Quick

EXTRA HEALTH BENEFITS
Lower Cholesterol
Better Blood Pressure
Stronger Immunity

Times: Prep: 6 min.
Cooking: 8 min.

Makes 4 servings.

Per serving: 161 calories, 2.8 g. fat (16% of calories), 0.9 g. dietary fiber, 37 mg. cholesterol, 100 mg. sodium.

Times: Prep: 10 min.
Baking: 20 min.

Makes 4 servings.

Per serving: 192 calories,
5.1 g. fat (24% of calories),
2.2 g. dietary fiber, 45 mg.
cholesterol, 225 mg. sodium.

SLIMMING STRATEGY

All in all, fish deserves its low-fat reputation. But not all sea creatures are created equal. The slimmest choices include cod, flounder, sole, haddock, red snapper, crab, shrimp, scallops and clams. Fattier fish include mackerel, salmon, bluefish, herring and some types of tuna. They're not off-limits—you just need to build them into your fat budget.

Lemon-Thyme Swordfish with Asparagus

A creamy low-fat lemon-thyme sauce accents this oven-poached swordfish. And the simply steamed asparagus adds color and fiber to help round out the meal. All you need to add is rice or another starch and some nonfat dinner rolls.

- ½ **cup reduced-fat cottage cheese**
- 2 **tablespoons skim milk**
  - **Juice of 1 lemon**
- 1 **teaspoon minced fresh parsley**
- 1 **teaspoon dried basil**
- 1½ **teaspoons dried thyme**
- 4 **swordfish steaks (1 pound total), cut 1" thick**
- 1 **cup water**
- 1 **bay leaf**
- 1 **pound fresh asparagus spears, steamed**
  - **Lemon slices (optional)**
  - **Thyme sprigs (optional)**

For the sauce, in a blender or food processor, blend or process the cottage cheese until creamy. Transfer the cottage cheese to a small bowl. Stir in the milk, 1½ teaspoons of the lemon juice, parsley, basil and ½ teaspoon of the dried thyme. Cover and chill in refrigerator while preparing the swordfish.

Place the swordfish in an 8" × 8" baking dish. Pour the water and 2 tablespoons of the remaining lemon juice into the dish. Add the bay leaf and sprinkle with the remaining 1 teaspoon of dried thyme. Cover the dish with foil. Bake at 350° about 20 minutes or until the fish flakes easily when tested with a fork and is opaque all the way through.

To serve, carefully transfer the swordfish to a serving platter. Arrange the asparagus next to the fish. If desired, garnish with the lemon slices and sprigs of thyme. Serve with the sauce.

Chef's Note: When buying asparagus, look for straight stalks with closed tips. If the stalks are thin, break off the tough section at the bottom. If they're thick, use a vegetable peeler to pare off tough skin, then cut off any really fibrous stem ends. Steam the spears in a saucepan with a tight-fitting lid for 10 to 15 minutes or until crisp-tender.

Lemon-Thyme Swordfish with Asparagus

EXTRA HEALTH BENEFITS
Better Blood Pressure
Stronger Immunity

Times: Prep: 10 min.
Baking: 15 min.

Makes 4 servings.

Per serving: 116 calories,
2.4 g. fat (19% of calories),
0.3 g. dietary fiber, 49 mg.
cholesterol, 100 mg. sodium.

Sage-Baked Cod

Just a tad of sage-flavor margarine adds a lot of richness and flavor to this fish without really contributing much fat.

> 4 **skinless cod fillets (about 4 ounces each and ½" thick)**
>   **Ground black pepper (to taste)**
> 4 **lemon slices**
> 4 **large green onions, thinly sliced**
> ¼ **cup defatted low-sodium chicken broth**
> 1 **tablespoon reduced-calorie margarine, softened**
> 2 **teaspoons minced fresh sage or ½ teaspoon dried sage**
> ½ **teaspoon paprika**
> ½ **teaspoon onion powder**
>   **Pinch of ground black pepper**

Place the cod in a single layer in a 13" × 9" baking dish, folding under any thin edges of the fillets. Sprinkle the cod with the desired amount of pepper. Then place the lemon slices on top and sprinkle with the onions.

Pour the broth around the cod. Cover the dish with foil and bake at 350° for 15 to 20 minutes or until the fish flakes easily when tested with a fork and is opaque all the way through.

Meanwhile, in a small bowl, stir together the margarine, sage, paprika, onion powder and pinch of pepper.

To serve, use a slotted spatula or spoon to carefully transfer the cod to a serving platter. Spread the margarine mixture on top of the hot fillets.

Poached Red Snapper

Adding seasonings such as fennel and bay leaves to the poaching liquid subtly flavors fish without contributing calories or fat. Before using the fennel, lightly crush it using a mortar and pestle to release its mild licorice flavor.

> 4 **cups water**
>   **Juice of 1 lemon**
> 1 **tablespoon fennel seeds**
> 1 **bay leaf**
> 2 **drawn and scaled red snappers (1 pound each)**

In a fish poacher or oval roaster, combine the water, lemon juice, fennel seeds and bay leaf. Bring to a boil. Carefully add the red snappers. Return to a boil, then reduce the heat. Cover and gently simmer about 15 minutes or until the fish flakes easily when tested with a fork and is opaque all the way through.

Using a slotted spoon or spatula, carefully transfer the red snappers to a serving platter.

Chef's Note: Complete this easy fish meal by serving linguine or spaghetti with marinara sauce, a tossed salad and crusty whole-grain bread.

Mariner's Salad

Here's a smart way to use leftover fish. Almost any white fish— cod, flounder, haddock, halibut or the like—will do. So will cooked shrimp or crab.

  5 cups torn spinach
12 ounces cooked white fish, cut into 1" chunks
  1 carrot, cut into 1½"-long julienne pieces
  ¼ cup sliced green onions
  ⅔ cup low-fat plain yogurt
  2 tablespoons lemon juice
  1 tablespoon minced fresh parsley
  1 clove garlic, minced
  1 lemon, sliced (optional)

In a large bowl, gently combine the spinach, fish, carrots and onions.

For the dressing, in a small bowl, stir together the yogurt, lemon juice, parsley and garlic. Drizzle the dressing over the spinach mixture. Gently toss until coated.

To serve, mound the mixture on salad plates. If desired, garnish each serving with lemon slices.

Makes 4 servings.

Per serving: 227 calories, 3 g. fat (13% of calories), 0 g. dietary fiber, 84 mg. cholesterol, 144 mg. sodium.

Quick

EXTRA HEALTH BENEFITS
Cancer Protection
Stronger Immunity

Time: Prep: 13 min.

Makes 4 servings.

Per serving: 141 calories, 1.6 g. fat (10% of calories), 2.6 g. dietary fiber, 49 mg. cholesterol, 155 mg. sodium.

Salmon en Papillote with Horseradish Cream

EXTRA HEALTH BENEFIT
Stronger Immunity

Times: Prep: 15 min.
Baking: 20 min.

Makes 4 servings.

Per serving: 263 calories,
7.1 g. fat (25% of calories),
3.7 g. dietary fiber, 48 mg.
cholesterol, 344 mg. sodium.

En papillote refers to cooking food in parchment paper. It's a simple yet exquisite way to prepare quick-cooking ingredients such as these salmon fillets. If you don't have parchment on hand, use foil.

¼ **cup reduced-fat cottage cheese**
1 **tablespoon prepared horseradish**
½ **teaspoon minced fresh parsley**
12 **ounces skinless salmon fillets (about ½" thick)**
  Lemon-pepper seasoning (to taste)
2 **small zucchini, bias-sliced into ¼"-thick slices**
2 **carrots, cut into 1½"-long julienne pieces**
4 **slices French bread**

For the sauce, in a blender or small food processor, blend or process the cottage cheese until creamy. Transfer the cottage cheese to a small bowl. Stir in the horseradish and parsley. Cover and chill in the refrigerator while preparing the salmon.

Cut parchment paper into 4 squares, 12" each. Fold each square in half, then trim into large hearts. Open the paper hearts.

Cut the salmon into 4 equal pieces. Place a piece on half of each paper heart. Sprinkle with the desired amount of lemon-pepper seasoning. Layer the zucchini and carrots on top of the salmon.

For each packet, fold the paper over the fish and vegetables and align the edges. Make a small fold at the top edge, crease and repeat to make a double seal. Work your way around the edge, making a double seal. When you reach the pointed end, twist the parchment to hold the folds in place. Make sure the edges are tightly sealed.

Place the packets on a large cookie sheet. Bake at 400° about 20 minutes or until the paper is browned and puffed. Carefully cut a large X in the top of each packet and fold back the points. Check to see if the fish flakes easily when tested with a fork and the vegetables are crisp-tender. If not, close the packets and bake about 3 minutes more.

To serve, transfer the packets to dinner plates. Open the packets and top each serving with the horseradish sauce. Serve with the French bread.

Salmon en Papillote with Horseradish Cream

EXTRA HEALTH BENEFITS
Better Blood Pressure
Cancer Protection
Stronger Immunity

Times: Prep: 5 min.
Cooking: 5 min.
Baking: 15 min.

Makes 4 servings.

Fish Fillets with Rapid Ratatouille

Ratatouille is a traditional French eggplant and vegetable mixture that usually contains lots of olive oil. This lighter version cooks the vegetables in tomato sauce.

- 1 can (8 ounces) low-sodium tomato sauce
- 1 cup peeled and cubed eggplant
- 1 medium tomato, seeded and chopped
- 1 small yellow summer squash or zucchini, thinly sliced
- 1 stalk celery, thinly sliced
- 1 teaspoon dried Italian seasoning
- ⅛ teaspoon hot-pepper sauce
- 4 skinless orange roughy, cod or sole fillets (about 4 ounces each and ½" thick)

In a medium saucepan, stir together the tomato sauce, eggplant, tomatoes, summer squash or zucchini, celery, Italian sea-

Hooking the Right Cut

When you're shopping for fish, it's helpful to know some of the terms used by markets and fishmongers. Here are some expressions that you might hear.

Drawn. This doesn't refer to the picture of the fish on the display case. It's a whole fish with its internal organs removed. It may still need to be scaled.

Dressed. This fish has been gutted, scaled and possibly boned. A pan-dressed fish has had its head, fins and tail removed.

Steak. A crosscut slice of one inch or more from a dressed fish. There may or may not be a center section of bones, depending upon how large the fish is. A rib steak comes from the front half of the fish; the tail steak, naturally, comes from the back half.

Fillet. The side of the fish that has been cut away from the ribs and backbone. This is probably the form you buy most often and is certainly what you get when purchasing flounder, sole and orange roughy, for example.
Depending upon the species, there may be a row of pin bones that will need to be removed. Pull them out with your fingers or with tweezers or needle-nose pliers reserved for kitchen use.

Chunks. These are sections or pieces of a large dressed fish. They may contain some of the backbone and rib bones.

soning and hot-pepper sauce. Bring to a boil, then reduce the heat. Cover and simmer about 5 minutes or until the vegetables are tender. Remove from the heat.

Spray a 12" × 7½" baking dish with no-stick spray. Place the fish in a single layer in the baking dish, folding under any thin edges of the fillets. Spoon the vegetable mixture on top of the fish.

Cover the dish with foil and bake at 350° for 15 to 20 minutes or until the fish flakes easily when tested with a fork and is opaque all the way through.

Per serving: 148 calories, 1.6 g. fat (10% of calories), 2.6 g. dietary fiber, 55 mg. cholesterol, 122 mg. sodium.

Orange-Marinated Halibut

The tangy marinade used here gives the halibut a delightful citrus flavor. The fish is especially good served on a bed of steamed shredded zucchini. For variety, replace the halibut with tuna steaks.

EXTRA HEALTH BENEFITS
Better Blood Pressure
Stronger Immunity

Times: Prep: 14 min.
Marinating: 1 hr.
Broiling: 9 min.

Makes 4 servings.

Per serving: 135 calories, 2.7 g. fat (19% of calories), 0.1 g. dietary fiber, 36 mg. cholesterol, 97 mg. sodium.

- 4 **halibut steaks (4 ounces each), cut 1" thick**
- ½ **teaspoon grated orange peel**
- ¼ **cup orange juice**
- 1 **tablespoon lime or lemon juice**
- 1 **tablespoon nonfat clear Italian salad dressing**
- 1 **teaspoon Dijon mustard**

Place the halibut in a single layer in a baking dish. In a small bowl, stir together the orange peel, orange juice, lime or lemon juice, salad dressing and mustard. Pour over the halibut. Cover the baking dish with plastic wrap and marinate in the refrigerator for 1 hour, turning the halibut over after 30 minutes.

Spray the rack of a broiling pan with no-stick spray. Drain the halibut, reserving the marinade. Place the halibut on the rack and brush with the reserved marinade. Broil 3" to 4" from the heat for 5 minutes. Turn the halibut over and brush again with the marinade. Broil for 4 to 7 minutes more or until the fish flakes easily when tested with a fork and is opaque all the way through.

Chef's Note: To simplify cleanup when broiling fish—or any other food, for that matter—line the pan with foil. Then coat the broiling rack with no-stick spray. The rack will be easy to wash, and the bottom pan will stay clean.

Times: Prep: 13 min.
Baking: 10 min.

Makes 4 servings.

Per serving: 164 calories,
3.8 g. fat (22% of calories),
0.5 g. dietary fiber, 57 mg.
cholesterol, 211 mg. sodium.

SLIMMING STRATEGY

Add spice to your life!
Spices are the most con-
centrated forms of fla-
vor—exactly what your
taste buds need when
your stomach is growling.
Research has shown that
good taste, not monot-
ony, is the key to losing
weight.

Cod with Italian
Crumb Topping

Cod with Italian Crumb Topping

*Here's a low-fat version of gratinéed fish. Plain fillets are
sprinkled with an easy crumb topping and baked quickly in a
hot oven. They're a terrific alternative to breaded, fried fish.*

¼	**cup fine dry bread crumbs**
2	**tablespoons grated Parmesan cheese**
1	**tablespoon cornmeal**
1	**teaspoon olive oil**
½	**teaspoon dried Italian seasoning**
⅛	**teaspoon garlic powder**
⅛	**teaspoon ground black pepper**
4	**skinless cod fillets (about 4 ounces each and ½" thick)**
1	**egg white, lightly beaten**

In a small shallow bowl, stir together the bread crumbs,
cheese, cornmeal, oil, Italian seasoning, garlic powder and pepper; set aside.

Spray the rack of a broiling pan with no-stick spray. Place the
cod on the rack, folding under any thin edges of the fillets.
Brush with the egg white, then spoon the crumb mixture evenly
on top.

Bake at 450° for 10 to 12 minutes or until the fish flakes easily
when tested with a fork and is opaque all the way through.

Spinach-Stuffed Flounder with Mushrooms and Feta

You could use the stuffing for these flounder fillets with other types of fish, including sole and orange roughy. The feta cheese used in the filling has a distinct, robust flavor, so you can get away with using just a small amount.

- 8 **large fresh mushrooms, sliced**
- 8 **ounces spinach, coarsely chopped**
- 1 **tablespoon finely crumbled feta cheese**
- 4 **skinless flounder fillets (about 4 ounces each and ¼"–½" thick)**
- 2 **cups hot cooked couscous**
     Watercress sprigs (optional)
     Lemon wedges (optional)

Spray an unheated medium skillet with no-stick spray. Heat the skillet over medium heat. Add the mushrooms and cook about 5 minutes or until the liquid released from the mushrooms has evaporated, stirring occasionally.

Add the spinach to the skillet. Cook and stir about 2 minutes or until the spinach is wilted. Remove from the heat and drain. Sprinkle the feta cheese over the vegetables, then stir it in.

To assemble the fish rolls, place one-quarter of the spinach mixture onto the wide end of each fillet. Carefully roll the fillet around the spinach mixture. Use wooden toothpicks to hold the end of each roll in place.

Spray an 8" × 8" baking dish or pie plate with no-stick spray. Place the fish rolls, seam side down, in the baking dish or pie plate. Add 2 tablespoons of water. Loosely cover with foil.

Bake at 350° for 15 to 20 minutes or until the fish flakes easily when tested with a fork and is opaque all the way through.

Serve the fish rolls on a bed of couscous. If desired, garnish each serving with the watercress sprigs and lemon wedges.

Quick

Extra Health Benefits
Cancer Protection
Blood Building
Stronger Immunity

Times: Prep: 13 min.
Baking: 15 min.

Makes 4 servings.

Per serving: 231 calories, 2.6 g. fat (10% of calories), 6.2 g. dietary fiber, 58 mg. cholesterol, 181 mg. sodium.

Slimming Strategy

For years, behavioral psychologists have been urging us to chew food longer. Why? The longer you chew, the more time your stomach has to register that it's full. Also, chewing creates currents of air. That forces odors into the nose and helps send a message to your brain that you're satisfied.

Pike Stuffed with Bulgur and Zucchini

EXTRA HEALTH BENEFIT
Stronger Immunity

Times: Prep: 6 min.
Cooking: 13 min.
Baking: 15 min.

Makes 4 servings.

Per serving: 152 calories,
1.8 g. fat (11% of calories),
2.4 g. dietary fiber, 54 mg.
cholesterol, 108 mg. sodium.

The stuffing for these fillets has a savory nutty flavor that comes from bulgur rather than high-fat nuts. When choosing your fillets, be sure to get thin, pliable ones that can easily be rolled around the filling.

⅓ **cup bulgur**
⅔ **cup defatted low-sodium chicken broth**
¼ **teaspoon dried sage**
⅛ **teaspoon garlic powder**
 Pinch of ground black pepper
⅓ **cup shredded zucchini**
2 **green onions, thinly sliced**
4 **skinless walleye pike fillets (about 4 ounces each and ¼"–½" thick)**

Place the bulgur in a colander and rinse under cold running water. Drain and transfer to a small bowl.

In a small saucepan, bring the broth to a boil. Stir in the bulgur, sage, garlic powder and pepper. Cover and cook over low heat for 10 minutes. Then stir in the zucchini and onions. Cover and cook about 3 minutes more or until the bulgur is tender and the water is absorbed.

To assemble the fish rolls, spoon about ¼ cup of the bulgur mixture onto the wide end of each fillet. Carefully roll the fillet around the bulgur mixture. Use wooden toothpicks to hold the end of each roll in place.

Spray an 8" × 8" baking dish with no-stick spray. Place the fish rolls upright in the baking dish. Cover the dish with foil. Bake at 350° for 15 to 20 minutes or until the fish flakes easily when tested with a fork and is opaque all the way through.

Chef's Note: For variety, make 2 fish stacks instead of 4 rolls. Spread the filling over 2 of the fillets and cover them with the remaining 2. Bake at 350° for 20 to 30 minutes, then cut the pieces crosswise in half to serve.

Potluck Salmon and Pasta

When you're going to a potluck dinner, take along this easy casserole. It's sure to be a favorite among the guests—and you'll know there's at least one buffet selection you can eat without blowing your eating plan.

    4 cups water
 1½ cups corkscrew pasta (rotini)
 1½ cups frozen mixed peas and carrots
    1 stalk celery, thinly sliced
  ¼ cup finely chopped onions
 1½ cups skim milk
    2 tablespoons unbleached flour
  ¾ cup (3 ounces) shredded reduced-fat cheddar cheese
  ¾ teaspoon dried basil
  ⅛ teaspoon ground black pepper
    1 can (7 ounces) skinless, boneless salmon, drained
    2 tablespoons fine dry bread crumbs
  ¼ teaspoon paprika

In a medium saucepan, bring the water to a boil. Add the pasta. Cover and return to a boil. Reduce the heat and gently boil, covered, for 5 minutes.

Stir in the peas and carrots, celery and onions. Return to a boil, then reduce the heat to medium. Cover and cook for 5 minutes or until the pasta and vegetables are tender. Drain well.

Meanwhile, spray a medium saucepan with no-stick spray. In the saucepan, use a wire whisk to stir together the milk and flour. Cook and stir over medium heat just until the mixture thickens and begins to gently boil. Remove from the heat and stir in the cheese, ½ teaspoon of the basil and the pepper. Stir until the cheese is melted. Then stir in the salmon and the pasta mixture.

Spray an 11" × 7" baking dish with no-stick spray. Transfer the salmon mixture to the baking dish.

In a small bowl, stir together the bread crumbs, paprika and the remaining ¼ teaspoon of basil. Sprinkle the crumb mixture on top of the salmon mixture. Bake at 350° for 25 to 30 minutes or until heated through.

Chef's Note: If you don't have an 11" × 7" baking dish, use a 1½-quart round casserole.

EXTRA HEALTH BENEFITS
Blood Building
Stronger Immunity

Times: Prep: 30 min.
Baking: 25 min.

Makes 4 servings.

Per serving: 345 calories, 5.9 g. fat (15% of calories), 3.8 g. dietary fiber, 30 mg. cholesterol, 377 mg. sodium.

SLIMMING STRATEGY

Sometimes saying a simple phrase to yourself can have an amazing effect on your attitude. When you look at an overloaded buffet table, tell yourself "I'm a person who doesn't eat very much." It just might make you think twice about digging in with both hands. And remember that you're not saying you don't like to eat, just that you can be satisfied with a reasonable amount.

Flounder Baked over Herbed Rice

EXTRA HEALTH BENEFIT
Stronger Immunity

Times: Prep: 15 min.
Cooking: 35 min.
Baking: 20 min.

Makes 4 servings.

Per serving: 311 calories,
3.5 g. fat (10% of calories),
3.7 g. dietary fiber, 55 mg.
cholesterol, 143 mg. sodium.

*To save time when making this dish, prepare the rice ahead.
Then it will be a quick matter to bake the fillets.*

2 **cups defatted low-sodium chicken broth**
1 **cup brown rice**
1 **cup thinly sliced fresh mushrooms**
1 **medium carrot, shredded**
⅓ **cup finely chopped onions**
¾ **teaspoon dried marjoram**
⅛ **teaspoon ground black pepper**
4 **skinless flounder fillets (about 4 ounces each and
   ¼"–½" thick)**
   Pinch of paprika

In a medium saucepan, bring the broth to a boil. Stir in the
rice, mushrooms, carrots, onions, marjoram and pepper. Bring to
a boil, then reduce the heat. Cover and simmer about 35 minutes or until the rice is almost tender and the
water is absorbed.

Spray a 12" × 7½" baking dish with no-stick
spray. Spoon the rice mixture into the baking
dish. Then place the flounder in a single layer on
top of the rice mixture, folding under any thin
edges of the fillets. Sprinkle with the paprika.

Cover the dish with foil and bake at 350° for 20
to 24 minutes or until the fish flakes easily when
tested with a fork and is opaque all the way
through.

Chef's Note: When buying fish, trust your nose.
Fresh fish usually has a faint odor, but it's a clean,
fresh scent. If you can discern a "fishy" smell,
don't buy the product.

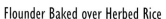
Flounder Baked over Herbed Rice

Salmon-Veggie Burgers

When you want a change of pace from meat burgers, try these fish patties. They're great with lettuce and tomatoes in a bun. They're also good for a more formal dinner. Serve the patties on a mixture of steamed julienned carrots and parsnips. Then drizzle nonfat cucumber or ranch-style salad dressing over the patties.

**EXTRA HEALTH BENEFIT
Stronger Immunity**

Times: Prep: 13 min.
Cooking: 10 min.

Makes 3 servings.

Per serving: 252 calories, 6.7 g. fat (23% of calories), 3.9 g. dietary fiber, 36 mg. cholesterol, 794 mg. sodium.

¼ cup fat-free egg substitute or 2 lightly beaten egg whites
1 small carrot, shredded
1 small onion, finely chopped
1 tablespoon sunflower seeds, ground
2 teaspoons minced fresh parsley or ½ teaspoon dried parsley
   Pinch of dried thyme
   Pinch of dried tarragon
1 can (7 ounces) salmon, drained, flaked and skin removed
3 tablespoons nonfat mayonnaise
3 whole-wheat hamburger buns, split and toasted
3 lettuce leaves
3 tomato slices

In a medium bowl, stir together the egg substitute or egg whites, carrots, onions, sunflower seeds, parsley, thyme and tarragon.

Crush the bones in the salmon. Add the salmon with the bones to the vegetable mixture. Mix until well combined. Form the salmon mixture into 3 patties.

Spray an unheated, medium no-stick skillet with no-stick spray. Heat the skillet over medium heat. Add the patties and cook for 5 minutes. Turn the patties over and cook for 5 to 8 minutes more or until lightly browned and cooked through.

To serve, spread the mayonnaise on the buns and serve the patties in the buns with the lettuce and tomatoes.

Chef's Note: To julienne carrots and parsnips, peel them and then cut them lengthwise into ⅛"-thick slices. Cut those into 2"-long pieces. Finish by cutting the pieces lengthwise into ⅛"-wide matchsticks.

Times: Prep: 18 min.
Broiling: 5 min.

Makes 4 servings.

Per serving: 260 calories, 3.4 g. fat (12% of calories), 2.4 g. dietary fiber, 26 mg. cholesterol, 822 mg. sodium.

SLIMMING STRATEGY

Buy canned tuna packed in water to avoid the extra calories of added oil. If you already have oil-packed tuna in the pantry that you want to use up, place it in a strainer and rinse well with cold water to remove the extra oil.

Tuna and Zucchini Melts

Here's another tuna sandwich, this one a lighter update of an old classic. The zucchini boosts the sandwich's fiber content and adds extra crunch to the filling.

　1　**can (9¼ ounces) tuna (packed in water), drained**
　½　**cup nonfat mayonnaise**
　¼　**cup finely chopped celery**
　¼　**cup shredded zucchini**
　2　**green onions, thinly sliced**
　1　**teaspoon prepared mustard**
　¼　**cup (1 ounce) shredded reduced-fat cheddar cheese**
　4　**English muffins, split and toasted**
　8　**tomato slices**

In a medium bowl, stir together the tuna, mayonnaise, celery, zucchini, onions and mustard until well combined. Then stir in the cheese.

Spread about ¼ cup of the tuna mixture on each English muffin half. Then place the muffins on the rack in a broiling pan. Broil 3" to 4" from the heat about 4 minutes or until the tuna mixture is heated through. Then top each with a tomato slice and broil for 1 to 2 minutes more or until the tomatoes are heated through.

Chef's Note: It's easy to toast all of the English muffin halves at the same time. Arrange them on the rack in a broiling pan and broil for a few minutes, until lightly brown.

Broiled Barbecued Sea Bass

The homemade barbecue sauce really makes this recipe! It's slightly tangy and a little spicy—and nowhere near as high in calories as commercial varieties. You can also use this recipe for swordfish, shark or tuna steaks.

  1 **can (8 ounces) low-sodium tomato sauce**
  3 **tablespoons canned diced green chili peppers or jalapeño peppers**
  2 **tablespoons nonfat clear Italian salad dressing**
  1 **tablespoon finely chopped onions**
  1 **tablespoon honey**
  2 **teaspoons reduced-sodium Worcestershire sauce**
  4 **sea bass steaks (4 ounces each and 1" thick)**

For the sauce, in a small bowl, stir together the tomato sauce, chili or jalapeño peppers, salad dressing, onions, honey and Worcestershire sauce. Transfer 1 cup of the mixture to a small saucepan and set aside until just before serving.

Spray the rack of a broiling pan with no-stick spray. Place the bass on the rack. Broil 3" to 4" from the heat for 4 minutes. Turn the bass over and generously brush with the remaining sauce. Broil for 6 to 8 minutes more or until the fish flakes easily when tested with a fork, brushing occasionally with the remaining sauce.

Just before serving, bring the sauce in the saucepan just to a boil. Serve the warm sauce with the bass.

Chef's Note: On a bright summer day, grill the bass instead of broiling it. Spray the unheated grill rack with no-stick spray. Light the grill according to the manufacturer's instructions. Then place the fish on the rack and grill, uncovered, directly over the coals for 8 to 12 minutes or until done.

Broiled Barbecued Sea Bass

Extra Health Benefit
Stronger Immunity

Times: Prep: 12 min.
Broiling: 10 min.

Makes 4 servings.

Per serving: 191 calories, 5.1 g. fat (25% of calories), 1.0 g. dietary fiber, 58 mg. cholesterol, 189 mg. sodium.

Grilled Snapper with Tomato Salsa and Black Beans

Grilled Snapper with Tomato Salsa and Black Beans

If you're short on time, broil the fish instead of grilling it—you won't have to wait for the grill to heat up.

¾ **cup chopped tomatoes**

2 **tablespoons minced fresh cilantro or fresh parsley**

1 **tablespoon balsamic vinegar**

2 **red snapper fillets with skin (4 ounces each and ½" thick)**

1 **cup canned black beans, rinsed, drained and heated**
   Lime wedges (optional)
   Cilantro or parsley sprigs (optional)

For the salsa, in a small bowl, stir together the tomatoes, minced cilantro or parsley and vinegar. Cover and let stand at room temperature to blend the flavors while grilling or broiling the red snapper.

To grill: To prepare the grill for cooking, spray the unheated grill rack with no-stick spray. Then light the grill according to the manufacturer's directions. Place the rack on the grill. Place the fillets on the rack, skin side down, over the coals. Grill, uncovered, about 5 minutes or until the fish flakes easily when tested with a fork and is opaque all the way through.

To broil: Spray the rack of a broiling pan with no-stick spray. Place the red snapper on the rack, skin side down. Broil 4" from the heat about 5 minutes or until done.

To serve, spoon the salsa over the red snapper and serve with the beans. If desired, garnish each serving with the lime wedges and cilantro or parsley sprigs.

Quick

EXTRA HEALTH BENEFIT
Cancer Protection

Times: Prep: 5 min.
Grilling/broiling: 5 min.

Makes 2 servings.

Per serving: 264 calories, 2.2 g. fat (8% of calories), 0.7 g. dietary fiber, 42 mg. cholesterol, 625 mg. sodium.

SLIMMING STRATEGY

Expand your culinary horizons with dishes from Mexico, India and Middle Eastern countries. These foods usually feature rice or beans and only small amounts of meat, fish or poultry—all of which combines to give you meals that are low in fat and high in fiber.

Taste the Difference

Are you all at sea when it comes to choosing fish that'll tickle your taste buds? Flounder no more. Here are some tips to guide your selection.

Cod. Delicate in flavor, cod has medium-firm flesh. Atlantic cod, harvested in waters from Virginia to the Arctic, tends to be a bit sweeter than Pacific cod.

Catfish. If farm raised, catfish has a delicate to mild flavor with a slightly sweet taste. Wild catfish usually has a richer flavor that may not be to everyone's liking.

Flounder and sole. These two fish are sweet and delicate. Because of their similarities, they are interchangeable in many recipes.

Grouper. Both the red and black species are delicate to mild in flavor. Because its meat is firm and doesn't easily break apart during cooking, this fish is excellent for chowders, stews and grilling.

Haddock. Like cod and flounder, haddock has a delicate flavor. Serve it poached, steamed or grilled with either a mild sauce or a sprinkling of lemon juice and salt-free seasoning.

Halibut. This fish has a delicate, sweet flavor. Because it's a fine-grained, medium-firm fish, it's ideal for kabobs and stir-fries.

Mahimahi. Also known as dolphinfish (no relation to Flipper), mahimahi ranks among the most popular finfish

these days. That's due in part to its flavorful, moderately fatty, medium-firm flesh.

Monkfish. Nicknamed "poor man's lobster," monkfish has the mild flavor and firm flesh characteristic of its namesake. For best results, don't overcook it or you'll lose that texture.

Orange roughy. Orange roughy has delicate flesh, similar to founder, and a mild flavor that's perhaps a shade stronger than flounder. Native to New Zealand, it's become a favorite in this country.

Red snapper. This fish is lean and moist with a delicate flavor. Fish harvested at two to four pounds have metallic pink skin. But as they grow larger, their skin darkens, hence the name red snapper.

Salmon. Depending upon the species, salmon can range from mild to full flavored. Atlantic salmon tends to be the lightest in flavor, followed by coho, chum, pink, sockeye and chinook or king.

Swordfish. Usually sold in steak form, swordfish has a full flavor; its firm texture is similar to tuna. It's ideal for kabobs.

Tuna. Tuna ranges from mild to rich in flavor and from dusky white to dark red in color. As you might expect, lighter-colored pieces have the milder flavor.

Tex-Mex Tuna
with Pineapple-Cilantro Salsa

The crowning glory of this Tex-Mex dish is the easy pineapple-cilantro salsa. It's equally delicious with other fish as well as grilled shrimp or scallops.

> 1 **can (8 ounces) crushed pineapple (packed in juice)**
> 1 **tablespoon minced fresh cilantro or parsley**
> 2 **teaspoons canola oil**
> ¼ **teaspoon ground cumin**
> ⅛ **teaspoon ground nutmeg**
> ⅛ **teaspoon ground red pepper**
> 4 **tuna steaks (1 pound total), cut 1" thick**

In a strainer over a small bowl, drain the pineapple. Transfer the pineapple to another small bowl.

To the pineapple, add the cilantro or parsley; set aside. To the juice, add the oil, cumin, nutmeg and pepper.

Spray the rack of a broiling pan with no-stick spray. Place the tuna on the rack. Brush with the juice mixture. Broil 3" to 4" from the heat for 4 minutes. Turn over and brush again with the juice mixture. Broil for 6 to 8 minutes more or until the fish flakes easily when tested with a fork, brushing occasionally with the juice mixture. Serve with the salsa.

Chef's Note: If you're using frozen fish steaks, thaw them before broiling. The safest method is to place the unopened package in the refrigerator for 8 hours or overnight. When you buy frozen fish, make sure the package is rock solid, with no soft spots. And be wary of boxes that have noticeable frost or ice crystals on them. They indicate that the fish has thawed and refrozen.

Quick

EXTRA HEALTH BENEFITS
Better Blood Pressure
Stronger Immunity

Times: Prep: 13 min.
Broiling: 10 min.

Makes 4 servings.

Per serving: 143 calories, 2.1 g. fat (14% of calories), 0.3 g. dietary fiber, 45 mg. cholesterol, 38 mg. sodium.

Tex-Mex Tuna
with Pineapple-Cilantro Salsa

Teriyaki
Swordfish Kabobs

Sensational Fish and Seafood

Teriyaki Swordfish Kabobs

Swordfish has a dense, meaty texture that's ideal for kabobs. Here we pair the fish with red peppers and pineapple for a double dose of vitamin C.

1 **pound swordfish steaks, cut 1" thick**
1 **can (15¼ ounces) pineapple chunks (packed in juice)**
2 **tablespoons reduced-sodium soy sauce**
2 **teaspoons canola oil**
1 **teaspoon sesame seeds, toasted**
½ **teaspoon ground ginger**
1 **small sweet red pepper, cut into 1" pieces**

Cut the swordfish into ¾" pieces. Remove and discard the skin and bones. Place the swordfish in a large self-closing bag; set aside.

In a strainer over a small bowl, drain the pineapple; set aside. Transfer ⅓ cup of the juice to another small bowl. (Reserve the remaining juice for another use.) To the ⅓ cup of juice, stir in the soy sauce, oil, sesame seeds and ginger. Pour over the swordfish in the bag. Seal the bag and marinate in the refrigerator for 30 to 45 minutes, turning the bag occasionally.

Spray the rack of a broiling pan with no-stick spray. Drain the swordfish well and discard the marinade.

Thread the swordfish, pineapple chunks and pepper pieces onto metal skewers, leaving a small space between the pieces. Place the kabobs on the broiler pan. Broil 3" to 4" from the heat for 4 to 6 minutes or until the fish flakes easily when tested with a fork and is opaque all the way through.

Chef's Note: To toast the sesame seeds, place them in a thin layer in a shallow baking pan. Bake at 350° for a few minutes or until golden; shake the pan once or twice as the seeds bake and also as they cool to keep hot spots from burning them.

EXTRA HEALTH BENEFIT
Stronger Immunity

Times: Prep: 14 min.
Marinating: 30 min.
Broiling: 4 min.

Makes 4 servings.

Per serving: 248 calories, 7.3 g. fat (26% of calories), 1.4 g. dietary fiber, 44 mg. cholesterol, 404 mg. sodium.

SLIMMING STRATEGY

Almost any way you measure it, fish is a wise choice. But spare your fish the deep fryer. Fried fillets are about 65 percent fat; the same fish when baked contains less than half that much.

Green and Gold Stir-Fry of Shrimp

What a beautiful dish!

12	**ounces shrimp, peeled and deveined**
½	**teaspoon grated orange peel**
¾	**cup orange juice**
2	**tablespoons reduced-sodium soy sauce**
1	**tablespoon cornstarch**
2	**teaspoons honey**
1	**tablespoon canola oil**
1	**teaspoon grated ginger root**
1	**medium onion, cut into thin wedges**
1	**small yellow summer squash, thinly sliced**
1	**cup broccoli florets**
1	**cup snow peas, ends and strings removed**
3	**cups hot cooked rice or couscous**

Pat the shrimp dry with paper towels; set aside. In a small bowl, stir together the orange peel, orange juice, soy sauce, cornstarch and honey; set aside.

Spray an unheated, large no-stick stir-fry pan or skillet with no-stick spray. Add 1 teaspoon of the oil and swirl to coat the bottom of the pan or skillet. Heat over medium-high heat. Add the ginger and stir-fry for 30 seconds. Then add the onions, squash, broccoli and snow peas. Stir-fry about 4 minutes or until the vegetables are crisp-tender. Transfer to a plate.

Add the remaining 2 teaspoons of oil to the pan or skillet and heat over medium-high heat. Then add the shrimp and stir-fry about 2 minutes or until the shrimp turn pink. Push the shrimp to the edge of the pan or skillet.

Add the juice mixture to the center of the pan or skillet. Cook and stir until the mixture thickens and begins to gently boil. Then return the vegetables to the pan or skillet and stir in the shrimp. Cook and stir about 1 minute more or until the vegetables are heated through. Serve the shrimp mixture over the rice or couscous.

Chef's Note: If you can't find peeled and deveined shrimp, buy 1 pound of shrimp in the shell. Use your fingers to pull off the shells. Then use the tip of a sharp paring knife to make a small slit down the back of each; pull out the tiny black vein that may be present.

EXTRA HEALTH BENEFITS
Blood Building
Stronger Immunity

Times: Prep: 15 min.
Cooking: 8 min.

Makes 4 servings.

Per serving: 389 calories, 5.4 g. fat (13% of calories), 4.6 g. dietary fiber, 109 mg. cholesterol, 420 mg. sodium.

SLIMMING STRATEGY

Although shrimp contains more cholesterol than fish, it's very low in fat—especially saturated fat—so it's a perfectly good diet-wise food. If you're concerned about the cholesterol count, remember that doctors say saturated fat raises your body's cholesterol level more than dietary cholesterol does.

Shrimp with Broccoli Rabe and Fettuccine

Broccoli rabe is a delicious vegetable that resembles thin leafy stalks of broccoli. Its distinctive bitter flavor blends well with shrimp.

Extra Health Benefits
Blood Building
Stronger Immunity

Times: Prep: 10 min.
Cooking: 18 min.

Makes 4 servings.

Per serving: 471 calories, 7.4 g. fat (14% of calories), 4.7 g. dietary fiber, 110 mg. cholesterol, 353 mg. sodium.

10	ounces fettuccine
1	small bunch broccoli rabe, tough stems removed
2	teaspoons olive oil
½	cup reconstituted and chopped sun-dried tomatoes
1	tablespoon pine nuts
4	cloves garlic, minced
¼	teaspoon crushed red pepper
12	ounces medium shrimp, peeled and deveined
1	cup canned chick-peas (garbanzo beans), rinsed and drained
½	cup defatted low-sodium chicken broth
2½	tablespoons balsamic vinegar
2	tablespoons finely shredded Parmesan cheese

Cook the fettucine according to the package directions, but without adding the salt.

Meanwhile, remove and discard the outer leaves from the broccoli rabe. Cut into bite-size pieces; set aside.

Add the oil to a large no-stick skillet and heat over medium heat. Add the broccoli rabe, tomatoes, pine nuts, garlic and pepper. Cook and stir for 5 to 7 minutes or until the broccoli rabe is crisp-tender, adding 1 to 2 tablespoons of water if necessary to prevent sticking.

Stir in the shrimp, chick-peas, broth and vinegar. Cook, uncovered, for 4 to 6 minutes more or until the liquid is slightly reduced and the shrimp have turned pink.

Drain the fettuccine, rinse with hot water and drain again. Transfer to a large serving bowl. Add the broccoli rabe mixture and toss until well mixed. Before serving, sprinkle with the cheese.

Chef's Note: Other names for broccoli rabe include broccoli di rape, broccoli raab, brocoletti di rape and rapini.

Sunshine Shrimp Kabobs

Just a small amount of oil is used in the sauce to keep the shrimp moist during broiling. Use canola oil, because it has a bland flavor that won't overpower the other ingredients in this dish.

- 3 **large carrots, cut diagonally into 1" pieces**
- 1 **small yellow or green pepper, cut into 1" pieces**
- ¼ **cup water**
- 12 **ounces medium shrimp, peeled and deveined**
- ½ **teaspoon grated orange peel**
- ½ **cup orange juice**
- 2 **teaspoons canola oil**
- 2 **teaspoons minced fresh thyme or ¾ teaspoon dried thyme**

In a small saucepan, combine the carrots, peppers and water. Bring to a boil, then reduce the heat. Cover and simmer for 3 minutes, then drain well.

Thread the shrimp, carrots and peppers onto metal skewers, leaving a small space between the pieces. Spray the rack of a broiling pan with no-stick spray. Place the kabobs on the rack.

In a small bowl, stir together the orange peel, orange juice, oil and thyme. Generously brush the kabobs with the juice mixture. Broil 3" to 4" from the heat for 2 minutes. Turn the kabobs over and brush again with the juice mixture. Broil for 2 to 3 minutes more or until the shrimp turn pink.

Chef's Note: For an elegant dinner, serve these colorful kabobs on a bed of long-grain and wild rice.

EXTRA HEALTH BENEFITS
Better Blood Pressure
Stronger Immunity

Times: Prep: 17 min.
Cooking: 3 min.
Broiling: 4 min.

Makes 4 servings.

Per serving: 139 calories, 3.7 g. fat (24% of calories), 2.3 g. dietary fiber, 109 mg. cholesterol, 126 mg. sodium.

Sunshine Shrimp Kabobs

Curried Prawns and New Potatoes over Rice

You can make this dish as spicy as you like by varying the amount of curry powder. For even more kick, choose Madras curry powder, which tends to be spicier.

　8　**new potatoes, quartered**
　¾　**cup defatted low-sodium chicken broth**
1–2　**teaspoons curry powder**
1½　**teaspoons onion powder**
　⅛　**teaspoon garlic powder**
　1　**cup frozen peas**
　12　**ounces shrimp, peeled, deveined and cooked**
　½　**cup nonfat plain yogurt**
　2　**tablespoons unbleached flour**
　3　**cups hot cooked long-grain rice**

In a large saucepan, combine the potatoes, broth, curry powder, onion powder and garlic powder. Bring to a boil, then reduce the heat. Cover and cook for 6 minutes. Stir in the peas. Cover and cook for 3 minutes more or just until the vegetables are tender.

Stir the shrimp into the vegetable mixture. Return to a boil. Meanwhile, in a small bowl, stir together the yogurt and flour.

Stir the yogurt mixture into the shrimp mixture. Cook and stir until the mixture gently boils. Then cook and stir for 1 minute more. Serve over the rice.

Chef's Note: If you can't find new potatoes in your market, use 2 or 3 medium potatoes and cut them into 1" pieces before cooking.

Bayou Shrimp and Oysters

Oysters add a fillip of rich flavor to this Creole shrimp dish.

¾ cup defatted low-sodium chicken broth
1 medium onion, chopped
2 stalks celery, chopped
2 medium tomatoes, seeded and chopped
2 cloves garlic, minced
1 tablespoon minced fresh basil or 1 teaspoon dried basil
1 teaspoon reduced-sodium Worcestershire sauce
½ teaspoon hot-pepper sauce
8 ounces shrimp, peeled and deveined
4 ounces shucked oysters, drained
2 tablespoons water
4 teaspoons cornstarch
3 cups hot cooked brown rice

In a large saucepan, stir together the broth, onions, celery, tomatoes, garlic, basil, Worcestershire sauce and hot-pepper sauce. Bring to a boil, then reduce the heat. Cover and simmer about 10 minutes or until the vegetables are tender.

Stir in the shrimp and oysters. Cook, uncovered, over low heat about 4 minutes or until the shrimp turn pink and the oysters are opaque.

Meanwhile, in a small bowl, stir together the water and cornstarch. Then stir into the shrimp mixture. Cook and stir over low heat until the mixture thickens and begins to gently boil. Cook and stir for 2 minutes more. Serve the shrimp mixture over the rice.

EXTRA HEALTH BENEFITS
Blood Building
Stronger Immunity

Times: Prep: 18 min.
Cooking: 16 min.

Makes 4 servings.

Per serving: 280 calories, 3.3 g. fat (11% of calories), 4.2 g. dietary fiber, 80 mg. cholesterol, 149 mg. sodium.

SLIMMING STRATEGY

Don't let numbers trip you up. Although doctors recommend a diet that gets less than 30 percent of calories from fat, not every food you eat has to beat that number. And sometimes a high percentage is downright misleading. Oysters, for instance, weigh in at 33 percent——but they contain so few grams of fat that the percentage is meaningless.

Safety First

Seafood is extremely perishable. And spoiled fish can do more than leave a bad taste in your mouth——it can make you sick. Here are some ways to ensure that the finfish and shellfish you buy make it to your table in fine flavor and good health (yours).

• Never let seafood sit in a hot car. Either go straight home and refrigerate it or have the fish market pack it in ice for you. (And even then, don't dally getting home.)

• Store all seafood in the refrigerator at 32° to 38° for no more than a day or two. Very often, the area right under the freezer and the meat compartment are the coldest parts.

• To store fresh fish, remove it from its package, rinse it under cold water and pat it dry with paper towels. Place the fish in a single layer on a wire rack in a shallow pan and cover the whole container tightly with plastic wrap. If you leave the fish sitting in its own juices, the flesh will deteriorate more rapidly.

• Refrigerate live clams, mussels and oysters in a container covered with a clean, damp towel. Do not put them in an airtight container. Their shells may open naturally but should close tightly when tapped. If they don't, discard them.

• Store shucked oysters, scallops and clams in the refrigerator with ice packed around the container.

• Store frozen products at 0° and use within two months. Thaw in the refrigerator, or defrost in your microwave (follow the manufacturer's directions carefully to keep from cooking portions of the fish).

• Wash your hands thoroughly with hot soapy water before and after handling raw seafood.

• Don't use the plate that held the raw product to serve it in unless you wash it well. Raw juices will contaminate the cooked product.

• Just before cooking, scrub the shells of mussels, clams and oysters. Rinse shucked oysters, mussels, clams, shrimp, scallops and such under cold water to remove any surface bacteria.

• If marinating seafood, do so in the refrigerator, never at room temperature.

• Although you don't want to overcook seafood, it's important to make sure it's done. The flesh of fish will be opaque and begin to flake easily when tested with a fork at the thickest part. Mussels, clams and oysters in the shell will open; discard any that stay shut. Shrimp will curl up and turn pink. Scallops will become opaque.

Cream-Sauced Seafood over Fettuccine

Evaporated skim milk and chicken broth—thickened with flour—produce a really creamy sauce that's superlow in fat.

  8 ounces fettuccine
  1 cup defatted low-sodium chicken broth
  6 green onions, thinly sliced
  1 tablespoon minced fresh basil
  1 clove garlic, minced
  ⅛ teaspoon ground black pepper
  1 cup evaporated skim milk
  3 tablespoons unbleached flour
  8 ounces shrimp, peeled, deveined and cooked
  4 ounces cooked crabmeat or lobster meat
  1 cup snow peas, ends and strings removed

Cook the fettuccine according to the package directions, but without adding the salt.

Meanwhile, spray an unheated medium saucepan with no-stick spray. In the saucepan, combine the broth, onions, basil, garlic and pepper. Bring to a boil.

In a medium bowl, use a wire whisk to stir together the milk and flour until smooth. Then stir into the broth mixture. Cook and stir over medium heat until the mixture thickens and begins to gently boil. Cook and stir for 1 minute more.

Stir in the shrimp, crabmeat or lobster and snow peas. Cook and stir about 3 minutes or until the seafood is heated through. Serve over the fettuccine.

EXTRA HEALTH BENEFITS
Blood Building
Stronger Immunity

Times: Prep: 22 min.
Cooking: 10 min.

Makes 4 servings.

Per serving: 401 calories, 3.0 g. fat (7% of calories), 1.3 g. dietary fiber, 109 mg. cholesterol, 230 mg. sodium.

Cream-Sauced Seafood over Fettuccine

EXTRA HEALTH BENEFITS
Cancer Protection
Stronger Immunity

Times: Prep: 10 min.
Cooking: 4 min.

Makes 4 servings.

Per serving: 118 calories,
2.4 g. fat (18% of calories),
1.5 g. dietary fiber, 28 mg.
cholesterol, 177 mg. sodium.

Herbed Scallops with Tomatoes

Thyme, rosemary and a touch of red pepper complement the scallops and tomatoes in this dish. For healthy accompaniments, round out the meal with couscous and a big tossed salad.

12 ounces scallops
 1 tablespoon reduced-calorie margarine
 ¾ teaspoon dried thyme
 ¼ teaspoon dried rosemary
 ⅛ teaspoon ground red pepper
 1 large onion, cut into thin wedges
 2 large tomatoes, cut into thin wedges
 1 tablespoon lemon juice

Pat the scallops dry with paper towels. Then cut any large scallops into 1" pieces. In a large skillet, melt the margarine with the thyme, rosemary and pepper over medium-high heat, stirring constantly.

Add the scallops and onions. Cook and stir about 3 minutes or until the scallops are opaque. (If the scallops water out during cooking, use a slotted spoon to remove the scallops and onions. Cook the liquid over medium heat until most of it has evaporated. Then return the scallops and onions to the skillet.)

Add the tomatoes and lemon juice. Cook about 1 minute or just until the tomatoes are heated through, stirring occasionally.

Key West Crab Salad

EXTRA HEALTH BENEFIT
Stronger Immunity

Time: Prep: 19 min.

Makes 4 servings.

Per serving: 181 calories, 4.2 g. fat (20% of calories), 4.1 g. dietary fiber, 85 mg. cholesterol, 279 mg. sodium.

This will win rave reviews at your next luncheon. (And no one will even guess that this is a low-fat dish!)

- 3 **cups torn spinach**
- 2 **cups torn leaf lettuce**
- 1 **cup finely shredded cabbage**
- 2 **medium oranges, peeled and sectioned**
- 1 **small red onion, sliced and separated into rings**
- 12 **ounces cooked crabmeat, broken into bite-size chunks**
- ½ **teaspoon grated orange peel**
- 3 **tablespoons orange juice**
- 2 **tablespoons balsamic vinegar**
- 2 **teaspoons olive or canola oil**
- 1 **teaspoon minced fresh tarragon or ¼ teaspoon dried tarragon**

In a large bowl, combine the spinach, lettuce, cabbage, oranges and onions. Add the crabmeat and gently toss until combined; set aside.

In small jar with a tight-fitting cover, combine the orange peel, orange juice, vinegar, oil and tarragon. Cover and shake until well combined. Pour over the spinach mixture and gently toss until coated.

Chef's Note: For variety, replace the crab with cooked fresh tuna, shrimp or lobster.

Key West Crab Salad

Pasta with Red Clam Sauce

Clams are quite low in calories, fat and cholesterol. And the canned ones used in this recipe are ultraconvenient for perking up tomato sauce.

- 8 **ounces fettuccine or spaghetti**
- 1 **can (16 ounces) low-sodium stewed tomatoes (with juices)**
- 1 **can (8 ounces) low-sodium tomato sauce**
- 1 **teaspoon onion powder**
- 1 **teaspoon dried Italian seasoning**
- ¼ **teaspoon celery seeds**
- ⅛ **teaspoon ground black pepper**
- 1 **large carrot, shredded**
- 2 **teaspoons cornstarch**
- 1 **can (6½ ounces) chopped clams, rinsed and drained**

Cook the fettuccine or spaghetti according to the package directions, but without adding the salt. Drain, rinse with hot water and drain again.

Meanwhile, drain and set aside 2 tablespoons of the juice from the tomatoes. In a medium saucepan, combine the tomatoes (with remaining juices), tomato sauce, onion powder, Italian seasoning, celery seeds and pepper. Bring to a boil and stir in the carrots. Reduce the heat, cover and simmer for 5 minutes.

In a small bowl, stir together the cornstarch and the reserved 2 tablespoons of tomato juice. Then stir the cornstarch mixture and clams into the tomato mixture. Cook and stir over medium heat until the mixture thickens and begins to gently boil. Cook and stir for 2 minutes more. Serve over the pasta.

Chef's Note: For a real treat—when you've got the time—steam some small clams, such as littleneck or butter clams, remove them from their shells and add them to the tomato sauce.

Quick

EXTRA HEALTH BENEFITS
Blood Building
Stronger Immunity

Times: Prep: 14 min.
Cooking: 7 min.

Makes 4 servings.

Per serving: 313 calories, 1.5 g. fat (4% of calories), 2.2 g. dietary fiber, 17 mg. cholesterol, 75 mg. sodium.

SLIMMING STRATEGY

Quite often, the directions for cooking pasta call for adding oil to the water. That's to keep the noodles from sticking together. But if you stir the pasta occasionally as it cooks and are careful not to overcook it, you really won't need the oil. As an extra precaution, however, you could give the drained noodles a spritz of no-stick spray and toss them lightly.

Steamed Clams with Lemon Dipping Sauce

Steamed Clams
with Lemon Dipping Sauce

This tangy dipping sauce is a delicious and healthy alternative to the lemon butter typically served with steamed clams.

> 4 **cups water**
> 18 **cherrystone clams, scrubbed**
> 2 **tablespoons lemon juice**
> 1 **tablespoon honey**
> 2 **teaspoons cornstarch**

Bring 3½ cups of the water to a boil in a 4-quart Dutch oven. Place the clams in a steamer basket and set the basket in the Dutch oven, making sure the basket sits above the water. Cover the Dutch oven and steam for 5 to 10 minutes or until the clams open and the flesh is plump. Discard any clams that did not open.

Meanwhile, for the sauce, in a small saucepan, use a wire whisk to stir together ½ cup of the water, the lemon juice, honey and cornstarch. Cook and stir over medium heat until the mixture thickens and begins to gently boil. Cook and stir for 2 minutes more. Serve with the clams.

Chef's Note: When buying clams in the shell, look for those that are tightly closed. That indicates they're alive. If the shells are slightly agape, tap them lightly with your finger. They should close—don't buy them if they remain open. The same advice applies to mussels and oysters.

Quick

EXTRA HEALTH BENEFITS
Better Blood Pressure
Cancer Protection
Blood Building
Stronger Immunity

Times: Prep: 10 min.
Steaming: 5 min.
Cooking: 2 min.

Makes 2 servings.

Per serving: 180 calories, 1.8 g. fat (9% of calories), 0.2 g. dietary fiber, 62 mg. cholesterol, 116 mg. sodium.

Lean Vegetarian Cuisine

Broccoli and White
Beans Baked in Phyllo
(page 230)

Vegetarian Paella

EXTRA HEALTH BENEFITS
Lower Cholesterol
Blood Building
Stronger Immunity

Times: Prep: 5 min.
Cooking: 9 min.
Standing: 10 min.

Makes 4 servings.

Per serving: 444 calories,
8.7 g. fat (17% of calories),
11.5 g. dietary fiber, 0 mg.
cholesterol, 247 mg. sodium.

Slim down Spain's national dish by adding lots of vegetables and using tofu instead of the traditional fatty sausages. Cut preparation time by using quick-cooking couscous, which takes less time than rice.

  2   teaspoons canola oil
  8   ounces firm tofu, cubed
  1   large sweet red pepper, cut into strips
  1   cup chopped onions
  2   cloves garlic, minced
2½   cups crushed canned tomatoes (with juices)
  1   package (10 ounces) frozen artichoke hearts, thawed
1½   cups frozen corn
  1   cup frozen peas
1½   cups defatted low-sodium chicken broth
  ½   teaspoon dried thyme
  ⅛   teaspoon ground saffron
  1   cup couscous

Add the oil to a paella pan or large skillet and heat over medium heat. Add the tofu, peppers, onions and garlic. Cook and stir for 4 to 5 minutes or until the tofu is golden.

Stir in the tomatoes (with juices), artichokes, corn and peas. Bring to a boil, then reduce the heat. Simmer, uncovered, for 5 to 7 minutes or until the vegetables are tender and the liquid slightly thickens.

Add the broth, thyme and saffron. Bring to a boil, then stir in the couscous. Remove the pan or skillet from the heat. Cover and let stand for 10 minutes. Before serving, use a fork to fluff the couscous.

Chef's Note: Be sure to use a paella pan or large skillet because couscous expands a great deal when cooked. For a nuttier taste, use whole-wheat couscous. You can find it at health-food stores.

SLIMMING STRATEGY

Tofu is a high-protein soy-bean product that can substitute for meat in many recipes. Although it contains fat (5.5 grams in 3 ounces), the fat is mostly the healthy mono-unsaturated and poly-unsaturated types. And there's no cholesterol.

Red Peppers Stuffed with Saffron Rice and Feta

Saffron gives the rice stuffing in these peppers the yellow color and distinctive flavor of Spanish paella.

Quick

EXTRA HEALTH BENEFITS
Lower Cholesterol
Stronger Immunity

Times: Cooking: 2 min.
Prep: 10 min.
Broiling: 10 min.

Makes 4 servings.

Per serving: 253 calories, 7.1 g. fat (24% of calories), 4.1 g. dietary fiber, 14 mg. cholesterol, 161 mg. sodium.

  4 medium sweet red peppers
2½ cups cooked rice
  4 ounces feta cheese, crumbled
½ cup chopped green onions
¼ cup pimento-stuffed olives, slightly chopped
¼ cup defatted low-sodium chicken broth
  3 tablespoons slivered almonds
½ teaspoon cumin
⅛ teaspoon ground saffron

Bring a large saucepan of water to a boil. Slice off the stem ends of the peppers and remove the seeds and membranes.

Place the peppers in the boiling water for 2 minutes, remove and rinse with very cold water. Drain well and transfer to an 8" × 8" baking pan.

In a medium bowl, combine the rice, cheese, onions, olives, broth, almonds, cumin and saffron. Spoon into the peppers. Broil 3" to 4" from the heat for 10 to 12 minutes.

Red Peppers Stuffed
with Saffron Rice and Feta

Lean Vegetarian Cuisine

Creole Couscous with Cucumbers in Spicy Sour Cream

EXTRA HEALTH BENEFITS
Lower Cholesterol
Blood Building
Stronger Immunity

Times: Prep: 10 min.
Cooking: 19 min.

Makes 4 servings.

Per serving: 419 calories,
4.3 g. fat (9% of calories),
16.4 g. dietary fiber, 0 mg.
cholesterol, 161 mg. sodium.

Here's a recipe with true Creole flavor but without the fat that's sometimes the hallmark of this cuisine.

   1 **small bunch broccoli**
   2 **teaspoons olive oil**
   1 **cup thinly sliced carrots**
  ½ **cup chopped onions**
   1 **can (16 ounces) low-sodium stewed tomatoes (with juices)**
   2 **tablespoons low-sodium tomato paste**
  ⅛ **teaspoon ground red pepper**
   1 **cup nonfat sour cream**
  ¼ **cup seeded and chopped cucumbers**
  ½ **teaspoon ground cumin**
 1½ **cups defatted low-sodium chicken broth**
  ½ **teaspoon dried thyme**
   1 **cup couscous**
   1 **package (10 ounces) frozen okra, thawed**
   1 **cup canned red kidney beans, rinsed and drained**

Remove and discard the outer leaves and stalks from the broccoli. Separate the florets into small pieces; set aside.

Add the oil to a large no-stick skillet and heat over medium heat. Add the broccoli, carrots and onions. Cook and stir for 5 to 7 minutes or until the vegetables are crisp-tender. Add the tomatoes (with juices), tomato paste and pepper. Bring to a boil, then reduce the heat. Simmer, uncovered, for 10 minutes, stirring frequently.

Meanwhile, in a small bowl, stir together the sour cream, cucumbers and cumin; set aside.

In a medium saucepan, bring the broth and thyme to a boil. Stir in the couscous. Remove the saucepan from the heat. Cover and let stand for 5 minutes.

Add the okra and beans to the tomato mixture. Bring to a boil, then reduce the heat. Cover and simmer for 4 to 5 minutes or until the okra is tender (do not overcook).

To serve, use a fork to fluff the couscous. Spoon the couscous

SLIMMING STRATEGY

Beware of the "fudge factor." This is the tendency to underestimate how much you eat and overestimate how much you exercise. One researcher found that a group of dieters honestly believed they ate an average of 1,000 calories a day but really were consuming nearly 2,100 calories. So until you can eyeball a portion size correctly, measure out your food.

onto a large platter. Then spoon the tomato mixture on top. Serve with the sour cream mixture.

Chef's Note: If you'd like, you can use fresh okra. Buy about a pound of small, young pods about 3" long. Look for pods that are clean, fresh and bright and that snap crisply when broken in half. Trim off the ends and slice the pods into ½" pieces. Add as directed in the recipe and simmer just until tender.

Quick-Stuffed Tomatoes

Here's a perfect dish to serve when summer-fresh tomatoes and herbs are plentiful.

   4 **large tomatoes**
 1½ **cups defatted low-sodium chicken broth**
  ½ **cup sun-dried tomatoes, chopped**
   1 **cup couscous**
  ¼ **cup (1 ounce) shredded nonfat mozzarella cheese**
  ¼ **cup chopped and loosely packed fresh basil**
   2 **tablespoons minced fresh mint**
  ¼ **teaspoon ground black pepper**

Cut the fresh tomatoes crosswise in half and scoop out the pulp. Coarsely chop the pulp; set aside. Invert the tomato shells on paper towels to drain.

In a small saucepan, bring the broth and sun-dried tomatoes to a boil. Remove the saucepan from the heat and stir in the couscous. Cover and let stand for 5 minutes.

Stir in the cheese, basil, mint and pepper. Then gently stir in the tomato pulp.

Place the tomato shells in an 11" × 7" baking dish. Spoon the couscous mixture into the shells, pressing the mixture firmly into the shells. Bake at 375° for 25 to 30 minutes or until heated through.

Chef's Note: To assure the success of this recipe, select firm, ripe tomatoes. Make sure to leave the shells thick enough so they won't crack when you stuff them.

EXTRA HEALTH BENEFITS
Lower Cholesterol
Better Blood Pressure
Cancer Protection
Stronger Immunity

Times: Prep: 15 min.
Baking: 25 min.

Makes 4 servings.

Per serving: 253 calories, 1.3 g. fat (4% of calories), 9.6 g. dietary fiber, 1 mg. cholesterol, 123 mg. sodium.

Bombay Rice with Mango Salsa

EXTRA HEALTH BENEFITS
Blood Building
Stronger Immunity

Times: Prep: 10 min.
Cooking: 20 min.

Makes 4 servings.

Per serving: 424 calories,
7.7 g. fat (16% of calories),
4.8 g. dietary fiber, 25 mg.
cholesterol, 378 mg. sodium.

Treat your taste buds to an unexpected flavor combination. The sweetness of the mangoes and raisins is accentuated by the saltiness of the feta cheese in this not-so-typical Indian entrée.

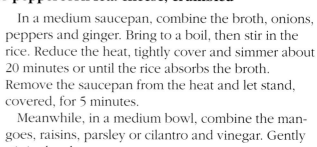

- 2½ **cups defatted low-sodium chicken broth**
- 1 **cup chopped green onions**
- 1 **cup chopped sweet red peppers**
- 1 **tablespoon grated ginger root**
- 1 **cup long-grain rice**
- 1 **medium ripe mango, peeled and coarsely chopped**
- 1 **cup raisins**
- ½ **cup chopped and loosely packed parsley or cilantro**
- 2 **teaspoons red wine vinegar**
- 4 **ounces peppercorn feta cheese, crumbled**

In a medium saucepan, combine the broth, onions, peppers and ginger. Bring to a boil, then stir in the rice. Reduce the heat, tightly cover and simmer about 20 minutes or until the rice absorbs the broth. Remove the saucepan from the heat and let stand, covered, for 5 minutes.

Meanwhile, in a medium bowl, combine the mangoes, raisins, parsley or cilantro and vinegar. Gently stir in the cheese.

Gently stir the mango mixture into the rice. Use a fork to fluff and separate the rice.

Chef's Note: For variety and a little added heat, sprinkle the rice with crushed red pepper.

Bombay Rice
with Mango Salsa

Hawaiian Fried Rice

Popular throughout Asia, fried rice is a flavorful way to use up leftovers. The only drawback is that it's often high in fat. To come up with this skinny version, we cut back on oil and used egg substitute instead of whole eggs.

¼ **cup defatted low-sodium chicken broth**
2 **tablespoons reduced-sodium soy sauce**
1 **tablespoon grated ginger root**
2 **teaspoons hoisin sauce**
¼ **teaspoon crushed red pepper**
3 **teaspoons peanut oil**
1 **cup fat-free egg substitute**
8 **ounces snow peas, ends and strings removed**
1 **cup drained canned baby corn**
½ **cup drained canned sliced water chestnuts**
4 **cups cooked rice**
1 **cup canned pineapple chunks (packed in juice), drained**

In a small bowl, stir together the broth, soy sauce, ginger, hoisin sauce and pepper; set aside.

Add 1 teaspoon of the oil to a wok or large no-stick skillet and heat over medium heat. Add the egg substitute and cook until it begins to set. Using a large spatula, lift and turn the egg so it cooks evenly. Continue cooking until set but still glossy and moist. Transfer to a plate. Wipe the wok or skillet with a paper towel.

Add the remaining 2 teaspoons of oil and heat over medium-high heat. Add the snow peas, corn and water chestnuts. Stir-fry for 2 to 3 minutes or until the vegetables are crisp-tender. Push the vegetables to the edge of the wok or skillet.

Add the rice and stir-fry about 2 minutes or until the rice begins to brown. Stir in the pineapple, egg, broth mixture and vegetables. Stir-fry about 5 minutes or until the mixture is heated through and the sauce slightly thickens.

Chef's Note: To garnish, sprinkle with a few chopped peanuts and top with cilantro leaves.

EXTRA HEALTH BENEFITS
Lower Cholesterol
Stronger Immunity

Times: Prep: 10 min.
Cooking: 12 min.

Makes 4 servings.

Per serving: 344 calories, 5.5 g. fat (14% of calories), 5.4 g. dietary fiber, 0 mg. cholesterol, 737 mg. sodium.

A Grains Glossary

Nutritionists recommend eating lots of foods rich in complex carbohydrates and fiber. And grains certainly fit the bill. These hunger-appeasing little nuggets are excellent sources of energy, and they're quite low in fat. You'd be well advised to incorporate the following grains into your everyday meals.

Barley. This oblong, beige grain, which dates back to the Stone Age, has a mild flavor and is appealingly chewy if not overcooked. One of the most popular forms is pearl barley, which has had its outer hull removed. Barley is available in medium-pearled and quick-cooking forms.

Buckwheat groats. Groats are whole buckwheat kernels. When roasted, they're called kasha and have a nutty flavor. Kasha is an important ingredient in Russian cooking, but it deserves a place in many American dishes as well.

Bulgur and cracked wheat. These grains, both forms of wheat berries, also have a nutty flavor. Bulgur has been steamed, dried and crushed. Cracked wheat is the whole berry that's been broken into fragments.

Cornmeal. As the name implies, cornmeal has a corn flavor. It's simply dried corn kernels that have been finely ground. Look for cornmeal in yellow, white and blue varieties.

Couscous. A granular product akin to pasta, couscous is made from semolina wheat that's rolled into tiny pellets, then dried. It cooks very quickly.

Grits. Grits can be any ground grain, such as corn, oats or rice. Hominy grits, from corn, are the most common type.

Millet. An ancient cereal grain, millet has a great nutty, cornmeal-like flavor. Its tiny, round, yellow kernels may be familiar to you as part of birdseed.

Rice. An important food worldwide, rice comes in different lengths—long, medium and short. Brown rice has had only its outer hull removed, leaving it with a beige color and a pleasantly nutty flavor. White rice has received more processing, including enrichment to replace lost nutrients. Both types come in regular and quick-cooking forms.

Rolled oats. To make rolled oats, oat kernels are steamed and flattened. They come in many forms. Old-fashioned (or regular) oats take about 15 minutes to cook; quick-cooking take about 5 minutes. Instant oatmeal requires no cooking, just the addition of boiling water.

Quinoa. This grain contains more protein than any other type. The tiny, ivory-colored, bead-shaped grain expands to four times its original volume during cooking. It has a delicate, almost bland flavor similar to couscous.

Wild rice. This is not a true rice, even though it's generally treated as one. It's the seed of an aquatic grass. Because it's difficult to produce, it's very expensive. A chewy texture and nutty flavor are its hallmarks. It's often combined with white or brown rice.

Rice-Crust Pizza

Try something out of the ordinary—pizza made with a rice crust. It's lower in calories than pizza that's made with a traditional bread crust, and it's even easier to prepare.

> 1   **cup coarsely grated carrots**
> ½   **cup reduced-fat cottage cheese**
> ⅓   **cup whole-wheat or unbleached flour**
> 2   **tablespoons finely chopped onions**
> 3   **teaspoons minced fresh basil or 1 teaspoon dried basil**
> 2½ **cups cooked and cooled brown rice**
> 1   **cup canned low-sodium tomato sauce**
> 1½ **cups (6 ounces) shredded reduced-fat mozzarella cheese**

For the crust, place the carrots in a strainer. Place an unopened can of fruit or vegetables on top to squeeze the excess liquid from the carrots. Let drain for 20 minutes, then pat dry with paper towels.

In a large bowl, stir together the cottage cheese, flour, onions and 1½ teaspoons of the fresh basil or ½ teaspoon of the dried basil. Then stir in the carrots and rice.

Spray a 13" × 9" baking pan with no-stick spray. Spread the crust mixture in the bottom and about ¼" up the sides of the pan. Bake at 350° for 25 minutes. Then broil 4" from the heat about 2 minutes or until the crust is browned, without burning the carrots.

Spread the tomato sauce on the crust and top with the cheese. Then sprinkle with the remaining 1½ teaspoons of fresh basil or ½ teaspoon of dried basil. Bake at 350° for 15 to 20 minutes or until the cheese is bubbly and light brown. Slice and serve.

Chef's Note: To jazz up this pizza, scatter 1 cup of chopped cooked vegetables over the tomato sauce. Sprinkle with the cheese and bake as directed. Broccoli, artichoke hearts, carrots, cauliflower, peppers, onions and mushrooms are good choices.

EXTRA HEALTH BENEFIT
Stronger Immunity

Times: Prep: 27 min.
Baking: 40 min.
Broiling: 2 min.

Makes 8 servings.

Per serving: 167 calories, 4.2 g. fat (23% of calories), 2.6 g. dietary fiber, 13 mg. cholesterol, 172 mg. sodium.

Rice-Crust Pizza

Tabbouleh with White Beans and Spinach

Tabbouleh is a Middle Eastern salad made with bulgur. Here we've added beans to transform this side dish into a hearty but low-calorie entrée.

½ **cup bulgur**
½ **cup hot water**
¼ **cup lemon juice**
1½ **cups minced fresh parsley**
5 **green onions, chopped**
1 **cup cooked white beans or canned small white beans, rinsed and drained**
1 **tablespoon olive oil**
1 **tablespoon water**
2 **cups fresh spinach leaves**
2 **tomatoes, sliced**
Lemon peel curls (optional)
Parsley sprigs (optional)

Place the bulgur in a colander and rinse under cold running water. Drain and transfer it to a medium bowl. Add the hot water and lemon juice and stir until combined. Let stand at room temperature for 20 minutes.

Stir in the minced parsley and onions.

In a small bowl, stir together the beans, oil and 1 tablespoon water. Add to the bulgur mixture. Gently toss until well combined. If desired, cover and chill in the refrigerator about 2 hours to blend the flavors.

To serve, arrange the spinach and tomato slices on plates. Mound the tabbouleh on top. If desired, garnish with lemon peel curls and parsley sprigs.

Chef's Note: Tabbouleh keeps well for up to 1 week. Actually, the flavor improves during storage, so you might want to make a double batch.

Millet-Cake Melts
with Sun-Dried Tomatoes

EXTRA HEALTH BENEFITS
Better Blood Pressure
Stronger Immunity

Times: Prep: 15 min.
Cooking: 30 min.

Makes 4 servings.

Per serving: 279 calories,
8.3 g. fat (27% of calories),
5.6 g. dietary fiber, 15 mg.
cholesterol, 84 mg. sodium.

A modest amount of Jarlsberg cheese and some sun-dried tomatoes add the crowning touch to these no-meat patties.

- 10 **sun-dried tomatoes**
- 2 **teaspoons olive oil**
- ¼ **cup finely chopped green onions**
- ¼ **cup shredded carrots**
- 2 **cloves garlic, minced**
- 2 **teaspoons dried thyme**
- 1½ **cups defatted low-sodium chicken broth**
- ⅔ **cup millet**
- ½ **cup fat-free egg substitute**
- ½ **teaspoon lemon-herb salt-free seasoning**
- 4 **slices reduced-fat Jarlsberg cheese (about 1 ounce each), halved**

In a small bowl, cover the tomatoes with boiling water; soak for 4 minutes. Drain the tomatoes and finely chop them; set aside.

Add 1 teaspoon of the oil to a small saucepan and heat over medium heat. Add the onions, carrots and garlic. Cook and stir about 2 minutes or until the vegetables are tender.

Add the thyme. Cook and stir for 1 minute. Then add the broth and bring to a boil. Stir in the millet. Reduce the heat, cover and simmer for 20 to 25 minutes or until the millet is tender and the water is absorbed. Remove the saucepan from the heat and let stand, covered, for 5 minutes.

In a blender or small food processor, blend or process half of the millet and the egg substitute until smooth. Stir the millet mixture into the remaining millet. Then stir in the lemon-herb seasoning. Form the mixture into 8 patties.

Add the remaining 1 teaspoon of oil to a large no-stick skillet and heat over medium heat. Add the patties and cook for 4 to 5 minutes on each side or until golden. Then place a piece of the cheese and equal amounts of the tomatoes on top of each patty. Cover and cook 1 minute more or until the cheese melts.

Chef's Note: Millet is the small round grain frequently found in birdseed. But it's great people food, too, with more protein than wheat, rice or corn. If you can't find it at your supermarket, try a health-food store or specialty market.

Spaghetti Squash Stuffed with Vegetables and Goat Cheese

Make this one-dish meal when summer-ripe vegetables abound. Serve it with crusty bread and tomato wedges tossed with a no-oil French dressing.

 1 large spaghetti squash (about 3 pounds)
 4 slices low-calorie whole-grain bread
 ½ teaspoon dried basil
 ½ teaspoon dried oregano
 ¼ teaspoon garlic powder
 2 cups green beans cut into 1" pieces, blanched
 2 cups coarsely shredded zucchini
 1 cup coarsely shredded carrots
 4 ounces herbed soft goat cheese, crumbled
 2 tablespoons minced fresh dill
 ½ teaspoon fennel seeds

Place the squash in a very large saucepan or Dutch oven and add enough water to cover. Bring to a boil, then reduce the heat. Simmer, uncovered, for 30 to 60 minutes or until the squash is tender when pierced with a fork. Drain the squash, then cut it lengthwise in half. Set aside until cool enough to handle.

Meanwhile, in a blender or food processor, blend or process the bread, basil, oregano and garlic powder until the mixture forms fine crumbs; set aside.

Discard the seeds from the squash. Use a fork to shred and remove the pulp from the skin. Transfer the pulp to a large bowl; set the squash shell aside. Add the beans, zucchini, carrots, cheese, dill and fennel seeds to the pulp. Use the fork to toss until combined.

Fill both halves of the squash shell evenly with the vegetable mixture. Sprinkle the crumb mixture on top. Bake at 350° for 15 to 25 minutes or until heated through.

EXTRA HEALTH BENEFITS
Lower Cholesterol
Blood Building
Stronger Immunity

Times: Prep: 12 min.
Cooking: 30 min.
Baking: 15 min.

Makes 4 servings.

Per serving: 249 calories, 4.8 g. fat (16% of calories), 4.3 g. dietary fiber, 14 mg. cholesterol, 232 mg. sodium.

SLIMMING STRATEGY

If you've got a cold, put your weight-loss program on hold. Minor illnesses may require a modest increase in foods rich in vitamins and minerals. There's a good chance you'll feel better faster if you make sure you're meeting your calorie needs in a properly balanced diet.

Asparagus-Artichoke Lasagna Rolls

This is a portion-controlled recipe, so you have no excuse for eating more than your share!

EXTRA HEALTH BENEFIT
Stronger Immunity

Times: Prep: 17 min.
Cooking: 4 min.
Baking: 15 min.

Makes 4 servings.

Per serving: 253 calories, 5.8 g. fat (19% of calories), 0.4 g. dietary fiber, 17 mg. cholesterol, 313 mg. sodium.

LASAGNA ROLLS

  8 **lasagna noodles**
16 **asparagus spears**
  2 **cups reduced-fat ricotta cheese**
½ **cup thawed and finely chopped frozen artichoke hearts**
½ **cup chopped arugula**
  2 **tablespoons grated Parmesan cheese**
½ **cup (2 ounces) finely shredded nonfat mozzarella cheese**

SAUCE

1¼ **cups skim milk**
  2 **tablespoons nonfat dry milk**
  1 **tablespoon cornstarch**
  1 **tablespoon minced fresh basil**
    Pinch of ground white pepper

For the lasagna rolls: Cook the noodles according to the package directions, but without adding the salt. Drain, rinse with cold water and drain again.

Meanwhile, bring a medium saucepan of water to a boil. Break off and discard the tough portions of the asparagus stems. Add the asparagus to the boiling water. Cook about 1 minute or until blanched. Immediately drain and rinse with very cold water to stop the cooking; set aside.

In a medium bowl, combine the ricotta cheese, artichokes, arugula and Parmesan cheese. Spray an 11" × 7" baking pan with no-stick spray.

To assemble the rolls, spread each noodle with some of the cheese mixture. Place 2 asparagus spears horizontally across a short end of each noodle. Then roll up from the short end to enclose the filling. Place the rolls, seam side down, in the baking pan. Sprinkle with the mozzarella cheese. Cover with foil and bake at 350° for 15 to 20 minutes or until heated through.

For the sauce: Meanwhile, in a small bowl, use a wire whisk to stir together ¼ cup of the skim milk, the dry milk and cornstarch until dissolved.

SLIMMING STRATEGY

There are now reduced-fat and nonfat versions of practically every dairy product imaginable. And while they're a great technological advance, sometimes they lose more than fat during the transformation—they lose flavor. To compensate, manufacturers often add extra salt. If you're watching your sodium intake, seek out low-sodium versions of other ingredients in your recipes to keep from exceeding your limit.

In a small saucepan, bring the remaining 1 cup of milk to a boil. Then use the wire whisk to stir in the cornstarch mixture. Cook and stir for 1 to 2 minutes or until the mixture slightly thickens and begins to gently boil. Cook and stir for 2 minutes more. Remove the saucepan from the heat and stir in the basil and pepper. Serve over the lasagna rolls.

Chef's Note: To make ahead, assemble the rolls and refrigerate until you're ready to bake them.

Three-Cheese Lasagna

Would you believe it? There are three separate cheeses in this lasagna, but it still has less than 3 grams of fat per serving!

- 12 **lasagna noodles**
- 1¾ **cups reduced-fat cottage cheese**
- 1 **cup nonfat ricotta cheese**
- ½ **cup fat-free egg substitute or 4 lightly beaten egg whites**
- ¼ **cup grated Parmesan cheese**
- ¼ **cup toasted wheat germ**
- 1 **cup cooked cauliflower or broccoli florets, sliced**
- 2 **cups canned low-sodium tomato sauce**

Cook the noodles according to the package directions, but without adding the salt. Drain the noodles, rinse with cold water and drain again. Lay the noodles flat until ready to use.

In a medium bowl, stir together the cottage cheese, ricotta cheese, egg substitute or egg whites, Parmesan cheese and wheat germ.

To assemble the lasagna, spray a 13" × 9" baking dish with no-stick spray. Place one-third of the noodles in the baking dish and spread with half of the cheese mixture. Top with ½ cup of the cooked cauliflower or broccoli and ½ cup of the tomato sauce.

Top with another one-third of the noodles. Repeat layering with the remaining cheese mixture, vegetables and another ½ cup of tomato sauce. Finally, top with the remaining noodles and tomato sauce.

Cover with foil and bake at 375° for 20 minutes. Remove the foil and bake about 20 minutes more or until heated through. Let the lasagna stand for 10 to 15 minutes before serving.

EXTRA HEALTH BENEFITS
Cancer Protection
Stronger Immunity

Times: Prep: 26 min.
Baking: 40 min.
Standing: 10 min.

Makes 9 servings.

Per serving: 182 calories, 2.5 g. fat (12% of calories), 1.8 g. dietary fiber, 5.9 mg. cholesterol, 580 mg. sodium.

EXTRA HEALTH BENEFITS
Blood Building
Stronger Immunity

Times: Prep: 10 min.
Cooking: 15 min.

Makes 4 servings.

Per serving: 431 calories,
10.1 g. fat (21% of calories),
2.1 g. dietary fiber, 27 mg.
cholesterol, 168 mg. sodium.

Asparagus and Orange Linguine

This light meal really hits the spot on a hot day.

       2 **cups part-skim ricotta cheese**
      ½ **cup evaporated skim milk**
      ½ **cup nonfat plain yogurt**
       2 **tablespoons grated orange peel**
     10 **ounces linguine**
       1 **pound asparagus**
       2 **teaspoons olive oil**
       1 **cup sliced green onions**
    1½ **tablespoons grated ginger root**
       1 **medium orange, peeled and sectioned**

In a blender or small food processor, blend or process the ricotta cheese, milk, yogurt and orange peel until smooth; set aside.

Bring a large saucepan of water to a boil. Add the linguine. Slightly reduce the heat. Boil, uncovered, for 9 to 11 minutes or until the linguine is tender but firm. Drain, rinse with hot water and drain again.

Meanwhile, break off and discard the tough portions of the asparagus stems. Slice the asparagus into 2" pieces. Add the oil to a large no-stick skillet and heat over medium-high heat. Add the asparagus, onions and ginger. Cook and stir for 4 to 5 minutes or until the asparagus is crisp-tender. Stir in the cheese mixture. Cook for 2 to 3 minutes more or until heated through, stirring occasionally.

Add the linguine and oranges to the skillet. Gently toss until coated.

Chef's Note: This ricotta sauce is very versatile. You can even make it ahead and store it in the refrigerator to use over baked white or sweet potatoes and other types of pasta. Rewarm it over low heat to keep it from curdling.

Baked Cheese Polenta with Artichokes

Polenta, a staple of northern Italy, is a fancy name for corn-meal mush. Often it's served as a first course or a side dish, but here it's a skinny main dish.

6 cups water
1 jar (6 ounces) marinated artichoke hearts, drained
1 cup (4 ounces) shredded reduced-fat Monterey Jack cheese
3 tablespoons canned diced green chili peppers
¼ teaspoon ground black pepper
2 cups polenta or coarse-grain yellow cornmeal
2 tablespoons grated Parmesan cheese
½ teaspoon garlic powder
1 medium tomato, thinly sliced

In a large saucepan, bring the water to a boil.

Meanwhile, in a medium bowl, combine the artichokes, Monterey Jack cheese, chili peppers and black pepper. Set aside. Spray an 8" × 8" baking pan with no-stick spray; set aside.

Using a wire whisk, slowly stir the polenta or cornmeal into the boiling water. Reduce the heat to low. Cook for 5 to 10 minutes or until thick and creamy, stirring frequently. Stir in the Parmesan cheese and garlic powder. Remove the saucepan from the heat and stir in the artichoke mixture.

Spread the polenta mixture in the baking pan. Top with the tomato slices. Bake at 350° for 30 to 35 minutes or until golden. Let stand for 5 minutes before serving.

Chef's Note: Be sure to let the polenta stand for at least 5 minutes after baking, otherwise it will be difficult to cut into individual portions.

Baked Cheese Polenta with Artichokes

Eggs in Potato-Cheese Nests

These cheese-flavored eggs are just as good for brunch as they are for a light dinner.

  3 **medium potatoes, cubed**
  1 **stalk celery, finely chopped**
 ½ **cup skim milk**
  1 **tablespoon unbleached flour**
 ½ **cup reduced-fat ricotta cheese**
  1 **green onion, finely chopped**
  1 **tablespoon minced fresh parsley**
1½ **cups fat-free egg substitute**
 ¼ **cup (1 ounce) shredded part-skim Muenster cheese**
 ½ **teaspoon paprika**
      Parsley sprigs (optional)

Place the potatoes and celery in a medium saucepan and add enough water to cover. Bring to a boil, then reduce the heat. Gently boil about 20 minutes or until the vegetables are very tender. Drain the vegetables and mash them; set aside.

Meanwhile, in a medium skillet, use a wire whisk to stir together the milk and flour. Cook and stir over medium heat until the mixture thickens and begins to gently boil. Cook and stir for 1 minute more. Transfer the sauce to a blender or food processor. Add the ricotta cheese and blend or process on low speed until smooth.

Stir the cheese mixture, onions and minced parsley into the potato mixture.

Spray 6 (6- or 8-ounce) custard cups with no-stick spray. Divide the potato mixture among the cups. Using a spoon, make a depression large enough to hold ¼ cup of the egg substitute. Place the cups on a large cookie sheet, then pour the egg substitute into the depressions. Sprinkle the tops with the Muenster cheese and paprika.

Bake at 375° for 20 to 25 minutes or until a knife inserted near the center of a cup comes out clean. If desired, garnish with parsley sprigs.

EXTRA HEALTH BENEFITS
Better Blood Pressure
Cancer Protection
Stronger Immunity

Times: Prep: 26 min.
Baking: 20 min.

Makes 6 servings.

Per serving: 134 calories, 2.5 g. fat (17% of calories), 1.5 g. dietary fiber, 9 mg. cholesterol, 150 mg. sodium.

SLIMMING STRATEGY

When buying reduced-fat cheese, choose brands with no more than 5 grams of fat per ounce. Also, be aware that brands vary considerably in taste and texture. Try different types until you find ones you really like. Remember that if your taste buds aren't satisfied, you'll probably end up overeating in an attempt to compensate.

Times: Prep: 10 min.
Baking: 15 min.

Makes 4 servings.

Per serving: 156 calories,
3.2 g. fat (18% of calories),
0.7 g. dietary fiber, 10 mg.
cholesterol, 713 mg. sodium.

Chilies Rellenos

*The addition of beans to this favorite Mexican side dish
turns it into a main course.*

  4 **large egg whites**
  ⅛ **teaspoon cream of tartar**
  1 **cup fat-free egg substitute**
  4 **canned whole green chili peppers**
  ½ **cup chopped tomatoes**
  1 **cup canned small white beans, rinsed and drained**
  1 **cup (4 ounces) shredded reduced-fat Monterey Jack
cheese**

Spray 4 individual au gratin dishes or shallow baking dishes
with no-stick spray; set aside.

In a medium bowl, use an electric mixer to beat the egg whites
and cream of tartar on medium speed until the egg whites form
stiff peaks but are not dry. Fold in the egg substitute. Spread half

Chilies Rellenos

of the mixture in the bottom of the au gratin or baking dishes.

To assemble, open the peppers so that they lie flat and place them on top of the egg mixture. Sprinkle the tomatoes, beans and cheese on top of the peppers. Then carefully spread the remaining egg mixture on top to cover.

Bake at 350° for 15 to 20 minutes or until the egg mixture is lightly brown and set.

Chef's Note: To garnish the chilies rellenos, top them with nonfat plain yogurt and sprinkle with chopped green onions or additional green chili peppers.

Spaghetti Frittata

Here's a novel use for leftover spaghetti. For a complete and easy meal, accompany the frittata with toasted English muffins and a salad made of bitter greens, such as watercress and arugula.

  1 **cup fat-free egg substitute**
  3 **tablespoons skim milk**
  2 **tablespoons grated Parmesan cheese**
  ½ **teaspoon dry mustard**
  ½ **teaspoon dried basil**
  ¼ **teaspoon garlic powder**
  ⅛ **teaspoon ground white pepper**
  2 **cups cooked and coarsely chopped spaghetti**
  1 **cup coarsely shredded zucchini**
  ½ **cup chopped green onions**

Spray the bottom and sides of a 9" pie plate with no-stick spray; set aside.

In a large bowl, use a wire whisk to stir together the egg substitute, milk, cheese, mustard, basil, garlic powder and pepper. Stir in the spaghetti, zucchini and onions. Transfer to the pie plate.

Bake at 350° for 10 minutes. Gently stir the egg mixture, then bake for 15 to 20 minutes more or until a knife inserted near the center comes out clean. Let stand 5 minutes before cutting. Cut into wedges to serve.

EXTRA HEALTH BENEFITS
Lower Cholesterol
Stronger Immunity

Times: Prep: 10 min.
Baking: 25 min.
Standing: 5 min.

Makes 4 servings.

Per serving: 131 calories, 1.5 g. fat (10% of calories), 2.5 g. dietary fiber, 3 mg. cholesterol, 147 mg. sodium.

Herbed Zucchini Frittata

Herbed Zucchini Frittata

Being short on time is no excuse to eat poorly. This nutritious entrée, for instance, can be on the table in less than 15 minutes.

- 2 **small zucchini**
- 1 **teaspoon water**
- 2 **green onions, finely chopped**
- 1 **tablespoon minced fresh basil or 1 teaspoon dried basil**
- 1½ **teaspoons minced fresh marjoram or ½ teaspoon dried marjoram**
- 1½ **cups fat-free egg substitute**
- 2 **tablespoons grated Parmesan cheese**
  Tomato wedges (optional)
  Small basil sprigs (optional)

Cut each zucchini lengthwise into quarters, then thinly slice each quarter.

Place the water in a 10" broiler-proof skillet, then add the zucchini and onions. Cook over low heat about 3 minutes or just until the vegetables are crisp-tender. Drain; discard the cooking liquid. Stir in the basil and marjoram.

Carefully pour the egg substitute over the zucchini and onions. Cook over low heat until the mixture begins to set. Using a spatula, lift the edges to allow the uncooked egg mixture to flow underneath. Continue cooking until nearly set but still moist on top. Sprinkle with the cheese.

Broil 4" from the heat about 1 minute or until the top is lightly browned and the egg mixture is set. To serve, cut into 4 wedges. If desired, garnish each serving with tomato wedges and a small sprig of basil.

Quick

EXTRA HEALTH BENEFIT
Lower Cholesterol

Times: Prep: 4 min.
Cooking: 8 min.
Broiling: 1 min.

Makes 4 servings.

Per serving: 69 calories, 1.1 g. fat (14% of calories), 1.8 g. dietary fiber, 2 mg. cholesterol, 181 mg. sodium.

SLIMMING STRATEGY

One simple change cut 300 calories, 30 grams of fat and 1,278 milligrams of cholesterol from this typical frittata recipe. What was it? Using egg substitute in place of whole eggs.

Meatless Moussaka

EXTRA HEALTH BENEFITS
Better Blood Pressure
Blood Building
Stronger Immunity

Times: Prep: 5 min.
Baking: 30 min.

Makes 4 servings.

Per serving: 235 calories,
6.3 g. fat (22% of calories),
7.8 g. dietary fiber, 2 mg.
cholesterol, 126 mg. sodium.

Here's a new twist on a traditional Greek favorite. It's much leaner than a standard recipe, which could easily cost you 50 grams of fat per serving. Using tofu instead of lamb and omitting the rich egg and cream sauce made the biggest difference.

- 1 **large red onion, thinly sliced and separated into rings**
- 1 **medium eggplant (1–1¼ pounds), cut crosswise into ½"-thick rounds**
- 2 **medium zucchini, thinly sliced**
- 8 **ounces firm tofu, crumbled**
- ¼ **cup minced fresh basil**
- 2 **tablespoons minced fresh parsley**
- 3 **cups low-sodium tomato sauce**
- ½ **teaspoon hot-pepper sauce**
- 2 **tablespoons grated Parmesan cheese**

Layer the onions, eggplant and zucchini in the bottom of an 11" × 7" baking dish. Sprinkle the tofu over the vegetables. Then top with the basil and parsley.

Stir together the tomato sauce and hot-pepper sauce. Pour over the tofu and vegetables. Bake at 350° for 30 to 40 minutes or until bubbly and the vegetables are tender. Sprinkle with the cheese before serving.

Chef's Note: Freezing tofu will give it a more chewy, meatlike texture. To freeze, drain the tofu and cut the large block into thick slices. Freeze the slices in a single layer until solid, then let them thaw. Crumble before using.

Tofu Layered with Three Cheeses

Thin slices of tofu replace the noodles in this variation of lasagna.

¼ cup plus 2 tablespoons low-sodium tomato sauce
1 large egg white, lightly beaten
1 cup nonfat ricotta cheese
¼ cup grated Parmesan cheese
¼ teaspoon ground nutmeg
¼ teaspoon ground white pepper
10 ounces firm tofu
8 slices tomato
½ cup chopped and loosely packed fresh basil
1 cup (4 ounces) shredded nonfat mozzarella cheese

Spread ¼ cup of the tomato sauce in the bottom of an 8" × 8" baking dish; set aside.

In a medium bowl, stir together the egg white, ricotta cheese, Parmesan cheese, nutmeg, pepper and the remaining 2 tablespoons of tomato sauce; set aside. Squeeze the tofu to remove excess moisture, then cut into 8 slices.

To assemble the lasagna, place 4 of the tofu slices in the baking dish. On top of the tofu, layer half of each in the following order: the ricotta mixture, tomato slices, basil and mozzarella cheese. Repeat layering with the remaining tofu, the ricotta mixture, tomatoes, basil and cheese.

Bake at 350° for 15 to 20 minutes or until bubbly and the cheese is melted. Let stand for 5 minutes before cutting.

Chef's Note: Tofu has a high water content. You'll have better results in cooking if you remove some of the excess moisture. One method is to cut the tofu into slices about ½" or less thick and then place the pieces between layers of paper towels. Press gently. Repeat with new paper towels until the towels no longer get very wet. This technique is especially useful for this recipe; the lasagna will become watery if you don't remove some of the moisture.

Quick

EXTRA HEALTH BENEFITS
Blood Building
Stronger Bones

Times: Prep: 10 min.
Baking: 15 min.
Standing: 5 min.

Makes 4 servings.

Per serving: 76 calories, 3.1 g. fat (34% of calories), 1.6 g. dietary fiber, 10 mg. cholesterol, 424 mg. sodium.

SLIMMING STRATEGY

Know your weaknesses. Your problem may not be overeating. It may be a weakness for certain fattening foods like cheeses, cream sauces, pastries or chocolate. Once you've identified your problem foods, you'll find it easier to resist them and reward yourself in other ways.

Broiled Vegetable Kabobs

Here's a meatless kabob that'll fool even meat lovers. The soy sauce in the marinade gives the tofu cubes a light tan color similar to pork or veal.

12 ounces firm tofu, cut into 1" cubes
 1 medium yellow summer squash, cut into 1" pieces
16 cherry tomatoes
16 radishes
 1 medium green pepper, cut into 1" pieces
¾ cup pineapple juice
 1 tablespoon lime juice
 1 tablespoon reduced-sodium soy sauce
 2 cloves garlic, crushed
¼ teaspoon ground allspice
   Pinch of ground red pepper
 2 cups hot cooked brown rice

Spray an unheated, large no-stick skillet with no-stick spray. Heat the skillet over medium heat. Add the tofu and cook for 4 to 5 minutes or until golden on all sides, stirring frequently.

Transfer the tofu to a large bowl. Add the squash, tomatoes, radishes and green peppers. In a small bowl, stir together the pineapple juice, lime juice, soy sauce, garlic, allspice and red pepper. Pour over the tofu mixture and gently toss until well coated. Marinate at room temperature for at least 15 minutes to blend the flavors.

Spray the rack of a broiling pan with no-stick spray. Drain the tofu mixture, reserving the marinade. Alternately thread the tofu and vegetables onto 8 skewers. Place the kabobs on the rack and brush with the reserved marinade. Broil 3" to 4" from the heat for 8 to 10 minutes or until the vegetables are tender, brushing with any of the remaining marinade and turning frequently. Serve each kabob on a bed of rice.

Chef's Note: To keep tofu sweet and fresh, store it in the refrigerator immersed in water. Change the water every other day. The tofu will last for up to 2 weeks.

EXTRA HEALTH BENEFITS
Blood Building
Stronger Immunity

Times: Prep: 15 min.
Marinating: at least 15 min.
Cooking: 4 min.
Broiling: 8 min.

Makes 4 servings.

Per serving: 293 calories, 8.8 g. fat (25% of calories), 5.1 g. dietary fiber, 0 mg. cholesterol, 179 mg. sodium.

SLIMMING STRATEGY

It's hip to be square—or at least to eat three square meals a day. Eating balanced meals will keep you from getting hungry and can prevent binge eating.

Red, White and Green Pizza

Tired of tomato sauce on your pizzas? Try this sauce made from roasted red peppers and basil.

  1 jar (7 ounces) roasted red peppers (with liquid)
 ¼ cup loosely packed fresh basil leaves
  1 tablespoon balsamic vinegar
  1 large Boboli Italian bread shell
  2 teaspoons olive oil
  2 Italian frying peppers, cut into strips (wear disposable gloves when handling)
  1 green pepper, cut into strips
  1 sweet red pepper, cut into strips
  1 cup canned white beans, rinsed and drained
  1 cup thawed frozen chopped spinach, squeezed to remove excess moisture
  1 cup (4 ounces) shredded part-skim mozzarella cheese

In a blender or small food processor, blend or process the roasted peppers (with liquid), basil and vinegar until smooth.

Place the bread shell on a large cookie sheet or pizza stone. Spread with the roasted pepper mixture; set aside.

Add the oil to a large no-stick skillet and heat over medium heat. Add the Italian, green and sweet red peppers. Cook and stir for 4 to 5 minutes or until the peppers are tender.

To assemble the pizza, sprinkle the cooked peppers, beans, spinach and cheese on top of the bread shell. Bake at 425° for 15 to 20 minutes or until the cheese is melted and the crust is golden.

Chef's Note: A Boboli shell is a commercial bread product that makes the perfect base for pizza. It is not, however, as low in fat as a homemade crust made without oil. So be sure to take that into consideration when balancing your daily fat budget.

EXTRA HEALTH BENEFITS
Lower Cholesterol
Blood Building
Stronger Immunity

Times: Prep: 20 min.
Baking: 15 min.

Makes 4 servings.

Per serving: 452 calories, 10.1 g. fat (18% of calories), 4.6 g. dietary fiber, 10 mg. cholesterol, 911 mg. sodium.

Times: Prep: 24 min.
Baking: 6 min.

Makes 12 bundles or 4 servings.

Per serving (3 bundles): 312 calories, 6.7 g. fat (19% of calories), 2.2 g. dietary fiber, 0 mg. cholesterol, 111 mg. sodium.

Slimming Strategy

When the urge to snack strikes, go for a walk. Or at least wait awhile before giving in to your craving—maybe you'll decide the splurge isn't worth it.

Broccoli and White Beans Baked in Phyllo

These pastry bundles are quite flaky, thanks to the use of phyllo dough. But unlike many phyllo recipes, which call for lots of butter or margarine between the layers, this one uses only a little.

- 2 teaspoons olive oil
- 2 cups broccoli florets
- 1 medium sweet red pepper, chopped
- 1 cup chopped green onions
- 1 cup canned small white beans, rinsed and drained
- ½ cup cooked orzo
- 1 tablespoon Dijon mustard
- 1 tablespoon lemon juice
- 12 sheets (13" × 9" each) frozen phyllo dough, thawed
- 2 tablespoons reduced-calorie margarine, melted
  Scallion greens cut into long, thin strips (optional)

For the filling, add the oil to a large no-stick skillet and heat over medium heat. Add the broccoli, peppers and onions. Cook and stir for 4 to 5 minutes or just until the vegetables are tender. Remove the skillet from the heat. Stir in the beans, orzo, mustard and lemon juice; set aside.

Place the phyllo in a stack on a large piece of wax paper. Cover with plastic wrap and then a damp kitchen towel to prevent drying out.

To assemble the bundles, place 2 sheets of the phyllo on another piece of wax paper. Brush with some of the margarine. Then top with 2 more sheets of the phyllo and brush with more of the margarine. Using a sharp knife, cut the prepared stack into 4 rectangles. Place ¼ cup of the filling in the center of each rectangle. To enclose the filling, bring the 4 corners up and together, then pinch and twist slightly.

Place the finished bundles in muffin cups. Repeat assembling bundles with the remaining phyllo, filling and margarine. Brush the tops with any remaining margarine. Bake at 375° for 6 to 8 minutes or until golden. If desired, tie a scallion green around the top of each bundle.

Like grains and pasta, beans are a perfect diet food. They're high in fiber and protein but very low in fat. There's also an endless variety to choose from, and they come canned or dried.

If you're using canned beans, rinse them well to remove excess sodium. If you opt for dried beans, you'll have to soak them before cooking. Let them stand overnight in a bowl of cold water or boil them for two minutes, then set aside for one hour. Either way, you can cook the beans immediately or drain them and freeze for future use. (To freeze: Spread the beans on a cookie sheet and freeze until they're as hard as marbles; transfer to plastic bags.)

To ease the gas-producing effect of beans, introduce them to your diet gradually. That way, your body will have a chance to adjust to the new digestive environment that beans create. Changing the water a few times during the soaking and cooking process will also help.

If gas is still a problem, check the antacid section of your pharmacy, supermarket or health-food store for a product called Beano. This is a food enzyme that will help you digest beans more easily. Just add three to eight drops to your first bite of food and that should do the trick.

Here are some of the most common types of beans, along with cooking information. The yields are based on one cup of dried legumes.

Black beans. Popular in South American, Caribbean and Mexican dishes, black beans are often served with rice. Cook for 45 to 60 minutes. Yield: 2½ cups.

Black-eyed peas. Used extensively in Southern cooking, black-eyed peas have a pealike flavor and buttery texture. You can sometimes find them fresh, and they're available frozen. Cook the dried beans for 1 hour. Yield: 2½ cups.

Chick-peas (or garbanzo beans). Chick-peas are essential for Middle Eastern hummus. They're also ideal in antipastos and minestrone. Cook for 2½ hours. Yield: 3¼ cups.

Kidney beans. These come in various shades of red and are a staple in three-bean salads and chili. Cook for 1½ hours. Yield: 2½ cups.

Lentils. Many colors of lentils are available, including green, brown and orange. They don't need soaking. Lentils are indispensable for Indian cooking. Cook for 30 minutes. Yield: 2¾ cups.

Lima beans. Limas have a rich, buttery flavor. Look for both small and large beans. They're also available fresh and frozen. Cook the dried limas for 30 minutes. Yield: 2½ hours.

Pea beans. The smallest of the white beans, pea beans are the bean of choice for Boston baked beans. Cook for 45 to 60 minutes. Yield: 2½ cups.

Pinto beans. These are popular in Mexican dishes like chili and refried beans. Cook for 1½ hours. Yield: 2 cups.

Vegetable and Black Bean Chili

EXTRA HEALTH BENEFITS
Lower Cholesterol
Blood Building
Stronger Immunity

Times: Prep: 10 min.
Cooking: 24 min.

Makes 4 servings.

Per serving: 255 calories,
3.5 g. fat (11% of calories),
5.1 g. dietary fiber, 0 mg.
cholesterol, 186 mg. sodium.

Hungry for authentic Southwestern chili flavor? Try this low-fat, meatless version. Serve it with cornbread and rice.

- 2 teaspoons olive oil
- 1 medium eggplant, cubed
- 1 medium sweet red pepper, chopped
- 1 medium zucchini, coarsely chopped
- ½ cup chopped onions
- 1 tablespoon chili powder
- 1 teaspoon ground cumin
- 3 cups crushed canned tomatoes (with juices)
- 1 can (15 ounces) black beans, rinsed and drained
- 1 cup frozen corn or drained canned corn

Add the oil to a Dutch oven and heat over medium heat. Add the eggplant. Cook and stir about 5 minutes or until the eggplant is just tender. Stir in the peppers, zucchini, onions, chili powder and cumin. Cook and stir for 4 to 5 minutes more or until the vegetables are tender.

Stir in the tomatoes (with juices), beans and corn. Bring to a boil, then reduce the heat. Partially cover and simmer for 15 to 20 minutes or until thick.

Chef's Note: The longer the chili simmers, the thicker it'll get and the more intense the flavors will be.

Vegetable and
Black Bean Chili

Falafel Burgers

Here are lean burgers that'll supply you with lots of energy to get through the day. Serve them with sliced tomatoes and cucumbers or in pita bread with alfalfa sprouts and nonfat yogurt.

- ⅓ **cup reduced-fat cottage cheese**
- ¼ **cup fat-free egg substitute or 2 lightly beaten egg whites**
- 2 **tablespoons minced fresh parsley**
- 1 **teaspoon ground cumin**
- 1 **teaspoon ground coriander**
- 2 **cloves garlic, minced**
- ¾ **teaspoon chili powder**
- ¼ **teaspoon Oriental sesame oil**
- 1 **cup cooked chick-peas (garbanzo beans) or 1 cup canned chick-peas, rinsed and drained**
- ½ **cup toasted wheat germ**

In a blender or food processor, blend or process the cottage cheese, egg substitute or egg whites, parsley, cumin, coriander, garlic, chili powder and oil until smooth.

Add the chick-peas and blend or process on low speed until smooth. (If necessary, stop and scrape down the sides of the container.) Stir in the wheat germ.

Spray an unheated medium skillet with no-stick spray. Heat the skillet over medium heat. Form the chick-pea mixture into 4 patties. Add to the skillet. Cook about 6 minutes on each side or until the patties are golden and cooked throughout.

Quick

EXTRA HEALTH BENEFITS
Lower Cholesterol
Better Blood Pressure
Stronger Immunity

Times: Prep: 6 min.
Cooking: 12 min.

Makes 4 servings.

Per serving: 149 calories, 3.2 g. fat (19% of calories), 2.4 g. dietary fiber, 1 mg. cholesterol, 108 mg. sodium.

SLIMMING STRATEGY

Make dining an event. Set the table with your good dishes, glassware and linens. (Or use pretty paper products.) Don't forget a centerpiece—it can be as simple as some fresh flowers from your backyard or the grocery store. The point is to help you pay attention to the food, as you would at a fine restaurant, instead of consuming your meal unconsciously.

Spaghetti Squash with Red Beans and Tomato Sauce

EXTRA HEALTH BENEFITS
Lower Cholesterol
Cancer Protection
Blood Building
Stronger Immunity

Times: Prep: 10 min.
Baking: 30 min.
Cooking: 30 min.

Makes 4 servings.

Per serving: 206 calories, 1.8 g. fat (8% of calories), 11.3 g. dietary fiber, 0 mg. cholesterol, 139 mg. sodium.

Spaghetti squash is a vegetable oddity—when cooked, the flesh forms into natural strands that resemble spaghetti. But there's nothing odd about this easy main course.

> 1   **spaghetti squash (2 pounds)**
> 3   **large tomatoes, chopped**
> 1   **medium onion, chopped**
> 1   **large sweet red pepper, chopped**
> 2   **teaspoons reduced-sodium soy sauce**
> 2   **cups cooked red kidney beans or 2 cups canned red kidney beans, rinsed and drained**
> 1½ **teaspoons dried marjoram**
> 1   **teaspoon dried basil**
> ½   **teaspoon dried oregano**

Cut the squash lengthwise in half and remove the seeds. Place the squash, cut side down, in a large baking dish. Use a fork to prick the skin. Bake at 350° about 30 minutes or until the squash is tender.

Meanwhile, for the sauce, in a blender or food processor, blend or process the tomatoes, onions, peppers and soy sauce until smooth. Transfer the mixture to a large skillet.

Spaghetti Squash
with Red Beans
and Tomato Sauce

Add the beans, marjoram, basil and oregano. Bring to a boil, stirring frequently. Reduce the heat, cover and simmer for 30 minutes, stirring occasionally.

Use a fork to shred and remove the pulp from the squash. Transfer the pulp to a serving bowl. Serve the sauce over the squash.

Chef's Note: If you don't have spaghetti squash or prefer a more traditional entrée, serve the meatless Italian sauce over regular pasta. Use any shape you want.

Good Earth Casserole

Lentils are prized for their versatility and ease of preparation. Like other members of the legume family, they're powerhouses of nutrition—low in fat and calories, yet high in fiber, protein and complex carbohydrates. Here they're combined with barley and cauliflower to make an easy casserole.

    1   **can (28 ounces) salt-free stewed tomatoes (with juices)**
    4   **cups cauliflower florets**
    2   **cups coarsely chopped Swiss chard**
    1   **cup lentils, sorted and rinsed**
    ½   **cup pearl barley**
    ½   **cup water**
    1   **tablespoon balsamic vinegar**
 1½   **cups (6 ounces) shredded reduced-fat Monterey Jack cheese**
    2   **tablespoons dry seasoned bread crumbs**

Spray a 3- to 4-quart casserole with no-stick spray. In the casserole, combine the tomatoes (with juices), cauliflower, Swiss chard, lentils, barley, water and vinegar.

Cover and bake at 350° for 50 to 60 minutes or until the lentils are tender and the liquid is absorbed.

Uncover and sprinkle with the cheese and bread crumbs. Bake about 5 minutes more or until the cheese melts.

Chef's Note: When buying cauliflower, look for heavy heads with white florets and green leaves. Avoid those with brown spots or speckles and yellowed leaves. Store in a plastic bag in the refrigerator and use within four days.

EXTRA HEALTH BENEFITS
Lower Cholesterol
Blood Building
Stronger Immunity

Times: Prep: 5 min.
Baking: 55 min.

Makes 4 servings.

Per serving: 444 calories, 5.5 g. fat (11% of calories), 11.9 g. dietary fiber, 15 mg. cholesterol, 193 mg. sodium.

Fennel and White Beans au Gratin

You can enjoy the richness of a cheese sauce without the addition of fat by using a sharp-flavored cheese like Asiago. Just a small amount of this cheese goes a long way. If Asiago is unavailable, use provolone cheese.

2 tablespoons reduced-calorie margarine
1½ tablespoons unbleached flour
1 cup skim milk
¼ cup defatted low-sodium chicken broth
3 tablespoons grated Asiago cheese
1 teaspoon dried thyme
¼ teaspoon paprika
⅛ teaspoon ground white pepper
4 cups coarsely chopped fennel
8 ounces canned white beans, rinsed and drained
½ cup chopped red onions

Spray 4 individual au gratin or shallow baking dishes with no-stick spray; set aside.

Melt the margarine in a small saucepan. Using a wire whisk, stir in the flour. Cook and stir over medium heat for 1 minute, then stir in the milk and broth. Cook and stir for 3 to 4 minutes or until the sauce thickens. Remove the saucepan from the heat and stir in the cheese, thyme, paprika and pepper; set aside.

Place equal amounts of the fennel, beans and onions in each of the au gratin or baking dishes. Pour the sauce over each. Bake at 350° for 20 to 25 minutes or until the fennel is tender.

EXTRA HEALTH BENEFITS
Blood Building
Stronger Immunity

Times: Prep: 10 min.
Cooking: 4 min.
Baking: 20 min.

Makes 4 servings.

Per serving: 196 calories, 5.2 g. fat (23% of calories), 5 g. dietary fiber, 4.7 mg. cholesterol, 523 mg. sodium.

SLIMMING STRATEGY

The next time you're painting the kitchen, keep in mind the influence of color: Calm, soothing colors, such as cool blue, slow your eating. Warm colors do the opposite. (Can you guess why fast-food restaurants are often orange?) You might also consider serving your food on dark-brown, blue, dull gray or plain white plates.

Vegetable-Stuffed Cabbage Leaves

Filled cabbage rolls are a classic dish enjoyed by many cultures. Here we make a departure from the usual recipes by using bulgur and mashed potatoes instead of meat as the stuffing.

½ **cup bulgur**
1 **cup boiling water**
8 **large green cabbage leaves**
1 **cup cooked mashed potatoes**
1 **cup frozen chopped broccoli, thawed**
1 **cup frozen lima beans, thawed**
¼ **cup purchased pesto**
2 **cups canned salt-free stewed tomatoes (with juices)**
1 **cup (4 ounces) finely shredded nonfat mozzarella cheese**

Place the bulgur in a colander and rinse under cold running water. Drain; transfer it to a large bowl. Add the boiling water and let stand for 20 minutes. Then drain the bulgur and squeeze out any excess water; set aside.

In a large saucepan with a tight-fitting lid, bring about 1" of water to a boil. Place the cabbage leaves in a steamer basket and set in the saucepan, making sure the basket sits above the water. Cover and steam for 5 to 8 minutes or just until the leaves are soft enough to bend. Remove the leaves and set aside.

To the bulgur, add the potatoes, broccoli, lima beans and pesto. Mix until well combined.

To assemble the cabbage rolls, spoon about ⅓ cup of the potato mixture in the center of each cabbage leaf. Fold in the sides of each leaf to form a bundle that encloses the filling.

Spread the tomatoes (with juices) in the bottom of an 11" × 7" baking dish. Place the rolls, seam side down, in the dish. Sprinkle with the cheese. Cover with foil and bake at 350° about 20 minutes or until bubbly and heated through.

Chef's Note: For variety, use different types of cabbage, such as Napa, savoy or red.

EXTRA HEALTH BENEFIT
Stronger Immunity

Times: Prep: 27 min.
Baking: 20 min.

Makes 4 servings.

Per serving: 274 calories, 8.4 g. fat (23% of calories), 8.9 g. dietary fiber, 10 mg. cholesterol, 624 mg. sodium.

Risotto of Radicchio and Arugula

EXTRA HEALTH BENEFITS
Lower Cholesterol
Blood Building
Stronger Immunity

Times: Prep: 15 min.
Cooking: 36 min.

Makes 6 servings.

Per serving: 387 calories,
4.7 g. fat (11% of calories),
1 g. dietary fiber, 2 mg. cholesterol, 229 mg. sodium.

Risotto is an Italian specialty that's made by stirring small amounts of hot broth into rice as it cooks. This step takes a little work on your part, but the delicious creamy flavor and texture of the dish are well worth the effort.

   2 **cups chopped tomatoes**
   2 **cups seeded and chopped cucumbers**
   1 **can (15 ounces) cannellini beans, rinsed and drained**
   ½ **cup chopped red onions**
   ¼ **cup chopped and loosely packed fresh basil**
   2 **tablespoons minced fresh parsley**
   1 **tablespoon balsamic vinegar**
   ¼ **teaspoon ground black pepper**
   4 **cups defatted low-sodium chicken broth**
   1 **tablespoon olive oil**
   ½ **cup chopped shallots**
   2 **cups Arborio rice**
   1 **cup chopped radicchio**
   1 **cup chopped arugula**
   2 **tablespoons grated Parmesan cheese**

In a medium bowl, stir together the tomatoes, cucumbers, beans, onions, basil, parsley, vinegar and pepper; set aside.

Bring the broth to a boil in a large saucepan. Meanwhile, add the oil to another large saucepan. Heat over medium heat, then add the shallots. Cook and stir for 4 to 5 minutes or until the shallots are tender.

Add the rice to the shallots and stir until coated with the oil. Then add ½ cup of the hot broth to the rice, cooking and stirring until the broth is absorbed. Repeat adding the broth, using ½ cup at a time and cooking and stirring until the broth is absorbed each time. Adding the broth should take 30 to 35 minutes or until the rice is tender but not dry in appearance.

Stir in the radicchio, arugula and cheese. Cook for 2 minutes more or until the greens are wilted.

To serve, spoon the rice mixture onto dinner plates and top each serving with an equal amount of the tomato mixture.

Times: Prep: 10 min.
Cooking: 9 min.

**Makes 12 pancakes or
4 servings.**

**Per serving (3 pan-
cakes):** 183 calories, 4.7 g.
fat (22% of calories), 2.4 g.
dietary fiber, 1 mg. cholesterol, 265 mg. sodium.

SLIMMING STRATEGY

Remember that fat—any
fat—contains twice as
many calories as an equal
weight of carbohydrates
or protein. And fat can
add up fast. An extra
tablespoon used to grease
a pan contributes almost
14 grams of fat. That's
why you should take
advantage of no-stick
pans and sprays whenever
you can.

Griddle Cakes of Black Beans and Spaghetti

*Pancakes are no longer just for breakfast. Here's a savory
version you'll enjoy for dinner. Serve them with cantaloupe
or mango wedges for a colorful accompaniment.*

1 **cup nonfat plain yogurt**
½ **cup salsa**
2 **tablespoons minced fresh cilantro**
1 **cup finely chopped cooked spaghetti**
1 **cup canned black beans, rinsed and drained**
½ **cup coarsely chopped green peppers**
⅓ **cup fat-free egg substitute**
¼ **cup finely chopped red onions**
1 **tablespoon canola oil**

For the sauce, in a small bowl, stir together the yogurt, salsa
and cilantro; set aside.

In a medium bowl, stir together the spaghetti, beans, peppers,
egg substitute and onions.

To make the pancakes, spray an unheated, large no-stick skillet with no-stick spray. Add 1 teaspoon of the oil and heat over
medium heat. Add the spaghetti mixture to the skillet, using a
scant ¼ cup for each pancake. Flatten slightly and cook about
4 minutes or until the tops appear set. Carefully turn the pancakes over and cook for 3 to 4 minutes more or until golden.
Repeat cooking more pancakes, using the remaining batter and
adding 1 teaspoon of the remaining oil to the skillet between
batches. Serve with the sauce.

Stuffed Acorn Squash Aztec

Quinoa is a high-protein grain of ancient origins. In this up-to-date dish, it's stuffed into acorn squash for a satisfying one-dish meal.

> 2 medium acorn squash (1¾–2 pounds each)
> 1¼ cups defatted low-sodium chicken broth
> ½ cup quinoa
> 2 teaspoons canola oil
> 1½ cups shredded red cabbage
> 1 medium onion, chopped
> 1 tablespoon honey
> 1 tablespoon cider vinegar
> ½ cup canned black beans, rinsed and drained
> ½ cup golden raisins

Cut each squash in half lengthwise. Remove and discard the seeds. Place the squash, cut side down, in a large baking dish. Bake at 375° about 45 minutes or just until the pulp is tender when tested with a fork.

Meanwhile, bring 1 cup of the broth to a boil in a medium saucepan. Stir in the quinoa, then reduce the heat. Cover and simmer for 20 to 25 minutes or until the liquid is absorbed. Remove the saucepan from the heat and let stand, covered, for 5 minutes. Use a fork to fluff the quinoa.

Add the oil to a medium no-stick skillet and heat over medium heat. Add the cabbage and onions. Cook and stir for 4 to 5 minutes or until the vegetables are tender. Stir in the remaining ¼ cup of broth, the honey and vinegar. Bring to a boil, then reduce the heat. Simmer, uncovered, for 5 minutes or until the liquid has evaporated. Remove the skillet from the heat and stir in the quinoa, beans and raisins.

Spoon the mixture evenly into the squash halves. Bake at 375° for 10 to 15 minutes more or until heated through.

EXTRA HEALTH BENEFITS
Lower Cholesterol
Blood Building
Stronger Immunity

Times: Prep: 6 min.
Cooking: 29 min.
Baking: 55 min.

Makes 4 servings.

Per serving: 424 calories, 4.8 g. fat (9% of calories), 9.4 g. dietary fiber, 0 mg. cholesterol, 148 mg. sodium.

Fusille Primavera in Spicy Peanut Sauce

EXTRA HEALTH BENEFITS
Blood Building
Stronger Immunity

Times: Prep: 16 min.
Cooking: 13 min.

Makes 4 servings.

Per serving: 417 calories,
10.8 g. fat (23% of calories),
4.6 g. dietary fiber, 2 mg.
cholesterol, 188 mg. sodium.

This creamy pasta is reminiscent of sesame noodles, a popular Chinese dish often served cold. We've cut fat by mixing peanut butter with nonfat sour cream to extend its nutty flavor.

     3 **tablespoons smooth peanut butter**
     3 **tablespoons nonfat sour cream**
     2 **teaspoons rice vinegar**
     1 **teaspoon reduced-sodium soy sauce**
   1/8 **teaspoon ground red pepper**
    10 **ounces fusille**
     2 **teaspoons Oriental sesame oil**
     8 **ounces snow peas, ends and strings removed and cut into julienne pieces**
     1 **cup green onions cut into 1" pieces**
     1 **cup cherry tomatoes, halved**
     1 **tablespoon sesame seeds, toasted**

In a blender or small food processor, blend or process the peanut butter, sour cream, vinegar, soy sauce and pepper until well combined. Transfer the mixture to a small bowl and set aside.

Cook the fusille according to the package directions, but without adding the salt.

Meanwhile, add the oil to a large no-stick skillet and heat over medium heat. Add the snow peas, onions and tomatoes. Cook and stir for 4 to 5 minutes or until the vegetables are crisp-tender.

To serve, drain the fusille, reserving 1 tablespoon of the cooking water. Rinse with hot water and drain again. Transfer the fusille to a large bowl.

Stir the reserved tablespoon of water into the peanut butter mixture. Then add the peanut butter mixture and vegetables to the fusille. Toss until coated. Before serving, sprinkle with the sesame seeds.

Chef's Note: Fusille is a spiral-shaped spaghetti. If you can't find it, use another textured pasta. It's the nooks and crannies that trap the creamy sauce and make eating this dish easier.

Stocking Up

Some people who prefer meatless meals like to go all the way, avoiding even stock or broth made from animal products. If you're among them, replace the chicken broth called for in these recipes with vegetable broth. You can buy it in some supermarkets and at health-food stores. Or you can make your own, using the following recipe. Freeze the broth in half- or one-cup portions so you always have some on hand.

Vegetable Broth

    8 cups cold water
    5 medium carrots, halved
    4 medium tomatoes, quartered
    3 medium onions, halved
    3 stalks celery, halved
    ½ bunch parsley
    1 clove garlic, minced

In a 3- to 4-quart saucepan, combine the water, carrots, tomatoes, onions, celery, parsley and garlic. Bring to a boil, then reduce the heat. Cover and simmer for 1 hour.

Let stand for 30 minutes, then strain the broth through a large sieve. Cool the broth, then refrigerate or freeze it.

Makes 8 cups.

Times: Prep: 10 min.
Cooking: 1 hr.
Standing: 30 min.

Full-Flavored Soups and Stews

Cioppino (page 266)

Chinese Vegetable-Shrimp Soup

EXTRA HEALTH BENEFIT
Lower Cholesterol

Times: Prep: 16 min.
Cooking: 20 min.

Makes 6 side-dish servings.

Per serving: 48 calories, 1.2 g. fat (22% of calories), 0.8 g. dietary fiber, 16 mg. cholesterol, 108 mg. sodium.

Here's an easy way to make low-cal soup—just let ginger and soy sauce jazz up chicken stock, then stir in some vegetables and shrimp.

> 4 **cups defatted chicken stock or low-sodium chicken broth**
> 2 **cups peeled and chopped cucumbers**
> 3 **shiitake mushrooms, rinsed and slivered**
> ½ **cup canned bamboo shoots, slivered**
> ½ **cup shredded spinach**
> ½ **cup chopped shrimp**
> 1 **teaspoon reduced-sodium soy sauce**
> 1 **clove garlic, halved**
> 1 **slice ginger root, cut ¼" thick**

In a large saucepan, combine the stock or broth, cucumbers, mushrooms, bamboo shoots, spinach, shrimp, soy sauce, garlic and ginger. Bring to a boil, then reduce the heat. Gently simmer, uncovered, for 20 minutes. Remove the garlic and ginger before serving.

Soup of A to Z

Quick

EXTRA HEALTH BENEFIT
Lower Cholesterol

Times: Prep: 9 min.
Cooking: 3 min.

Makes 4 side-dish servings.

Per serving: 58 calories, 0.8 g. fat (11% of calories), 1.8 g. dietary fiber, 0 mg. cholesterol, 33 mg. sodium.

This soup is letter perfect, combining apples and zucchini into a quick lunch. Round out your lean meal with a light sandwich, such as grilled chicken.

> 1½ **cups defatted chicken stock or low-sodium chicken broth**
> ½ **cup unsweetened apple juice**
> 1 **small zucchini, thinly sliced**
> 1 **small apple, cored and thinly sliced**
> 2 **green onions, thinly sliced**
> ½ **teaspoon grated lemon peel**
> ⅛ **teaspoon ground nutmeg**

In a medium saucepan, combine the stock or broth, apple juice, zucchini, apples, onions, lemon peel and nutmeg. Cover and bring to a boil, then reduce the heat. Simmer about 3 minutes or until the zucchini and apples are crisp-tender.

Chef's Note: Use whatever type of apple you like best. Granny Smith, Jonagold, Golden Delicious and Winesap are just a few of the varieties that would work well.

Zucchini Bisque

This chilled soup is the perfect mealtime opener during the hot summer months. Serve it with a few low-fat crackers.

> 3 small zucchini, cubed
> 1 small green pepper, chopped
> 6 green onions, sliced diagonally
> 2¼ cups defatted chicken stock or low-sodium chicken broth
> 1 cup skim milk
> Pinch of ground red pepper
> Dill sprigs (optional)

In a large skillet, combine the zucchini, green peppers, onions and 2 tablespoons of the stock or broth. Cover and cook over medium-low heat about 10 minutes or until the vegetables are tender, stirring occasionally. (If necessary, add more stock or broth during cooking to prevent the vegetables from browning.)

Transfer the vegetable mixture and the remaining stock or broth to a blender or food processor. Blend or process on low speed until smooth.

Return the mixture to the skillet. Cover and bring to a boil, then reduce the heat. Simmer for 5 minutes. Remove from the heat and stir in the milk and red pepper.

Cover and chill in the refrigerator for at least 1 hour. Serve in small bowls. If desired, garnish the top of each serving with a sprig of dill.

EXTRA HEALTH BENEFITS
Lower Cholesterol
Cancer Protection
Stronger Immunity

Times: Prep: 6 min.
Cooking: 15 min.
Chilling: at least 1 hr.

Makes 4 side-dish servings.

Per serving: 74 calories, 1.2 g. fat (13% of calories), 3.1 g. dietary fiber, 1 mg. cholesterol, 81 mg. sodium.

Times: Prep: 5 min.
Cooking: 5 min.

Makes 4 side-dish servings.

Per serving: 107 calories, 1.6 g. fat (14% of calories), 1.7 g. dietary fiber, 11 mg. cholesterol, 129 mg. sodium.

Cheese Tortellini Soup

Using ready-made cheese tortellini lets you get this soup on the table fast. If you would like an even leaner soup, use plain pasta such as rotelle or short fusille.

3 cups defatted beef stock or low-sodium beef broth
1 cup frozen cheese tortellini
1 cup frozen peas
2 tablespoons chopped sun-dried tomatoes
¾ teaspoon dried basil
¼ teaspoon dried oregano

In a medium saucepan, combine the stock or broth, tortellini, peas, tomatoes, basil and oregano. Cover and bring to a boil, then reduce the heat. Simmer for 5 to 6 minutes or until the tortellini are tender.

Is It Soup Yet?

Your family won't have to ask that if you take advantage of the soups in this chapter that have the "quick" symbol. For times when you want to speed up your own recipes, turn to your microwave. Here are some quick tips for converting your favorite recipes.

• Reduce the amount of liquid in your conventional recipe by one-fourth, since very little of the liquid will evaporate.

• Cut meat and vegetables into small, uniform pieces so they'll cook evenly and quickly.

• Microwave clear soups or brothy chicken-and-vegetable soups on high power (100%).

• Use medium power (50%) and longer cooking times for soups based on less tender cuts of meats, such as beef cubes. Start by cooking the beef in liquid to cover until tender. Then add vegetables and seasonings.

• When making fish or shellfish soups, cook the rest of the ingredients first. Then add the seafood and use medium power (50%); cook just until opaque. Allow a few minutes' standing time to complete the cooking process.

• Soups or chowders that are made with milk can be microwaved on high power. Choose a container that will hold double the volume to avoid boilovers.

• When precooking vegetables for pureed soups, use high power and little or no liquid.

Fennel Vichyssoise

Fennel adds a delicate anise flavor to this variation of the classic cold soup. But that's not the only difference. A standard vichyssoise would contain heavy cream, making it high in fat.

EXTRA HEALTH BENEFITS
Lower Cholesterol
Cancer Protection
Stronger Immunity

Times: Prep: 16 min.
Cooking: 23 min.

Makes 8 side-dish servings.

Per serving: 115 calories, 1 g. fat (7% of calories), 2.3 g. dietary fiber, 1 mg. cholesterol, 136 mg. sodium.

4 **cups defatted chicken stock or low-sodium chicken broth**
3 **large leeks (white part only), chopped**
1 **large onion, chopped**
1 **large fennel bulb, chopped**
4 **large potatoes, peeled and cubed**
2 **teaspoons reduced-sodium soy sauce**
1 **cup skim milk**
 Small watercress or Italian parsley sprigs (optional)

In a large saucepan, combine 2 tablespoons of the stock or broth, the leeks, onions and fennel. Cook over low heat for 3 to 4 minutes or until the vegetables are wilted, stirring often. (If necessary, add more of the stock or broth during cooking to prevent the vegetables from browning.)

Add the remaining stock or broth, the potatoes and soy sauce. Cover and bring to a boil, then reduce the heat. Simmer about 20 minutes or until all of the vegetables are very tender. Remove from the heat and stir in the milk.

Transfer the mixture in small batches to a blender or food processor. Blend or process on low speed until smooth. If desired, chill the soup in the refrigerator before serving.

Serve in small bowls. If desired, garnish the top of each serving with a sprig of watercress or parsley.

Chef's Note: Leeks are grown in sandy soil and often have a fair amount of dirt between the layers. Here's one easy way to remove it. Trim the root end and tough green leaves from each leek. Split it lengthwise, then cut into slices. Place about 4" of cold water in your sink, add the leeks and swish them around until they look clean. The sand will fall to the bottom and the leeks will float, so you can easily scoop them up.

SLIMMING STRATEGY

Cut down on calorie consumption at dinnertime by starting off with a bowl of soup. In one study, a bowl of tomato soup, served as an appetizer, reduced later calorie intake by 25 percent. Other starters, including cheese on crackers and fruit, didn't fare nearly as well.

Sweet Potato and Parsnip Soup

Both sweet potatoes and parsnips have a pleasantly sweet flavor that lifts this soup out of the ordinary.

 3 cups defatted chicken stock or low-sodium chicken broth
¾ cup coarsely shredded sweet potatoes
¾ cup coarsely shredded parsnips
 2 tablespoons minced fresh chives
¾ teaspoon dried fines herbes
   Pinch of ground black pepper
 1 small tomato, seeded and chopped
½ cup shredded Chinese cabbage

In a medium saucepan, combine the stock or broth, sweet potatoes, parsnips, chives, fines herbes and pepper. Cover and bring to a boil, then reduce the heat. Simmer for 12 to 15 minutes or until the vegetables are tender.

Stir in the tomatoes and cabbage. Simmer for 1 to 2 minutes more or until heated through.

Chef's Note: Fines herbes is a dried seasoning that's usually made from a blend of chervil, parsley, chives and tarragon. If you can't find the blend, use a scant ¼ teaspoon of each of the dried components.

EXTRA HEALTH BENEFITS
Lower Cholesterol
Cancer Protection
Stronger Immunity

Times: Prep: 21 min.
Cooking: 13 min.

Makes 4 side-dish servings.

Per serving: 88 calories, 1.3 g. fat (13% of calories), 1.1 g. dietary fiber, 0 mg. cholesterol, 76 mg. sodium.

Georgian Split Pea Soup

*The Georgia referred to here is in Russia, where a low-cost
soup like this would be standard peasant fare. But there's
nothing commonplace about the robust flavor of this filling
soup.*

 3 **cups water**
 1 **large tomato, chopped**
 1 **large carrot, sliced diagonally**
 ½ **cup shredded cabbage**
 ¼ **cup dried yellow split peas, sorted and rinsed**
 ¼ **cup pearl barley**
 2 **tablespoons minced fresh parsley**
 1 **teaspoon reduced-sodium soy sauce**
 1 **clove garlic, minced**

In a blender or food processor, blend or process 1 cup of the
water and the tomatoes until smooth. Transfer to a large saucepan. Add the remaining 2 cups of water, the carrots, cabbage,
split peas, barley, parsley, soy sauce and garlic.

Cover and bring to a boil, then reduce the heat. Simmer about
1¼ hours or until the barley is tender.

Mexican Vegetable Soup

Salsa is the secret ingredient that adds flavor without fat.

 1 **package (10 ounces) frozen French-style green beans**
 3 **cups defatted chicken stock or low-sodium chicken
    broth**
 1 **cup frozen crinkle-cut carrots**
 1 **tablespoon lime juice**
 ½ **cup mild salsa**
    Minced fresh parsley or cilantro

Place the frozen beans in a colander and run cold water over
them until they separate.

In a medium saucepan, combine the beans, stock or broth and
carrots and lime juice. Cover and bring to a boil, then reduce the

heat. Simmer about 5 minutes or until the vegetables are tender, stirring occasionally.

Serve garnished with the salsa and parsley or cilantro.

Chef's Note: Don't turn up your nose at frozen vegetables. They often give fresh veggies a run for their money in the health department. Because they're processed just hours after being picked, they retain nutrients that so-called fresh produce might lack if it's been in transit for a week or more.

Per serving: 68 calories, 1.2 g. fat (14% of calories), 2.5 g. dietary fiber, 0 mg. cholesterol, 391 mg. sodium.

Mexican Vegetable Soup

SLIMMING STRATEGY

Do you have a habit of tasting food as you cook? To keep from eating more than is wise, use an infant feeding spoon. That tiny spoonful will give you just enough to evaluate the seasonings but not enough to take in a lot of calories.

Corn Chowder

EXTRA HEALTH BENEFITS
Cancer Protection
Stronger Immunity

Times: Prep: 9 min.
Cooking: 8 min.

**Makes 4 side-dish
servings.**

Per serving: 118 calories,
1.2 g. fat (8% of calories),
0.4 g. dietary fiber, 1.8 mg.
cholesterol, 118 mg. sodium.

*You'll really appreciate this soul-warming soup when the
winter winds are howling outside.*

　1　**small sweet red pepper, finely chopped**
　3　**green onions, finely chopped**
　1　**shallot, finely chopped**
　2　**cups fresh or thawed frozen corn**
1¾　**cups skim milk**
　1　**tablespoon unbleached flour**
　1　**teaspoon reduced-sodium soy sauce**
　　Pinch of ground nutmeg

Spray an unheated large saucepan with no-stick spray. Heat
the saucepan over medium heat. Add the chopped red peppers,
onions and shallots. Cook and stir about 3 minutes or until the
peppers are crisp-tender. Remove from the heat and set aside.

In a blender or food processor, blend or process 1 cup of the
corn, 1 cup of the milk and the flour on low speed until smooth.
(If necessary, stop and scrape down the sides of the container.)

Stir the blended corn mixture, the remaining 1 cup of corn and
¾ cup of milk, the soy sauce and nutmeg into the pepper mixture. Bring just to a boil over medium heat, then reduce the heat
to low. Gently simmer, uncovered, for 5 minutes.

Corn Chowder

Chicken Vegetable Soup with Shells

Here's an old-fashioned homemade chicken soup that's a lot lower in fat and calories than Grandma's.

6 cups defatted chicken stock or low-sodium chicken broth

12 ounces skinless, boneless chicken breasts, cut into 1" pieces

1 large onion, thinly sliced

1 teaspoon poultry seasoning

½ teaspoon dried savory

¼ teaspoon ground black pepper

¾ cup tiny shell macaroni

3 cups frozen mixed broccoli, cauliflower and carrots or other mixed vegetables

In a medium saucepan, combine the stock or broth, chicken, onions, poultry seasoning, savory and pepper. Cover and bring to a boil, then reduce the heat. Simmer for 10 minutes, stirring occasionally.

Stir in the macaroni. Return to a boil, then reduce the heat. Cover and simmer for 5 minutes, stirring occasionally.

Stir in the vegetables. Return to a boil, then reduce the heat. Cover and simmer for 5 minutes or until the vegetables are crisp-tender, stirring occasionally.

Chef's Note: To keep the preparation time low, buy chicken breasts that are already skinned and boned. If you'd rather do the prep work yourself, start with about 1½ pounds of bone-in, skin-on breasts.

Quick

**EXTRA HEALTH BENEFIT
Stronger Immunity**

Times: Prep: 10 min.
Cooking: 20 min.

Makes 4 main-dish servings.

Per serving: 296 calories, 4.1 g. fat (12% of calories), 6.3 g. dietary fiber, 49 mg. cholesterol, 261 mg. sodium.

SLIMMING STRATEGY

You can add creamy body—but no fat—to most any soup by stirring in cooked and pureed white beans, potatoes, cauliflower, corn, carrots, onions or rice.

Times: Prep: 15 min.
Cooking: 8 min.

Makes 4 main-dish servings.

Per serving: 299 calories, 6 g. fat (18% of calories), 4.9 g. dietary fiber, 52 mg. cholesterol, 336 mg. sodium.

Pasta e Fagioli with Beef

If you're in the mood for minestrone, try this quick version. To keep the fat and calories down, we used ground sirloin instead of fattier ground beef.

12 **ounces ground sirloin beef**
2½ **cups defatted beef stock or low-sodium beef broth**
1½ **teaspoons dried Italian seasoning**
¼ **teaspoon onion powder**
⅛ **teaspoon garlic powder**
½ **cup elbow macaroni**
1 **can (16 ounces) low-sodium stewed tomatoes (with juices), cut up**
1 **can (16 ounces) kidney beans, rinsed and drained**

In a large saucepan, cook the ground beef over medium heat about 5 minutes or until browned, stirring occasionally. Drain in a strainer or colander, then transfer to a large plate lined with three layers of paper towels. Blot with additional paper towels.

Return the beef to the saucepan. Stir in the stock or broth, Italian seasoning, onion powder and garlic powder. Cover and bring to a boil. Stir in the macaroni. Return to a boil, then reduce the heat. Cover and simmer for 8 minutes or until the macaroni is just tender.

Stir in the tomatoes (with juices) and kidney beans. Return to a boil to heat through.

Chef's Note: For a treat, sprinkle a little grated Parmesan cheese over each serving.

SLIMMING STRATEGY

Make your own low-fat croutons by very lightly brushing whole-grain bread slices with a mixture of olive oil, garlic powder and dried herbs. Cut into cubes, place on a cookie sheet and bake at 300°, stirring often, for 10 to 20 minutes or until crisp.

Lemon-Asparagus Soup

Lemon juice and black pepper give a subtle flavor boost to the asparagus in this soup.

2½ **cups defatted chicken stock or low-sodium chicken broth**
 1 **package (10 ounces) frozen cut asparagus**
 ½ **cup instant mashed potato flakes**
 1 **tablespoon lemon juice**
 ⅛ **teaspoon cracked black pepper**
 1 **tablespoon minced fresh parsley**

In a medium saucepan, combine the stock or broth and asparagus. Cover and bring to a boil, then reduce the heat. Simmer for 3 minutes.

Stir in the potato flakes, lemon juice and pepper. Then cover and simmer for 1 to 2 minutes or until the asparagus is just tender. Stir in the parsley.

Chef's Note: By all means, use fresh asparagus when it's in season. Start with 1 pound of spears. Break off and discard the tough portions of the stems, then bias-slice the stalks into 1" pieces. Cook for the same amount of time as the frozen.

Quick

EXTRA HEALTH BENEFITS
Lower Cholesterol
Better Blood Pressure
Cancer Protection

Times: Prep: 9 min.
Cooking: 4 min.

Makes 4 side-dish servings.

Per serving: 59 calories, 1.2 g. fat (17% of calories), 1.5 g. dietary fiber, 0 mg. cholesterol, 54 mg. sodium.

Lemon-Asparagus Soup

Curried Chicken and Rice Soup

Buttermilk adds a pleasant tang to this exotic soup.

EXTRA HEALTH BENEFIT
Stronger Immunity

Times: Prep: 20 min.
Cooking: 36 min.

Makes 4 main-dish servings.

Per serving: 237 calories, 3.6 g. fat (14% of calories), 3.3 g. dietary fiber, 35 mg. cholesterol, 215 mg. sodium.

- 4 **cups defatted chicken stock or low-sodium chicken broth**
- 2 **medium carrots, thinly sliced**
- 2 **stalks celery, thinly sliced**
- ½ **teaspoon curry powder**
- ⅛ **teaspoon ground red pepper**
- ½ **cup brown rice**
- 8 **ounces skinless, boneless chicken breasts, cut into 1" pieces**
- 2 **cups thinly sliced mushrooms**
- 1 **cup buttermilk**

In a large saucepan, combine the stock or broth, carrots, celery, curry powder and pepper. Cover and bring to a boil over medium-high heat. Stir in the rice. Return to a boil, then reduce the heat. Cover and simmer for 15 minutes, stirring occasionally.

Stir in the chicken. Return to a boil, then reduce the heat. Cover and simmer for 15 minutes, stirring occasionally. Stir in the mushrooms. Cover and simmer for 5 minutes more.

Stir in the buttermilk. Cook and stir about 1 minute or just until heated through.

SLIMMING STRATEGY

Don't be scared by the name: Buttermilk is low in fat and calories—as long as it doesn't contain added cream, whole milk or butter flakes. (Check the label.) Buttermilk got its name because it was the low-fat fluid left after butter was churned. Use it in soups, baked goods, mashed potatoes, noodle dishes and more.

Times: Prep: 16 min.
Cooking: 5 min.

**Makes 4 main-dish
servings.**

Per serving: 216 calories,
5.7 g. fat (24% of calories),
0.6 g. dietary fiber, 52 mg.
cholesterol, 84 mg. sodium.

Potage of Beef and Mixed Vegetables

*All this filling soup needs to round out a meal is some
French bread and a tossed salad.*

> 12 ounces ground sirloin beef
> 4 cups defatted beef stock or low-sodium beef broth
> 1 teaspoon dried marjoram
> ¼ teaspoon ground black pepper
> 1½ cups frozen mixed vegetables
> 1 cup frozen small whole onions
> 1 cup frozen hash brown potatoes with no fat

In a large saucepan, cook the ground beef over medium heat
about 5 minutes or until browned, stirring occasionally. Drain in
a strainer or colander, then transfer to a large plate lined with
three layers of paper towels. Blot with additional paper towels.

Return the beef to the saucepan. Stir in the stock or broth,
marjoram and pepper. Cover and bring to a boil. Stir in the
mixed vegetables, onions and potatoes. Return to a boil, then
reduce the heat. Cover and simmer for 5 minutes or until the
vegetables are just tender, stirring occasionally.

Chef's Note: Change this recipe to suit your family's taste by
using whichever assortment of frozen mixed vegetables they
enjoy most. You may need to adjust the cooking time slightly.
Just check the directions on the package and add or subtract
time from the 5-minute cooking time listed in this recipe.

Hungarian Barley Soup

Using quick-cooking barley and ground pork really saves time here.

    4 ounces lean ground pork
    5 cups defatted chicken stock or low-sodium chicken broth
1⅓ cups quick-cooking barley
    1 teaspoon onion powder
    1 teaspoon dried marjoram
    ¼ teaspoon garlic powder
       Few dashes of hot-pepper sauce
    1 medium green pepper, cut into ½" pieces
    1 medium carrot, coarsely shredded

In a large saucepan, cook the ground pork over medium heat about 5 minutes or until no longer pink, stirring occasionally. Drain in a strainer or colander, then transfer to a large plate lined with three layers of paper towels. Blot with additional paper towels.

Return the pork to the saucepan. Stir in the stock or broth, barley, onion powder, marjoram, garlic powder and hot-pepper sauce. Cover and bring to a boil, then reduce the heat. Simmer for 5 minutes.

Stir in the peppers and carrots. Cover and simmer about 5 minutes more or until the vegetables are crisp-tender.

Chef's Note: If you should overseason a soup or stew with salt, add a few slices of raw potato and let stand for 10 minutes. The potato will absorb some of the excess sodium, so you can throw it out with the slices.

Quick

EXTRA HEALTH BENEFIT
Stronger Immunity

Times: Prep: 10 min.
Cooking: 10 min.

Makes 4 main-dish servings.

Per serving: 286 calories, 8.8 g. fat (25% of calories), 5.9 g. dietary fiber, 20 mg. cholesterol, 127 mg. sodium.

SLIMMING STRATEGY

There's no telling how fatty ground pork is. To take control of the situation, pick out a pork loin and ask the butcher to grind it for you (or do it yourself at home).

Salmon Chowder with Dill

EXTRA HEALTH BENEFIT
Stronger Immunity

Times: Prep: 25 min.
Cooking: 14 min.

Makes 4 main-dish
servings.

Per serving: 303 calories,
7.9 g. fat (23% of calories),
3.9 g. dietary fiber, 39 mg.
cholesterol, 206 mg. sodium.

This fish soup is so rich you won't believe how well it fits into your weight-loss plan. Light cream cheese is the secret ingredient that imparts a delicious creamy texture without contributing excess calories or fat.

8 ounces skinless salmon fillets (about ½"-inch thick)
4 cups defatted chicken stock or low-sodium chicken broth
2 teaspoons dried dillweed
⅛ teaspoon garlic powder
3 medium potatoes, peeled and cut into ½" pieces
1 cup frozen peas
1 medium leek, thinly sliced
3 ounces light cream cheese, softened
½ cup skim milk
¼ cup unbleached flour
   Cracked black pepper

Remove and discard the bones from the salmon and cut it into 1" pieces; set aside.

In a large saucepan, combine the stock or broth, dillweed and garlic powder. Cover and bring to a boil. Stir in the potatoes, peas and leeks. Return to a boil, then reduce the heat. Cover and simmer about 10 minutes or until the potatoes are almost tender. Stir in the salmon. Cover and simmer about 3 minutes more or until the fish flakes easily when tested with fork.

In a small bowl, stir together the cream cheese, milk and flour. Stir about ½ cup of the hot soup into the cream cheese mixture. Then stir the cream cheese mixture into the soup in the saucepan. Bring to a boil, stirring constantly, then reduce the heat. Cook for 1 minute more. Sprinkle with the pepper before serving.

Chef's Note: In a pinch, you can substitute canned salmon for the fresh fish. Before adding it, drain it well and remove the skin. Flake the flesh and crush the bones (which are soft enough to eat and contribute valuable calcium). Then add the salmon at the very end and cook for 1 minute to heat through.

SLIMMING STRATEGY

Treat yourself! Plan to reward yourself after every 2-, 3- or 5-pound weight loss. And make the rewards more grand as you go along. Just don't let food be your payoff.

Extra Health Benefit
Stronger Immunity

Times: Prep: 9 min.
Cooking: 5 min.

Makes 4 main-dish servings.

Per serving: 341 calories, 10.5 g. fat (27% of calories), 0.8 g. dietary fiber, 35 mg. cholesterol, 226 mg. sodium.

New England Fish Chowder

Here's a Yankee favorite that can be ready in 14 minutes—a plus for those who are frugal with their time.

2½ **cups defatted chicken stock or low-sodium chicken broth**
 1 **teaspoon onion powder**
 ½ **teaspoon dried Italian seasoning**
 ¼ **teaspoon garlic powder**
10 **ounces skinless cod or other mild fish fillets, cut into ¾" pieces**
 2 **cups frozen hash brown potatoes with onions and peppers**
 1 **can (12 ounces) evaporated skim milk**
 2 **tablespoons unbleached flour**

In a large saucepan, combine the stock or broth, onion powder, Italian seasoning and garlic powder. Cover and bring to a boil over medium-high heat.

Add the fish and potatoes. Return to a boil, then reduce the heat. Cover and simmer for 3 to 4 minutes or until the fish flakes when tested with a fork and is opaque all the way through, stirring occasionally.

In a small bowl, stir together ¼ cup of the milk and the flour. Stir into the fish mixture. Then stir in the remaining milk. Cook and stir over medium heat until the mixture thickens and begins to gently boil. Cook and stir for 1 minute more.

Chef's Note: To use frozen instead of fresh fish, add the whole fillets before the potatoes and simmer for 5 minutes. Then add the potatoes. Return to a boil and continue as directed in the recipe. As the fish thaws, break it up with a wooden spoon.

Tuna-Broccoli Chowder

Evaporated skim milk gives this soup a creamy appearance that you'd ordinarily associate with heavy cream—but at a fraction of the calories and fat.

1½ **cups defatted chicken stock or low-sodium chicken broth**
3 **tablespoons unbleached flour**
1 **teaspoon onion powder**
½ **teaspoon dried basil**
⅛ **teaspoon ground black pepper**
1 **can (12 ounces) evaporated skim milk**
2 **cups frozen cut broccoli**
1 **can (6 ounces) tuna (packed in water), drained**

In a small jar with a tight-fitting cover, combine the stock or broth and flour. Cover and shake until well combined. (Or combine the stock or broth and flour in a blender and process until smooth.)

Pour the mixture into a medium saucepan. Stir in the onion powder, basil and pepper. Cook and stir over medium heat until the mixture thickens and begins to gently boil. Slowly stir in the milk and broccoli. Cook and stir over medium heat about 10 minutes or until the broccoli is tender.

Stir in the tuna and heat through.

Quick

EXTRA HEALTH BENEFITS
Lower Cholesterol
Cancer Protection
Stronger Immunity

Times: Prep: 8 min.
Cooking: 10 min.

Makes 4 main-dish servings.

Per serving: 164 calories, 1.4 g. fat (7% of calories), 3.8 g. dietary fiber, 3.4 mg. cholesterol, 170 mg. sodium.

SLIMMING STRATEGY

When using canned broth, be sure to remove the fat that you find floating on the top. The easiest way is to place the can in the refrigerator until the fat hardens. Then lift off the fat with a spoon. You might even want to keep a few cans of broth in the fridge so they're ready when you need them.

Cioppino

EXTRA HEALTH BENEFITS
Blood Building
Stronger Immunity

Times: Prep: 9 min.
Cooking: 38 min.

Makes 4 main-dish servings.

Per serving: 238 calories, 3.3 g. fat (13% of calories), 1.3 g. dietary fiber, 158 mg. cholesterol, 318 mg. sodium.

Created years ago by San Francisco's Italian immigrants, cioppino (chub-PEE-noh) is a rich tomato stew chock-full of seafood. This low-fat version features shrimp, clams and haddock. For real Frisco flair, serve it with plenty of sourdough bread.

1 small onion, chopped
4 green onions, sliced
2 small cloves garlic, minced
1½ cups defatted chicken stock or low-sodium chicken broth
2 canned plum tomatoes (with juices), chopped
¼ cup minced fresh parsley
1 bay leaf
⅛ teaspoon dried thyme
Pinch of dried rosemary
Pinch of ground red pepper
Pinch of ground black pepper
8 ounces medium shrimp, peeled and deveined
8 littleneck clams, scrubbed
8 ounces skinless haddock fillets, cut into 1½" pieces
Minced fresh parsley (optional)

Spray an unheated medium saucepan with no-stick spray. Heat the saucepan over medium heat. Add the onions, green onions and garlic. Cook and stir over medium heat about 3 minutes or until the onions are tender.

Add the stock or broth, tomatoes (with juices), ¼ cup parsley, bay leaf, thyme, rosemary, red pepper and black pepper. Cover and bring to a boil. Reduce the heat. Simmer for 30 minutes.

Add the shrimp, clams and haddock. Cover and bring just to a boil, then reduce the heat. Gently simmer about 5 minutes or until the shrimp turn pink, the clams open and the fish flakes easily when tested with a fork and is opaque all the way through.

Remove and discard the bay leaf and any unopened clams. Serve in soup bowls. If desired, garnish the top of each serving with the additional parsley.

Chef's Note: If you'd like an even heartier dish, serve the soup over cooked spaghetti.

SLIMMING STRATEGY

Try including a high-carbohydrate food—like pasta or bread without butter—with your soup or stew to lessen your fat craving, so you won't be as likely to want a high-fat dessert later on.

Nouvelle French Onion Soup

One simple change eliminated a ton of calories and fat from classic onion soup: We cooked the onions in a pan coated with no-stick spray rather than sautéing them in a pool of butter and oil. To further lighten the dish, we used a small amount of reduced-fat mozzarella instead of a heavy topping of Swiss cheese.

2 **large onions, thinly sliced and separated into rings**
4 **cups defatted chicken stock or low-sodium chicken broth**
4 **cups defatted beef stock or low-sodium beef broth**
1 **clove garlic, minced**
1 **bay leaf**
4 **slices French bread or whole-wheat bread, toasted**
4 **slices (¾ ounce each) reduced-fat mozzarella cheese**

Spray an unheated large saucepan with no-stick spray. Heat the saucepan over medium heat. Add the onions and reduce the heat to low. Cook about 10 minutes or until the onions are tender and translucent, stirring often.

Add the chicken and beef stocks or broths, garlic and bay leaf. Cover and bring to a boil, then reduce the heat. Simmer for 40 minutes. Remove and discard the bay leaf.

Meanwhile, place the bread on a rack in a broiler pan. Top each slice with a piece of cheese. Broil 4" from the heat about 1 minute or until the cheese is melted.

To serve, ladle the soup into bowls. Top with the bread.

Chef's Note: Turn this into a complete meal with the addition of a spinach and tomato salad tossed with low-fat vinaigrette.

EXTRA HEALTH BENEFITS
Stronger Bones
Stronger Immunity

Times: Prep: 8 min.
Cooking: 50 min.
Broiling: 1 min.

Makes 4 main-dish servings.

Per serving: 282 calories, 7.5 g. fat (24% of calories), 2.1 g. dietary fiber, 12 mg. cholesterol, 393 mg. sodium.

Curried Lentil Soup

Here's a tasty way to add fiber to your diet.

Times: Prep: 10 min.
Cooking: 1 hr.

Makes 4 main-dish servings.

Per serving: 166 calories, 0.9 g. fat (4% of calories), 6.5 g. dietary fiber, 0 mg. cholesterol, 53 mg. sodium.

½ cup chopped onions
½ cup chopped celery
½ cup chopped carrots
3 cups water
1 can (16 ounces) low-sodium tomatoes (with juices), cut up
¾ cup lentils, sorted and rinsed
2 teaspoons curry powder
2 tablespoons low-fat yogurt (optional)

In a blender or food processor, puree the onions, celery and carrots.

Transfer the mixture to a large saucepan. Add the water, tomatoes (with juices), lentils and curry powder. Cover and bring to a boil, then reduce the heat. Simmer for 1 hour.

Serve in soup bowls. If desired, spoon a dollop of the yogurt on top of each serving.

Chef's Note: Unlike most other legumes, lentils don't need to be soaked before being cooked. Simply rinse them well and pick them over to remove any small stones or other debris.

Savory Turkey Soup

Popeye would love this one! It contains plenty of his favorite vegetable.

Times: Prep: 13 min.
Cooking: 5 min.
Standing: 1 min.

Makes 4 main-dish servings.

Per serving: 210 calories, 4.1 g. fat (17% of calories), 4.7 g. dietary fiber, 49 mg. cholesterol, 212 mg. sodium.

4 cups defatted chicken stock or low-sodium chicken broth
1 can (8 ounces) low-sodium tomato sauce
1 teaspoon dried savory
½ teaspoon onion powder
⅛ teaspoon ground black pepper
2 cups cooked turkey breast cut into ½" pieces
1 package (10 ounces) frozen mixed peas and carrots
2 cups torn spinach

In a large saucepan, combine the stock or broth, tomato sauce, savory, onion powder and pepper. Cover and bring to a boil.

Stir in the turkey and peas and carrots. Return to a boil, then reduce the heat. Cover and simmer about 5 minutes or until the vegetables are crisp-tender. Remove from the heat.

Stir in the spinach. Cover and let stand about 1 minute or just until the spinach starts to wilt.

Chef's Note: Spinach needs to be washed very well before using to remove the sand that's so often present. To save time, look for ready-to-use spinach. This product has been prewashed and trimmed, so all you have to do is tear up the leaves before adding them to the soup.

Savory Turkey Soup

Six-Bean Soup

If you don't have all six beans on hand, use whatever you've got. Just make sure you end up with three cups of uncooked beans.

EXTRA HEALTH BENEFITS
Lower Cholesterol
Better Blood Pressure
Cancer Protection
Stronger Immunity

Times: Prep: 15 min.
Standing: 1 hr.
Cooking: 1¼ hr.

Makes 9 main-dish servings.

Per serving: 305 calories, 3.2 g. fat (9% of calories), 1.6 g. dietary fiber, 0 mg. cholesterol, 146 mg. sodium.

½ cup dried kidney beans, sorted
½ cup dried navy beans, sorted
½ cup dried great northern beans, sorted
½ cup dried lima beans, sorted
½ cup dried pinto beans, sorted
½ cup dried chick-peas (garbanzo beans), sorted
12 cups water
12 cups defatted chicken stock or low-sodium chicken broth
2 medium onions, chopped
3 cloves garlic, minced
1 tablespoon dried oregano
2 teaspoons dried rosemary
1½ teaspoons dried sage
1 teaspoon dried savory
½ teaspoon ground black pepper
3 medium carrots, thinly sliced
1 medium turnip, peeled and cut into ½" pieces

In a colander, rinse the kidney, navy, great northern, lima, pinto and garbanzo beans.

In a 6-quart Dutch oven, combine the beans and water. Cover and bring to a boil, then reduce the heat. Simmer for 2 minutes. Remove from the heat and let stand for 1 hour. (Or you can combine the beans and water and let stand overnight.)

Drain the beans and return them to the Dutch oven. Stir in the stock or broth, onions, garlic, oregano, rosemary, sage, savory and pepper. Cover and bring to a boil, then reduce the heat. Simmer for 1 hour, stirring occasionally.

Stir in the carrots and turnips. Cover and return to a boil, then reduce the heat. Simmer about 15 minutes more or until the beans and vegetables are tender.

Chef's Note: Like many other soups, this one freezes well. Chill it, then pack it into pint containers. To reheat, place the frozen block and a little water in a saucepan. Place over medium heat and stir frequently until thawed and hot.

SLIMMING STRATEGY

Beans can chase away hunger. One Swiss study showed that dieters who included a bean dish with each meal were less likely to desire a snack 3 hours later. Those who didn't eat beans were ready to nosh.

Turkey Ragout over Rice

For a hearty winter dinner, there's nothing better than this mixture of turkey, tomatoes and green peppers served over steaming rice.

> 1 **pound skinless, boneless turkey breast, cut into 1" cubes**
> 1¼ **cups water**
> 1 **cup chopped tomatoes**
> 1 **cup chopped onions**
> 1 **cup chopped green peppers**
> 1 **clove garlic, minced**
> 2 **tablespoons lemon juice**
> 1 **teaspoon dried Italian seasoning**
> ½ **teaspoon ground black pepper**
> 2 **teaspoons cornstarch**
> 4 **cups hot cooked rice**

Spray a large saucepan with no-stick spray. Heat the saucepan over medium heat. Add the turkey, then cook and stir just until all sides of the turkey cubes are browned. Add 1 cup of the water, the tomatoes, onions, green peppers, garlic, lemon juice, Italian seasoning and black pepper. Reduce the heat, cover and simmer for 12 to 15 minutes or until the turkey is no longer pink.

In a small bowl, stir together the cornstarch and the remaining ¼ cup of water. Then stir the mixture into the saucepan. Cook and stir over medium heat until the mixture thickens and begins to gently boil. Then cook and stir for 2 minutes. Serve over the rice.

EXTRA HEALTH BENEFITS
Better Blood Pressure
Cancer Protection
Blood Building
Stronger Immunity

Times: Prep: 12 min.
Cooking: 14 min.

Makes 4 main-dish servings.

Per serving: 329 calories, 2.3 g. fat (7% of calories), 2.5 g. dietary fiber, 68 mg. cholesterol, 84 mg. sodium.

Ragout of Butternut Squash

EXTRA HEALTH BENEFITS
Lower Cholesterol
Blood Building
Stronger Immunity

Times: Prep: 20 min.
Cooking: 49 min.

Makes 4 main-dish servings.

Per serving: 466 calories, 5.6 g. fat (10% of calories), 7.8 g. dietary fiber, 0 mg. cholesterol, 631 mg. sodium.

The main star of this thick, rich vegetable stew is butternut squash. It's low in fat and calories but high in beta-carotene, a nutrient that may help prevent certain types of cancer.

2	teaspoons olive oil
½	teaspoon cumin seeds
½	teaspoon mustard seeds
1	medium butternut squash, peeled and cubed (4 cups)
½	cup defatted low-sodium chicken broth
1	can (28 ounces) tomatoes (with juices), crushed
1	can (15 ounces) pinto beans, rinsed and drained
¼	cup chopped fresh cilantro
2	tablespoons chili sauce
1½	cups shredded cabbage
1	cup drained canned corn
1–2	tablespoons fresh lime juice
4	cups hot cooked brown rice

Add the oil to a large Dutch oven and heat over medium heat. Add the cumin and mustard seeds. Cook and stir for 1 minute, then add the squash. Cook and stir for 2 minutes, then stir in the broth. Reduce the heat, cover and simmer for 12 to 15 minutes or just until the squash is tender.

Add the tomatoes (with juices), beans, cilantro and chili sauce. Bring to a boil, then reduce the heat. Simmer, uncovered, for 30 to 40 minutes or until the mixture thickens.

Stir in the cabbage, corn and lime juice. Simmer, uncovered, about 5 minutes more or until the cabbage is tender. Serve over the rice.

Ragout of Butternut Squash

Shamrock Stew

Let the luck of the Irish guide your weight-loss efforts! This easy stew needs only a slice or two of soda bread to turn it into a full meal.

1 **pound boneless beef chuck arm steak, cut 1" thick and trimmed of all visible fat**
3 **cups water**
2 **cups defatted beef stock or low-sodium beef broth**
1 **bay leaf**
3 **cups sliced carrots**
1 **cup peeled and cubed turnips**
1 **cup peeled and cubed potatoes**
1 **medium onion, sliced and separated into rings**
½ **teaspoon ground black pepper**
¼ **cup unbleached flour**
2 **teaspoons dried marjoram**

Cut the beef into 1" cubes. In a large saucepan, combine the beef, water, stock or broth and bay leaf. Cover and bring to a boil, then reduce the heat. Simmer for 1¼ hours.

Add the carrots, turnips, potatoes, onions and pepper. Cover and return to a boil, then reduce the heat. Simmer about 30 minutes or until the vegetables are tender. Skim the fat from the stew. Remove and discard the bay leaf.

Remove about 1 cup of the liquid. In a small bowl, use a wire whisk to stir the liquid into the flour until smooth and free of lumps. Then stir into the stew. Add the marjoram. Cook and stir over medium-high heat until the stew thickens and begins to gently boil. Cook and stir for 1 minute more.

EXTRA HEALTH BENEFITS
Blood Building
Stronger Immunity

Times: Prep: 16 min.
Cooking: 1¾ hr.

Makes 4 main-dish servings.

Per serving: 333 calories, 8.4 g. fat (23% of calories), 6.6 g. dietary fiber, 93 mg. cholesterol, 167 mg. sodium.

Pork and Vegetable Stew with Cornmeal Dumplings

Dumplings ordinarily add unwanted fat to stews, but these fluffy cornmeal dumplings contain only a small amount of oil.

STEW

- 12 ounces lean boneless pork, trimmed of all visible fat
- 2 teaspoons canola oil
- 2 medium onions, cut into thin wedges
- 1 clove garlic, minced
- 4 cups defatted beef stock or low-sodium beef broth
- 1 teaspoon dried marjoram
- ½ teaspoon dried thyme
- ¼ teaspoon ground black pepper
- 2 cups peeled and cubed sweet potatoes
- 2 cups frozen peas
- 3 tablespoons unbleached flour
- 3 tablespoons cold water

DUMPLINGS

- ¼ cup unbleached flour
- ¼ cup cornmeal
- 1 tablespoon minced fresh parsley
- ¾ teaspoon baking powder
- ⅛ teaspoon dried marjoram
- 3 tablespoons skim milk
- 1 tablespoon canola oil

For the stew: Cut the pork into 1" pieces. Spray an unheated 4-quart Dutch oven with no-stick spray. Add the oil and swirl to coat the bottom. Heat over medium-high heat. Add the pork, onions and garlic. Cook and stir until the meat is well browned.

Stir in the stock or broth, marjoram, thyme and pepper. Cover and bring to a boil, then reduce the heat. Simmer about 30 minutes or until the meat is almost tender.

Stir in the sweet potatoes. Cover and simmer for 20 minutes. Stir in the peas. Cover and simmer about 5 minutes more or until the vegetables are just tender.

In a small bowl, combine the flour and water. Stir into the

EXTRA HEALTH BENEFITS
Blood Building
Stronger Immunity

Times: Prep: 23 min.
Cooking: 1 hr. 10 min.

Makes 5 main-dish servings.

Per serving: 412 calories, 11.4 g. fat (25% of calories), 6.7 g. dietary fiber, 38 mg. cholesterol, 203 mg. sodium.

SLIMMING STRATEGY

From cooking expert Jeanne Jones, author of Eating Smart, comes this suggestion: Wear slightly snug clothes when you're in the kitchen. You'll be more aware of your body and less apt to taste too much of everything as you cook.

pork mixture. Cook and stir over medium heat until the mixture thickens and begins to gently boil. Cook and stir for 1 minute more.

For the dumplings: While the stew is cooking, in a small bowl, stir together the flour, cornmeal, parsley, baking powder and marjoram. In another small bowl, stir together the milk and oil. Add to the flour mixture and stir with a fork just until all the flour is moistened.

Spoon the cornmeal mixture into five mounds on top of the stew. Reduce the heat, cover and simmer for 10 to 12 minutes or until the dumplings are no longer doughy in the center.

Chef's Note: Use a toothpick to check the doneness of the dumplings. Carefully poke the toothpick into the center of one. If no dough clings to the toothpick, the dumplings are done. If some dough clings, cover the pot and cook the dumplings for 1 or 2 minutes longer. Then check again with a clean toothpick.

Pork and Vegetable Stew with Cornmeal Dumplings

Beef Stew with Potatoes and Parsnips

EXTRA HEALTH BENEFITS
Better Blood Pressure
Blood Building
Stronger Immunity

Times: Prep: 23 min.
Cooking: 1 hr. 50 min.

Makes 4 main-dish servings.

Per serving: 317 calories,
6.3 g. fat (18% of calories),
5.9 g. dietary fiber, 48 mg.
cholesterol, 111 mg. sodium.

Apple juice adds an unexpected hint of sweetness to this savory stew.

2	teaspoons canola oil
12	ounces beef top round, trimmed of all visible fat and cut into 1" pieces
2	medium onions, thinly sliced
2½	cups reduced-sodium vegetable juice cocktail
1	cup unsweetened apple juice
1½	cups water
1	teaspoon dried basil
1	teaspoon dried thyme
¼	teaspoon dried sage
⅛	teaspoon ground black pepper
3	medium potatoes, peeled and cut into 1" pieces
2	small parsnips, peeled and cut into ¾" pieces
1	large carrot, sliced
1	stalk celery, sliced

Spray an unheated 4-quart Dutch oven with no-stick spray. Add the oil and swirl to coat the bottom. Heat over medium heat. Add the beef and onions and cook until the meat is well browned, stirring frequently.

Stir in the vegetable juice and apple juice, water, basil, thyme, sage and pepper. Cover and bring to a boil, then reduce the heat. Simmer for 1¼ hours or until the meat is almost tender, stirring occasionally.

Stir in the potatoes, parsnips, carrots and celery. Cover and bring to a boil, then reduce the heat. Simmer for 35 to 40 minutes more or until the meat and vegetables are tender.

SLIMMING STRATEGY

Vegetable juices make a savory, low-fat, low-cal base for soups and stews. Tomato juice and vegetable juice cocktail are good choices, but so are carrot and other flavors that you might find at a health-food store or make at home. If you're monitoring your salt intake, look for reduced-sodium versions.

Moroccan Lamb Stew

Even lamb, which tends to be quite fatty, can fit into a weight-loss program. Here we use the loin, which is one of the leaner cuts, and supplement it with lots of vegetables. Serve this tasty stew as is or over couscous for true Moroccan flavor.

    2 teaspoons canola oil
    8 ounces boneless lamb loin, trimmed of all visible fat
      and cut into 1" pieces
    2 cloves garlic, minced
    ¼ cup unbleached flour
    5 cups defatted beef stock or low-sodium beef broth
    1 can (6 ounces) low-sodium tomato paste
    1 tablespoon paprika
    ¼ teaspoon ground black pepper
    2 bay leaves
    1 small rutabaga, peeled and cut into ½" pieces
    1 small acorn squash, peeled and cut into ½" pieces
    2 medium onions, cut into thin wedges
 1½ cups frozen corn
    ½ cup nonfat plain yogurt

Spray a 4-quart ovenproof Dutch oven with no-stick spray. Add the oil and swirl to coat the bottom. Heat over medium heat. Add the lamb and garlic. Cook and stir until the meat is well browned.

Stir in the flour. Then stir in the stock or broth, tomato paste, paprika, pepper and bay leaves. Cover and bring to a boil, then transfer to the oven. Bake, covered, at 350° for 45 minutes. Stir in the rutabagas, squash, onions and corn. Cover and bake about 45 minutes more or until the meat and vegetables are tender, stirring occasionally.

Add the yogurt, stirring until well mixed. Remove and discard the bay leaves before serving.

Chef's Note: If you aren't sure that the handles on your Dutch oven are ovenproof, protect them by wrapping them with at least two layers of heavy foil.

SLIMMING STRATEGY

The leanest cuts of lamb: Shanks have 153 calories and 5.7 grams fat in 3 ounces of cooked meat. Cuts like sirloin chops, sirloin roast and loin chops all have 173 calories and 7.8 grams fat. Just be sure to trim as much visible fat as possible before cooking and to spoon or blot off any fat that appears after cooking.

Skinny Side Dishes

Tossed salad with Peppery Balsamic Vinaigrette (page 306), Cranberry Vinaigrette (page 307), Dilled Cucumber Dressing (page 309) and Tomato Vinaigrette (page 306)

EXTRA HEALTH BENEFITS
Lower Cholesterol
Cancer Protection
Stronger Immunity

Times: Prep: 8 min.
Cooking: 4 min.

Makes 4 servings.

Per serving: 27 calories,
0.3 g. fat (8% of calories),
1.9 g. dietary fiber, 0 mg.
cholesterol, 166 mg. sodium.

Broccoli and Red Pepper Stir-Fry

The molasses, soy sauces and ginger give broccoli and peppers out-of-the-ordinary appeal.

> 8 ounces fresh broccoli
> 1 tablespoon water
> 1 tablespoon reduced-sodium soy sauce
> 1 teaspoon molasses
> ¼ teaspoon ground ginger
> ⅛ teaspoon cracked black pepper
> 1 small sweet red pepper, cut into bite-size strips

Cut the broccoli florets into bite-size pieces and thinly slice the stems. In a small bowl, combine the water, soy sauce, molasses, ginger and black pepper; set aside.

Spray an unheated large skillet with no-stick spray. Heat the skillet over medium-high heat. Add the broccoli to the skillet and stir-fry for 1 minute. Add the red peppers and stir-fry for 3 to 4 minutes or until the vegetables are just tender.

Add the soy sauce mixture to the vegetables. Gently toss until coated.

EXTRA HEALTH BENEFITS
Lower Cholesterol
Better Blood Pressure
Cancer Protection
Blood Building
Stronger Immunity

Times: Prep: 10 min.
Cooking: 5 min.

Makes 4 servings.

Per serving: 52 calories,
1.4 g. fat (21% of calories),
2.9 g. dietary fiber, 0 mg.
cholesterol, 25 mg. sodium.

Fresh Asparagus and Onion Sauté

These stir-fried vegetables get their nutty flavor and crunch from a sprinkle of toasted wheat germ—a low-fat alternative to nuts.

> 1 pound fresh asparagus
> 1 small onion, sliced
> 1 tablespoon water
> 2 teaspoons reduced-calorie margarine
> ½ teaspoon dried thyme
> ⅛ teaspoon lemon-pepper seasoning
> 1 tablespoon toasted wheat germ

Break off and discard the tough portion of the asparagus stems. Bias slice the asparagus into 1" pieces.

Spray an unheated large skillet with no-stick spray. Heat the skillet over medium-high heat. Add the asparagus and onions.

Cook and stir about 5 minutes or until the vegetables are crisp-tender.

Add the water, margarine, thyme and lemon-pepper seasoning. Stir until the margarine is melted and the vegetables are coated. Transfer to a serving dish. Sprinkle with the wheat germ.

Chef's Note: You may need to slightly reduce the cooking temperature if the vegetables are getting too brown on the outside but are still crunchy on the inside.

Fresh Asparagus and Onion Sauté

Orange Beets

Here's a delicious low-fat alternative to buttered beets.

EXTRA HEALTH BENEFITS
Lower Cholesterol
Better Blood Pressure
Cancer Protection
Stronger Immunity

Times: Prep: 12 min.
Cooking: 35 min.

Makes 6 servings.

Per serving: 60 calories,
0.2 g. fat (3% of calories),
1.8 g. dietary fiber, 0 mg.
cholesterol, 50 mg. sodium.

5 medium beets
2 oranges
½ cup orange juice
2 tablespoons water
1 teaspoon cornstarch
  Pinch of ground nutmeg

To cook the beets, cut off the roots. Then cut off the tops, leaving 2" of the stems. Place the beets in a large saucepan and add water to cover. Bring to a boil, then reduce the heat. Simmer about 35 minutes or until the beets are tender.

Meanwhile, peel and section the oranges; set aside. In a small saucepan, bring the orange juice to a boil. Stir together the 2 tablespoons water and cornstarch until dissolved. Using a wire whisk, slowly stir into the boiling orange juice. Reduce the heat to medium-low. Cook and stir until the mixture thickens and begins to gently boil. Cook and stir for 1 minute more. Gently stir in the oranges and nutmeg. Heat through and keep warm until ready to serve.

Drain the beets. Holding the hot beets with a fork, use a sharp knife to remove the skin. Slice the beets and arrange on individual serving dishes. Pour the orange mixture over the beets and arrange the oranges on top.

Chef's Note: If fresh beets are unavailable, substitute 24 ounces of canned beet slices. Just heat the beets, drain and top with the orange sauce.

Orange Beets

Dilled Brussels Sprouts in Cream Sauce

You might not think of dill in conjunction with brussels sprouts, but it complements the flavor of these little cabbages quite well. Light cream cheese used in the sauce gives it a rich, creamy texture without contributing too much fat.

12 ounces fresh brussels sprouts or 1 package (10 ounces) frozen brussels sprouts
⅓ cup skim milk
1 teaspoon cornstarch
1 teaspoon minced fresh dill or ¼ teaspoon dillweed
⅛ teaspoon garlic powder
⅛ teaspoon cracked black pepper
1 ounce light cream cheese, cut into cubes
10 cherry tomatoes, halved

Cut the fresh brussels sprouts in half. In a small saucepan, bring a small amount of water to a boil. Add the brussels sprouts and cook, covered, about 10 to 12 minutes or until the brussels sprouts are crisp-tender. Drain, reserving ¼ cup of the cooking liquid. (Or cook the frozen brussels sprouts according to the package directions, but without adding any salt. Drain, reserving ¼ cup of the cooking liquid. Cut large brussels sprouts in half.) Set aside.

Meanwhile, in a small bowl, stir together the milk, cornstarch, dill, garlic and pepper. Add to the saucepan and stir in the reserved cooking liquid. Cook and stir over medium heat until the mixture thickens and begins to gently boil.

Stir in the cream cheese and cook and stir until it melts. Add the brussels sprouts and tomatoes. Gently toss until coated. Cook just until heated through.

Chef's Note: You'll find fresh brussels sprouts in the supermarket almost all year-round, but they're most plentiful between October and April. Look for small, compact, bright green heads. If cooking them whole, cut a small ✕ in the root end so they'll cook more evenly.

EXTRA HEALTH BENEFITS
Better Blood Pressure
Cancer Protection
Stronger Immunity

Times: Prep: 6 min.
Cooking: 14 min.

Makes 4 servings.

Per serving: 75 calories, 2.1 g. fat (22% of calories), 4.2 g. dietary fiber, 6 mg. cholesterol, 64 mg. sodium.

SLIMMING STRATEGY

Walk it off! Plan to get in at least an extra mile of walking every day to help burn calories and bring you closer to your weight goal. A few simple changes in your routine may be all that's needed: Park a few blocks from work, take a walk at lunchtime, use stairs instead of the elevator. Such small steps will have a cumulative effect.

Basil Cauliflower and Sweet Peppers

So easy to make, and so low in fat and calories!

EXTRA HEALTH BENEFITS
Lower Cholesterol
Better Blood Pressure
Cancer Protection
Stronger Immunity

Times: Prep: 5 min.
Steaming: 10 min.

Makes 4 servings.

Per serving: 17 calories,
0.2 g. fat (8% of calories),
1.5 g. dietary fiber, 0 mg.
cholesterol, 8 mg. sodium.

- 2 **cups small cauliflower florets**
- 1 **small sweet red pepper, cut into thin strips**
- 1 **tablespoon minced fresh basil or 1 teaspoon dried basil**

In a large saucepan with a tight-fitting lid, bring about 1" of water to a boil. Place the cauliflower in a steamer basket. Arrange the peppers on top. Set the basket in the saucepan, making sure the basket sits above the water. Cover and steam for 10 to 15 minutes or until the cauliflower is crisp-tender.

Transfer the cauliflower and peppers to a serving bowl. Sprinkle with the basil and gently toss until combined.

Whipped Carrots and Potatoes

Here's a three-in-one vegetable dish that'll have 'em guessing what's in it.

EXTRA HEALTH BENEFITS
Lower Cholesterol
Better Blood Pressure
Cancer Protection
Stronger Immunity

Times: Prep: 15 min.
Cooking: 25 min.

Makes 4 servings.

Per serving: 70 calories,
0.7 g. fat (8% of calories),
2.8 g. dietary fiber, 0 mg.
cholesterol, 35 mg. sodium.

- 3 **medium carrots, sliced**
- 1 **small potato, peeled and sliced**
- 1 **small onion, chopped**
- 1 **tablespoon skim milk**
- 1 **teaspoon reduced-calorie margarine**
- ¼ **teaspoon dried tarragon**
- ⅛ **teaspoon ground black pepper**

Place the carrots, potatoes and onions in a small saucepan and add enough water to cover. Bring to a boil, then reduce the heat. Cover and simmer about 25 minutes or until the vegetables are very tender. Drain, then transfer to a medium bowl.

Using an electric mixer on low speed or a potato masher, beat or mash the vegetables. Add the milk, margarine, tarragon and pepper. Beat or mash until nearly smooth. If necessary, return the mixture to the saucepan and reheat over low heat, stirring frequently.

Chef's Note: For a fancy presentation, transfer the warm vegetable puree to a pastry bag fitted with a large star tip. Then pipe a mound of the mixture onto each dinner plate. You could also use this as a topping for shepherd's pie or other casseroles.

Whipped Carrots and Potatoes

Lemony Peas and Spinach

Plain-Jane peas can get a little boring. Perk them up with a splash of lemon, some tiny onions and a bit of spinach.

 1   **package (10 ounces) frozen peas**
½   **cup frozen small whole onions**
 1   **teaspoon reduced-calorie margarine**
¼   **teaspoon grated lemon peel**
 1   **teaspoon lemon juice**
     Pinch of cracked black pepper
 2   **cups torn spinach**

In a small saucepan, cook the peas and onions according to the directions on the pea package, but without adding the salt. Drain, reserving 1 tablespoon of the cooking liquid.

Add the margarine, lemon peel, lemon juice, pepper and the reserved cooking liquid to the saucepan. Gently toss until the margarine is melted and the vegetables are coated.

Stir in the spinach. Cover and let stand about 1 minute or until the spinach just starts to wilt.

Chef's Note: When grating the lemon peel, be careful not to get any of the underlying white part. It will add a bitter taste to the vegetables.

Quick

EXTRA HEALTH BENEFITS
Lower Cholesterol
Cancer Protection
Stronger Immunity

Times: Prep: 6 min.
Cooking: 4 min.
Standing: 1 min.

Makes 4 servings.

Per serving: 67 calories, 0.9 g. fat (11% of calories), 5 g. dietary fiber, 0 mg. cholesterol, 137 mg. sodium.

Zucchini in Fresh Tomato Sauce

Whether you grow your own zucchini and tomatoes or pick them up at the farmers' market, here's a low-fat way to savor these bountiful summer staples.

EXTRA HEALTH BENEFITS
Lower Cholesterol
Better Blood Pressure
Cancer Protection

Times: Prep: 18 min.
Cooking: 10 min.

Makes 4 servings.

Per serving: 50 calories,
1.5 g. fat (24% of calories),
2.1 g. dietary fiber, 4 mg.
cholesterol, 41 mg. sodium.

1	small onion, thinly sliced
2	medium tomatoes, seeded and chopped
1	tablespoon minced fresh parsley
½	teaspoon dried oregano
¼	teaspoon dried marjoram
⅛	teaspoon cracked black pepper
1½	cups zucchini sliced ¼" thick
2	tablespoons shredded part-skim mozzarella cheese

Spray an unheated large skillet with no-stick spray. Heat the skillet over medium heat. Add the onions. Cook and stir for 4 minutes. Stir in the tomatoes, parsley, oregano, marjoram and pepper. Cook about 2 minutes or until heated through, stirring occasionally.

Stir in the zucchini. Cover and cook for 4 to 5 minutes more or until the zucchini is crisp-tender.

Transfer the mixture to a serving dish. Sprinkle the cheese over the top.

Chef's Note: To seed tomatoes quickly and easily, cut them into wedges, then squeeze each wedge in your hand to remove the seeds.

SLIMMING STRATEGY

Beat the munchies by keeping such foods as frozen beans, snap peas and spinach on hand in the freezer. When you feel the need to snack, heat them in a microwave oven, add a sprinkle of vinegar and eat. That way, you'll be able to snack and it'll be nutritious.

Baked Potatoes
with Chive and Cheese Topping

So who needs butter on a baked potato when there's a creamy low-fat topping like this one around?

- 4 **medium baking potatoes**
- ¼ **cup nonfat cottage cheese**
- 2 **tablespoons minced fresh chives**
- 2 **tablespoons nonfat plain yogurt**
- 1 **tablespoon grated Parmesan cheese**
- ⅛ **teaspoon dried basil**

Wash and scrub the potatoes, then pat dry. Prick with a fork. Bake at 400° for 40 to 60 minutes or until the potatoes are tender.

Meanwhile, for the topping, in a blender or small food processor, blend or process the cottage cheese, chives, yogurt, Parmesan cheese and basil on low speed until smooth. Cover and chill in the refrigerator until serving time.

To serve, cut an ✕ in the top of each potato. Push in the ends and use a fork to lightly fluff the pulp. Spoon the cheese topping on top of each serving.

Chef's Note: When buying potatoes, choose ones that are fairly clean but have not been washed. Washed potatoes spoil quicker. If you intend to bake them, look for potatoes that are about the same size so they'll cook in the same amount of time.

Extra Health Benefits
Lower Cholesterol
Better Blood Pressure
Cancer Protection
Stronger Immunity

Times: Prep: 3 min.
Baking: 40 min.

Makes 4 servings.

Per serving: 127 calories, 0.6 g. fat (4% of calories), 3 g. dietary fiber, 2 mg. cholesterol, 71 mg. sodium.

Perfect Mashed Potatoes

Here are mashed potatoes that are as creamy as the ones Mom used to make—but with only a fraction of the fat. To serve four, peel and cube about 2 pounds of all-purpose, baking or yellow-fleshed potatoes. Place in a large saucepan, cover with cold water, bring to a boil and cook for 20 minutes or until tender. Drain well and mash with a potato masher or an electric mixer. (Don't use a food processor; the potatoes will turn gummy.) Whip in enough evaporated skim milk, nonfat sour cream or buttermilk to get the creamy texture you're looking for. Add a few grindings of black pepper. Serve the potatoes plain or topped with snipped chives, minced parsley or paprika.

Maple-Spiced Winter Vegetables

Make this your new Thanksgiving standard—a slimming replacement for candied yams.

1½ **cups peeled and cubed sweet potatoes**
  1 **cup peeled and cubed kohlrabi**
  ½ **cup sliced leeks**
  ⅓ **cup unsweetened apple juice**
  1 **teaspoon reduced-calorie maple-flavored syrup**
  ½ **teaspoon cornstarch**
  ⅛ **teaspoon ground cinnamon**
  ⅛ **teaspoon ground ginger**

Place the sweet potatoes in a medium saucepan and add enough water to cover. Bring to a boil, then reduce the heat. Cover and simmer for 10 minutes. Add the kohlrabi and leeks. Cover and simmer about 10 minutes more or until the vegetables are just tender. Drain, then transfer to a large bowl and set aside.

Meanwhile, in a small bowl, stir together the apple juice, syrup, cornstarch, cinnamon and ginger.

Transfer the apple juice mixture to the saucepan. Cook and stir

Maple-Spiced
Winter Vegetables

over medium heat until the mixture thickens and begins to gently boil. Cook and stir for 1 minute more.

Add the cooked vegetables to the apple juice mixture. Gently toss until coated, then heat through.

Chef's Note: Kohlrabi is a member of the cancer-preventing crucifer family. It looks like a pale green or red-purple beet with dark green leaves and a large single root. When selecting kohlrabi, look for small ones, because large specimens often have a woody texture. Make sure there are no soft spots on the bulb or yellowing of the leaves.

Sweet-and-Sour Pea Pods and Carrots

A purchased sweet-and-sour sauce gives these vegetables their Chinese restaurant panache. To keep the calories down, we've diluted the sauce with orange juice.

- 2 **cups fresh snow peas or 1 package (6 ounces) frozen snow peas, thawed**
- ⅓ **cup orange juice**
- 1 **tablespoon bottled sweet-and-sour sauce**
- ½ **teaspoon cornstarch**
- ¼ **teaspoon aniseed, crushed**
- 3 **medium carrots, cut into julienne strips**
- 4 **green onions, bias sliced into 1" pieces**

If using fresh snow peas, remove the ends and strings. In a small bowl, combine the orange juice, sweet-and-sour sauce, cornstarch and aniseed; set aside.

Spray an unheated large skillet with no-stick spray. Heat the skillet over medium-high heat. Add the carrots. Cook and stir for 4 minutes. Add the fresh or thawed snow peas and onions. Cook and stir for 1 to 2 minutes more or until the vegetables are crisp-tender.

Stir in the orange juice mixture. Cook and stir until the mixture thickens and begins to gently boil. Cook and stir for 2 minutes more.

Chef's Note: The easiest way to trim fresh pea pods is to snap off the tip, without breaking the string. Use the tip to pull the string all the way off the pod.

EXTRA HEALTH BENEFITS
Lower Cholesterol
Better Blood Pressure
Cancer Protection
Stronger Immunity

Times: Prep: 18 min.
Cooking: 8 min.

Makes 6 servings.

Per serving: 48 calories, 0.2 g. fat (4% of calories), 2.6 g. dietary fiber, 0 mg. cholesterol, 23 mg. sodium.

Times: Prep: 8 min.
Cooking: 7 min.

Makes 4 servings.

Per serving: 19 calories,
0.2 g. fat (8% of calories),
1.2 g. dietary fiber, 0 mg.
cholesterol, 6 mg. sodium.

SLIMMING STRATEGY

Find out what's eating
you—before you
overeat. Too often, a case
of the blues leads directly
to a bag of chips, brown-
ies or some other high-fat
"soother." A change in
attitude may rouse you
from your rut and extin-
guish your food cravings.

Caraway Summer Squash

*The combination of caraway seeds, dry mustard and black
pepper brings out the best in summer squash.*

¼ **cup nonfat plain yogurt**
1 **teaspoon cornstarch**
2 **tablespoons skim milk**
¼ **teaspoon caraway seeds**
⅛ **teaspoon dry mustard**
 Pinch of ground black pepper
2 **cups yellow summer squash or zucchini sliced**
 ¼" **thick**
1 **cup halved fresh mushrooms**

In a small bowl, stir together the yogurt and cornstarch. Stir in
the milk, caraway seeds, mustard and pepper; set aside.

Spray an unheated large skillet with no-stick spray. Heat the
skillet over medium-high heat. Add the yellow squash or zucchini. Cook and stir for 2 minutes, then add the mushrooms. Cook
and stir for 2 to 3 minutes more or until the vegetables are crisp-
tender.

Stir in the yogurt mixture. Cook and stir until the mixture thickens and begins to gently boil. Cook and stir for 2 minutes more.

Chef's Note: For an eye-catching presentation, use 1 cup summer squash and 1 cup zucchini.

Broiled Tomatoes

Here's a simple side dish for when you're in a hurry. Pair these tomato slices with broiled chicken breasts and you've got a meal in minutes.

- 2 **medium tomatoes, cut into 8 slices, ½" thick**
- 2 **tablespoons nonfat Italian salad dressing**
- 1 **tablespoon minced fresh cilantro or parsley**
- 2 **teaspoons lime juice**
   Pinch of ground black pepper
   Cilantro or parsley sprigs

Place the tomato slices on the rack in a broiler pan; set aside.

In a small bowl, stir together the Italian dressing, minced cilantro or parsley, lime juice and pepper. Spoon on top of the tomato slices.

Broil about 4" from the heat for 4 to 5 minutes or until the tomatoes are heated through. Arrange two tomato slices on each dinner plate and garnish with the cilantro or parsley sprigs.

Chef's Note: Before you turn on the broiler, remember to check the cooking distance. Use a ruler and measure from the top of the food on the rack in the broiler pan to the bottom of the heat source.

Broiled Tomatoes

Quick

EXTRA HEALTH BENEFITS
Lower Cholesterol
Better Blood Pressure
Cancer Protection

Times: Prep: 10 min.
Broiling: 4 min.

Makes 4 servings.

Per serving: 16 calories, 0.2 g. fat (10% of calories), 0.8 g. dietary fiber, 0 mg. cholesterol, 13 mg. sodium.

SLIMMING STRATEGY

Season vegetables with a spicy alternative to salt. Combine ½ teaspoon ground red pepper, 1 tablespoon garlic powder and 1 teaspoon <u>each</u> of dried basil, marjoram, thyme, parsley, savory, mace, onion powder, ground black pepper and sage. Place the mixture in a shaker and keep it on the table or near the stove.

Jícama, Romaine and Tomato with Hot-Pepper Dressing

EXTRA HEALTH BENEFITS
Lower Cholesterol
Cancer Protection

Time: Prep: 13 min.

Makes 4 servings.

Per serving: 55 calories,
1.5 g. fat (24% of calories),
0.9 g. dietary fiber, 4 mg.
cholesterol, 186 mg. sodium.

The jícama, chili peppers and seasonings give this version of a tossed salad great Mexican flavor.

2 cups torn romaine lettuce
1 medium tomato, cut into thin wedges
1 cup bite-size jícama strips
2 tablespoons shredded reduced-fat cheddar cheese
2 tablespoons nonfat mayonnaise
2 tablespoons skim milk
2 tablespoons canned diced green chili peppers
1 clove garlic, minced
¼ teaspoon dried oregano
¼ teaspoon ground cumin
⅛ teaspoon hot-pepper sauce

Salad Bar Savvy

Here's how to end up with a supernutritious meal instead of a dietary disaster the next time you sidle up to the salad bar.

• Go for "green" greens. The darker the lettuce, the higher the nutrient value. Romaine lettuce, for example, has more calcium, iron, vitamin C and vitamin A than pale iceberg lettuce. Other colorful choices might include kale, spinach, watercress and arugula. Don't forget parsley—you <u>can</u> eat enough to make a difference.

• Load up on lots of fiber-rich vegetables and fruits to boost your fiber intake. Carrots, snap beans, legumes (such as lentils, chick-peas and kidney beans), green peas, red cabbage, broccoli, cauliflower, sweet corn, apples and oranges are all low in calories and fat.

• Take it easy on the cheese. Eat only as much as a mouse would, about a tablespoon.

• If you want a little protein, choose shrimp, crabmeat, or turkey or chicken breast. All of these get only about 20 percent of their calories from fat.

• Skip the croutons, bacon bits, chow mein noodles and salads made with mayonnaise. They're much too high in calories and fat!

• Dress your salad with just a little vinegar, a squirt of fresh lemon juice or a nonfat or reduced-calorie dressing.

In a salad bowl, combine the romaine, tomatoes, jícama and cheese; set aside.

In a small bowl, stir together the mayonnaise, milk, chili peppers, garlic, oregano, cumin and hot-pepper sauce.

Drizzle the mayonnaise mixture over the romaine mixture. Gently toss until lightly coated.

Chef's Note: Jícama is a root vegetable of Mexican origin that looks like a big brown turnip. It has a thin skin that covers crisp, white flesh. Peel off the skin before cutting the flesh. You'll be able to find jícama in the produce department of most large supermarkets.

Garden Salad with Quick-Draw Dressing

We've combined ketchup and vinegar to create a no-fat Western-style dressing for this salad. The flavors complement grilled meat or poultry and corn on the cob, making this a slimming accompaniment for your next barbecue.

3   **cups torn leaf lettuce**
1   **small cucumber, sliced**
½   **small red onion, sliced and separated into rings**
3   **tablespoons reduced-calorie and -sodium ketchup**
1   **teaspoon vinegar**
1   **teaspoon water**
¼   **teaspoon paprika**
⅛   **teaspoon ground black pepper**

In a salad bowl, combine the lettuce, cucumbers and onions; set aside.

In a small bowl, stir together the ketchup, vinegar, water, paprika and pepper.

Drizzle the ketchup mixture over the lettuce mixture. Gently toss until lightly coated.

Quick

EXTRA HEALTH BENEFITS
Lower Cholesterol
Cancer Protection
Stronger Immunity

Time: Prep: 8 min.

Makes 4 servings.

Per serving: 29 calories, 0.3 g. fat (7% of calories), 1.6 g. dietary fiber, 0 mg. cholesterol, 92 mg. sodium.

Fuji Salad

Fuji Salad

Here's an Oriental vegetable salad that's dressed in rice vinegar, ginger and soy sauce. If you wonder where the speck of fat comes from—it's in the vegetables. Even carrots and peas contain minute amounts of fat.

- 2 **cups sliced daikon**
- 1 **cup sliced carrots**
- 1 **cup sugar snap peas, ends and string removed**
- ½ **cup chopped sweet red peppers**
- ¼ **cup rice vinegar**
- 1 **tablespoon reduced-sodium soy sauce**
- ½ **teaspoon grated ginger root**
- 1 **clove garlic, minced**

In a large saucepan with a tight-fitting lid, bring about 1" of water to a boil. Place the daikon and carrots in a steamer basket and set the basket in the saucepan, making sure the basket sits above the water. Cover and steam for 5 minutes. Remove the basket and let the vegetables stand until cool.

In a large bowl, combine the daikon, carrots, peas and red peppers. In a small jar with a tight-fitting cover, combine the vinegar, soy sauce, ginger and garlic. Cover and shake until well combined. Pour over the vegetables and toss until coated.

Chef's Note: A daikon is a Japanese radish that looks like a large white carrot and has a mild radish flavor. If daikons are unavailable, you can substitute red radishes or the white icicle variety.

Quick

EXTRA HEALTH BENEFITS
Lower Cholesterol
Cancer Protection
Stronger Immunity

Times: Prep: 9 min.
Steaming: 5 min.

Makes 4 servings.

Per serving: 48 calories, 0.2 g. fat (4% of calories), 2.6 g. dietary fiber, 0 mg. cholesterol, 187 mg. sodium.

SLIMMING STRATEGY

Are you still a member of the clean plate club? Resign! Too many people continue to clean their plates because of old messages they received as children. As a result, they eat more than they would if they let their appetite be their guide.

Time: Prep: 7 min.

Makes 4 servings.

Per serving: 43 calories, 0.9 g. fat (17% of calories), 1.5 g. dietary fiber, 1 mg. cholesterol, 60 mg. sodium.

SLIMMING STRATEGY

Spritz your salad. You'll use less dressing if you spray it on, so look for salad sprays—low-calorie dressings in pump-type bottles. To make your own, mix up a low-oil vinaigrette and place it in a pump bottle. But leave out the herbs or any other ingredient that would clog the pump—add those directly to your salad.

Asparagus and Tomato with Yogurt-Cheese Dressing

Using frozen asparagus makes this vegetable salad extra quick and supereasy.

1 package (10 ounces) frozen cut asparagus
1 medium tomato, chopped
2 tablespoons sliced green onions
3 tablespoons nonfat plain yogurt
1 tablespoon grated Parmesan cheese
1 teaspoon prepared mustard
  Leaf lettuce

Place the frozen asparagus in a colander. Rinse under warm running water until the pieces separate and begin to thaw. Drain well.

In a medium bowl, combine the asparagus, tomatoes and onions; set aside.

In a small bowl, stir together the yogurt, cheese and mustard. Add to the asparagus mixture and toss until well coated.

To serve, line salad plates with the lettuce leaves and spoon the asparagus mixture on top.

Chef's Note: If you love mustard and keep several kinds on hand, use one of them instead of plain yellow mustard. A spicy coarse mustard or a garlic-flavored one would be great in this salad.

Green and White Vegetable Salad

Calling all garlic lovers—here's the salad for you. This salad uses about six cloves!

3 cups halved green beans
3 cups cauliflower florets
3 cups broccoli florets
2 tablespoons sesame seeds
1 tablespoon minced garlic
3 tablespoons defatted low-sodium chicken broth
2 tablespoons vinegar
1 tablespoon honey
1 tablespoon reduced-sodium soy sauce

In a large saucepan with a tight-fitting lid, bring about 1" of water to a boil. Place the beans, cauliflower and broccoli in a steamer basket and set the basket in the saucepan, making sure the basket sits above the water. Cover and steam for 10 to 15 minutes or until the vegetables are crisp-tender. (Do not overcook.) Rinse the vegetables under cold water until they are cool, then drain well.

Meanwhile, spray an unheated small skillet with no-stick spray. Heat the skillet over low heat. Add the sesame seeds and garlic. Cook and stir for 1 to 2 minutes or until the sesame seeds are lightly toasted. (Do not allow the garlic to brown or it will taste bitter.) Remove the skillet from the heat and stir in the broth, vinegar, honey and soy sauce until well combined.

Transfer the steamed vegetables to a shallow container. Drizzle the broth mixture over the vegetables and toss until coated. Cover and refrigerate for 4 to 6 hours before serving, gently tossing the vegetables occasionally. Gently toss again before serving.

EXTRA HEALTH BENEFITS
Lower Cholesterol
Cancer Protection
Stronger Immunity

Times: Prep: 16 min.
Steaming: 10 min.
Chilling: 4 hr.

Makes 6 servings.

Per serving: 74 calories, 1.8 g. fat (19% of calories), 2.9 g. dietary fiber, 0 mg. cholesterol, 126 mg. sodium.

SLIMMING STRATEGY

Imported whole-grain crackers like Ry-Krisp are a low-fat salad accompaniment. And when broken up, they can substitute for high-fat croutons.

Serendipitous Spinach Salad

EXTRA HEALTH BENEFITS
Lower Cholesterol
Better Blood Pressure
Cancer Protection
Stronger Immunity

Time: Prep: 16 min.

Makes 4 servings.

Per serving: 62 calories,
0.4 g. fat (5% of calories),
2.4 g. dietary fiber, 0 mg.
cholesterol, 62 mg. sodium.

When you're looking for a new salad idea, try this change of pace—apples and grapes tossed with spinach and topped with a creamy honey-lime dressing. For variety, substitute peaches and kiwifruit for the other fruit.

- 4 **cups torn spinach**
- 1 **medium apple or pear, cored and coarsely chopped**
- ¼ **cup seedless red grapes, halved**
- ¼ **cup sliced celery**
- ¼ **cup nonfat plain yogurt**
- 1 **tablespoon honey**
- ¼ **teaspoon grated lime peel**

In a salad bowl, combine the spinach, apples or pears, grapes and celery; set aside.

In a small bowl, stir together the yogurt, honey and lime peel. Drizzle over the spinach mixture. Gently toss until lightly coated.

Confetti Bulgur Salad

EXTRA HEALTH BENEFITS
Lower Cholesterol
Better Blood Pressure
Cancer Protection
Stronger Immunity

Times: Standing: 1 hr.
Prep: 25 min.
Chilling: at least 2 hr.

Makes 4 servings.

Per serving: 94 calories,
0.7 g. fat (6% of calories),
5.2 g. dietary fiber, 0 mg.
cholesterol, 29 mg. sodium.

We've combined bulgur with a mixture of vegetables to create this hearty fiber-rich salad. Serve it with grilled chicken breasts or lean pork.

- ½ **cup bulgur**
- ½ **cup defatted low-sodium chicken broth**
- 1 **small cucumber, seeded and chopped**
- 1 **medium tomato, chopped**
- 1 **medium carrot, shredded**
- 3 **green onions, thinly sliced**
- 3 **tablespoons lime juice**
- ¾ **teaspoon chili powder**
- **Pinch of garlic powder**

Place the bulgur in a colander and rinse under cold running water. Drain and transfer to a small bowl. In a small saucepan, bring the broth to a boil. Stir into the bulgur and let stand for 1 hour.

Stir in the cucumbers, tomatoes, carrots and onions.

In another small bowl, stir together the lime juice, chili powder and garlic powder. Pour over the bulgur mixture and stir until combined.

Cover and chill the mixture in the refrigerator for at least 2 hours before serving, stirring occasionally. Stir before serving.

Chef's Note: To fit this salad into a busy schedule, do most of the work the night before. Mix the vegetables and refrigerate them in one bowl. Mix the broth and bulgur in another bowl and refrigerate that also. Early the next day, combine the vegetables and bulgur, stir in the remaining ingredients and let the salad chill until dinner.

Confetti Bulgur Salad

EXTRA HEALTH BENEFITS
Lower Cholesterol
Better Blood Pressure
Cancer Protection
Stronger Immunity

Time: Prep: 8 min.

Makes 4 servings.

Per serving: 67 calories,
0.3 g. fat (3% of calories),
2.6 g. dietary fiber, 0 mg.
cholesterol, 17 mg. sodium.

Florida Slaw

Who would ever think of adding citrus fruit to coleslaw? You would—from now on.

> 1 **can (8 ounces) grapefruit sections (packed in juice)**
> 1 **medium orange, peeled and sliced**
> 2 **cups preshredded coleslaw mixture**
> ½ **cup halved strawberries**
> 2 **tablespoons nonfat Italian salad dressing**
> 1 **tablespoon orange juice**
> 2 **teaspoons honey**
> ⅛ **teaspoon ground cinnamon**

Drain the juice from the grapefruit into a small bowl. Set the juice aside. Cut the orange slices into bite-size pieces.

In a salad bowl, combine the grapefruit, oranges, coleslaw mixture and strawberries; set aside.

In a small jar with a tight-fitting cover, combine 1 tablespoon of the grapefruit juice, the salad dressing, orange juice, honey and cinnamon. Cover and shake until well combined.

Drizzle the dressing mixture over the fruit mixture. Gently toss until well coated.

EXTRA HEALTH BENEFITS
Lower Cholesterol
Cancer Protection

Times: Prep: 11 min.
Chilling: at least 1 hr.

Makes 4 servings.

Per serving: 100 calories,
2.7 g. fat (24% of calories),
3.2 g. dietary fiber, 0 mg.
cholesterol, 20 mg. sodium.

Sultan's Garden Salad

Balsamic vinegar and tarragon give this colorful salad a savory yet slightly sweet flavor.

> ½ **cup defatted low-sodium chicken broth**
> ⅓ **cup couscous**
> 1 **cup chopped fresh broccoli**
> ¾ **cup sliced fresh mushrooms**
> ¼ **cup sliced radishes**
> 2 **tablespoons balsamic vinegar**
> 2 **teaspoons canola oil**
> ¼ **teaspoon dried tarragon**
> ⅛ **teaspoon ground black pepper**

Bring the broth to a boil in a small saucepan. Remove the saucepan from the heat and stir in the couscous. Let stand for 10 minutes.

Meanwhile, in a salad bowl, combine the broccoli, mushrooms and radishes; set aside.

In a small jar with a tight-fitting cover, combine the vinegar, oil, tarragon and pepper. Cover and shake until well combined.

Pour the vinegar mixture over the vegetable mixture. Toss until well coated. Stir in the couscous mixture. Cover and chill in the refrigerator for at least 1 hour before serving. Stir before serving.

Chef's Note: Couscous is made up of tiny semolina beads and is a staple in North African cooking. Look for it in the pasta or rice section of your supermarket.

Fruited Pasta Salad with Lemon-Poppy Seed Dressing

The creamy poppy seed dressing used here is easy on the waistline—it's made from low-fat lemon yogurt. For variety, stir up the dressing and serve it over a mixture of your favorite fruits.

EXTRA HEALTH BENEFITS
Lower Cholesterol
Better Blood Pressure

Time: Prep: 30 min.

Makes 6 servings.

Per serving: 79 calories, 0.7 g. fat (8% of calories), 2.2 g. dietary fiber, 1 mg. cholesterol, 16 mg. sodium.

1½ **cups cooked shell macaroni**
  2 **cups torn bibb or Boston lettuce**
  1 **small pear, cored and coarsely chopped**
  1 **cup sliced fresh strawberries**
⅓ **cup sliced celery**
⅓ **cup low-fat lemon yogurt**
  1 **tablespoon orange juice**
½ **teaspoon poppy seeds**

If the macaroni is still warm, rinse it under cold running water until cool. Drain well.

In a salad bowl, combine the macaroni, lettuce, pears, strawberries and celery; set aside.

In a small bowl, stir together the yogurt, orange juice and poppy seeds. Add to the macaroni mixture. Gently toss until coated.

Chef's Note: To keep this recipe low in sodium, be sure to omit the salt when you're cooking the macaroni.

Fresh Fruit with Orange Mayonnaise

Just a spoonful of orange marmalade adds a delightful sweet note—but no fat—to this refreshing fruit combination.

> 2 **medium oranges, peeled and sliced**
> 2 **medium apples, cored and thinly sliced**
> 1 **cup fresh blueberries**
> ¼ **cup nonfat mayonnaise**
> 2 **tablespoons low-calorie orange marmalade**
> ¼ **teaspoon ground nutmeg**

On a serving platter, arrange the oranges and apples. Sprinkle with the blueberries and set aside.

In a small bowl, stir together the mayonnaise, marmalade and nutmeg. Serve the mayonnaise with the fruit.

Sunshine Tossed Salad

This pineapple dressing uses only a tad of oil to help the dressing cling to the greens but not your waist.

> 1 **can (8 ounces) pineapple slices (packed in water or juice)**
> 2 **cups torn iceberg lettuce**
> 1 **small carrot, shredded**
> 1 **tablespoon raisins**
> 2 **tablespoons white vinegar**
> 1½ **teaspoons canola oil**
> ¼ **teaspoon grated lemon peel**
> ¼ **teaspoon celery seeds**

Drain the juice from the pineapple into a small bowl. Set the juice aside. Cut the pineapple into bite-size pieces.

In a salad bowl, combine the pineapple, lettuce, carrots and raisins; set aside.

In a small jar with a tight-fitting cover, combine 2 tablespoons of the pineapple juice, the vinegar, oil, lemon peel and celery seeds. Cover and shake until well combined.

Drizzle the juice mixture over the lettuce mixture. Toss until coated.

Salad of Gingered Fruit and Spinach

Salad of Gingered Fruit and Spinach

A creamy ginger-lime dressing adds the crowning touch to this colorful salad.

- ⅓ cup nonfat plain yogurt
- 1 tablespoon lime juice
- ¼ teaspoon grated ginger root
- ½ small cantaloupe or ⅓ honeydew melon
- ½ cup blueberries
- 2 tablespoons chopped red onions
- 8 large spinach leaves
- 2 green onions, sliced (optional)

For the dressing, in a small bowl, stir together the yogurt, lime juice and ginger. Cover and chill in the refrigerator while preparing the fruit.

To prepare the fruit, use a melon baller to remove the melon from the cantaloupe or honeydew. In a medium bowl, combine the melon balls, blueberries and red onions. Toss gently until well combined.

To serve, line four salad plates or bowls with the spinach leaves. Spoon the fruit mixture on top and drizzle with the dressing. If desired, garnish the tops of the salads with the green onions.

EXTRA HEALTH BENEFITS
Lower Cholesterol
Better Blood Pressure
Cancer Protection
Stronger Immunity

Time: Prep: 6 min.

Makes 4 servings.

Per serving: 50 calories, 0.4 g. fat (6% of calories), 1.4 g. dietary fiber, 0 mg. cholesterol, 33 mg. sodium.

SLIMMING STRATEGY

One of the best things about a nice big salad is that you can munch on it for a long, long time. To satisfy your craving to eat, select foods that require a lot of chewing—like carrots, celery, jicama, kale, spinach and raw broccoli and cauliflower. These foods are often the highest in fiber and the lowest in fat.

Here's alarming news—those few tablespoons of salad dressing you add to your salad can be a major factor in your total fat and calorie intake. Just 2 tablespoons of regular blue cheese dressing, for instance, can add 154 calories and 16 grams of fat (93 percent of calories) to your daily allotment.

Commercial nonfat and low-fat dressings are certainly an alternative. But for those times when you want an honest-to-goodness homemade dressing, try our low-fat offerings.

Quick

EXTRA HEALTH BENEFIT
Lower Cholesterol

Time: Prep: 7 min.

**Makes 1 cup or
8 servings.**

Per 2 tablespoons:
16 calories, 0.2 g. fat (12% of calories), 0 g. dietary fiber, 0 mg. cholesterol, 84 mg. sodium.

Quick

EXTRA HEALTH BENEFIT
Better Blood Pressure

Time: Prep: 7 min.

**Makes ⅓ cup or
4 servings.**

Per 4 teaspoons: 7 calories, 0.2 g. fat (18% of calories), 0.2 g. dietary fiber, 0 mg. cholesterol, 36 mg. sodium.

Peppery Balsamic Vinaigrette

½ cup defatted low-sodium chicken broth
¼ cup balsamic vinegar
2 tablespoons reduced-calorie and -sodium ketchup
2 tablespoons prepared mustard
½ teaspoon dried savory
½ teaspoon dried thyme
¼ teaspoon ground red pepper

In a small jar with a tight-fitting cover, combine the broth, vinegar, ketchup, mustard, savory, thyme and pepper. Cover and shake until well combined. To store, refrigerate for up to 1 week. Shake well before serving.

Tomato Vinaigrette

½ cup peeled and chopped tomatoes
2 tablespoons white wine vinegar
½ teaspoon dried basil
½ teaspoon dried thyme
½ teaspoon Dijon mustard

In a blender or small food processor, blend or process the tomatoes, vinegar, basil, thyme and mustard on medium to high speed about 25 seconds or until well combined. To store, transfer the vinaigrette to a jar with a tight-fitting cover and refrigerate for up to 2 days. Shake well before serving.

Cranberry Vinaigrette

- 1 tablespoon powdered fruit pectin
- ¼ teaspoon lemon-pepper seasoning
- ¼ teaspoon poppy seeds
- ⅔ cup cranberry juice cocktail
- 1 tablespoon white vinegar
- 1 tablespoon honey

In a small bowl, stir together the fruit pectin, lemon-pepper seasoning and poppy seeds. Then stir in the cranberry juice, vinegar and honey. Cover and chill at least 1 hour before serving. To store, cover tightly and refrigerate for up to 3 days. Stir well before serving.

Chef's Note: It's the small amount of fruit pectin that gives this dressing body that you'd normally get from an oil emulsion.

EXTRA HEALTH BENEFITS
Lower Cholesterol
Better Blood Pressure
Cancer Protection

Times: Prep: 10 min.
Chilling time: at least 1 hr.

**Makes ½ cup or
4 servings.**

Per 2 tablespoons:
46 calories, 0.1 g. fat (2% of calories), 0 g. dietary fiber, 0 mg. cholesterol, 5 mg. sodium.

Orange Vinaigrette

- ¼ cup orange juice
- 2 tablespoons balsamic vinegar
- 1 tablespoon Dijon mustard
- 2 teaspoons honey
- ⅛ teaspoon cracked black pepper

In a small jar with a tight-fitting cover, combine the orange juice, vinegar, mustard, honey and pepper. Cover and shake until well combined. To store, refrigerate for up to 1 week. Shake well before serving.

Chef's Note: This vinaigrette goes particularly well with fruit salads.

Quick

EXTRA HEALTH BENEFITS
Lower Cholesterol
Better Blood Pressure

Time: Prep: 5 min.

**Makes ½ cup or
4 servings.**

Per 2 tablespoons:
28 calories, 0.2 g. fat (6% of calories), 0.1 g. dietary fiber, 0 mg. cholesterol, 64 mg. sodium.

Creamy Italian Herb Dressing

¼ **cup nonfat plain yogurt**
¼ **cup nonfat mayonnaise**
¼ **cup skim milk**
½ **teaspoon dried Italian seasoning**
¼ **teaspoon garlic powder**

In a small bowl, stir together the yogurt, mayonnaise, milk, Italian seasoning and garlic powder. To store, cover tightly and refrigerate for up to 1 week.

Creamy Blue Cheese Dressing

1 **cup nonfat cottage cheese**
2 **tablespoons crumbled blue cheese**
2 **tablespoons skim milk**
1 **clove garlic, minced**

In a blender or food processor, blend or process the cottage cheese, blue cheese, milk and garlic on low speed for 20 seconds (the blue cheese will still be chunky). To store, cover tightly and refrigerate for up to 1 week.

Chef's Note: It takes only a small amount of blue cheese to give big flavor to this low-fat version of a fatty favorite.

Dilled Cucumber Dressing

½ cup nonfat plain yogurt
½ cup peeled, seeded and finely chopped cucumber
1 tablespoon minced fresh chives
1 teaspoon Dijon mustard
1½ teaspoons dillweed
½ teaspoon cider vinegar

In a small bowl, stir together the yogurt, cucumber, chives, mustard, dillweed and vinegar. To store, cover tightly and refrigerate for up to 1 week.

Chef's Note: This dressing also makes an excellent dip for raw vegetables or a sauce for fish.

Quick

EXTRA HEALTH BENEFITS
Lower Cholesterol
Better Blood Pressure

Time: Prep: 4 min.

Makes 1 cup or 8 servings.

Per 2 tablespoons:
10 calories, 0.1 g. fat (8% of calories), 0 g. dietary fiber, 0 mg. cholesterol, 29 mg. sodium.

Curried Chutney Dressing

¼ cup nonfat plain yogurt
¼ cup nonfat sour cream
¼ cup skim milk
1 tablespoon chutney, chopped
½ teaspoon curry powder
¼ teaspoon ground ginger

In a small bowl, stir together the yogurt, sour cream, milk, chutney, curry powder and ginger. To store, cover tightly and refrigerate for up to 1 week.

Chef's Note: If the dressing is too thick after being refrigerated, stir in a little more skim milk.

Quick

EXTRA HEALTH BENEFITS
Lower Cholesterol
Better Blood Pressure

Time: Prep: 8 min.

Makes ½ cup or 4 servings.

Per 2 tablespoons:
34 calories, 0.1 g. fat (3% of calories), 0.1 g. dietary fiber, 1 mg. cholesterol, 30 mg. sodium.

Lemon-Almond Biscotti
(page 316) and
Blackberry Parfaits
(page 325)

Pineapple Chiffon Pie with Strawberry Sauce

No one will believe how low in fat this luscious pie is!

CRUST
4 sheets phyllo dough (13" × 9" each)

FILLING
1 package (0.6 ounce) sugar-free pineapple gelatin
½ cup boiling water
⅓ cup frozen pineapple juice concentrate, thawed
1 can (12 ounces) evaporated skim milk

SAUCE
2½ cups sliced strawberries
1 tablespoon maple syrup or thawed pineapple juice concentrate

For the crust: Drape 1 sheet of the phyllo dough across a 9" pie plate. Press into the plate and fold the overhanging edges toward the center, crumpling them slightly to fit. Lightly spray the dough with no-stick spray. Repeat layering and spraying with the remaining sheets of phyllo dough.

Bake the crust at 375° for 5 to 7 minutes or until the shell is golden brown. Transfer the pie plate to a wire rack to cool.

For the filling: In a large bowl, stir together the gelatin and boiling water until the gelatin dissolves. Then stir in the pineapple juice concentrate and milk. Cover and refrigerate until the mixture mounds on a spoon.

Using an electric mixer, beat the gelatin mixture on high speed about 5 minutes or until fluffy. Pour into the crust. Cover and refrigerate for 2 to 2½ hours or until set.

For the sauce: Place 1½ cups of the strawberries and the maple syrup or pineapple juice concentrate in a blender or food processor. Blend or process on medium speed until smooth. Transfer to a small bowl. Stir in the remaining 1 cup of strawberries.

To serve, cut the pie into wedges and spoon the sauce over each serving.

Chef's Note: If you have any leftover sauce, serve it over angel food cake. Or heat the sauce and serve it on top of frozen yogurt.

Orange Angel Torte

Low-fat vanilla yogurt makes a luscious, sweet-tangy filling for this torte.

- 1 **cup low-fat vanilla yogurt**
- 7 **egg whites**
- ½ **teaspoon cream of tartar**
- 1½ **teaspoons grated orange peel**
- ½ **teaspoon vanilla**
- 5 **tablespoons honey**
- ¾ **cup unbleached flour, sifted**

Place a strainer lined with cheesecloth over a deep bowl. Spoon the yogurt into the strainer. Let stand in the refrigerator to allow the liquid to drain out.

Meanwhile, place the egg whites in a large bowl. Let stand at room temperature for 30 minutes.

Using an electric mixer, beat the egg whites on high speed until foamy. Add the cream of tartar, ½ teaspoon of the orange peel and the vanilla. Then beat on medium speed until the egg whites form soft peaks. Add 2 tablespoons of the honey, 1 tablespoon at a time, and continue beating on medium speed until the egg whites form stiff peaks but are not dry.

Sprinkle 1 tablespoon of the flour over the egg whites and fold in using a wire whisk or large spatula. Repeat sprinkling and folding in the flour until all of it is used.

Spray an 8" × 4" loaf pan with no-stick spray. Spoon the batter into the pan. Using a thin knife, cut through the batter to remove any large air pockets. Bake at 325° for 30 to 35 minutes or until the cake springs back when lightly touched. Invert the pan onto a wire rack and let the cake cool completely.

For the filling, transfer the drained yogurt to a small bowl. Discard the liquid. Stir in the remaining 1 teaspoon of orange peel and the remaining 3 tablespoons of honey.

To assemble the torte, remove the cake from the pan. Cut the cake horizontally into two even layers. Place the bottom layer on a serving platter and spread ¼ cup of the yogurt mixture on top. Then place the remaining layer on top and drizzle with the remaining yogurt mixture.

EXTRA HEALTH BENEFITS
Lower Cholesterol
Better Blood Pressure

Times: Standing: 30 min.
Prep: 20 min.
Baking: 30 min.
Cooling: 1½ hr.

Makes 10 servings.

Per serving: 101 calories, 0.5 g. fat (4% of calories), 0.3 g. dietary fiber, 1 mg. cholesterol, 67 mg. sodium.

SLIMMING STRATEGY

Give yourself a pep talk. When the cheesecake-laden dessert trolley rolls by in a restaurant, focus on what you won't gain if you abstain. Tell yourself that "thin" tastes better than the too-fatty desserts.

EXTRA HEALTH BENEFITS
Lower Cholesterol
Better Blood Pressure

Time: Prep: 5 min.

Makes 10 cookies

Per cookie: 66 calories,
0.6 g. fat (8% of calories),
2 g. dietary fiber, 0 mg. cholesterol, 1 mg. sodium.

No-Bake Fruit Cookies

If you don't have time to bake regular cookies, whip up a batch of these easy treats.

10 **dried apricots, cut up**
10 **pitted prunes, cut up**
½ **cup rolled oats or chopped walnuts**
 2 **tablespoons apple juice**
 1 **teaspoon ground cinnamon**

In a blender or food processor, blend or process the apricots, prunes and oats or walnuts until finely chopped. Stir in the apple juice and cinnamon. Shape into 10 balls. Cover and store the cookies in a cool, dry place.

EXTRA HEALTH BENEFITS
Lower Cholesterol
Cancer Protection
Stronger Immunity

Times: Standing: 30 min.
Prep: 20 min.
Baking: 30 min.
Cooling: 1½ hr.

Makes 12 servings.

Per serving: 121 calories,
0.6 g. fat (4% of calories),
2.5 g. dietary fiber, 0 mg.
cholesterol, 76 mg. sodium.

Cocoa Angel Food Cake

Lose weight and have your cake, too—as long as it's an angel food cake. Angel cakes are low in calories because they're made from egg whites and no added fat. This choco- late version is a delicious departure from the usual.

1½ **cups egg whites (about 12 egg whites)**
 ¾ **cup sifted whole-wheat pastry flour or sifted unbleached flour**
 ¼ **cup unsweetened cocoa powder**
 1 **teaspoon cream of tartar**
 1 **teaspoon vanilla**
 ½ **cup honey**
    Fresh fruit (such as strawberries, raspberries, blueberries or peaches)

Place the egg whites in a 5- or 6-quart bowl. Let stand at room temperature for 30 minutes.

Meanwhile, sift the flour and cocoa powder together 4 times; set aside.

Using an electric mixer, beat the egg whites on high speed until foamy. Add the cream of tartar and vanilla. Then beat on medium speed until the egg whites form soft peaks. Add the honey, 1 tablespoon at a time, and continue beating on medium speed until the egg whites form stiff peaks but are not dry.

Sift ¼ of the flour mixture over the egg whites and fold in using a wire whisk or large spatula. Repeat sifting and folding in the flour 3 more times.

Spoon the batter into an ungreased 10" tube pan with a removable bottom. Use a thin knife to cut through the batter to remove any large air pockets. Bake at 350° for 30 to 35 minutes or until the cake springs back when lightly touched. Invert the pan onto a wire rack and let cool for at least 1½ hours. Then remove the cake from the pan. Slice and serve with the fresh fruit.

Chef's Note: To differently flavor this cocoa cake, use 1 teaspoon of a flavor extract (such as almond, cherry, peppermint or orange) instead of the vanilla.

Cocoa Angel Food Cake

Lemon-Almond Biscotti

Biscotti are twice-baked Italian cookies that are usually lower in fat than other cookies. But this version goes one step better, using egg whites instead of whole eggs and only a small amount of oil.

EXTRA HEALTH BENEFITS
Lower Cholesterol
Better Blood Pressure

Times: Prep: 10 min.
Baking: 55 min.
Cooling: 15 min.

Makes 40 cookies.

Per cookie: 58 calories, 0.8 g. fat (13% of calories), 0.5 g. dietary fiber, 0 mg. cholesterol, 21 mg. sodium.

3 **cups unbleached flour**
½ **cup cornmeal**
2 **teaspoons baking powder**
3 **lightly beaten egg whites**
½ **cup honey**
2 **tablespoons canola oil**
1 **teaspoon almond extract**
½ **cup lemon juice**

In a medium bowl, stir together the flour, cornmeal and baking powder. In a large bowl, stir together the egg whites, honey, oil and almond extract.

Using a wire whisk, stir the flour mixture into the egg white mixture and add enough of the lemon juice to form a pliable dough. Divide the dough in half. Form each portion into a 12" roll.

Line a cookie sheet with parchment paper. Place the rolls 5" apart on the cookie sheet. Slightly flatten each roll to ½" high.

Bake at 350° for 35 to 40 minutes or until the tops are firm to the touch. Remove from the oven and let cool for 3 minutes. Using a serrated knife, cut each log diagonally into ½"-thick slices.

Place the slices, cut side down, on the cookie sheet and bake at 350° for 10 to 15 minutes or until golden brown. Then turn the slices over and bake for 10 to 15 minutes more or until golden brown. Transfer the cookies to a wire rack and let stand until completely cool. Then store in an airtight container.

SLIMMING STRATEGY

If you must eat cookies, keep in mind that hard cookies like gingersnaps and vanilla wafers tend to have less fat than soft-textured cookies. (Fig bars are a notable low-fat exception.)

Georgia Peach Soufflé

This no-yolk dessert soufflé is brimming with peach flavor. For a special presentation, arrange thinly sliced peaches on individual dessert plates and spoon the soufflé on top.

> 5 **egg whites**
> 3 **peaches, peeled, pitted and chopped (about 1½ cups)**
> 3 **tablespoons honey**
> 1 **tablespoon lemon juice**
> ½ **teaspoon ground nutmeg**
>   **Pinch of ground cinnamon**

Place the egg whites in a large bowl. Let stand at room temperature for 30 minutes.

Meanwhile, in a blender or food processor, puree the peaches.

In a small saucepan, stir together the peaches and honey. Cook and stir over medium-low heat about 20 minutes or until thickened. Remove from the heat and stir in the lemon juice and nutmeg. Transfer the peach mixture to a medium bowl and let cool to lukewarm.

Using an electric mixer, beat the egg whites until they form stiff peaks but are not dry. Using a wire whisk, fold ⅓ of the egg whites into the peach mixture. Then gently fold the peach mixture into the remaining egg whites. Spoon into an ungreased 1½-quart soufflé dish. Sprinkle the cinnamon on top.

Place the soufflé dish in a baking pan, then place the pan on the bottom rack of the oven. Pour 1" of hot water into the pan. Bake at 300° for 50 to 60 minutes or until a knife inserted near the center comes out clean. (Do not open the oven door until near the end of the baking time. Otherwise, the soufflé may fall.)

Chef's Note: If fresh peaches are not available, use thawed frozen peaches or well-drained canned peaches (packed in water or juice).

Extra Health Benefits
Lower Cholesterol
Better Blood Pressure

Times: Prep: 40 min.
Baking: 50 min.

Makes 8 servings.

Per serving: 50 calories, 0.1 g. fat (1% of calories), 0.5 g. dietary fiber, 0 mg. cholesterol, 35 mg. sodium.

Slimming Strategy
Runaway appetites may be tamed by a set schedule. Training your body to be hungry at certain times—by eating at the same times every day—might also lessen between-meal hunger pangs.

Sweet Potato Pudding

They don't call 'em sweet potatoes for nothing! These taters make great pumpkin-like desserts, like this dense custardy pudding.

2 **medium sweet potatoes (8 ounces total), peeled and cubed**
¼ **cup skim milk**
1 **tablespoon honey**
½ **teaspoon ground cinnamon**
½ **teaspoon vanilla**
1 **tablespoon shredded coconut, toasted**

Place the potatoes in a medium saucepan and add enough water to cover. Bring to a boil, then reduce the heat. Simmer, uncovered, about 20 minutes or until the potatoes are tender; drain.

In a food processor, puree the potatoes with the milk, honey, cinnamon and vanilla.

To serve, spoon the mixture into dessert dishes and top each serving with some of the coconut. Serve immediately.

Currant Kisses
and Sweet Potato
Pudding

Currant Kisses

These easy cookies are incredibly low in calories and have virtually no fat! If currants don't tickle your fancy, use snipped dried apricots, mixed fruit bits, dried cherries or dried blueberries.

  2 **egg whites**
¼ **cup dried currants**
  1 **teaspoon lemon juice**
  2 **teaspoons honey**

Place the egg whites in a medium bowl. Let stand at room temperature for 30 minutes.

Meanwhile, in a small bowl, pour enough warm water over the currants to cover. Let stand in the warm water until softened, then drain well.

Using an electric mixer, beat the egg whites on high speed until foamy. Add the lemon juice. Then beat on medium speed until the egg whites form soft peaks. Add the honey, 1 teaspoon at a time, and continue beating on medium speed until the egg whites form stiff peaks but are not dry. Fold in the currants.

Line a cookie sheet with parchment or brown paper. Spray the paper with no-stick spray. Drop the meringue mixture by level tablespoons 1" apart onto the paper. Bake at 275° about 20 minutes or just until lightly browned. Turn off the oven and leave the cookies in the oven for 1 hour with the door closed.

Remove the cookies from the oven and let cool. Then remove them from the paper. Store the cookies in a tightly covered container so they won't become soggy.

EXTRA HEALTH BENEFITS
Lower Cholesterol
Better Blood Pressure

Times: Standing: 30 min.
Prep: 11 min.
Baking: 1 hr. 20 min.
Cooling: 10 min.

Makes 30 cookies.

Per cookie: 3 calories, < 0.1 g. fat (1% of calories), 0 g. dietary fiber, 0 mg. cholesterol, 4 mg. sodium.

SLIMMING STRATEGY

One way to cut fat in baked goods is to replace the nuts with chopped dried fruit, as we have in these meringue cookies. An alternative method is to use only half the amount of nuts and toast them to bring out their flavor. Also, when the nuts are finely chopped, the flavor will be evenly distributed throughout the baked product.

EXTRA HEALTH BENEFITS
Lower Cholesterol
Better Blood Pressure
Cancer Protection
Blood Building
Stronger Immunity

Time: Prep: 4 min.

Makes 4 servings.

Per serving: 51 calories,
0.4 g. fat (6% of calories),
2.1 g. dietary fiber, 1 mg.
cholesterol, 23 mg. sodium.

Strawberries with Creamy Banana Sauce

Pureed bananas make a wonderfully rich, creamy sauce that you can serve over other fruit. Just be sure to serve the sauce soon after it's made, otherwise the bananas will turn brown.

> 2 **cups halved strawberries**
> ½ **cup nonfat plain yogurt**
> ⅓ **medium banana, cut up**
> ½ **teaspoon honey**
> ¼ **teaspoon vanilla**

Place the strawberries in 4 small dessert dishes.

In a blender or small food processor, blend or process the yogurt, bananas, honey and vanilla until smooth. Spoon over the strawberries. Serve immediately.

Chef's Note: The banana sauce is also good over angel food cake (try it with the Cocoa Angel Food Cake on page 314).

EXTRA HEALTH BENEFITS
Lower Cholesterol
Better Blood Pressure
Cancer Protection

Time: Prep: 7 min.

Makes 8 servings.

Per serving: 153 calories,
1.1 g. fat (6% of calories),
0.6 g. dietary fiber, 4 mg.
cholesterol, 33 mg. sodium.

Bubbly Fruit Cup with Raspberry Sherbet

Think of this as a fruity ice-cream soda in a bowl.

> 1 **can (15¼ ounces) pineapple chunks (packed in juice)**
> ¼ **cup honey**
> 1 **can (11 ounces) mandarin oranges (packed in water), drained**
> 1 **large banana, sliced**
> 1 **pint (2 cups) raspberry sherbet**
> 1 **bottle (10 ounces) club soda**

Drain the pineapple, reserving ¼ cup of the juice. In a medium bowl, stir together the reserved juice and the honey. Add the oranges and bananas and gently toss until coated.

To serve, spoon the fruit mixture into 8 dessert dishes. Top with a scoop of the sherbet. Then pour the club soda over each serving and serve immediately.

Chocolate Soufflé

Chocoholics will love this one! These individual soufflés are so rich in chocolate flavor that it's hard to believe they have only 136 calories.

> 3 **egg whites**
> ¼ **cup unsweetened cocoa powder**
> 2 **tablespoons cornstarch**
> 1 **teaspoon ground cinnamon**
> ¾ **cup milk**
> ½ **cup reduced-calorie maple-flavored syrup**
> 2 **egg yolks, lightly beaten**
> ½ **teaspoon cream of tartar**

Place the egg whites in a large bowl. Let stand at room temperature for 30 minutes.

Meanwhile, spray 6 (5- or 6-ounce) soufflé dishes or custard cups with no-stick spray; set aside.

In a medium saucepan, stir together the cocoa powder, cornstarch and cinnamon. Then stir in the milk and maple syrup. Cook and stir over medium heat for 4 to 8 minutes or until heated through.

Remove the saucepan from the heat and slowly stir about ¼ of the cocoa mixture into the egg yolks. Then stir the yolk mixture into the cocoa mixture in the saucepan. Set aside.

Add the cream of tartar to the egg whites. Using an electric mixer, beat on high speed until the egg whites form soft peaks.

Gently fold ¼ of the egg whites into the cocoa mixture. Then gently fold in the remaining egg whites. Spoon the mixture evenly into the soufflé dishes or custard cups.

Place the dishes or cups on a cookie sheet. Bake at 400° for 15 to 20 minutes or until the soufflés are puffed and a knife inserted near the center comes out clean. Serve immediately.

Extra Health Benefit
Better Blood Pressure

Makes 6 servings.

Times: Prep: 40 min. Baking: 15 min.

Makes 6 servings.

Per serving: 136 calories, 2.8 g. fat (18% of calories), 0 g. dietary fiber, 73 mg. cholesterol, 50 mg. sodium.

Slimming Strategy

Cocoa powder gives baked goods great chocolate flavor—without the high amount of fat that chocolate would contribute.

Extra Health Benefits
Lower Cholesterol
Better Blood Pressure

Times: Prep: 6 min.
Microwaving: 3 min.
Standing: 3 min.

Makes 4 servings.

Per serving: 110 calories, 2 g. fat (16% of calories), 2.2 g. dietary fiber, 0 mg. cholesterol, 45 mg. sodium.

New-Wave Streusel Apples

When you need a fast dessert to satisfy a sweet craving, try these microwave-baked apples.

¼ **cup nonfat plain yogurt**
1 **tablespoon honey**
2 **medium cooking apples**
2 **tablespoons quick-cooking oats**
1 **tablespoon brown sugar**
1 **tablespoon reduced-calorie margarine, softened**
½ **teaspoon ground cinnamon**

In a small bowl, stir together the yogurt and honey. Cover and refrigerate until ready to serve.

Core the apples to within ½" of the bottom. Peel the top ⅓ of each apple.

In a custard cup or another small bowl, combine the oats, brown sugar, margarine and cinnamon. Spoon into the centers of the apples.

Place the apples in a small microwave-proof dish. Cook in a microwave oven on high power (100%) for 3 to 6 minutes or until

---

Are You Addicted to Sweets?

When you give up eating sweets, do you experience strong cravings, headaches or irritability? Your cravings may be linked to neurochemicals triggered by certain foods that make you feel better.

So what can you do to cope with these cravings? Try satisfying your desire with a piece of nonchocolate candy. This type of sweet is not nearly as fattening as a dessert like ice cream or cake. And eating just a piece now and then may make it easier for you to stick with your weight-loss program. Here are a few low-cal candies to choose from.

- Butterscotch disk (0.2 oz.)—22 calories
- Breath gum (1 piece)—5 calories
- Breath mint (1 piece)—7 calories
- Caramel (1 piece)—39 calories
- Cinnamon bears (9 pieces)—48 calories
- Jelly beans (4 pieces)—52 calories
- Lollipop (1)—60 calories
- Toffee (1 piece)—60 calories

the apples are nearly tender, rotating the dish a half-turn halfway through cooking. Cover with plastic wrap and let stand for 3 minutes to finish cooking.

To serve, cut each apple lengthwise in half and transfer to dessert dishes. Top each serving with 1 tablespoon of the yogurt mixture.

Chef's Note: Cooking apples—like Cortland, Granny Smith, Rome Beauty, Winesap and York—hold their shape well when baked and are a better choice than McIntosh, Empire and other varieties that turn soft and mushy quickly.

SLIMMING STRATEGY

Play the wait-and-see trick. When you long for something sweet, wait 10 minutes. If you still crave it, try to wait 10 minutes more. If you simply can't wait, have one of the low-fat desserts in this book, or reach for a piece of low-cal candy (see the list on the opposite page).

New-Wave Streusel Apples

Chilled Strawberry Swirl

Think of this as a dessert soup.

- **4 cups medium strawberries**
- **2 tablespoons apple juice**
- **2 tablespoons nonfat plain yogurt**

Set 4 of the strawberries aside for the garnish. In a blender or food processor, puree the remaining strawberries with the apple juice. Cover and chill in the refrigerator for at least 3 hours before serving.

Just before serving, pour the strawberry mixture into dessert dishes. Add small dollops of the yogurt and swirl lightly with a fork.

For the garnish, make three slices in each of the reserved strawberries (from the pointed end to, but not through, the stem end). Fan out each strawberry and gently place on top of the strawberry mixture.

EXTRA HEALTH BENEFITS
Lower Cholesterol
Cancer Protection

Times: Prep: 8 min.
Chilling: at least 3 hr.

Makes 4 servings.

Per serving: 52 calories, 0.6 g. fat (9% of calories), 3.9 g. dietary fiber, 0.1 mg. cholesterol, 7 mg. sodium.

Honey and Spice Yogurt

Here's an easy low-fat dessert cheese you can make yourself. Serve it with fresh fruit or as a low-calorie spread on bread wafers.

- **2 containers (8 ounces each) nonfat plain yogurt (made without gelatin)**
- **¼ cup honey**
- **2 teaspoons ground cinnamon**

For the yogurt cheese, line a fine-mesh sieve with a double thickness of cheesecloth or a coffee filter. Place over a bowl. Spoon the yogurt into the sieve. Refrigerate about 8 hours or overnight, until all the extra whey has drained from the yogurt.

Discard the liquid in the bowl. Transfer the yogurt to a clean bowl. Add the honey and cinnamon.

EXTRA HEALTH BENEFITS
Lower Cholesterol
Better Blood Pressure

Times: Prep: 10 min.
Chilling: 8 hr.

Makes 1 cup or 4 servings.

Per serving: 102 calories, 0.2 g. fat (2% of calories), 0.1 g. dietary fiber, 1 mg. cholesterol, 51 mg. sodium.

Blackberry Parfaits

At the peak of blackberry season in midsummer, finish off an evening meal with these beautiful layered parfaits.

> 2 **cups fresh blackberries**
> ¼ **cup honey**
> 1 **container (8 ounces) nonfat or low-fat lemon yogurt**

Set 4 of the blackberries aside for the garnish. In a blender or small food processor, blend or process the remaining blackberries and honey until smooth.

In 4 (6-ounce) parfait glasses, evenly layer the blackberry mixture and the yogurt. Garnish each serving with a reserved whole blackberry.

Chef's Note: If blackberries are unavailable, enjoy this luscious dessert with raspberries, blueberries or sliced strawberries or peaches.

Quick

EXTRA HEALTH BENEFITS
Lower Cholesterol
Better Blood Pressure
Cancer Protection

Time: Prep: 4 min.

Makes 4 servings.

Per serving: 119 calories, 0.2 g. fat (2% of calories), 3.7 g. dietary fiber, 1 mg. cholesterol, 29 mg. sodium.

Blackberry Parfaits

Cherry-Cheese Crêpes

Crêpes sound fattening, but they needn't be. This version features a rich-tasting, low-fat filling made from dark sweet cherries, nonfat cottage cheese and yogurt.

EXTRA HEALTH BENEFITS
Lower Cholesterol
Stronger Immunity

Times: Prep: 8 min.
Standing: 2 hr.
Cooking: 16 min.

Makes 4 servings.

Per serving: 128 calories,
0.4 g. fat (3% of calories),
1.3 g. dietary fiber, 2 mg.
cholesterol, 93 mg. sodium.

CRÊPES
- ¾ **cup skim milk**
- ¼ **cup fat-free egg substitute**
- ½ **teaspoon honey**
- ¼ **cup unbleached flour**
- ¼ **cup whole-wheat flour**

FILLING
- ⅓ **cup nonfat cottage cheese**
- ⅓ **cup nonfat plain yogurt**
- ½ **teaspoon honey**
- ½ **teaspoon vanilla**
- 1 **cup pitted dark sweet cherries**

For the crêpes: In a medium bowl, use a wire whisk to stir together the milk, egg substitute and honey. In a small bowl, stir together the unbleached flour and whole-wheat flour.

Gradually stir the flour mixture into the milk mixture just until combined. Cover and let stand at room temperature for 2 hours. (This allows the flour particles to swell and soften to produce lighter crêpes.)

Spray an unheated, small no-stick skillet with no-stick spray. Heat the skillet over medium heat until a drop of water sizzles and evaporates upon contact.

Holding the pan in one hand, ladle about 3 tablespoons of the batter into it with the other hand. Immediately rotate the pan so the batter forms an even circle in the bottom of the pan. Cook for 1 to 2 minutes or until the edges begin to brown and the batter is set. Using a rubber spatula, loosen the edges and carefully flip the crêpe over. Cook the other side for 45 seconds, then transfer it to a plate. Repeat with the remaining batter to make 8 crêpes.

For the filling: In a blender or food processor, blend or process the cottage cheese, yogurt, honey and vanilla until smooth. Add the cherries and blend or process in short pulses until the cherries are finely chopped but not pureed.

To assemble: Spoon about 2 tablespoons of the filling on the center of each crêpe. Roll up the crêpes and place them on dessert plates. Spoon a dollop of the remaining filling on top of each serving.

Chef's Note: For variety, use ¾ cup peeled, pitted and chopped peaches or sliced strawberries instead of the cherries.

Cherry-Cheese Crêpes

EXTRA HEALTH BENEFITS
Lower Cholesterol
Cancer Protection

Times: Prep: 8 min.
Cooking: 2 min.

Makes 4 servings.

Per serving: 139 calories,
1.2 g. fat (7% of calories),
2.5 g. dietary fiber, 0 mg.
cholesterol, 33 mg. sodium.

SLIMMING STRATEGY

When you want the
crunch and nutty flavor of
nuts—without the fat
most varieties carry—
use Grape-Nuts cereal.
A quarter cup (1 ounce)
has only 110 calories and
no fat. An ounce of wal-
nuts, by comparison, has
182 calories and almost
18 grams of fat.

Peach Crunch

*"Crunch" is the right word! The topping on these peaches lets
you derive great chewing satisfaction from a low-fat dessert.*

- ½ **cup nonfat plain yogurt**
- 1 **tablespoon apple pie spice**
- 1 **teaspoon margarine**
- ½ **cup Grape-Nuts cereal**
- 2 **teaspoons honey**
- 1 **package (16 ounces) frozen unsweetened peach slices
  or 3½ cups peeled, pitted and sliced fresh peaches**

In a small bowl, stir together the yogurt and 1½ teaspoons of
the apple pie spice. Cover and refrigerate until ready to serve.

Spray a small skillet with no-stick spray. Add the margarine and
heat over medium heat until melted.

Meanwhile, in another small bowl, combine the cereal, honey
and the remaining 1½ teaspoons of apple pie spice.

Add the cereal mixture to the skillet. Cook and stir about 2 minutes or until the margarine is absorbed. Remove the skillet from
the heat.

To serve, spoon the peaches into 4 individual dessert bowls.
Top each with 2 tablespoons of the yogurt mixture and sprinkle
with 2 tablespoons of the cereal mixture.

Chef's Note: To thaw frozen peaches in minutes, use your
microwave oven. Plan on about 3 to 4 minutes per pound on high
power (100%).

Hot-Fudge Sundaes

A dieter's dream come true—the guilt-free sundae!

- 3 tablespoons unsweetened cocoa powder
- 3 tablespoons reduced-calorie maple-flavored syrup
- 2 tablespoons cornstarch
- 1 cup water
- 2 teaspoons vanilla
- 3 cups frozen low-fat vanilla yogurt

In a small saucepan, stir together the cocoa powder, maple syrup and cornstarch. Then stir in the water.

Bring the mixture to a boil over medium-high heat, stirring constantly. Reduce the heat to medium. Cook and stir about 1 minute or until the mixture slightly thickens. Remove from the heat and stir in the vanilla. Serve hot over the frozen yogurt.

Chef's Note: If you like, you can substitute Dutch cocoa powder for the unsweetened cocoa. The Dutch powder has been treated with alkali to partially neutralize cocoa's natural acidity. The result is a more mellow flavor and a darker color.

Quick

EXTRA HEALTH BENEFITS
Lower Cholesterol
Better Blood Pressure

Times: Prep: 5 min.
Cooking: 1 min.

Makes 6 servings.

Per serving: 112 calories, 0.3 g. fat (3% of calories), 0 g. dietary fiber, 0 mg. cholesterol, 31 mg. sodium.

Dreamy Dessert Shakes

Indulge in the following sensational fruity drinks. These low-fat frozen treats are so incredibly creamy you won't miss the ice cream usually found in shakes.

- Freeze 1" chunks of bananas and fresh peach wedges in a single layer in a self-closing bag. When you're ready for a quick drink, place ½ cup of each fruit in a blender. Turn on the blender and slowly add ½ cup of skim milk. Taste the mixture. If you would like it sweeter, add a little honey. Per serving: 132 calories, 0.6 g. fat (4% of calories), 2.3 g. dietary fiber, 2 mg. cholesterol, 64 mg. sodium.
- Freeze 1" chunks of bananas, peaches or strawberries in a single layer in a self-closing bag. Then place 1 cup of the frozen fruit in a blender with ½ cup orange juice and ½ cup nonfat vanilla or plain yogurt. Blend until frothy. Per serving: 235 calories, 0.6 g. fat (2% of calories), 3.3 g. dietary fiber, 3 mg. cholesterol, 72 mg. sodium.

Fruit Kabobs with Pineapple Yogurt

When you're looking for a fruit dessert that's light, simple and a little different, make these tiny fruit kabobs.

1 cup chopped pineapple
¼ cup apple juice
¼ cup nonfat plain yogurt
2 small bananas, cut into ½"-thick slices
1 tablespoon orange juice
2 kiwifruits, peeled and cut into ½"-thick slices
1 cup small strawberries, melon balls and blackberries

For the dip, in a small saucepan, bring the pineapple and apple juice to a boil. Reduce the heat, cover and simmer for 10 minutes, stirring occasionally. Let stand about 25 minutes or until cool.

Transfer the pineapple mixture to a blender or food processor. Add the yogurt and blend or process until smooth. If desired, cover and chill in the refrigerator before serving.

Place the bananas in a small bowl. Drizzle with the orange juice, then gently toss until coated. Cut the kiwi slices into quarters.

For the kabobs, thread the bananas, kiwi, strawberries, melon balls and blackberries onto 4" bamboo skewers. Serve with the dip.

Chef's Note: Save time in the kitchen by purchasing fresh pineapple that's already been peeled and cored.

EXTRA HEALTH BENEFITS
Lower Cholesterol
Better Blood Pressure
Cancer Protection
Blood Building
Stronger Immunity

Times: Prep: 12 min.
Cooking: 10 min.
Cooling: 25 min.

Makes 4 servings.

Per serving: 123 calories, 0.8 g. fat (5% of calories), 3.7 g. dietary fiber, <1 mg. cholesterol, 15 mg. sodium.

SLIMMING STRATEGY

Fiber is filling! Boost your intake with such low-cal fresh fruits as blackberries (7.2 grams dietary fiber per cup), figs (5 grams in three medium), pears (4.3 grams each), raspberries (6 grams per cup) and strawberries (3.9 grams per cup).

EXTRA HEALTH BENEFITS
Cancer Protection
Lower Cholesterol
Better Blood Pressure

Time: Prep: 2 min.

Makes 2 servings.

Per serving: 31 calories, 0.2 g. fat (5% of calories), 0.9 g. dietary fiber, 0 mg. cholesterol, 1 mg. sodium.

Strawberry-Banana Sodas

Here's a fruity low-cal refresher that can be a satisfying snack as well as a quick dessert.

½ **ripe banana, sliced and frozen**
4 **large strawberries, halved and frozen**
1½ **cups sparkling mineral water**
2 **medium strawberries (optional)**

In a blender or food processor, blend or process the bananas, strawberries and mineral water on medium speed until smooth.

To serve, pour into 2 chilled glasses. If desired, garnish the rims with the remaining strawberries.

Chef's Note: Keep bananas and strawberries in the freezer and you'll always be ready to whip up these simple drinks.

Pink Pops

EXTRA HEALTH BENEFITS
Lower Cholesterol
Better Blood Pressure

Times: Prep: 8 min.
Freezing: 6 hr.

Makes 4 pops.

Per pop: 67 calories, 0.2 g. fat (3% of calories), 1.3 g. dietary fiber, 0 mg. cholesterol, 8 mg. sodium.

Here's a no-sugar pop you can easily make at home. For variety, use strawberries, peaches or mango.

¾ **cup black or red raspberries**
½ **cup frozen apple juice concentrate, thawed**
½ **cup water**

In a blender or food processor, puree the raspberries, apple juice and water on a low speed.

Using a fine sieve, strain the mixture. Discard the seeds. If necessary, let the mixture stand until the foam goes down.

Ladle the fruit mixture into 4 (3-ounce) paper cups. Cover and freeze until partially frozen. Insert a fruit-pop mold stick or wooden frozen ice-pop stick in each pop and freeze about 6 hours or until completely frozen.

To serve, remove the frozen pop from the mold or peel away the paper cup.

Fresh-Fruit Frozen Yogurt

You can easily make your own no-sugar flavored yogurt. Choose the fruit you like best. Raspberries, blueberries, pitted sweet cherries and chopped kiwifruit, peaches and apricots work especially well.

> **1 cup nonfat plain yogurt**
> **1 cup fresh fruit**
> **1 tablespoon honey**
> **1 teaspoon vanilla**

Freeze the yogurt for 3 to 4 hours or until almost frozen.

In a blender or food processor, puree the fruit, honey and vanilla. Break the frozen yogurt into small chunks and add it to the blender or food processor. Blend or process on low speed just until smooth.

Transfer the mixture to a 9" × 5" loaf pan. Cover and freeze for 3 to 4 hours or until frozen.

Before serving, break the frozen mixture into small chunks and transfer it to the blender or food processor. Blend or process on low speed just until smooth. Serve immediately.

Chef's Note: To make a frozen yogurt pie, blend the frozen yogurt with the pureed fruit as directed. Then transfer the mixture to a 9" graham cracker crumb pie shell and freeze until firm. When ready to serve, dip a sharp knife into hot water and cut the pie into wedges.

EXTRA HEALTH BENEFITS
Lower Cholesterol
Better Blood Pressure

Times: Prep: 7 min.
Freezing: 6 hr.

Makes 4 servings.

Per serving: 67 calories, 0.3 g. fat (4% of calories), 1.4 g. dietary fiber, 1 mg. cholesterol, 44 mg. sodium.

SLIMMING STRATEGY
Never eat foods—especially frozen desserts—out of their original containers. It's too easy to lose track of how much you've consumed.

Peach Ice Milk

EXTRA HEALTH BENEFITS
Lower Cholesterol
Better Blood Pressure

Times: Prep: 18 min.
Cooking: 10 min.
Chilling: 2 hr.
Freezing: 30 min.

**Makes 8 cups or
16 servings.**

Per ½ cup: 70 calories,
0.1 g. fat (2% of calories),
0.5 g. dietary fiber, 1 mg.
cholesterol, 34 mg. sodium.

This extraordinary ice milk has all the luxury of a premium ice cream but with a lot less fat.

> 2 **cups mashed ripe fresh peaches or frozen unsweet-
>   ened peach slices (about 1 pound)**
> ½ **cup honey**
> ½ **cup fat-free egg substitute**
> 2 **tablespoons unbleached flour**
> 3 **cups skim milk**
> 1 **tablespoon almond extract**

In a medium bowl, stir together the peaches and ¼ cup of the honey. Cover and let stand for 15 minutes.

In a large bowl, use an electric mixer to beat the egg substitute on medium speed until foamy. While continuing to beat, slowly add the flour. Then slowly beat in the remaining ¼ cup of honey. Add the milk and beat until well mixed.

Transfer the mixture to a large saucepan. Cook and stir over medium-low heat about 10 minutes or until the mixture slightly thickens. Remove from the heat and let cool.

Stir in the peach mixture and almond extract. Cover and refrigerate about 2 hours or until thoroughly chilled. Then freeze in a 5-quart ice-cream freezer according to the manufacturer's instructions.

If desired, to ripen the ice milk, remove the dasher and scrape the ice milk down from the sides of the container. Plug the hole in the lid with a cork, then replace the lid on the container. Repack the container in the freezer with additional ice and salt, using the same proportions as before. Let ripen about 1 hour before serving.

Chef's Note: If you like, you can eat the ice milk immediately after it freezes. But ripening allows the flavors to blend and makes the ice milk firmer.

Sunset Compote

If you can't live on a tropical island, here's a dessert that will at least make you feel as if you're on one.

- 1   medium papaya, peeled, seeded and cubed
- 2   kiwifruits, peeled and sliced
- 4   cups strawberries, quartered
- 2   tablespoons lime juice
- ¼   teaspoon almond extract
- 2   tablespoons toasted and chopped pistachios

In a medium bowl, combine the papaya, kiwi and strawberries. Drizzle with the lime juice and almond extract. Gently toss until coated.

To serve, divide the fruit mixture among 6 dessert dishes. Sprinkle each with the pistachios.

Quick

EXTRA HEALTH BENEFITS
Lower Cholesterol
Better Blood Pressure
Cancer Protection
Stronger Immunity

Time: Prep: 10 min.

Makes 6 servings.

Per serving: 82 calories, 2 g. fat (20% of calories), 4.2 g. dietary fiber, 0 mg. cholesterol, 4 mg. sodium.

SLIMMING STRATEGY

Try not to eat too much sugar. It tends to make you crave more and more. Satisfy your sweet tooth with fresh fruit instead. Or try sweetening desserts with fruit juices. White grape and apple juices provide lots of sweetness and more nutrients than white sugar.

Happy, Healthy Holidays

Salsa-Grilled Steak (page 338),
Red Potato and Artichoke
Salad (page 340), Creamy
Chive Coleslaw (page 341)

Fourth-of-July Barbecue

- Crudités with nonfat yogurt dip
- Salsa-Grilled Steak (below) or Grilled Chicken with Sweet Onion Relish (opposite page)
- Corn on the cob
- Red Potato and Artichoke Salad (page 340)
- Creamy Chive Coleslaw (page 341)
- Watermelon
- Iced tea with lemon

Salsa-Grilled Steak

EXTRA HEALTH BENEFIT
Stronger Immunity

Times: Prep: 22 min.
Marinating: at least 2 hr.
Grilling: 15 min.
Standing: 10 min.

Makes 4 servings.

Per serving: 156 calories, 4.5 g. fat (26% of calories), 0 g. dietary fiber, 63 mg. cholesterol, 205 mg. sodium.

Marinating round steak in a mixture of salsa and vinegar helps tenderize and flavor the meat.

2 **cups hot-style salsa**
2 **tablespoons canned diced green chili peppers**
2 **tablespoons red wine vinegar**
1 **tablespoon reduced-sodium Worcestershire sauce**
½ **teaspoon garlic powder**
1 **beef top round steak (about 12 ounces), cut 1" thick and trimmed of all visible fat**

In a blender or food processor, blend or process the salsa, chili peppers, vinegar, Worcestershire sauce and garlic powder until smooth.

Transfer the salsa mixture to a gallon-size self-closing plastic bag. Add the steak. Seal the bag and marinate in the refrigerator for at least 2 hours, turning the bag occasionally.

Meanwhile, to prepare the grill for cooking, spray the unheated grill rack with no-stick spray. Then light the grill according to the manufacturer's directions. Place the rack on the grill.

Remove the steak from the bag, reserving the marinade. Place the steak on the rack over the coals. Grill, uncovered, for 7 minutes. Turn the steak over and grill for 8 to 10 minutes more for medium-rare doneness, brushing frequently with the reserved marinade.

Let stand for 10 minutes before slicing, then slice the steak diagonally across the grain into thin slices.

Chef's Note: This marinade also works well with other lean meats, including pork loin and poultry.

Grilled Chicken with Sweet Onion Relish

The all-fruit spread in this relish adds a natural sweetness.

CHICKEN

- 2 pounds skinless chicken pieces
- ½ cup orange juice
- 2 tablespoons honey
- 1 tablespoon Dijon mustard
- 1 tablespoon grated ginger root
- 2 teaspoons reduced-sodium soy sauce

RELISH

- 1 tablespoon reduced-calorie margarine
- ½ cup chopped red onions
- ½ cup chopped green peppers
- ½ cup chopped tomatoes
- 3 tablespoons all-fruit orange spread
- 2 tablespoons chili sauce
- 1 tablespoon cider vinegar
- ½ teaspoon thyme

For the chicken: Rinse the chicken and pat dry with paper towels. Place the pieces in a large self-closing plastic bag. In a small bowl, stir together the orange juice, honey, mustard, ginger and soy sauce. Pour over the chicken. Seal and marinate in the refrigerator for at least 2 hours, turning the bag occasionally.

For the relish: In a small saucepan, melt the margarine. Add the onions and peppers. Cook and stir about 4 minutes or until the vegetables are tender. Stir in the tomatoes, fruit spread, chili sauce, vinegar and thyme. Cook and stir for 2 minutes more. Remove from the heat and set aside.

To prepare the grill for cooking, spray the unheated grill rack with no-stick spray. Then light the grill according to the manufacturer's directions. Place the rack on the grill.

Remove the chicken from the bag, reserving the marinade. Place the chicken on the rack over the coals. Grill, uncovered, for 15 to 20 minutes or until the chicken is no longer pink, turning and brushing with the reserved marinade frequently. Serve with the relish.

Chef's Note: Use this same recipe with fish fillets. But instead of marinating it for 2 hours, cut the time to 30 minutes and shorten the grilling time to 10 minutes or less.

EXTRA HEALTH BENEFIT
Stronger Immunity

Times: Prep: 22 min.
Marinating: at least 2 hr.
Grilling: 15 min.

Makes 4 servings.

Per serving: 317 calories, 8.3 g. fat (24% of calories), 1 g. dietary fiber, 93 mg. cholesterol, 422 mg. sodium.

SLIMMING STRATEGY

Discourage picnic and barbecue guests from bringing along fatty desserts. Suggest instead that everyone contribute to a community salad. Have guests bring tomatoes, carrots, beans and other low-fat ingredients. You can supply colorful greens and a selection of reduced-calorie or fat-free dressings.

Red Potato and Artichoke Salad

Here's a picnic classic that we've updated for today's health-conscious picnickers. Apple juice and water replace most of the oil in the marinade.

EXTRA HEALTH BENEFITS
Cancer Protection
Lower Cholesterol
Better Blood Pressure

Times: Prep: 10 min.
Cooking: 20 min.
Cooling: 30 min.
Chilling: at least 2 hr.

Makes 4 servings.

Per serving: 125 calories, 2.2 g. fat (15% of calories), 2 g. dietary fiber, 0 mg. cholesterol, 51 mg. sodium.

SALAD

1½   pounds red potatoes, scrubbed and quartered

1   package (10 ounces) frozen artichoke hearts, thawed and coarsely chopped

1   medium sweet red pepper, coarsely chopped

½   cup chopped red onions

½   cup frozen peas, thawed

2   tablespoons pitted and sliced ripe olives, drained

DRESSING

¼   cup coarsely chopped and loosely packed fresh basil

2   tablespoons water

2   tablespoons red wine vinegar

1   tablespoon olive oil

1   tablespoon apple juice

½   teaspoon dry mustard

¼   teaspoon garlic-and-herb salt-free seasoning

2   tablespoons minced fresh parsley (optional)

For the salad: Place the potatoes in a large saucepan and add enough water to cover. Bring to a boil, then reduce the heat. Cover and simmer about 20 minutes or until the potatoes are tender. Drain and let cool about 30 minutes.

In a large bowl, combine the potatoes, artichokes, peppers, onions, peas and olives.

For the dressing: In a small bowl, stir together the basil, water, vinegar, oil, apple juice, mustard and garlic-and-herb seasoning.

Pour the dressing over the potato mixture and toss until well coated. Cover and refrigerate for at least 2 hours before serving. If desired, sprinkle with the parsley just before serving.

Chef's Note: Make sure the cooked potatoes are completely cooled before combining the salad. Otherwise, the skins will come off when you toss the potatoes with the dressing.

SLIMMING STRATEGY

Artichokes are really low in calories, with virtually no fat—as long as they're not packed in oil or served with a fatty sauce. When buying canned or frozen artichoke hearts, read the label carefully to make sure you're getting only what you want. If you buy canned hearts packed in brine, rinse them well.

Happy, Healthy Holidays

Creamy Chive Coleslaw

Creamy is right! You won't believe this slaw is made with nonfat ingredients.

- ¾ **pound green cabbage, finely shredded**
- ¾ **pound red cabbage, finely shredded**
- 2 **medium carrots, coarsely shredded**
- ½ **cup finely chopped green onions**
- ½ **cup thinly sliced radishes**
- ½ **cup nonfat plain yogurt**
- ¼ **cup nonfat sour cream**
- 2 **tablespoons chopped fresh chives**
- 1 **tablespoon cider vinegar**
- 2 **teaspoons pickle relish**
- 1 **teaspoon honey**
- ½ **teaspoon dry mustard**
- ¼ **teaspoon celery seeds**
- ¼ **teaspoon freshly ground black pepper**
  Pinch of paprika

In a large bowl, combine the green and red cabbage, carrots, onions and radishes.

In a small bowl, stir together the yogurt, sour cream, chives, vinegar, relish, honey, mustard, celery seeds and pepper. Add to the cabbage mixture and toss until well combined. Cover and chill in the refrigerator for at least 1 hour before serving. Just before serving, sprinkle with the paprika.

Chef's Note: For an extra note of sweetness, add some chopped or thinly sliced sweet red, green or yellow peppers.

EXTRA HEALTH BENEFITS
Lower Cholesterol
Cancer Protection
Stronger Immunity

Times: Prep: 15 min.
Chilling: at least 1 hr.

Makes 4 servings.

Per serving: 104 calories, 0.6 g. fat (5% of calories), 5.2 g. dietary fiber, 1 mg. cholesterol, 108 mg. sodium.

SLIMMING STRATEGY

When dessert time rolls around, take a hike. Or join the softball game. Do anything to get yourself out of the path of temptation.

- Shrimp served on shredded lettuce with cocktail sauce
- Orange-Rosemary Roasted Turkey Breast (below)
- Wild Rice Stuffing with Cherries and Walnuts (opposite page)
- Baked sweet potato wedges sprinkled with cinnamon
- Steamed brussels sprouts
- Dilled cornbread squares
- Orange-Pumpkin Custard (page 344) with light whipped topping

Orange-Rosemary Roasted Turkey Breast

EXTRA HEALTH BENEFITS
Better Blood Pressure
Stronger Immunity

Times: Prep: 20 min.
Roasting: 2¼ hr.

**Makes 12 servings,
3 ounces each.**

Per serving: 125 calories,
0.8 g. fat (6% of calories),
0.2 g. dietary fiber, 72 mg.
cholesterol, 47 mg. sodium.

Preparing a turkey breast instead of a whole bird is less fuss. And, best of all, your leftovers will be white meat only.

- 1 fresh or frozen bone-in turkey breast (4–5 pounds)
- 1 small bunch flat parsley, finely chopped
- 1 small bunch fresh thyme, finely chopped
- 1 small bunch fresh rosemary, finely chopped
- 2 oranges
- 1 lemon
  Pinch of freshly ground black pepper
  Pinch of paprika

If using frozen turkey, thaw it. Rinse and pat dry with paper towels.

In a medium bowl, combine the parsley, thyme and rosemary. Grate the peel from the oranges and lemon, then set the oranges and lemon aside. Add the peels to the herb mixture and toss until combined.

Rub the herb mixture over the skin of the turkey. Place the turkey on a rack in a large roasting pan.

Cut the oranges and lemon in half and squeeze their juices over the turkey. Sprinkle with the pepper and paprika. Insert a meat thermometer in the thickest part of the breast.

Roast, uncovered, at 325° for 2¼ to 2½ hours or until the thermometer registers 170° to 175°, basting frequently with the pan juices. (If necessary, loosely cover the turkey with foil during roasting to avoid overbrowning.)

Let stand for at least 15 minutes before carving. Remove and discard the skin before serving. Cover and refrigerate the remaining turkey for another use.

Wild Rice Stuffing
with Cherries and Walnuts

This light rice stuffing is a welcome change from the heavier bread dressings usually found on Thanksgiving tables.

 1 **cup defatted low-sodium chicken broth**
 ½ **cup unsweetened apple juice**
 ⅔ **cup wild rice**
 1½ **teaspoons reduced-calorie margarine**
 4 **ounces sliced fresh mushrooms**
 ½ **cup chopped onions**
 1 **stalk celery, chopped**
 ½ **teaspoon dried thyme**
 Pinch of dried sage
 ½ **cup dried red cherries or light raisins**
 ¼ **cup chopped walnuts**

In a medium saucepan, bring the broth and juice to a boil. Meanwhile, rinse the rice with cold water.

Stir the rice into the broth mixture and return to a boil. Reduce the heat, cover and simmer for 45 to 50 minutes or until the rice is tender and the liquid is absorbed.

Meanwhile, in a medium no-stick skillet, melt the margarine. Add the mushrooms, onions, celery, thyme and sage. Cook and stir over medium heat about 4 minutes or until the vegetables are tender. Add the cherries or raisins and walnuts. Cook and stir for 2 minutes more. Remove from the heat and transfer to a large bowl. Add the rice and toss until well mixed.

Spray a 1-quart casserole with no-stick spray. Transfer the mixture to the casserole. Cover and bake at 325° about 30 minutes or until heated through.

Extra Health Benefit
Lower Cholesterol

Times: Prep: 12 min.
Cooking: 45 min.
Baking: 30 min.

Makes 8 servings.

Per serving: 121 calories, 3.1 g. fat (22% of calories), 1.3 g. dietary fiber, 0 mg. cholesterol, 106 mg. sodium.

Slimming Strategy

Bake your Thanksgiving stuffing in a casserole dish rather than stuffing it into the turkey. That way it won't soak up fatty drippings from the bird.

Orange-Pumpkin Custard

Extra Health Benefits
Lower Cholesterol
Better Blood Pressure
Cancer Protection
Stronger Immunity

Times: Prep: 5 min.
Cooking: 10 min.
Baking: 30 min.

Makes 8 servings.

Per serving: 106 calories,
0.9 g. fat (7% of calories),
1.9 g. dietary fiber, 1 mg.
cholesterol, 74 mg. sodium.

If pumpkin pie is a must on your Thanksgiving table, slim it down by eliminating the crust as we've done here. These individual puddings have the traditional pie flavor but with a lot less fat.

    1 **can (16 ounces) pumpkin**
    ½ **cup pitted and finely chopped prunes**
    ¼ **cup frozen apple juice concentrate, thawed**
    ¼ **cup frozen orange juice concentrate, thawed**
    2 **teaspoons reduced-calorie margarine**
    1 **cup evaporated skim milk**
    ½ **cup fat-free egg substitute**
    1 **tablespoon grated orange peel**
    2 **teaspoons pumpkin-pie spice**
    8 **Jack-Be-Little pumpkins (3½ inches in diameter)**

In a medium saucepan, stir together the pumpkin, prunes, apple and orange juice concentrate and margarine. Simmer, uncovered, for 15 minutes, stirring frequently. Transfer to a food processor. Add the milk, egg substitute, orange peel and spice. Process until smooth.

Cut off the tops of each pumpkin about 1" down. Scoop out the seeds. Place the shells in a 13" × 9" baking dish. Bake at 350° for 25 to 35 minutes or until the flesh is tender but the shells are not in danger of collapsing. Spoon the custard mixture into the shells.

Bake at 350° for 30 to 40 minutes or until a knife inserted near the center of a custard comes out clean.

Chef's Note: You may also bake the pumpkin mixture in 6-ounce custard cups. Place in a 13" × 9" baking pan and add 1" of hot water. Bake for 30 to 40 minutes.

Hanukkah Celebration

- Baked Vegetable Latkes (below) with unsweetened applesauce, nonfat sour cream or all-fruit spread
- Beef and Mushroom Barley (opposite page)
- Tzimmes
- Baked Apples Stuffed with Currants (page 348)
- Cranberry-juice poached pears

Baked Vegetable Latkes

Potato pancakes are a hallmark of Hanukkah, the Feast of Lights. Usually they're fried in oil, but here we've baked them to cut back on fat. And we've given them a nutrient boost by adding carrots, zucchini and parsnips.

EXTRA HEALTH BENEFITS
Lower Cholesterol
Better Blood Pressure
Cancer Protection
Stronger Immunity

Times: Prep: 10 min.
Baking: 10 min.

Makes about 20 latkes or 4 servings.

Per serving: 97 calories, 0.3 g. fat (2% of calories), 3.9 g. dietary fiber, 0 mg. cholesterol, 101 mg. sodium.

1 large potato, peeled
2 medium carrots, peeled
1 small zucchini
1 small parsnip, peeled
1 small onion
½ cup fat-free egg substitute
1½ tablespoons unbleached flour
½ teaspoon baking powder
¼ teaspoon freshly ground black pepper

For the batter, use a food processor or fine shredder to grate or finely shred the potato, carrots, zucchini, parsnip and onion. Squeeze any excess liquid from the vegetables and immediately transfer to a large bowl. Stir in the egg substitute, flour, baking powder and pepper; mix well.

Spray 2 large cookie sheets with no-stick spray. Using a tablespoon, spoon the batter onto the cookie sheets. Then use the back of the spoon to slightly flatten each latke. Bake at 425° for 10 to 15 minutes or until golden.

Beef and Mushroom Barley

Beef and barley are traditional Hanukkah foods. One way to keep beef dishes low in fat is by using lean cuts such as top round or eye of round.

- 2 cups water
- 2 cups defatted low-sodium beef broth
- 1 cup pearl barley
- 1 teaspoon dried thyme
- 2 cloves garlic, minced
- 1 teaspoon olive oil
- 6 ounces boneless lean beef top round or eye of round, cut into ½" cubes
- 2 cups quartered mushrooms
- 1 cup chopped green onions
- 1 cup thinly sliced carrots
- 1 cup chopped celery
- 1½ cups vegetable juice cocktail
- ½ cup chopped tomatoes

In a 2-quart saucepan, combine the water, broth, barley, thyme and garlic. Bring to a boil, then reduce the heat. Simmer, uncovered, for 20 minutes.

Meanwhile, spray an unheated, large no-stick skillet with no-stick spray. Then add the oil and heat over medium-high heat. Add the beef. Cook and stir for 3 to 5 minutes or until the beef is lightly browned.

Add the mushrooms, onions, carrots and celery to the skillet. Cook and stir for 2 to 3 minutes or until the vegetables are crisp-tender.

Drain the barley and discard the liquid. Add the barley to the skillet. Stir in the vegetable juice and tomatoes. Cover and simmer for 15 to 20 minutes or until the barley is just tender and the beef is cooked through.

Chef's Note: To save on last-minute preparation, make this dish ahead and reheat it later. To keep it from getting too dry, stir in a small amount of additional vegetable juice cocktail or beef broth as it warms.

EXTRA HEALTH BENEFITS
Blood Building
Stronger Immunity

Times: Prep: 10 min.
Cooking: 42 min.

Makes 4 servings.

Per serving: 347 calories, 5.4 g. fat (14% of calories), 11.5 g. dietary fiber, 38 mg. cholesterol, 422 mg. sodium.

SLIMMING STRATEGY

Find a fellow weight watcher and buddy up for the holidays. You can keep each other in line and motivated by phone, mail or in person. Doctors say that people who can talk about their weight-gain apprehensions are less likely to use food for comfort.

Baked Apples Stuffed with Currants

Indulge your sweet tooth with these low-fat fruit-filled apples.

EXTRA HEALTH BENEFITS
Lower Cholesterol
Better Blood Pressure
Cancer Protection

Times: Prep: 10 min.
Baking: 20 min.
Cooling: 10 min.

Makes 4 servings.

Per serving: 114 calories,
2 g. fat (14% of calories),
3.2 g. dietary fiber, 0 mg.
cholesterol, 2 mg. sodium.

- 4 small Granny Smith apples, cored
- ¼ cup dried currants
- 1 tablespoon coconut
- 1 tablespoon toasted and chopped walnuts
- ½ teaspoon ground cinnamon
- 2 teaspoons honey

Place each apple in a custard cup, then place the cups in an 8" × 8" baking pan.

In a small bowl, combine the currants, coconut, walnuts and cinnamon. Stir in the honey until well combined. Spoon evenly into the center of each apple.

Cover the pan with foil and bake at 350° for 20 to 25 minutes or until the apples are just tender when pierced with a fork. Let cool for 10 minutes before serving.

SLIMMING STRATEGY

Sit up straight! After your holiday dinner, don't take on the sofa slouch as you relax and visit with friends. Proper posture burns more calories than slumping over.

- Caesar Salad Noel (below)
- Herbed Pork Tenderloin with Della Robbia Sauce (page 351)
- Puree of Potatoes and Parsnips (page 352)
- Steamed carrots and green beans lightly sprinkled with toasted sesame seeds
- Whole-wheat dinner rolls with reduced-calorie margarine
- Cranberry-Peach Compote (page 353)
- Hot cider garnished with cinnamon sticks and orange wedges

Caesar Salad Noel

*The combination of flavors—olive oil, lemon juice, garlic
and cheese—is the signature of a Caesar salad. In this holiday salad, we kept the flavors but used buttermilk instead of
oil to create a creamy low-fat dressing.*

2 teaspoons Dijon mustard
1 teaspoon anchovy paste or 2 anchovy fillets, mashed
2 cloves garlic, crushed
1 cup buttermilk
2 tablespoons finely shredded provolone cheese
2 tablespoons minced fresh parsley
2 tablespoons defatted low-sodium chicken broth
2 tablespoons white wine vinegar
2 tablespoons olive oil
1 tablespoon lemon juice
6 cups torn Boston or bibb lettuce
6 cups torn spinach
2 cups thinly sliced radishes
1 cup coarsely shredded carrots
   Freshly ground black pepper (to taste)

In a medium bowl, stir together the mustard, anchovies and garlic. Using a wire whisk, stir in the buttermilk, cheese, parsley,
broth, vinegar, oil and lemon juice. Stir until well combined.

In a large bowl, combine the lettuce, spinach, radishes and carrots. Pour the mustard mixture over the lettuce mixture and toss
until well coated. Season to taste with the pepper.

EXTRA HEALTH BENEFITS
Lower Cholesterol
Blood Building
Stronger Immunity

Time: Prep: 25 min.

Makes 8 servings.

Per serving: 52 calories,
1.6 g. fat (25% of calories),
2.4 g. dietary fiber, 2 mg.
cholesterol, 151 mg. sodium.

Caesar Salad Noel (page 349)

Happy, Healthy Holidays

Herbed Pork Tenderloin with Della Robbia Sauce

Pork is a Christmas favorite in many households. Here we've taken lean pork tenderloin and infused it with the flavors of fresh herbs and garlic. Then we serve the pork with a colorful fruit sauce instead of gravy to keep the fat content down.

¼ cup loosely packed fresh mint leaves
6 sprigs fresh thyme
6 cloves garlic
1 tablespoon grated lemon peel
½ teaspoon freshly ground black pepper
2 tablespoons defatted low-sodium chicken broth
1½ teaspoons olive oil
2 pork tenderloins (10 to 12 ounces each)
1 cup apricot all-fruit spread
½ cup green grapes, halved
¼ cup apple juice
12 dried apricot halves, coarsely chopped
¼ cup dried currants
1 tablespoon grated orange peel
¼ teaspoon ground ginger

In a blender or small food processor, blend or process the mint, thyme, garlic, lemon peel and pepper until the mint and thyme are finely chopped. Add the broth and oil. Blend or process until the mixture forms a paste.

Place the pork on a rack in a roasting pan. Spread the herb paste on the pork. Pour 1" of water into the bottom of the pan. Then insert a meat thermometer near the center of one of the tenderloins. Roast, uncovered, about 30 minutes or until the thermometer registers 160°.

Meanwhile, in a medium saucepan, stir together the fruit spread, grapes, apple juice, apricots, currants, orange peel and ginger. Bring to a simmer. Simmer for 10 to 12 minutes or until the fruit is tender, stirring frequently.

Remove the pork from the oven. Loosely cover with foil and let stand for 10 minutes before carving. Serve with the fruit mixture as a sauce.

EXTRA HEALTH BENEFITS
Better Blood Pressure
Cancer Protection
Blood Building

Times: Prep: 10 min.
Roasting: 30 min.
Cooking: 10 min.

Makes 8 servings.

Per serving: 195 calories, 1.8 g. fat (8% of calories), 0.8 g. dietary fiber, 25 mg. cholesterol, 28 mg. sodium.

SLIMMING STRATEGY

Have a bite to eat <u>before</u> you head to the mall to Christmas shop. You'll be less likely to stop at a fast-food place and chow down on high-fat snacks or even a meal.

Puree of Potatoes and Parsnips

Butter-flavored granules boost the flavor of margarine in this two-vegetable combo.

2½ **pounds potatoes, peeled and cut into 2" pieces**
 1 **pound parsnips, peeled and cut into ¾" pieces**
 1 **cup skim milk**
 1 **tablespoon reduced-calorie margarine**
 3 **tablespoons Dijon mustard**
 1 **tablespoon prepared horseradish**
 1 **tablespoon butter-flavored granules**
 ⅛ **teaspoon ground white pepper**

Place the potatoes and parsnips in a large saucepan and add enough water to cover. Bring to a boil, then reduce the heat. Cover and simmer for 20 to 25 minutes or the vegetables are very tender.

Meanwhile, in a small saucepan, combine the milk, margarine, mustard, horseradish, butter-flavored granules and white pepper. Bring to a simmer and keep warm.

Drain the potatoes and parsnips. Transfer to a food processor and process until coarsely pureed. Add the milk mixture and process to desired consistency.

Chef's Note: If you don't have a food processor, use a food mill or blender to puree the vegetables. (If using a blender, puree small batches at a time.) Then transfer to a bowl and stir in the milk mixture.

Cranberry-Peach Compote

We reduced calories in this compote by cooking the fruit in juice rather than the conventional sugar syrup.

 1 cup orange juice
 ½ cup pineapple juice
 2 tablespoons honey
 1 tablespoon grated orange peel
 1 tablespoon grated ginger root
 ½ teaspoon ground cinnamon
 ¼ teaspoon ground nutmeg
 2 cups cranberries
 ½ cup light raisins
 8 dried apricot halves
 1 can (16 ounces) sliced peaches (packed in juice)

In a medium saucepan, combine the orange juice, pineapple juice, honey, orange peel, ginger, cinnamon and nutmeg. Bring to a boil. Stir in the cranberries, raisins and apricots. Reduce the heat and simmer, uncovered, for 10 to 12 minutes or until the cranberries begin to pop.

Place the peaches in a medium glass bowl. Pour the hot cranberry mixture over the peaches and gently stir just until combined. Cover and refrigerate for at least 4 hours before serving, or overnight.

Chef's Note: For an extra-special presentation, serve this colorful compote in your prettiest dessert bowls or wine goblets. If you like, top each serving with a spoonful of nonfat vanilla yogurt or a scoop of nonfat frozen yogurt.

EXTRA HEALTH BENEFITS
Lower Cholesterol
Better Blood Pressure
Cancer Protection
Stronger Immunity

Times: Prep: 10 min.
Cooking: 10 min.
Chilling: at least 4 hr.

Makes 8 servings.

Per serving: 119 calories, 0.3 g. fat (2% of calories), 0.6 g. dietary fiber, 0 mg. cholesterol, 5 mg. sodium.

SLIMMING STRATEGY
Play holiday tunes on your headset while you exercise. It's one way to keep exercise in your holiday plans.

The Gift You Give Yourself

There's one present nobody wants—those extra pounds that appear during the holidays. Here are some ways to give yourself the gift of better health and a more pleasing profile.

1. Do <u>unto</u> others as you would have them do <u>unto</u> you. Give something you would like to receive, possibly a fruit basket or some low-fat muffins. The favor just may be returned.

2. Take a light alternative, such as a vegetable or fruit plate, to a holiday party. Even nonalcoholic beer or sparkling grape juice makes a nice offering.

3. Be the designated driver. Save your friends and your waistline at the same time.

4. Order club soda with a twist of lime or lemon at cocktail parties. It looks like an alcoholic drink but doesn't set you back 70 to 150 calories.

5. Don't let family or friends pressure you into overindulging. When they say "You have nothing to worry about—you're so thin," reply, "The reason I'm thin is because I've worked hard to take off the weight, and I'm not going to blow it now."

6. Be assertive. Refuse food and drinks if you don't want them.

7. At a holiday buffet, limit the number of choices on your plate. Enjoy a few smart selections instead of giving in to overzealous sampling.

8. If you must eat candy, make it the hard varieties instead of chocolates. Hard candies are still high in sugar and calories but are usually fat-free and take longer to eat.

9. Keep your hands full of anything but food. Take along photos, a branch of mistletoe, a camera or anything else that will keep your hands occupied.

10. Plan a guilt-free event—organize a holiday dance party and serve a hearty buffet of veggies and low-fat dips.

11. Deliver holiday cards in person to your neighbors. Do it on foot and burn calories while you boost your community spirit.

12. Give party leftovers and gifts of cakes, cookies and chocolates to the local food shelter. You'll remove rich foods from your grasp and provide a rare treat to those in need.

13. Make meringue cookies or gingersnaps instead of cutout cookies. They're low in fat and give a different twist to holiday baking.

14. Bake your latkes (potato pancakes) for Hanukkah instead of frying them. (See the recipe on page 346.)

15. Keep your mind off food and your heart in the right place by volunteering. Soup kitchens, toy drives and other charitable endeavors can use all the help they can get.

16. Give your New Year's weight-loss resolution a trial run—start it before the holidays instead of after!

17. Try a new low-fat or no-fat food every day. It's better to experiment with them than with holiday cookies.

18. Help reduce temptation at the office. Coordinate treats so they're brought in on only one day during the week rather than trickling in every day.

19. Keep your fat-and-calorie diary up-to-date. For each day you succeed in staying within your budgets, set aside a dollar. On January 2, go out and buy yourself something special as a reward. But make sure it's not food!

20. If you slip a little on your weight-control program, don't dwell on it. That doesn't solve anything and can ruin your holiday fun. Just learn from the mistake. Most of all, keep your sense of humor and good cheer.

Happy, Healthy Holidays

New Year's Eve Dinner

- Roasted Peppers with Fresh Basil (below)
- Turkey Tonnato (page 356)
- Pilaf Florentine (page 357)
- Steamed artichoke hearts with lemon
- Crusty Italian bread
- Raspberry-Peach Flutes (page 358)
- Sparkling water or sparkling apple juice

Roasted Peppers with Fresh Basil

Here's a first-course salad with an Italian influence—sweet red peppers roasted, peeled and served on a bed of bitter greens.

3 sweet red peppers
1 tablespoon grated orange peel
½ cup orange juice
2 tablespoons balsamic vinegar
1 teaspoon honey
1 small red onion, chopped
1 navel orange, peeled and sectioned
¼ cup chopped and loosely packed fresh basil
1 bunch arugula, stems removed

To roast the peppers, cut them lengthwise in half and remove the stems, seeds and membranes. Place the pepper halves, cut sides down, on a cookie sheet. Broil 5" from the heat about 10 minutes or until the skins begin to blister. Then place in a clean paper bag, close it and let stand for 30 minutes.

Meanwhile, in a medium bowl, stir together the orange peel, orange juice, vinegar and honey. Then stir in the onions, oranges and basil.

Using a knife, pull off the skin from the peppers. Cut the peppers into 2" strips. Add to the orange mixture and gently toss until combined. Cover and marinate in the refrigerator for at least 1 hour, stirring occasionally.

To serve, line salad plates with the arugula leaves. Then top with the pepper mixture and drizzle the liquid over the greens.

EXTRA HEALTH BENEFITS
Lower Cholesterol
Better Blood Pressure
Cancer Protection
Stronger Immunity

Times: Prep: 37 min.
Marinating: at least 1 hr.

Makes 4 servings.

Per serving: 72 calories, 0.3 g. fat (4% of calories), 1.5 g. dietary fiber, 0 mg. cholesterol, 6 mg. sodium.

SLIMMING STRATEGY
Toast the new year with calorie-wise beverages. Try flavored sparkling water, sparkling apple juice, nonalcoholic champagne or fruit juice diluted with seltzer. You'll save on calories and still be able to share in the good times.

Turkey Tonnato

In Italian, tonnato *means "with tuna." In this low-fat dish, tender turkey cutlets are topped with a rich tomato-tuna sauce.*

EXTRA HEALTH BENEFITS
Blood Building
Stronger Immunity

Times: Prep: 7 min.
Cooking: 16 min.

Makes 4 servings.

Per serving: 253 calories, 4.4 g. fat (15% of calories), 2.1 g. dietary fiber, 68 mg. cholesterol, 464 mg. sodium.

- 4 turkey cutlets (5 ounces each)
- ¼ teaspoon garlic powder
- ¼ teaspoon ground black pepper
- ¼ cup defatted low-sodium chicken broth
- 1 cup chopped onions
- 2 cloves garlic, minced
- 3 anchovy fillets
- 2 cups crushed tomatoes (with juices)
- ¼ cup rinsed, pitted and coarsely chopped kalamata olives
- 2 tablespoons lemon juice
- 1 tablespoon minced fresh parsley
- 2 teaspoons capers, rinsed and drained
- 1 can (3 ounces) tuna (packed in water), drained

Rinse the turkey and pat dry with paper towels. Sprinkle both sides of the cutlets with the garlic powder and pepper.

Spray an unheated, large no-stick skillet with no-stick spray. Heat the skillet over medium-high heat. Add the turkey and cook for 4 minutes. Turn the cutlets over and cook for 4 to 6 minutes more or until no longer pink. Transfer to a serving platter and cover to keep warm.

In the skillet, bring the broth to a boil. Add the onions, garlic and anchovies. Reduce the heat and simmer for 1 to 2 minutes, mashing the anchovies with the back of a spoon until dissolved.

Stir in the tomatoes (with juices) and return to a boil. Reduce the heat and simmer, uncovered, for 4 to 5 minutes or until slightly thickened. Stir in the olives, lemon juice, parsley and capers. Simmer for 2 minutes more. Then add the tuna and simmer about 1 minute or until heated through.

To serve, spoon the tomato mixture over the turkey.

Chef's Note: For a change of pace, prepare only the sauce and serve it over rotelle, fettuccine or ziti as a side dish.

Pilaf Florentine

Spinach adds color and vitamins to this easy rice dish.

1½ teaspoons reduced-calorie margarine
 ¼ cup chopped green onions
 1 tablespoon pine nuts
 ½ cup long-grain white rice
1¼ cups defatted low-sodium chicken broth
 ½ cup chopped spinach
 1 tablespoon grated Parmesan cheese
 2 teaspoons grated lemon peel
   Pinch of ground nutmeg
   Pinch of ground white pepper

In a small saucepan, melt the margarine. Add the onions and pine nuts. Cook and stir over medium heat for 4 to 5 minutes or until the onions are tender. Add the rice. Cook and stir for 2 minutes more.

Stir in the broth, spinach, cheese, lemon peel, nutmeg and pepper. Bring to a boil, then reduce the heat. Cover and simmer for 20 to 25 minutes or until the rice is tender and the liquid is absorbed.

Remove from the heat and let stand, covered, for 5 minutes. Before serving, fluff with a fork.

EXTRA HEALTH BENEFITS
Lower Cholesterol

Times: Prep: 10 min.
Cooking: 20 min.
Standing: 5 min.

Makes 4 servings.

Per serving: 125 calories, 3 g. fat (22% of calories), 1 g. dietary fiber, 1 mg. cholesterol, 77 mg. sodium.

Time: Prep: 15 min.

Makes 4 servings.

Per serving: 123 calories, 1.9 g. fat (13% of calories), 3 g. dietary fiber, 0 mg. cholesterol, 36 mg. sodium.

SLIMMING STRATEGY

Have an active New Year's Eve party. Rent a skating rink, go bowling—do anything but sit around watching TV, snacking and drinking eggnog (which packs 19 grams of fat and 342 calories into 1 cup).

Raspberry-Peach Flutes

A truly elegant dessert doesn't have to be high in calories or fat. Here's a case in point. Simply serving frozen yogurt in fancy glasses and adding a few finishing touches creates a smashing dessert.

> 4 **cups fresh or frozen unsweetened sliced peaches**
> 2 **cups fresh or frozen unsweetened red raspberries**
> ¼ **cup shredded coconut**
> 1 **cup frozen nonfat vanilla yogurt**
> 1 **cup sparkling apple cider**
> **Fresh mint (optional)**

If using frozen peaches and raspberries, thaw them. Heat a small no-stick skillet over medium heat. Add the coconut. Cook and stir for 3 to 4 minutes or just until toasted. Remove the coconut from the skillet and set aside.

To serve, spoon the peaches and raspberries into champagne or wine glasses. Top each with small scoops of the frozen yogurt. Then pour the apple cider over each serving. Sprinkle with the coconut and, if desired, garnish with the mint.

Bitter Greens and Asparagus with Poppy Seed Dressing

Dijon mustard serves a dual purpose in the no-oil dressing. It adds flavor and helps thicken the dressing so that it'll cling better to the salad greens.

24 asparagus spears
6 small heads Belgian endive (1¾ pounds total), sliced into 1" pieces
4 cups watercress, trimmed
3 cups loosely packed arugula leaves
2 cups thinly sliced fresh mushrooms
½ cup unsweetened apple juice
¼ cup minced red onions
¼ cup water
¼ cup cider vinegar
4 teaspoons Dijon mustard
2 teaspoons poppy seeds

In a large skillet, bring 2" of water to a boil. Add the asparagus and return to a boil. Boil about 1 minute or just until the asparagus turns bright green. Immediately drain and rinse with cold water to stop further cooking. Chill in the refrigerator.

In a large bowl, combine the endive, watercress, arugula and mushrooms. In a small bowl, stir together the juice, onions, water, vinegar, mustard and poppy seeds.

To serve, place equal amounts of the greens on 8 salad plates. Top each with 3 asparagus spears, then drizzle with the juice mixture.

EXTRA HEALTH BENEFITS
Lower Cholesterol
Better Blood Pressure
Cancer Protection
Blood Building
Stronger Immunity

Time: Prep: 10 min.

Makes 8 servings.

Per serving: 65 calories, 1.1 g. fat (13% of calories), 1.8 g. dietary fiber, 0 mg. cholesterol, 71 mg. sodium.

SLIMMING STRATEGY

If you like to give Easter gifts, put some flowers in a basket rather than baking treats or making candy. This is a particularly good plan for cooks who frequently like to taste test their homemade goodies.

Seafood Quiche

EXTRA HEALTH BENEFITS
Better Blood Pressure
Stronger Immunity

Times: Prep: 18 min.
Baking: 50 min.
Standing: 5 min.

Makes 8 servings.

Per serving: 303 calories,
7.4 g. fat (23% of calories),
0.6 g. dietary fiber, 93 mg.
cholesterol, 450 mg. sodium.

A no-fat potato crust serves as the base of this seafood delight. You'll find it's just as crispy and elegant as a pastry crust.

    2 medium baking potatoes, peeled, coarsely shredded
      and soaked in cold water
    1 cup fat-free egg substitute
   ¼ cup + 1 tablespoon unbleached flour
    1 medium sweet red pepper, chopped
   ½ cup chopped green onions
    2 cloves garlic, minced
    1 cup cooked and flaked salmon or 1 can (7 ounces)
      salmon, drained, flaked and skin removed
    1 cup frozen baby shrimp, thawed or 1 can (4½ ounces)
      shrimp, drained
    1 tablespoon capers, rinsed and drained
 1½ cups skim milk
    1 tablespoon grated lemon peel
    1 teaspoon dried tarragon leaves
      Pinch of ground white pepper
    1 cup (4 ounces) shredded reduced-fat Jarlsberg cheese

Spray a 10" deep-dish pie plate with no-stick spray; set aside. Drain the potatoes well, squeezing excess liquid from them.

In a medium bowl, stir together the potatoes, ¼ cup of the egg substitute and ¼ cup of the flour. Pat the mixture in the bottom and up the sides of the pie plate. Bake at 450° about 5 minutes or until lightly browned. Remove the potato shell from the oven. Reduce the temperature to 325°.

Meanwhile, spray an unheated, large no-stick skillet with no-stick spray. Heat the skillet over medium heat. Add the red peppers, onions and garlic. Cook and stir about 4 minutes or until tender.

Crush the bones in the salmon. Add the salmon with the bones, the shrimp and capers to the onion mixture. Cook and stir for 2 minutes. Spoon into the potato shell; set aside.

In a medium bowl, use a wire whisk to combine the milk, the remaining ¾ cup egg substitute, the remaining 1 tablespoon flour, the lemon peel, tarragon and white pepper. Stir in the cheese.

Pour the mixture over the salmon mixture in the shell. Place on a cookie sheet and bake at 325° for 35 to 45 minutes or until a knife inserted near the center comes out clean. Let stand for 5 minutes before serving.

Chef's Note: To keep the potatoes from turning brown after they're shredded, transfer them immediately to a bowl of cold water. When you're ready to mix them with the egg substitute, drain well and pat dry with paper towels.

Seafood Quiche

Orange-Glazed Raisin-Oat Bread

EXTRA HEALTH BENEFITS
Lower Cholesterol
Stronger Immunity

Times: Prep: 10 min.
Baking: 25 min.
Cooling: 30 min.

Makes 12 servings.

Per serving: 151 calories,
0.4 g. fat (2% of calories),
1.6 g. dietary fiber, 0 mg.
cholesterol, 118 mg. sodium.

Yogurt replaces the margarine normally found in this quick bread, making it almost fat-free. Serve the bread plain or toasted. (Because there is a glaze on the bread, keep your toaster clean by toasting the slices under the broiler.) If you'd like, add an extra bit of sweetness by serving the bread with some all-fruit spread.

BREAD

- 1½ cups unbleached flour
- ¼ cup whole-wheat flour
- ¼ cup quick-cooking oats
- 1 teaspoon baking powder
- 1 teaspoon baking soda
- 1 teaspoon ground cinnamon
- 2 egg whites, lightly beaten
- ¾ cup nonfat plain yogurt
- ¼ cup honey
- 1 cup raisins

GLAZE

- 2 tablespoons honey
- 2 tablespoons orange juice

For the bread: Spray a 9" × 5" loaf pan with no-stick spray; set aside.

In a large bowl, stir together the unbleached flour and whole-wheat flour, oats, baking powder, baking soda and cinnamon. In a medium bowl, stir together the egg whites, yogurt and honey. Add to the flour mixture. Stir just until combined. Fold in the raisins.

Spoon the mixture into the loaf pan. Bake at 350° for 25 to 30 minutes or until a toothpick inserted near the center comes out clean. Let cool for 5 minutes in the pan on a wire rack. Remove the pan and partially cool the bread 10 to 15 minutes more.

For the glaze: Meanwhile, in a small bowl, stir together the honey and orange juice.

While the bread is still warm, use a cake tester or skewer to poke holes in the top. Spoon the glaze over the top, then let cool completely.

Chef's Note: This bread freezes well, so you can make it ahead. Bake it, glaze it and let it cool completely. Then wrap the bread in foil and place in a self-closing plastic bag. It will keep in the freezer for 2 months.

Two Weeks of Low-Fat Menus

This is what it all boils down to: What does a low-fat eating plan look like? Is it something you can really live with? Is it varied and interesting? Will you be satisfied? And can you still enjoy restaurant meals, takeout lunches, Sunday brunch and all the other pleasures that make life fun?

The answer is a resounding yes. Yes, you can be satisfied. Yes, you can eat out and throw parties. Yes, you *can* live happily ever after on a low-fat "diet."

To help you personalize an eating plan for your own situation, we had a nutritionist gear two weeks' worth of menus to three different calorie and fat budgets, using the recipes in this book. These menus will show you how easy it is to stay *under* your fat budget and within your calorie budget, even when enjoying treats such as dinner at your favorite restaurant and margarine spread on your bread or on top of your baked potato.

To use these menus, pick the daily calorie and fat budget that's closest to the weight-loss or maintenance plan you're following. Then adjust the menus as needed to tailor them to the exact fat and calorie intake for you. It might mean subtracting an item here and there or adding extra portions of whatever appeals to you.

Feel free, too, to make up your own menu plans using the recipes in this book. Supplement individual dishes as we did by adding easily prepared vegetables, grains, fruits, entrées and other items. That will simplify things for you in the kitchen and prove, once and for all, that eating healthy is not a complicated proposition.

So here's to your health—and to deliciously healthy dining.

Day 1: Sunday

		1,300 Calories (36 g. fat)	1,600 Calories (44 g. fat)	2,200 Calories (61 g. fat)
Brunch	Potato Frittata Italiano (p. 49)	1 serving	1 serving	2 servings
	Whole-wheat toast with reduced-calorie margarine	2 slices 1 tsp.	2 slices 2 tsp.	2 slices 2 tsp.
	Fresh fruit cup	1 cup	1 cup	1 cup
	Skim milk	1 cup	1 cup	1 cup
Dinner	Grilled Cornish Hens Teriyaki (p. 104)	1 serving	1 serving	2 servings
	Rice pilaf	¾ cup	1 cup	1½ cups
	Steamed broccoli spears	1 cup	1 cup	1 cup
	Whole-wheat roll with reduced-calorie margarine	1 roll —	2 rolls 2 tsp.	2 rolls 2 tsp.
	Sliced fresh strawberries with nonfat plain yogurt	1 cup 6 oz.	1 cup 6 oz.	1 cup 6 oz.
	Skim milk	½ cup	½ cup	½ cup
Snacks	Crispy Wonton Chips (p. 64)	1 serving	2 servings	2 servings
	Carrot sticks	1 cup	1 cup	1 cup
	Piquant Yogurt Cheese (p. 60)	1 serving	2 servings	2 servings
Daily Total	Calories	1,279	1,536	2,111
	Fat (g.)	20	27	38
	% Calories from Fat	14	17	16
	Dietary Fiber (g.)	34	38	38
	Cholesterol (mg.)	120	120	233
	Sodium (mg.)	1,581	1,846	2,514

Day 2: Monday

		1,300 Calories (36 g. fat)	1,600 Calories (44 g. fat)	2,200 Calories (61 g. fat)
Breakfast	Peach-Bran Muffin (p. 38)	1 muffin	2 muffins	2 muffins
	Fresh pear	1 medium	1 medium	1 medium
	Skim milk	1 cup	1 cup	1 cup
Lunch	Turkey breast and	1 oz.	1 oz.	1½ oz.
	Swiss cheese on	1 oz.	1 oz.	1½ oz.
	rye bread with	2 slices	2 slices	3 slices
	tomatoes, lettuce and mustard	as desired	as desired	as desired
	Fresh cut-up vegetables with	1 cup	1 cup	1 cup
	Madras Curry Dip (p. 62)	1 serving	1 serving	1 serving
Dinner	Lemon-Asparagus Soup (p. 257)	1 serving	1 serving	1 serving
	Hawaiian Fried Rice (p. 209)	1 serving	1 serving	1 serving
	French bread with	—	1 slice	2 slices
	reduced-calorie margarine	—	1 tsp.	1 tsp.
	Orange slices	1 orange	1 orange	1 orange
	Fortune cookie	1 cookie	1 cookie	1 cookie
Snacks	Cocoa Angel Food Cake (p. 314)	1 piece	2 pieces	2 pieces
	Fresh raspberries	½ cup	½ cup	½ cup
	Skim milk	½ cup	½ cup	½ cup
Daily Total	Calories	1,284	1,602	2,186
	Fat (g.)	23	30	42
	% Calories from Fat	16	17	17
	Dietary Fiber (g.)	26	31	38
	Cholesterol (mg.)	55	55	79
	Sodium (mg.)	1,745	2,096	3,246

Day 3: Tuesday

	1,300 Calories (36 g. fat)	1,600 Calories (44 g. fat)	2,200 Calories (61 g. fat)
Breakfast			
Bran flakes with	1 oz.	2 oz.	2 oz.
skim milk	¾ cup	1 cup	1 cup
Whole-wheat toast with	—	—	2 slices
reduced-calorie margarine	—	—	2 tsp.
Banana	1 medium	1 medium	1 medium
Lunch			
Waldorf Chicken Salad (p. 94)	1 serving	1 serving	1 serving
Whole-grain flatbread crackers	¾ oz.	1 oz.	1 oz.
Fresh green pepper strips	1 cup	1 cup	1 cup
Skim milk	1 cup	1 cup	1 cup
Dinner			
Pork Medallions in Spiced Tomato Sauce over Noodles (p. 145)	1 serving	1 serving	1 serving
Steamed green beans	1 cup	1 cup	1½ cups
Rye bread with	—	1 slice	2 slices
reduced-calorie margarine	—	1 tsp.	2 tsp.
New-Wave Streusel Apples (p. 322)	1 serving	1 serving	2 servings
Snacks			
Pretzels (with mustard)	1 oz.	2 oz.	2 oz.
Lime sparkling water	10 oz.	10 oz.	10 oz.
Daily Total			
Calories	1,293	1,604	2,203
Fat (g.)	17	22	40
% Calories from Fat	12	12	16
Dietary Fiber (g.)	21	26	39
Cholesterol (mg.)	121	122	182
Sodium (mg.)	1,407	2,316	3,086

Day 4:
Wednesday

		1,300 Calories (36 g. fat)	1,600 Calories (44 g. fat)	2,200 Calories (61 g. fat)
Breakfast	Fast-Track Breakfast (p. 46)	1 serving	1 serving	1 serving
	Toasted English muffin with	1 muffin	1 muffin	2 muffins
	peanut butter	1 Tbsp.	1 Tbsp.	2 Tbsp.
Lunch	Baked Potatoes with Chive and Cheese Topping (p. 287)	1 serving	1 serving	2 servings
	Spinach salad with	2 cups	2 cups	2 cups
	mandarin oranges and	½ cup	½ cup	½ cup
	nonfat Italian salad dressing	2 Tbsp.	2 Tbsp.	2 Tbsp.
Dinner	Grilled Snapper with Tomato Salsa and Black Beans (p. 183)	1 serving	2 servings	2 servings
	Yellow summer squash sautéed in	1 cup	1 cup	1 cup
	olive oil	1 tsp.	1 tsp.	1 tsp.
	Sourdough bread with	1 slice	1 slice	2 slices
	reduced-calorie margarine	1 tsp.	1 tsp.	2 tsp.
	Fresh blueberries	½ cup	½ cup	1 cup
Snacks	Skim milk	1 cup	1 cup	2 cups
	Fig bars	2 cookies	3 cookies	3 cookies
Daily Total	Calories	1,299	1,616	2,206
	Fat (g.)	25	28	42
	% Calories from Fat	17	16	17
	Dietary Fiber (g.)	19	20	31
	Cholesterol (mg.)	55	97	103
	Sodium (mg.)	2,202	2,872	3,718

Day 5: Thursday

		1,300 Calories (36 g. fat)	1,600 Calories (44 g. fat)	2,200 Calories (61 g. fat)
Breakfast	Fruited Bulgur (p. 42)	1 serving	1 serving	2 servings
	Skim milk	½ cup	½ cup	1 cup
Lunch	Roast beef on	2 oz.	2 oz.	2 oz.
	whole-wheat bread with	2 slices	2 slices	2 slices
	sprouts and mustard and	as desired	as desired	as desired
	reduced-calorie mayonnaise	—	1½ tsp.	1 Tbsp.
	Cherry tomatoes	1 cup	1 cup	1 cup
	Cauliflower florets (raw)	½ cup	½ cup	½ cup
	Grapes	20 grapes	20 grapes	20 grapes
	Nonfat plain yogurt	6 oz.	6 oz.	6 oz.
Dinner	Three-Cheese Lasagna (p. 217)	1 serving	2 servings	2 servings
	Garlic bread with	1 slice	2 slices	2 slices
	reduced-calorie margarine	1 tsp.	2 tsp.	2 tsp.
	Steamed carrot slices	1 cup	1 cup	1 cup
	Lemon sorbet	½ cup	½ cup	1 cup
Snacks	Air-popped popcorn with	3 cups	3 cups	3 cups
	reduced-calorie margarine	1 tsp.	1 tsp.	1 tsp.
Daily Total	Calories	1,292	1,596	2,196
	Fat (g.)	21	27	35
	% Calories from Fat	15	15	14
	Dietary Fiber (g.)	27	29	38
	Cholesterol (mg.)	58	66	78
	Sodium (mg.)	1,619	2,368	3,150

Day 6: Friday

	1,300 Calories (36 g. fat)	1,600 Calories (44 g. fat)	2,200 Calories (61 g. fat)
Breakfast			
Nonfat, sugar-free fruit-flavored yogurt	6 oz.	6 oz.	6 oz.
Plain bagel with	½ bagel	1 bagel	1 bagel
light cream cheese	1 Tbsp.	1½ Tbsp.	2 Tbsp.
Melon cubes	1 cup	1 cup	1½ cups
Lunch			
Chicken Vegetable Soup with Shells (p. 255)	1 serving	1 serving	1 serving
Crusty roll with	—	1 roll	2 rolls
reduced-calorie margarine	—	—	2 tsp.
Blackberries with cubed kiwifruit	1 cup	1 cup	1 cup
Dinner (at a restaurant)			
Filet mignon	4 oz.	6 oz.	8 oz.
Baked potato with	1 medium	1 medium	1 medium
sour cream	1 Tbsp.	1 Tbsp.	1 Tbsp.
Whole-wheat roll with	—	—	1 roll
butter	—	—	1 tsp.
Tossed salad with	2 cups	2 cups	2 cups
reduced-calorie salad dressing	2 Tbsp.	2 Tbsp.	2 Tbsp.
Ice milk	½ cup	½ cup	1 cup
Snacks			
Blazing Trail Mix (p. 70)	1 serving	1 serving	2 servings
Raspberry sparkling water	10 oz.	10 oz.	10 oz.
Daily Total			
Calories	1,304	1,603	2,182
Fat (g.)	29	38	53
% Calories from Fat	20	21	22
Dietary Fiber (g.)	24	28	38
Cholesterol (mg.)	164	214	263
Sodium (mg.)	1,161	1,511	2,215

Two Weeks of Low-Fat Menus

Day 7: Saturday

	1,300 Calories (36 g. fat)	1,600 Calories (44 g. fat)	2,200 Calories (61 g. fat)
Breakfast			
Grapefruit	½ medium	½ medium	½ medium
Poached egg	1 egg	2 eggs	2 eggs
Whole-wheat toast with	1 slice	2 slices	2 slices
reduced-calorie margarine	1 tsp.	2 tsp.	2 tsp.
Skim milk	½ cup	½ cup	1 cup
Lunch			
Falafel Burger (p. 233) on	1 patty	1 patty	2 patties
whole-wheat pita bread with	½ pita	½ pita	1 pita
chopped tomatoes and onions	½ cup	½ cup	½ cup
and sprouts			
Carrot sticks	1 cup	1 cup	1½ cups
Fresh pear	1 medium	1 medium	1 medium
Skim milk	1 cup	1 cup	1 cup
Dinner			
Spicy Barbecued Chicken Breasts (p. 88)	1 serving	1 serving	2 servings
Grilled new potato and vegetable skewers brushed with olive oil	1½ skewers	1½ skewers	2½ skewers
	1 tsp.	1 tsp.	1½ tsp.
Sourdough bread with	——	1 slice	2 slices
reduced-calorie margarine	——	1 tsp.	2 tsp.
Blackberry Parfait (p. 325)	1 serving	1 serving	1 serving
Snacks			
Nonfat, sugar-free fruit-flavored yogurt	6 oz.	6 oz.	6 oz.
Graham crackers	4 squares	4 squares	6 squares
Daily Total			
Calories	1,296	1,585	2,201
Fat (g.)	22	34	45
% Calories from Fat	15	19	18
Dietary Fiber (g.)	25	30	39
Cholesterol (mg.)	350	623	689
Sodium (mg.)	1,430	1,929	2,716

Day 8: Sunday

		1,300 Calories (36 g. fat)	1,600 Calories (44 g. fat)	2,200 Calories (61 g. fat)
Brunch	Oven-Crisped French Toast with Apricot Sauce (p. 53)	1 serving	1½ servings	2 servings
	Canadian bacon	1 oz.	2 oz.	2 oz.
	Fresh fruit cup	1 cup	1 cup	1 cup
	Skim milk	1 cup	1 cup	1 cup
Dinner	Sun-Dried Tomato Crostini with Goat Cheese (p. 67)	1 serving	1 serving	1 serving
	Rib Steaks with Papaya Salsa (p. 134)	1 serving	1 serving	2 servings
	Fresh Asparagus and Onion Sauté (p. 280)	1 serving	1 serving	2 servings
	Crusty roll with reduced-calorie margarine	1 roll 1 tsp.	1 roll 1 tsp.	2 rolls 2 tsp.
	Pineapple Chiffon Pie with Strawberry Sauce (p. 312)	1 serving	2 servings	2 servings
Snacks	Mozzarella cheese	1 oz.	1½ oz.	1 oz.
	Apple wedges	1 apple	1 apple	1 apple
Daily Total	Calories	1,306	1,601	2,184
	Fat (g.)	30	36	50
	% Calories from Fat	21	20	21
	Dietary Fiber (g.)	22	25	37
	Cholesterol (mg.)	111	138	198
	Sodium (mg.)	1,689	2,424	2,917

Day 9: Monday

		1,300 Calories (36 g. fat)	1,600 Calories (44 g. fat)	2,200 Calories (61 g. fat)
Breakfast	Fast-Track Breakfast (p. 46)	1 serving	1 serving	2 servings
	Whole-wheat toast with	1 slice	2 slices	2 slices
	jam	1½ tsp.	1½ Tbsp.	1½ Tbsp.
Lunch (at a fast-food restaurant)	Broiled chicken sandwich	1 sandwich	1 sandwich	1 sandwich
	Garden side salad with	1 salad	1 salad	1 salad
	reduced-calorie salad dressing	2 Tbsp.	2 Tbsp.	2 Tbsp.
	Skim milk	1 cup	1 cup	1 cup
Dinner	Fish Fillets with Rapid Ratatouille (p. 172)	1 serving	2 servings	2 servings
	Tiny new potatoes	3 potatoes	5 potatoes	6 potatoes
	Hard roll with	1 roll	1 roll	1 roll
	reduced-calorie margarine	1 tsp.	2 tsp.	2 tsp.
	Fresh peach slices	1 cup	1 cup	1 cup
	Ice milk	—	—	1 cup
Snacks	Frozen grapes	20 grapes	20 grapes	30 grapes
	Vanilla wafers	6 cookies	6 cookies	12 cookies
Daily Total	Calories	1,303	1,593	2,191
	Fat (g.)	24	28	38
	% Calories from Fat	17	16	16
	Dietary Fiber (g.)	17	25	28
	Cholesterol (mg.)	169	224	259
	Sodium (mg.)	1,510	1,715	2,068

Day 10: Tuesday

		1,300 Calories (36 g. fat)	1,600 Calories (44 g. fat)	2,200 Calories (61 g. fat)
Breakfast	Bagels to Go (p. 46)	1 serving	1 serving	1½ servings
	Orange	1 medium	1 medium	1 medium
Lunch	Mariner's Salad (p. 169)	1 serving	1 serving	2 servings
	Whole-wheat French bread with	1 slice	1 slice	2 slices
	reduced-calorie margarine	1 tsp.	1 tsp.	2 tsp.
	Nonfat, sugar-free fruit-flavored yogurt	8 oz.	8 oz.	8 oz.
Dinner	Cheese Tortellini Soup (p. 248)	1 serving	1 serving	1 serving
	Spaghetti with	1½ cups	1½ cups	2½ cups
	tomato-mushroom sauce	½ cup	¾ cup	1¼ cups
	Italian bread with	—	1 slice	2 slices
	reduced-calorie margarine	—	1 tsp.	1 tsp.
	Mixed green salad with	2 cups	2 cups	3 cups
	nonfat Italian dressing	1 Tbsp.	1 Tbsp.	1 Tbsp.
	Fresh strawberries	1 cup	1 cup	1 cup
Snacks	Good Morning Muffin (p. 36)	1 muffin	2 muffins	2 muffins
	Skim milk	1 cup	1 cup	1 cup
Daily Total	Calories	1,306	1,583	2,202
	Fat (g.)	16	22	30
	% Calories from Fat	11	13	12
	Dietary Fiber (g.)	24	29	39
	Cholesterol (mg.)	74	75	126
	Sodium (mg.)	1,663	2,140	3,222

Two Weeks of Low-Fat Menus

Day 11: Wednesday

	1,300 Calories (36 g. fat)	1,600 Calories (44 g. fat)	2,200 Calories (61 g. fat)
Breakfast			
Mini-square wheat cereal with	1 oz.	1 oz.	2 oz.
skim milk	¾ cup	1 cup	1 cup
Banana	½ medium	1 medium	1 medium
Lunch			
Tabbouleh with White Beans and Spinach (p. 212)	1 serving	1 serving	2 servings
Crusty roll with	—	1 roll	1 roll
reduced-calorie margarine	—	—	1 tsp.
Cantaloupe wedge	¼ melon	¼ melon	¼ melon
Skim milk	1 cup	1 cup	1 cup
Dinner			
Baked tortilla chips with	1 oz.	2 oz.	2 oz.
Fresh Tomato Salsa (p. 65)	1 serving	2 servings	2 servings
Chicken and Three-Pepper Fajitas (p. 92)	1 serving	1 serving	2 servings
Tangerine	1 medium	1 medium	1 medium
Snacks			
Angel food cake	1/12 cake	1/12 cake	1/12 cake
Frozen nonfat yogurt with	½ cup	½ cup	½ cup
chocolate ice-cream topping	1 Tbsp.	1 Tbsp.	1 Tbsp.
Daily Total			
Calories	1,311	1,599	2,212
Fat (g.)	15	18	30
% Calories from Fat	10	10	12
Dietary Fiber (g.)	20	27	41
Cholesterol (mg.)	56	57	106
Sodium (mg.)	682	1,035	1,172

Day 12: Thursday

	1,300 Calories (36 g. fat)	1,600 Calories (44 g. fat)	2,200 Calories (61 g. fat)
Breakfast			
Toasted whole-wheat English muffin with	½ muffin	1 muffin	2 muffins
jam	1 Tbsp.	1½ Tbsp.	3 Tbsp.
Nonfat, sugar-free fruit-flavored yogurt	6 oz.	6 oz.	6 oz.
Lunch			
Corned beef and	1 oz.	1 oz.	2 oz.
Swiss cheese on	1 oz.	1 oz.	1 oz.
rye bread with	2 slices	2 slices	2 slices
lettuce and mustard	as desired	as desired	as desired
Cauliflower florets (raw)	1 cup	1 cup	1 cup
Fresh apricots	3 medium	3 medium	3 medium
Currant Kisses (p. 319)	6 cookies	6 cookies	6 cookies
Skim milk	—	—	1 cup
Dinner			
Vegetarian Paella (p. 204)	1 serving	1 serving	1 serving
Whole-wheat roll with	—	1 roll	2 rolls
reduced-calorie margarine	—	1 tsp.	2 tsp.
Mixed salad greens with	2 cups	2 cups	3 cups
Tomato Vinaigrette (p. 306)	1 serving	1 serving	2 servings
Lime sorbet	½ cup	½ cup	1 cup
Snacks			
Italian Nachos (p. 74)	1 serving	2 servings	2 servings
Orange sparkling water	10 oz.	10 oz.	10 oz.
Daily Total			
Calories	1,303	1,593	2,205
Fat (g.)	26	31	41
% Calorie from Fat	18	18	17
Dietary Fiber (g.)	23	29	36
Cholesterol (mg.)	60	66	94
Sodium (mg.)	1,865	2,696	3,785

Two Weeks of Low-Fat Menus

Day 13: Friday

	1,300 Calories (36 g. fat)	1,600 Calories (44 g. fat)	2,200 Calories (61 g. fat)
Breakfast			
Frozen plain waffles with	2 (4") waffles	3 (4") waffles	4 (4") waffles
reduced-calorie pancake syrup	2 Tbsp.	3 Tbsp.	4 Tbsp.
Orange juice	½ cup	¾ cup	1 cup
Lunch			
Potage of Beef and Mixed Vegetables (p. 260)	1 serving	1 serving	2 servings
French bread with	1 slice	1 slice	2 slices
reduced-calorie margarine	1 tsp.	1 tsp.	2 tsp.
Tossed salad with	2 cups	2 cups	2 cups
nonfat salad dressing	2 Tbsp.	2 Tbsp.	2 Tbsp.
Skim milk	1 cup	1 cup	1 cup
Dinner			
Haddock in Creamy Orange-Basil Sauce (p. 163)	1 serving	1 serving	2 servings
Brown rice	½ cup	1 cup	1 cup
Steamed yellow summer squash	1 cup	1 cup	1 cup
Serendipitous Spinach Salad (p. 298)	1 serving	1 serving	1 serving
Snacks			
Nonfat plain yogurt	6 oz.	6 oz.	6 oz.
Banana	1 medium	1 medium	1 medium
Daily Total			
Calories	1,283	1,593	2,199
Fat (g.)	12	13	23
% Calories from Fat	8	7	9
Dietary Fiber (g.)	17	24	28
Cholesterol (mg.)	114	114	221
Sodium (mg.)	1,648	1,886	2,564

Day 14: Saturday

	1,300 Calories (36 g. fat)	1,600 Calories (44 g. fat)	2,200 Calories (61 g. fat)
Breakfast			
Oatmeal with	½ cup	½ cup	1 cup
sliced strawberries and	½ cup	½ cup	½ cup
brown sugar and	1 Tbsp.	1 Tbsp.	1 Tbsp.
skim milk	½ cup	1 cup	1 cup
Whole-wheat toast with	—	1 slice	1 slice
reduced-calorie margarine	—	1 tsp.	1 tsp.
Lunch			
Red, White and Green Pizza (p. 229)	1 serving	1 serving	2 servings
Grapes	20 grapes	30 grapes	30 grapes
Dinner			
Lamb Chops in Parchment (p. 151)	1 serving	2 servings	2 servings
Steamed brussels sprouts	1 cup	1 cup	1 cup
Crusty roll with	1 roll	1 roll	1 roll
reduced-calorie margarine	1 tsp.	1 tsp.	1 tsp.
Georgia Peach Soufflé (p. 317)	1 serving	1 serving	2 servings
Snacks			
Skim milk	1 cup	1 cup	1¼ cups
Whole-wheat toast with	1 slice	1 slice	1 slice
peanut butter	1 Tbsp.	1 Tbsp.	1 Tbsp.
Daily Total			
Calories	1,304	1,599	2,195
Fat (g.)	29	36	48
% Calories from Fat	20	20	20
Dietary Fiber (g.)	25	30	36
Cholesterol (mg.)	49	84	95
Sodium (mg.)	1,688	1,991	2,969

Calories and Fat at a Glance

What's the leanest cut of beef? What are the best choices at fast-food restaurants? How do cold cereals compare? The following tables tell all. As long as you know the fat and calorie figures for the foods you're eating, you can budget in occasional treats, convenience foods and trips to fast-food outlets.

The fast-food establishments are especially notorious for their fat-laden menu items. But you can still enjoy the convenience of dining at these places by choosing some of their lighter items. We've listed a good cross section of those foods here. To compare them with other menu items, see if the restaurants have nutrition information available. Many have pamphlets that are yours for the asking.

When you're in a hurry, frozen entrées can provide a quick and easy dinner—and many brands are low in calories and fat. Use this table to help you plan your purchases before leaving the house. You'll save time at the store and not be confused by the staggering array of items in the frozen-food case. Keep in mind that frozen entrées are often not complete meals. Round out your dinners with fresh vegetables, whole-grain bread, skim milk and fruit or low-fat yogurt.

Cereal is an excellent food choice when you're dieting. It's a good source of complex carbohydrates, fiber, vitamins and minerals. And it can make a nutritious dinner when you just want something light. (Don't overlook cereal's snack potential, either.) Use the table to help you wisely navigate your way through the overflowing cereal aisle.

Common Foods

Food	Amount	Calories	Total Fat (g)	% Calories From Fat
Beverages				
Carbonated Beverages				
Beer, nonalcoholic	12 oz.	73	0	0
Club soda/seltzer	12 oz.	0	0	0
Cola				
Regular	12 oz.	151	0.1	1
Sugar-free	12 oz.	2	0	0
Fruit and Vegetable Juices/Drinks				
Apple juice, unsweetened	8 oz.	111	0.3	2
Apricot nectar	8 oz.	141	0.2	1
Cranberry juice cocktail	8 oz.	144	0.3	2
Grapefruit juice				
Fresh	8 oz.	96	0.3	2
Canned, unsweetened	8 oz.	93	0.2	2
Orange juice				
Fresh	8 oz.	112	0.5	4
From frozen concentrate	8 oz.	112	0.1	1
Pineapple juice, unsweetened	8 oz.	139	0.2	0.7
Prune juice	8 oz.	181	0.1	0.4
Tomato juice	8 oz.	41	0.1	3
Vegetable juice cocktail	8 oz.	46	0.2	4
Hot Beverages				
Cocoa, sugar-free instant	6 oz.	48	0.4	8
Coffee, brewed or instant	6 oz.	4	0	0
Tea, brewed or herbal	6 oz.	2	0	0
Breads, Crackers and Muffins				
Breads				
Bagel, plain	1	156	1	5.2
Croutons, plain	¼ cup	30	0.5	15
English muffin, plain	1	134	1	7
French or Vienna bread	2 slices	138	1.6	10
Hamburger bun, white	1	123	2.2	16

Food	Amount	Calories	Total Fat (g)	% Calories From Fat
Hot dog bun, white	1	23	2.2	16
Mixed-grain bread	2 slices	130	2	14
Pita bread, whole-wheat	1	170	1.7	9
Pumpernickel bread	1 slice	80	1	11
Raisin bread	2 slices	142	2.2	14
Rye bread, American	2 slices	166	2.2	11
Tortillas				
Corn	2 medium	112	1.2	10
Flour	2 medium	228	5	20
Wheat bread, reduced-calorie	2 slices	92	1	10
White bread, reduced-calorie	2 slices	96	1.2	11

Crackers

Food	Amount	Calories	Total Fat (g)	% Calories From Fat
Butter-flavored (Ritz-type)	8	128	5	35
Graham	2 squares	110	2.6	22
Melba toast rounds, plain	6	110	0.8	7
Ry-Krisp, plain	1 triple cracker	84	0.2	2
Saltines				
Fat-free	10 squares	100	0	0
Plain	10 squares	120	3	25
Wheat				
Thin wafer	15	135	6	39
Triscuit	6	120	4	30

Muffins

Food	Amount	Calories	Total Fat (g)	% Calories From Fat
Blueberry, homemade	1	163	6.1	34
Bran, homemade	1	161	7.0	39
Corn, homemade	1	180	7.0	35

Quick Breads

Food	Amount	Calories	Total Fat (g)	% Calories From Fat
Banana bread, homemade	1 slice	195	6.3	29
Biscuits, plain or buttermilk				
Homemade	1	212	9.8	41
Low-fat, prepared from refrigerated dough	2	126	2.2	16
Regular, prepared from refrigerated dough	2	186	8	39

Food	Amount	Calories	Total Fat (g)	% Calories From Fat
Breads, Crackers and Muffins—continued	**Quick Breads—**continued			
Pancakes				
Homemade	3 (4")	258	11	38
"Light," prepared from mix	3 (4")	130	2	14
Popover, homemade	1	87	3.1	32
Waffles				
Plain, homemade	1 (7")	218	10.6	44
Plain, low-fat, frozen	2 (4")	160	2	11
Broths				
Beef, low-sodium, ready-to-serve	8 oz.	12	1.2	90
Chicken, low-sodium, ready-to-serve	8 oz.	41	1.9	42
Candy (also see page 322)				
Gumdrops	1 oz.	100	trace	NA
Milk chocolate	1 oz.	146	9	56
Cheeses				
American, reduced-fat	1 oz.	70	4	51
Blue, reduced-fat	1 oz.	76	4	47
Cheddar, reduced-fat	1 oz.	70	4	51
Colby, reduced-fat	1 oz.	70	4	51
Cottage cheese				
Nonfat	½ cup	80	0	0
1% milk fat	½ cup	82	1	10
2% milk fat	½ cup	101	2.2	19
Cream cheese				
Light	1 oz.	60	5	75
Nonfat	1 oz.	30	0	0
Monterey Jack, reduced-fat	1 oz.	80	5	56
Mozzarella				
Nonfat	1 oz.	40	0	0
Part-skim	1 oz.	80	6	68
Reduced-fat	1 oz.	65	3	42
Parmesan	1 Tbsp.	23	1.5	59

Food	Amount	Calories	Total Fat (g)	% Calories From Fat
Ricotta				
Nonfat	1/4 cup	40	0	0
Part-skim	1/4 cup	90	6	60
Reduced-fat	1/4 cup	70	3	39
Swiss, reduced-fat	1 oz.	80	5	56

Condiments

Food	Amount	Calories	Total Fat (g)	% Calories From Fat
Ketchup				
Reduced-calorie and -sodium	1 Tbsp.	10	0	0
Regular	1 Tbsp.	16	0	0
Mustard				
Dijon	1 tsp.	5	0.3	64
Prepared	1 tsp.	4	0.2	53
Pickles				
Dill	1 whole	12	0.1	9
Sweet	1 whole	41	0.1	2
Sweet relish	1 Tbsp.	19	0.1	3

Desserts and Toppings

Cakes

Food	Amount	Calories	Total Fat (g)	% Calories From Fat
Angel food, plain, homemade	1/12 cake	142	0.1	0.7
Chocolate, prepared from 94% fat-free mix	1/12 cake	200	4	18
Sponge, plain, homemade	1/12 cake	140	2	13
White, prepared from 94% fat-free mix	1/12 cake	180	3	15

Cookies and Bars

Food	Amount	Calories	Total Fat (g)	% Calories From Fat
Animal crackers	11	126	3.9	28
Brownies				
Homemade, without nuts	1 (2" square)	156	9.8	57
Prepared from 96% fat-free mix	1 (2" square)	200	2	9
Chocolate chip cookies				
Homemade	1 medium	138	8	52
Purchased, low-fat	1	128	4.4	31
Fig bar, purchased	1	56	1.2	19

Food	Amount	Calories	Total Fat (g)	% Calories From Fat

Desserts and Toppings—continued

Cookies and Bars—continued

Food	Amount	Calories	Total Fat (g)	% Calories From Fat
Gingersnaps, homemade	4 small	176	2.8	21
Lady fingers, purchased	3	120	3.0	19
Oatmeal cookies, with raisins, homemade	2 small	130	4.8	34

Frozen Desserts

Frozen yogurt, nonfat, all flavors	½ cup	100	0	0
Ice milk				
Chocolate, hard	½ cup	110	3	25
Chocolate, soft-serve	½ cup	142	4.3	27
Vanilla, hard	½ cup	92	2.8	28
Vanilla, soft-serve	½ cup	112	2.3	19
Sherbet, orange	½ cup	135	1.9	13

Gelatins

All fruit flavors				
Regular	½ cup	80	0	0
Sugar-free	½ cup	8	0	0

Puddings

Chocolate				
Regular, prepared from instant mix using skim milk	½ cup	147	1.2	7
Sugar-free, prepared from instant mix using skim milk	½ cup	87	1.2	12
Tapioca, prepared from mix using skim milk	½ cup	123	0.2	1
Vanilla				
Regular, prepared from instant mix using skim milk	½ cup	133	0.2	1
Sugar-free, prepared from instant mix using skim milk	½ cup	68	0.2	3

Toppings

Frozen whipped topping, thawed				
"Light"	2 Tbsp.	16	1	56
Regular, nondairy	2 Tbsp.	24	2	75

	Food	Amount	Calories	Total Fat (g)	% Calories From Fat
Eggs and Egg Substitute	Egg				
	White, uncooked	I large	17	0	0
	Whole, uncooked	I large	75	5	61
	Yolk, uncooked	I large	59	5.1	78
	Egg substitute, fat-free	¼ cup	25	0	0
Fats	Butter-flavored granules	½ tsp.	4	0	0
	Cooking oil				
	Canola	I Tbsp.	124	14	100
	Olive	I Tbsp.	119	14	100
	Margarine, reduced-calorie				
	Liquid	I Tbsp.	90	10	100
	Spread (tub)	I Tbsp.	70	7	100
	Stick	I Tbsp.	70	7	100
	No-stick spray	I spray (4 sec.)	2	trace	100
Fish and Shellfish	Fish				
	Catfish, farm-raised, cooked	3 oz.	129	6.8	47
	Cod, Atlantic, cooked	3 oz.	89	0.7	7
	Flounder or sole, cooked	3 oz.	99	1.3	12
	Grouper, cooked	3 oz.	100	1.1	10
	Haddock, cooked	3 oz.	95	0.8	7
	Halibut, cooked	3 oz.	119	2.5	19
	Mackerel, Pacific or Jack, cooked	3 oz.	171	8.6	45
	Mahimahi, cooked	3 oz.	93	0.8	8
	Monkfish, cooked	3 oz.	82	1.7	19
	Orange roughy, cooked	3 oz.	75	.76	9
	Perch, ocean, cooked	3 oz.	103	1.8	16
	Pike, northern, cooked	3 oz.	96	0.8	7
	Pollock, cooked	3 oz.	96	1.0	9
	Salmon				
	Atlantic, cooked	3 oz.	175	10.5	54
	Coho, cooked	3 oz.	151	7	42
	Pink, canned, with bones and liquid	3 oz.	114	5	39

Food	Amount	Calories	Total Fat (g)	% Calories From Fat

Fish and Shellfish— continued

Fish—continued

Food	Amount	Calories	Total Fat (g)	% Calories From Fat
Shark, mixed species, cooked	3 oz.	111	3.8	31
Snapper, mixed species, cooked	3 oz.	109	1.5	12
Surimi (imitation crabmeat), cooked	3 oz.	84	0.7	8
Swordfish, cooked	3 oz.	132	4.4	30
Trout, rainbow, cooked	3 oz.	128	4.9	35
Tuna				
Fresh, cooked	3 oz.	156	5.3	31
Light, canned (water-pack), drained	3 oz.	99	0.5	5
White, canned (water-pack), drained	3 oz.	116	2.1	16
Whiting, mixed species, cooked	3 oz.	98	1.4	13

Shellfish

Food	Amount	Calories	Total Fat (g)	% Calories From Fat
Clams, mixed species				
Canned, drained	3 oz.	126	1.7	12
Fresh, cooked	3 oz. (20 small)	133	1.8	12
Crab				
Alaskan King, cooked	3 oz.	82	1.3	1.4
Blue, cooked	3 oz.	87	1.5	16
Lobster, cooked	3 oz.	83	0.5	5
Mussels, blue, cooked	3 oz.	146	3.8	23
Oysters, Eastern, cooked	3 oz. (12 medium)	116	4.2	33
Scallops, mixed species, cooked	3 oz. (6 large)	75	0.6	7
Shrimp, mixed species, cooked	3 oz. (16 large)	84	0.9	10

Fruits

Food	Amount	Calories	Total Fat (g)	% Calories From Fat
Apples				
Dried	6 rings	98	0.1	1
Fresh	1 medium	81	0.5	6
Applesauce				
Canned, sweetened	½ cup	97	0.2	2
Canned, unsweetened	½ cup	53	0.1	1

Calories and Fat at a Glance

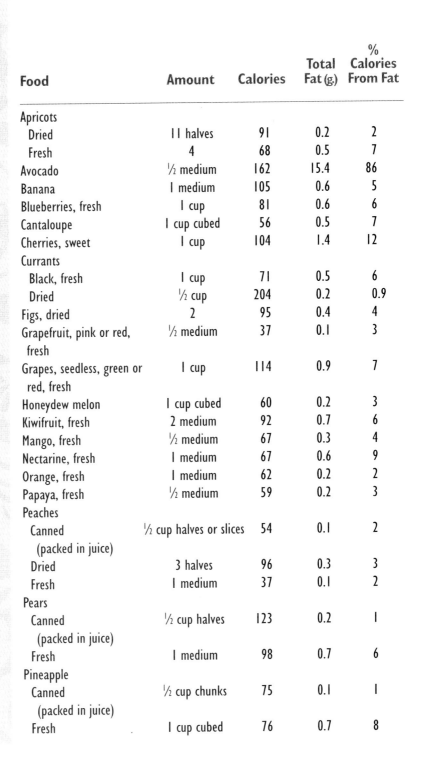

Food	Amount	Calories	Total Fat (g)	% Calories From Fat
Apricots				
Dried	11 halves	91	0.2	2
Fresh	4	68	0.5	7
Avocado	½ medium	162	15.4	86
Banana	1 medium	105	0.6	5
Blueberries, fresh	1 cup	81	0.6	6
Cantaloupe	1 cup cubed	56	0.5	7
Cherries, sweet	1 cup	104	1.4	12
Currants				
Black, fresh	1 cup	71	0.5	6
Dried	½ cup	204	0.2	0.9
Figs, dried	2	95	0.4	4
Grapefruit, pink or red, fresh	½ medium	37	0.1	3
Grapes, seedless, green or red, fresh	1 cup	114	0.9	7
Honeydew melon	1 cup cubed	60	0.2	3
Kiwifruit, fresh	2 medium	92	0.7	6
Mango, fresh	½ medium	67	0.3	4
Nectarine, fresh	1 medium	67	0.6	9
Orange, fresh	1 medium	62	0.2	2
Papaya, fresh	½ medium	59	0.2	3
Peaches				
Canned (packed in juice)	½ cup halves or slices	54	0.1	2
Dried	3 halves	96	0.3	3
Fresh	1 medium	37	0.1	2
Pears				
Canned (packed in juice)	½ cup halves	123	0.2	1
Fresh	1 medium	98	0.7	6
Pineapple				
Canned (packed in juice)	½ cup chunks	75	0.1	1
Fresh	1 cup cubed	76	0.7	8

Food	Amount	Calories	Total Fat (g)	% Calories From Fat
Fruits— continued				
Plums, fresh	2 medium	73	0.8	10
Prunes, dried	5 (1.5 oz.)	100	0.2	2
Raisins, seedless	¼ cup	120	0.2	2
Raspberries, fresh	1 cup	60	0.7	10
Rhubarb, fresh	1 cup diced	26	0.2	8
Strawberries, fresh	1 cup	45	0.6	11
Tangerine	1 medium	37	0.2	4
Watermelon	1 cup cubed	51	0.7	12

Grains, Hot Cereals and Pastas

Food	Amount	Calories	Total Fat (g)	% Calories From Fat
Grains				
Barley, pearled, cooked	½ cup	97	0.4	3
Bran				
Oat, raw	2 Tbsp.	29	0.8	25
Wheat, raw	2 Tbsp.	15	0.3	18
Bulgur wheat, cooked	½ cup	76	0.2	3
Couscous, cooked	½ cup	101	0.1	1
Grits, corn, cooked	½ cup	73	0.3	3
Rice				
Brown, cooked	½ cup	110	0.8	7
White, enriched, cooked	½ cup	133	0.2	1
Wild, cooked	½ cup	83	0.3	3
Wheat germ, toasted	2 Tbsp.	54	1.5	25
Hot Cereals				
Cream of wheat, quick-cooking, cooked	¾ cup	97	0.4	3
Farina, cooked	¾ cup	87	0.1	2
Oatmeal, cooked	¾ cup	109	1.8	15
Pastas				
Egg noodles, enriched, cooked	1 cup	213	2.4	10
Fettucine				
Dried, cooked	1 cup	220	3	12
Fresh, cooked	1 cup	195	3	14
Macaroni, enriched, cooked	1 cup	197	0.9	4
Spaghetti, enriched, cooked	1 cup	197	0.9	4

Food	Amount	Calories	Total Fat (g.)	% Calories From Fat
Tortellini				
Cheese, fresh, cooked	1 cup	480	10.6	20
Chicken, fresh, cooked	1 cup	462	17.3	34

Legumes

Food	Amount	Calories	Total Fat (g.)	% Calories From Fat
Baby lima beans				
Cooked from dried	½ cup	115	0.4	3
Frozen, cooked	½ cup	94	0.3	3
Black beans				
Canned, rinsed and drained	½ cup	125	0.5	4
Cooked from dried	½ cup	114	0.5	4
Chick-peas (garbanzo beans)				
Canned, rinsed and drained	½ cup	143	1.4	9
Cooked from dried	½ cup	134	2.1	14
Great northern beans, cooked from dried	½ cup	104	0.4	3
Lentils, cooked	½ cup	115	0.4	3
Navy beans, cooked from dried	½ cup	129	0.5	4
Pinto beans, cooked from dried	½ cup	117	0.4	3
Split peas, cooked from dried	½ cup	116	0.4	3
Tofu, regular	3 oz.	88	5.5	57

Meats

Food	Amount	Calories	Total Fat (g.)	% Calories From Fat
Beef				
Chuck arm, cooked (lean only)	3 oz.	183	7.1	35
Flank, cooked (lean only)	3 oz.	176	8.6	44
Ground beef, cooked (90% to 95% lean)	3 oz.	218	13.9	57
Loin, top, cooked (lean only)	3 oz.	176	8.0	41
Round cuts				
Bottom round, cooked (lean only)	3 oz.	178	7.0	35
Eye of round, cooked (lean only)	3 oz.	143	4.2	26
Round tip, cooked (lean only)	3 oz.	157	5.9	34
Top round, cooked (lean only)	3 oz.	153	4.2	25

Food	Amount	Calories	Total Fat (g)	% Calories From Fat
Meats—continued				
Beef—continued				
Shank cross cuts, cooked (lean only)	3 oz.	171	5.4	29
Sirloin, top, cooked (lean only)	3 oz.	165	6.1	33
Tenderloin, cooked (lean only)	3 oz.	179	8.5	43
Lamb				
Arm chop or roast, cooked (lean only)	3 oz.	173	9.2	47
Blade, cooked (lean only)	3 oz.	178	9.8	50
Leg chop or roast, cooked (lean only)	3 oz.	162	6.6	36
Loin, cooked (lean only)	3 oz.	172	8.3	44
Rib chop or roast, cooked (lean only)	3 oz.	197	11.3	52
Shank, cooked (lean only)	3 oz.	153	5.7	33
Sirloin, cooked (lean only)	3 oz.	173	7.8	40
Pork				
Bacon, cooked and drained	3 slices	109	9.4	77
Canadian bacon, cooked	2 slices	86	3.9	41
Ham				
Cured, cooked (lean only)	3 oz.	140	6.5	42
Canned, cooked (95% lean)	3 oz.	116	4.2	32
Loin cuts				
Center loin, cooked (lean only)	3 oz.	204	11.1	49
Tenderloin, cooked (lean only)	3 oz.	141	4.1	26
Top loin, cooked (lean only)	3 oz.	209	11.7	51

Calories and Fat at a Glance

Food	Amount	Calories	Total Fat (g.)	% Calories From Fat
Rib chop or roast, cooked (lean only)	3 oz.	219	12.7	52
Sirloin, cooked (lean only)	3 oz.	201	11.2	50
Rabbit				
Domestic, cooked (meat only)	3 oz.	167	6.8	37
Veal				
Arm roast or steak, cooked (lean only)	3 oz.	139	4.9	24
Blade, cooked (lean only)	3 oz.	146	5.8	36
Loin, cooked (lean only)	3 oz.	149	5.9	36
Rib chop or roast, cooked (lean only)	3 oz.	150	6.3	38
Round, top, cooked (lean only)	3 oz.	128	2.9	20
Sirloin, cooked (lean only)	3 oz.	143	5.3	33

Milk, Cream and Yogurt

Food	Amount	Calories	Total Fat (g.)	% Calories From Fat
Milk				
Buttermilk	8 oz.	99	2.2	20
Evaporated milk				
Low-fat	2 Tbsp.	28	0.8	9
Skim	2 Tbsp.	25	0.1	9
Nonfat dry (powder)	1/4 cup	109	0.2	2
1% fat	8 oz.	102	2.6	23
Skim	8 oz.	86	0.4	4
Cream				
Heavy	1 Tbsp.	52	5.6	97
Light	1 Tbsp.	30	2.9	89
Nondairy creamer (powdered)				
Low-saturated-fat	1 tsp.	8	0.3	33
Regular	1 tsp.	11	0.7	58
Sour cream				
Nonfat	2 Tbsp.	30	0	0
Reduced-calorie	2 Tbsp.	40	2	45

Food	Amount	Calories	Total Fat (g)	% Calories From Fat

Milk, Cream and Yogurt—
continued

Yogurt

Plain

Low-fat	I cup	144	3.5	22
Nonfat	I cup	127	0.4	3

Vanilla-flavored

Low-fat	I cup	200	3	I4
Nonfat, sugar-free	I cup	100	0	0

Nuts and Seeds

Almonds	I oz.	166	15	81
Cashews	I oz.	163	13	73
Coconut, sweetened, flaked	2 Tbsp.	71	4.8	61
Hazelnuts (filberts)	I oz.	179	17.8	89
Peanut butter				
Chunky or smooth	2 Tbsp.	188	16	76
Whipped	2 Tbsp.	143	12	76
Peanuts, dry-roasted	I oz.	170	15	79
Pecans, dried	I oz.	189	19.2	91
Pistachios, dried	I oz.	164	13.7	75
Pumpkin seeds, dried	I oz.	154	13	76
Sunflower kernels	I oz.	162	14	78
Walnuts, English	I oz.	182	17.6	87

Poultry

Chicken, broiler/fryer

Breast, cooked (meat only)	3 oz.	142	3.1	19
Drumstick, cooked (meat only)	3 oz.	151	5	30
Thigh, cooked (meat only)	3 oz.	163	7.2	40

Duck

Cooked (meat only)	3 oz.	172	9.6	50

Turkey

Bacon, cooked and drained	3 slices	90	6	60
Breast, cooked (white meat only)	3 oz.	115	0.6	4.7

Food	Amount	Calories	Total Fat (g)	% Calories From Fat
Dark meat only, cooked	3 oz.	137	3.7	24
Ham	2 oz.	73	2.9	36
Sausage, cooked (85% lean)	2 oz.	120	8	60
Tenderloin, cooked	3 oz.	132	1.8	12

Preserves and Sweeteners

Preserves

Food	Amount	Calories	Total Fat (g)	% Calories From Fat
Apple butter	1 Tbsp.	33	0.1	4
Fruit spread				
All-fruit, all flavors	1 Tbsp.	42	0	0
Low-sugar, all flavors	1 Tbsp.	24	0	0
Jam, all flavors, reduced-calorie	1 Tbsp.	42	0	0

Sweeteners

Food	Amount	Calories	Total Fat (g)	% Calories From Fat
Honey	1 tsp.	21	0	0
Sugar				
Brown	1 tsp.	11	0	0
Granulated	1 tsp.	15	0	0
Powdered, unsifted	1 tsp.	10	0	0
Syrup, pancake				
Reduced-calorie	2 Tbsp.	50	0	0
Regular	2 Tbsp.	100	0	0

Salad Dressings

Food	Amount	Calories	Total Fat (g)	% Calories From Fat
Blue cheese or Roquefort				
Nonfat	2 Tbsp.	40	0	0
Reduced-calorie	2 Tbsp.	6	0.3	54
French				
Nonfat	2 Tbsp.	40	0	0
Reduced-calorie	2 Tbsp.	44	1.9	39
Italian				
Nonfat	2 Tbsp.	12	0	0
Reduced-calorie	2 Tbsp.	32	2.9	84
Mayonnaise				
Nonfat	1 Tbsp.	8	0	0
Reduced-calorie	1 Tbsp.	22	2	84

Food	Amount	Calories	Total Fat (g.)	% Calories From Fat
Salad Dressings—continued				
Ranch-style				
Nonfat	2 Tbsp.	40	0	0
Reduced-calorie	2 Tbsp.	80	8	80
Thousand Island				
Nonfat	2 Tbsp.	32	0	0
Reduced-calorie	2 Tbsp.	60	4	60
Sauces				
Barbecue, ready-to-serve	2 Tbsp.	24	0.6	22
Salsa, ready-to-serve	2 Tbsp.	8	0	0
Soy, reduced-sodium	1 Tbsp.	13	0	0
Spaghetti, ready-to-serve	½ cup	136	5.9	39
Taco, ready-to-serve	1 Tbsp.	8	0	0
Tartar, ready-to-serve	2 Tbsp.	148	16.2	98
Tomato, canned	¼ cup	19	0.1	5
Snacks				
Chips				
Corn	30 (1 oz.)	153	9.5	53
Potato	13 (1 oz.)	140	9.5	61
Tortilla	10 (about 1 oz.)	150	8	48
Popcorn				
Air-popped	3 cups	69	0.9	12
Microwaved, low-fat	3 cups	81	4	44
Pretzels, thin sticks	1 oz.	110	1	8
Rice cakes, plain	2 (0.5 oz.)	70	0.4	5
Vegetables				
Artichoke, cooked	1 medium	60	0.2	3
Artichoke hearts, cooked	½ cup	42	0.1	3
Asparagus, cooked	½ cup	23	0.3	11
Beans, snap				
Cooked	½ cup	22	0.2	7
Raw	1 cup	34	0.1	3
Beets, cooked	½ cup sliced	38	0.2	1
Bok choy, raw	1 cup shredded	10	0.2	14

Food	Amount	Calories	Total Fat (g)	% Calories From Fat
Broccoli				
Cooked	½ cup chopped	22	0.3	11
Raw	1 cup chopped	12	0.2	11
Brussels sprouts, cooked	½ cup	30	0.4	12
Cabbage				
Cooked	½ cup shredded	17	0.3	17
Raw	1 cup shredded	18	0.2	10
Carrots				
Cooked	½ cup sliced	35	0.1	4
Raw	1 medium	31	0.1	4
Cauliflower				
Cooked	½ cup florets	14	0.3	18
Raw	1 cup florets	26	0.2	7
Celery, raw	1 medium stalk	6	0.1	8
Corn, sweet yellow, cooked	1 ear	83	1	11
Cucumbers, raw	1 cup sliced	14	0.1	6
Eggplant, cooked	½ cup cubed	13	0.1	7
Endive, raw	1 cup chopped	8	0.2	11
Lettuce				
Butterhead	1 cup shredded	8	0.1	15
Iceberg	1 cup shredded	9	0.1	15
Leaf	1 cup shredded	10	0.2	15
Romaine	1 cup shredded	9	0.1	12
Mushrooms				
Cooked	½ cup pieces	21	0.4	16
Raw	1 cup pieces	18	0.3	15
Okra, cooked	½ cup sliced	25	0.1	5
Onions, cooked	⅓ cup chopped	37	0.2	4
Pea pods (sugar snap or snow), cooked	½ cup	34	0.2	5
Peas, green, cooked	½ cup	67	0.2	3
Peppers, sweet, raw	½ cup chopped	14	0.1	6
Potatoes, cooked	½ cup cubed	93	0.1	1
Rutabagas, cooked	½ cup cubed	33	0.2	5

Food	Amount	Calories	Total Fat (g)	% Calories From Fat
Spinach				
Cooked	½ cup	21	0.2	10
Raw	1 cup chopped	24	0.4	15
Sprouts				
Alfalfa, raw	½ cup	5	0.1	22
Bean, canned, rinsed and drained	½ cup	7	trace	5
Squash				
Acorn, cooked	½ cubed	57	0.1	2
Yellow summer, cooked	½ cup sliced	18	0.3	14
Zucchini, cooked	½ cup sliced	14	0.1	3
Sweet potatoes, cooked	½ cup cubed	107	0.1	1
Tomatoes, raw	½ cup chopped	20	0.3	14
Turnips, cooked	½ cup cubed	14	0.1	4
Water chestnuts, canned, slices	½ cup	35	trace	1
Watercress	1 cup chopped	4	trace	10
Yams, cooked	½ cup	116	0.2	1

Vegetables—
continued

NOTE: All calorie and fat figures for cooked foods are based on using the leanest cooking method for preparation.

Fast Foods

Food	Amount	Calories	Total Fat (g)	% Calories From Fat

Arby's

Beverages

Food	Amount	Calories	Total Fat (g)	% Calories From Fat
Jamocha shake	1	368	10.5	22
Milk, 2% fat	8 oz.	121	4.4	33
Orange juice	6 oz.	82	0	0
Vanilla shake	1	330	11.5	31

Breakfast Items

Food	Amount	Calories	Total Fat (g)	% Calories From Fat
Biscuit, plain	1	280	14.9	48
Blueberry muffin	1	240	7	26
Cinnamon-nut Danish	1	360	11	28
Croissant, plain	1	260	15.6	54

Salads and Dressing

Food	Amount	Calories	Total Fat (g)	% Calories From Fat
Chef salad	1	205	9.5	42
Garden salad	1	117	5.2	40
Light Italian dressing	1 Tbsp.	23	1.1	4
Roast chicken salad	1	204	7.2	32

Sandwiches

Food	Amount	Calories	Total Fat (g)	% Calories From Fat
Arby Q	1	389	15.2	35
Grilled Chicken Barbecue	1	386	13.1	31
Ham 'n' Cheese	1	355	14.2	36
Junior Roast Beef	1	233	10.8	42
Light Roast Chicken Deluxe	1	276	7	23
Light Roast Turkey Deluxe	1	260	6	21

Soups

Food	Amount	Calories	Total Fat (g)	% Calories From Fat
Lumberjack Mixed Vegetable	1 cup	89	3.6	36
Old-Fashioned Chicken Noodle	1 cup	99	1.8	16

Other Menu Items

Food	Amount	Calories	Total Fat (g)	% Calories From Fat
Baked potato, plain	1	240	1.9	7
Chocolate chip cookies	3	390	12	28
Potato cakes	2	204	12	53

Food	Amount	Calories	Total Fat (g)	% Calories From Fat

Burger King

Beverages

Food	Amount	Calories	Total Fat (g)	% Calories From Fat
Milk, 2% fat	8 oz.	121	5	37
Orange juice	10 oz.	140	0	0

Breakfast Items

Food	Amount	Calories	Total Fat (g)	% Calories From Fat
Breakfast Buddy with Sausage, Egg and Cheese	1	255	16	56
Hash browns	1	213	12	51
Mini blueberry muffins (not available in all restaurants)	6	292	14	43

Salads and Dressing

Food	Amount	Calories	Total Fat (g)	% Calories From Fat
Chef salad	1	178	9	46
Chunky chicken salad	1	142	4	25
Garden salad	1	95	5	47
Reduced-calorie Italian dressing	2 Tbsp.	15	1	60

Sandwiches/Burgers

Food	Amount	Calories	Total Fat (g)	% Calories From Fat
BK Broiler chicken sandwich	1	280	10	32
Cheeseburger	1	300	14	42
Double cheeseburger	1	450	25	50
Hamburger	1	260	10	35
Whopper Jr.	1	330	19	52

Other Menu Items

Food	Amount	Calories	Total Fat (g)	% Calories From Fat
Baked potato, plain	1	210	0	0
Chicken Tenders	6 pieces	236	13	50

Chick-Fil-A

Salads

Food	Amount	Calories	Total Fat (g)	% Calories From Fat
Chargrilled Chicken Garden Salad	1	126	2.1	15
Tossed salad with light Italian dressing	1	43	1.2	25

Sandwiches

Food	Amount	Calories	Total Fat (g)	% Calories From Fat
Chargrilled Chicken Sandwich	1	258	4.8	17
Original Chicken Sandwich	1	360	8.5	21

	Food	Amount	Calories	Total Fat (g.)	% Calories From Fat
	Other Menu Items				
	Grilled 'n' Lites chicken	2 skewers	97	1.8	16
	Hearty Breast of Chicken Soup	1 cup	152	2.7	16
	Lemonade	10 oz.	138	trace	0
Dairy Queen/Brazier	**Desserts**				
	Frozen yogurt				
	Strawberry sundae	1	200	trace	5
	Vanilla cone	1	180	trace	4
	Ice milk				
	Banana split	1	510	11	19
	Chocolate cone	1	230	7	27
	Chocolate sundae	1	300	7	21
	Sandwiches/Burgers				
	BBQ beef sandwich	1	225	4	16
	Fish fillet sandwich	1	370	16	39
	Grilled chicken fillet sandwich	1	300	8	24
	Hamburger, single	1	310	13	38
Domino's	Pepperoni pizza	⅛ of 12" pizza	219	7.3	30
	Vegetable pizza	⅛ of 12" pizza	204	5.4	24
Hardee's/ Roy Rogers	**Breakfast Items**				
	Cinnamon 'n' raisin biscuit	1	320	17	48
	Ham biscuit	1	320	16	45
	Oat bran/raisin muffin	1	410	16	35
	Pancakes, plain	3	280	2	6
	Pancakes with bacon	3 pancakes, 2 bacon strips	350	9	23
	Rise 'n' Shine Biscuit	1	320	18	51
	Sandwiches				
	Combo sub	1	380	6	14
	Grilled chicken breast	1	310	9	26
	Hot Ham 'n' Cheese	1	330	12	33

Food	Amount	Calories	Total Fat (g)	% Calories From Fat

Hardee's/ Roy Rogers— continued

Sandwiches—continued

Food	Amount	Calories	Total Fat (g)	% Calories From Fat
Roast beef sub	1	370	5	12
Roy Rogers Roast Beef	1 large	360	11.9	30
Turkey sub	1	390	7	16

Other Menu Items

Food	Amount	Calories	Total Fat (g)	% Calories From Fat
Chicken Stix	6 pieces	210	9	38
Cool Twist cone, vanilla	1	180	4	20
French fries, regular	1	230	11	43
Grilled chicken salad	1	120	4	30

Kentucky Fried Chicken

Chicken

Extra Tasty Crispy Chicken

Food	Amount	Calories	Total Fat (g)	% Calories From Fat
Center breast	1 piece	342	19.7	52
Drumstick	1	204	13.9	61

Original Recipe

Food	Amount	Calories	Total Fat (g)	% Calories From Fat
Center breast	1 piece	283	15.3	49
Drumstick	1	146	8.5	52
Wing	1	178	11.7	59

Rotisserie Gold

Food	Amount	Calories	Total Fat (g)	% Calories From Fat
White-meat quarter (skin and wing removed)	1 piece	199	5.9	26

Other Menu Items

Food	Amount	Calories	Total Fat (g)	% Calories From Fat
Chicken Littles sandwich	1	169	10.1	54
Corn on the cob	1	176	3.1	16
Kentucky Nuggets	6 pieces	276	17.4	57

Little Caesar's

Cheese pizza

Food	Amount	Calories	Total Fat (g)	% Calories From Fat
Round	1/10 of 12" pizza	154	5	29
Square	1 (4") square	185	6	29

Sandwiches

Food	Amount	Calories	Total Fat (g)	% Calories From Fat
Ham and cheese	1	553	27	44
Tuna melt	1	610	31	46

Other Menu Items

Food	Amount	Calories	Total Fat (g)	% Calories From Fat
Crazy Bread, plain	1 (6") breadstick	98	1	9

	Food	Amount	Calories	Total Fat (g)	% Calories From Fat
Long John Silver's	**Dinners**				
	Baked fish with lemon-crumb topping (3-piece dinner with rice, green beans, slaw and a roll, no margarine)	1 dinner	610	13	19
	Light herb baked chicken	1 piece	120	4	30
	Other Menu Items				
	Batter-dipped chicken sandwich	1	280	8	26
	Lemon meringue pie	1 slice	340	9	24
	Ocean Chef Salad (no dressing)	1	110	1	8
McDonald's	**Breakfast Items**				
	Apple-bran muffin, fat-free	1	180	0	0
	Egg McMuffin	1	280	11	35
	English Muffin with fruit spread	1	170	4	21
	Burgers				
	McLean Deluxe	1	320	10	28
	McLean Deluxe with Cheese	1	370	14	34
	Salads and Dressing				
	Chunky chicken salad	1	150	4	24
	Light vinaigrette dressing	1 Tbsp.	12	0.5	38
	Side salad	1	30	1	30
	Other Menu Items				
	Chicken fajita	1	190	8	38
Pizza Hut	Beef pizza, hand-tossed	⅛ of 12" pizza	261	10	34
	Cheese pizza, hand-tossed	⅛ of 12" pizza	253	9	32
	Pepperoni pizza, hand-tossed	⅛ of 12" pizza	253	10	36
	Super Supreme pizza, hand-tossed	⅛ of 12" pizza	276	10	33
	Vegetable Lovers pizza, hand-tossed	⅛ of 12" pizza	222	7	28

Food	Amount	Calories	Total Fat (g)	% Calories From Fat
Roy Rogers				
See Hardee's				
Taco Bell				
Bean burrito	1	387	14	33
Beef burrito	1	431	21	44
Burrito Supreme	1	440	22	45
Chicken burrito	1	334	12	32
Combo Burrito	1	407	16	35
Wendy's				
Sandwiches/Burgers				
Grilled chicken sandwich	1	290	7	22
Hamburger, single, plain	1	350	15	39
Other Menu Items				
Baked potato				
Plain	1	300	trace	2
With broccoli and cheese	1	450	14	28
Chili	1 large	290	9	28
Frosty dairy dessert	1 small	340	10	20
Reduced-fat and -calorie Italian salad dressing	2 Tbsp.	80	7	79
Side salad	1	60	3	45

Frozen Entrées

	Food	Amount	Calories	Total Fat (g)	% Calories From Fat
The Budget Gourmet Light and Healthy	Chinese Style Vegetables and Chicken	9 oz.	280	7	23
	French Recipe Chicken	10 oz.	210	7	30
	Glazed Turkey	9 oz.	260	5	17
	Orange Glazed Chicken	9 oz.	290	3	9
	Rigatoni in Cream Sauce with Broccoli and Chicken	10.8 oz.	290	7	22
	Sirloin of Beef in Herb Sauce	9.5 oz.	250	9	32
Healthy Choice	**Entrées**				
	Beef Pepper Steak	9.5 oz.	250	4	15
	Chicken and Vegetables	11.5 oz.	280	3	10
	Chicken Fettucini	8.5 oz.	240	4	15
	Glazed Chicken Breast	8.5 oz.	220	3	12
	Roasted Turkey Breast and Mushrooms in Gravy	8.5 oz.	200	3	14
	Dinners				
	Breast of Turkey	10.5 oz.	260	3	10
	Chicken Parmigiana	11.5 oz.	290	6	19
	Mesquite Chicken	10.5 oz.	300	3	9
	Salisbury Steak	11.5 oz.	280	7	23
	Sirloin Beef with Barbecue Sauce	11 oz.	280	4	13
Lean Cuisine	Cheddar Bake with Pasta and Vegetables	11.5 oz.	230	7	27
	Glazed Chicken with Vegetable Rice	8.5 oz.	250	7	25
	Lasagna with Meat Sauce	10.3 oz.	280	6	19
	Macaroni and Cheese	9 oz.	290	9	28
	Three-Bean Chili with Rice	9 oz.	230	6	23

Food	Amount	Calories	Total Fat (g)	% Calories From Fat
Smart Ones from Weight Watchers				
Fiesta Chicken	8 oz.	210	1	4
Lasagna Florentine	10 oz.	190	1	5
Lemon Herb Chicken Piccata	7.5 oz.	160	1	6
Roast Turkey Medallions	8.5 oz.	200	1	5
Weight Watchers				
Broccoli and Cheese Baked Potato	10.5 oz.	270	6	20
Chicken Enchiladas Suiza	9 oz.	230	7	27
Chicken Fettucini	8.25 oz.	280	9	29
Fettucini Alfredo	8.5 oz.	220	6	25
Lasagna	10.25 oz.	270	6	20
Macaroni and Cheese	9 oz.	280	6	19

Cereals

Food	Amount	Calories	Total Fat (g)	% Calories From Fat
General Mills				
Cheerios	1 oz. (1¼ cups)	110	2	16
Fiber One	1 oz. (½ cup)	60	1	15
Raisin Nut Bran	1 oz. (½ cup)	100	2	1
Ripple Crisp Honey Bran	1 oz. (⅔ cup)	100	<1	0
Total Corn Flakes	1 oz. (1 cup)	110	<1	0
Total Raisin Bran	1 oz. (⅔ cup)	93	<1	6
Total, Whole Grain	1 oz. (1 cup)	100	1	1
Wheaties	1 oz. (1 cup)	100	<1	0
Health Valley				
Amaranth Flakes	1 oz. (½ cup)	90	0	0
Fat-Free Granola	1 oz. (⅓ cup)	90	0	0
Fruit & Fitness	2 oz. (1 cup)	220	4	16
Oat Bran Flakes	1 oz. (½ cup)	90	0	0
Oat Bran O's	1 oz. (¾ cup)	90	0	0
Kellogg's				
All-Bran	1 oz. (⅓ cup)	70	1	13
All-Bran with Extra Fiber	1 oz. (½ cup)	50	1	18
Bran Buds	1 oz. (⅓ cup)	70	1	13
Common Sense Oat Bran	1 oz. (¾ cup)	100	1	9
Complete Bran Flakes	1 oz. (⅔ cup)	90	0.5	5
Corn Flakes	1 oz. (1 cup)	100	0	0
Cracklin' Oat Bran	1 oz. (½ cup)	110	3	25
Frosted Mini-Wheats	1 oz. (4 biscuits)	100	0	0
Fruitful Bran	1 oz. (½ cup)	92	0	0
Kenmei Rice Bran	1 oz. (¾ cup)	110	1	8
Low-Fat Granola	1 oz. (⅓ cup)	110	2	16
Mueslix Crispy Blend	1 oz. (½ cup)	106	1.3	11
Nut & Honey Crunch	1 oz. (⅔ cup)	120	1	8
Nutri-Grain Raisin Bran	1 oz. (¾ cup)	93	0.7	7
Oatbake Raisin Nut	1 oz. (⅓ cup)	110	3	25
Product 19	1 oz. (1 cup)	100	0	0
Raisin Bran	1 oz. (½ cup)	86	0.7	7

Food	Amount	Calories	Total Fat (g.)	% Calories From Fat
Kellogg's— continued				
Rice Krispies	1 oz. (1 cup)	110	0	0
Special K	1 oz. (1 cup)	110	0	0
Nabisco				
100% Bran	1 oz. (⅓ cup)	70	1	13
Shredded Wheat	0.8 oz. (1 biscuit)	80	0.3	3
Shredded Wheat 'N Bran	1 oz. (⅔ cup)	90	0.5	5
Spoon-Size Shredded Wheat	1 oz. (⅔ cup)	90	0.6	6
Post				
Fruit & Fiber with Dates, Raisins, Walnuts and Oat Clusters	1 oz. (½ cup)	96	1.6	15
Grape-Nuts	1 oz. (¼ cup)	110	0	0
Great Grains Double Pecan	1 oz. (¼ cup)	94	2.4	23
Oat Flakes	1 oz. (⅔ cup)	107	1	8
Raisin Bran	1 oz. (½ cup)	87	0.7	7
Quaker Oats				
Crunchy Corn Bran	1 oz. (¾ cup)	90	1	10
Low-Fat Quaker 100% Natural	1 oz. (¼ cup)	110	2	16
Puffed Rice	1 oz. (2 cups)	100	0	0
Puffed Wheat	1 oz. (2 cups)	100	0	0
Toasted Oatmeal, original	1 oz. (⅔ cup)	100	1	1
Ralston Purina				
Chex				
Corn	1 oz. (1 cup)	111	0	0
Multi-Bran	1 oz. (⅔ cup)	100	1	9
100% Whole Grain Wheat	1 oz. (⅔ cup)	100	1	9
Rice	1 oz. (1⅛ cup)	110	0	0
Fruit Muesli	1 oz. (⅓ cup)	103	2	17

Credits

Carol Inouye   Illustration, p. 10

William Smith   Food Styling: p. v; Slim, Trim Appetizers and Snacks, p. 63; The Fairest Fowl (all recipe photos); Getting to the Meat of the Matter (all recipe photos); Lean Vegetarian Cuisine, pp. 211, 213, 219, 220, 222, 232, 234; Full-Flavored Soups and Stews (all recipe photos); Happy, Healthy Holidays, pp. 336-337.

Mariann Sauvion   Food Styling: Starting the Day Right (all recipe photos); Slim, Trim Appetizers and Snacks, pp. 58-59, 67, 72, 78, 84; Sensational Fish and Seafood (all recipe photos); Lean Vegetarian Cuisine, pp. 202-203, 205, 208, 224, 239; Skinny Side Dishes (all recipe photos); Light Delights (all recipe photos); Happy, Healthy Holidays, pp. 345, 350, 361.

Index

A

NOTE: Underscored page references indicate boxed text. **Boldface** references indicate illustrations and photographs. *Italic* references indicate tables.

C

D

E

Kitchen
  colors in, 236
  equipment, 27–30
Kiwifruit, *387*
  Fruit Kabobs with Pineapple Yogurt, 330, **331**
  Sunset Compote, 335
  Turkey, Macaroni and Fruit Salad, 116–17

L

Labels, food, 23–26, <u>26</u>, **26**, 82
  terms used on, 24–25
Lamb, 22
  Dolmades, 152–53, **152**
  fat and calories in, *29*, 277, *390*
  ground, <u>142</u>
  Lamb Chops in Parchment, **150**, 151
  leanest cuts, 277
  Moroccan Lamb Stew, 277
  Mustard-Yogurt Lamb Kabobs on a Bed of Couscous, **130–31**, 153
  Noisettes of Lamb, 154
Lasagna
  Asparagus-Artichoke Lasagna Rolls, 216–17
  Three-Cheese Lasagna, 217
Latkes, <u>354</u>
  Baked Vegetable Latkes, 346
Legumes. *See* Beans
Lemon
  Fruited Pasta Salad with Lemon-Poppy Seed Dressing, 301
  Grilled Lemon-Lime Turkey, 112–13
  Lemon-Almond Biscotti, **310–11**, 316
  Lemon-Asparagus Soup, 257, **257**
  Lemon-Garlic Roasted Cornish Hens, 100, **100**
  Lemon-Sesame Turkey Cutlets, 105, **105**
  Lemon-Thyme Swordfish with Asparagus, 166–67, **167**
  Lemony Peas and Spinach, 285

  Steamed Clams with Lemon Dipping Sauce, **200**, 201
Lentils, 23, <u>231</u>, *389*
  Curried Lentil Soup, 268
  Good Earth Casserole, 235
Lettuce, *395*
  Garden Salad with Quick-Draw Dressing, 293
  Jícama, Romaine and Tomato with Hot-Pepper Dressing, 292–93
  Sunshine Tossed Salad, 302
Linguine
  Asparagus and Orange Linguine, 218, **219**
Lobster, 22, *386*
  Cream-Sauced Seafood over Fettuccine, 195
Low-fat diet. *See* Weight-loss program

M

Macaroni, *388*
  Chicken Vegetable Soup with Shells, 255
  Fruited Pasta Salad with Lemon-Poppy Seed Dressing, 301
  Pasta e Fagioli with Beef, 256
  Turkey, Macaroni and Fruit Salad, 116–17
Mackerel, 166, *385*
Mahimahi, <u>184</u>, *385*
Mangoes, *387*
  Bombay Rice with Mango Salsa, 208, **208**
Maple
  Maple-Spiced Winter Vegetables, 288–89, **288**
Margarine, 21, *28, 385*
  softening, 162
Marinades, <u>113</u>
  salad dressings as, 76
  seafood safety and, <u>194</u>
Mayonnaise, 97, *393*
Meals, 4, 228, 295. *See also* Eating; Menus
  cutting prep time, 4–5

R

S